The Disturbed State of the Russian Realm

Duke Friedrich Ulrich of Braunschweig-Wolfenbüttel.
Herzog August Library, Wolfenbüttel

The Disturbed State
of the Russian Realm

CONRAD BUSSOW

TRANSLATED

AND EDITED BY

G. EDWARD ORCHARD

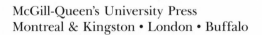

McGill-Queen's University Press
Montreal & Kingston • London • Buffalo

© McGill-Queen's University Press 1994
ISBN 0-7735-1165-2

Legal deposit second quarter 1994
Bibliothèque nationale du Québec
Printed in Canada on acid-free paper

This book has been published with the help of a
grant from the Canadian Federation for the
Humanities, using funds provided by the Social
Sciences and Humanities Research Council of Canada.
Publication has also been supported by the University
of Lethbridge.

Canadian Cataloguing in Publication Data

Bussow, Conrad, d. 1617
The disturbed state of the Russian realm
Translation of: Relatio: das ist summarische
Erzehlung vom eigentlichen Ursprung dieses itzigen
blutigen Kriegs-Wesens in Moscowiter-Land oder
Reussland.
Includes bibliographical references and index.
ISBN 0-7735-1165-2
1. Russia – History – Time of Troubles, 1598–1613.
I. Orchard, G.E. (George Edward). II. Title.
DK111.B8813 1994   947'.045   C94-900059-0

Typeset in Baskerville 10/12 by
Caractéra production graphique inc., Quebec City.

This work is dedicated
with affection and respect
to
Sir Keith Thomas
my former tutor, who
revealed to me the drama
and pathos of the seventeenth century.

Contents

Acknowledgments   xi
Introduction   xiii
Chronology   xxxix
Genealogy of the Polish and Swedish Vasas   xliii

THE DISTURBED STATE OF THE RUSSIAN REALM

  I   Prince Fedor Ivanovitch   7

 II   Concerning Tsar Boris Fedorovich, and How He Came
      to Rule   9

III   Fedor Borisovich, Son of Boris Fedorovich   44

IV   The First Dmitry and His Reign   48

 V   What Befell the Governor of Sandomir and the Poles
      after the Tsar's Murder   67

VI   How the Muscovites Dealt with the Tsaritsa and Her
      Father   71

VII What Happened to the Murdered Dmitry and His
Champion Lord Peter Fedorovich Basmanov, and also to
the 2,135 Poles, Who Willed that the Second Dmitry
Should Rescue Them in a Miraculous Fashion, and the
Miracles which Occurred When They Brought Dmitry's
Corpse 76

VIII True Evidence That This Dmitry Was Not the Son of
the Tyrant Ivan Vasilievich, but an Alien 81

IX–X Concerning Prince Vasily Shuisky and the Second
Dmitry, Who Sought to Overthrow Shuisky, and
Claimed to Be the Escaped Dmitry; Also Concerning
Sigismund III, King of Poland, How He Intervened, and
How His Son, His Royal Highness Prince Wladyslaw,
Was Offered the Muscovite Land and Throne 85

XI How Prince Grigory Shakhovskoy by Theft and
Falsehood Brought Great Harm to Tsar Shuisky 88

XII Concerning Ivan Isaevich Bolotnikov, Who Came to
Poland from Venice, and How in Poland a Certain
Person, Who Allowed Himself to Be Addressed as
Dmitry Tsar of Russia, Sent Him into Russia to Wage
War 91

XIII–XIV Concerning a Certain Cossack Sent to Poland to Urge
Dmitry to Make Haste, or to Commit Everything to the
King in Poland, and How a Certain Man from Shklov
Claimed to Be Dmitry and Came into Russia 100

XV How Russia in the Year 1609 Was Beset on All Sides by
War and Tribulation 117

XVI Concerning the Return of Skopin and the Arrival of
Jakob de la Gardie with Three Thousand
Foreigners 122

XVII   Concerning Aleksandr Jozef Lisowski, the Second
Dmitry's Commander over Several Thousand Cossacks,
and How He Proceeded with Them Too Deep Into the
Country, and How the Enemy Cut Off His Retreat to
the Encampment, and How for This Reason He Was
Compelled to Retreat to Suzdal, and How, Finally,
Having Effected a Wide Diversion, He Withdrew
Towards Pskov   124

XVIII   Concerning the Embassy of His Majesty the King of
Poland to the Poles in Dmitry's Encampment   126

XIX   Concerning Shuisky's Deposition; Also the Destruction
of the Second Dmitry and the Election of Lord
Wladyslaw, Son of King Sigismund of Poland   144

XX   What Occurred in the Year 1611 in Russia, Especially in
the Capital City of Moscow, and Why the Polish King
Did Not Allow His Son Wladyslaw, Who Had Been
Chosen Russian Tsar, to Proceed Thither, and What
Great Misfortune and Irreparable Harm Resulted
Therefrom   154

Appendices
1   Conrad Bussow's Missive to Duke Friedrich-Ulrich of
Brunswick, 28 November 1613   171

2   Conrad Bussow's Letter to J. Peparino, 3 February
1614   174

3   Bussow's Map of Moscow   177

Notes   181
Bibliography   225
Index   233

Acknowledgments

I should like to take this opportunity to express my thanks to those who have helped me in various ways in the preparation of this volume, which, with a number of hiatuses, has been almost a decade in the making. The University of Lethbridge granted me study leave for the academic session of 1984–85 and special funding for travel to Germany in 1989. My host institutions – the School of Slavonic and East European Studies, University of London; the Center for Russian and East European Studies, University of Illinois at Champaign-Urbana; and the Herzog August Bibliothek, Wolfenbüttel – provided me with a congenial research environment and kindly granted me permission to reproduce materials in their collections. For taking the time to read various drafts of my manuscript and make many helpful suggestions, I am indebted to Hugh F. Graham of California State College, Bakersfield (himself a translator of no mean repute), Edward C. Thaden of the University of Illinois at Chicago Circle, and Erich Donnert of the University of Halle, Germany. I would like to express my particular appreciation of the kindness and courtesy of Professor Wolfgang Milde of the Herzog August Bibliothek for his patience in answering my innumerable queries about early modern German chirographic style and orthography. Thomas Robinson of the University of Lethbridge deserves a special vote of thanks for rendering my crudely drawn sketch maps into reproducible form. A final acknowledgment must go out to the anonymous readers appointed by the publishers and granting agencies, as well as to Doris Cowan and Joan McGilvray, who put the finishing touches on this work.

Introduction

This is the first English translation of a major primary source on the Time of Troubles (1598–1613), the name given by historians to the combination of dynastic, social, and political crises that all but overwhelmed the Muscovite state.

The roots of the Time of Troubles go back to the disturbed reign of Ivan IV (1533–84), who became the ruler at the age of three when his father died prematurely. The early years of the reign were plagued with the usual problems attendant on the accession of a minor to the throne, as the realm was riven by factional strife among the boyar clans, while the young grand prince was neglected and treated with great contumacy.[1] Despite its shaky beginning, Ivan IV's reign showed much promise in the 1550s. The currency stabilized, and Russia was developing along lines parallel to those in evidence elsewhere in Europe.[2] The western frontier was secure, while the gunpowder revolution enabled Russia to assume the offensive against the successor states of the Golden Horde. With the conquest of Kazan (1552) Ivan justified the title of tsar, which he had assumed in 1547; Astrakhan was conquered in 1556, and the whole course of the Volga came under Russian control. The stage was set for the colonization of Siberia. The time had come to settle accounts with the Crimean khanate, which its Ottoman suzerain was in no position to protect. The Muscovite realm would then be safe on all sides, free to develop in peace and prosperity.

Unfortunately this auspicious movement in Russian history took a wrong turn. Against the better judgment of his advisers, Ivan IV, instead of completing the unfinished business to the south, attacked the Livonian territories to the west, which had been left undefended with the collapse of the Livonian Order in 1558. After initial successes, the Russian armies suffered heavy losses in men and territory.

Traditional historiography has seen far-sighted motives in Ivan's decision to embark upon the Livonian campaign. S.F. Platonov states that "the time was ripe for Moscow in the West, toward the seacoasts, and Ivan did not squander this opportunity to lay claim to part of the Livonian inheritance that was to become escheat ... No one in Russia was at all displeased that the war had begun."[3] More recently, R.G. Skrynnikov argued: "Russia had good reasons for starting the war. The wealthy Livonian towns long had monitored trade between Russia and the West. The Order and the German merchants were hampering the development of Russian commerce at a time when economic growth rendered it essential for Russia to establish close economic ties with the advanced countries of western Europe."[4]

Alexander Yanov, on the other hand, sees the "turn against the Germans" as Russia's cardinal error. "Its defeat in the Livonian war was no mere military setback. This was the political collapse of Muscovy."[5] Elsewhere the same author states:

Livonia had regressed so thoroughly ... that it must have seemed an overripe fruit which would fall of its own accord into the hands of the conqueror ... However, this was the deceptive weakness of a no-man's-land, situated between several strong predators, all of whom coveted its ports, its wealthy cities and its first-class fortresses: all waiting for one of the others – the stupidest – to take the initiative ... The one who struck first not only risked losing prestige by openly taking on the aggressor's role, but would also unite against himself a strong coalition of other predators, who would reap the spoils at the expense of the first under the guise of justice.[6]

This is precisely what happened. Muscovy lost not only its conquests in Livonia, but five key Russian cities as well.

While the Livonian war was being fought and lost, Ivan IV engaged in a bizarre scheme of social engineering which was to make his name a byword for bloody tyranny. In 1565 he organized a complex of crown estates called the *oprichnina*, from which, aided by a body of hand-picked black-robed henchmen, he established a reign of terror over the entire country. The purpose of this exercise remains unclear: the Russian historian who has studied the problem most thoroughly admits that "the *oprichnina* was not consistent during the seven years it existed; it did not pursue, either subjectively or objectively, a single goal, principle or plan."[7] If, as some historians have maintained, its aim was to destroy the boyar aristocracy, it failed; it merely shuffled the deck.[8] The attempt to explain the sack of Novgorod by the *oprichnina* in 1570 as a curtailment of "separatism" is equally unsatisfactory.

Gruesome though it was, the *oprichnina* was merely a symptom of a series of deeper-lying problems, not all of which were unique to Russia. As the prospect of easy and rapid victory in Livonia receded and Ivan found himself involved in a seemingly never-ending triangular contest with Poland and Sweden, taxation escalated to such an extent that the tsar was forced to convoke the Assembly of the Land (*zemskii sobor*) to obtain the co-operation of his subjects in raising more men and money for the war effort. The disorganization caused by the *oprichnina* was compounded by natural calamities such as plague, famine, and the total failure of the harvest in 1568 and 1569. As if these misfortunes were not enough, in 1571 the Crimean Tatars burned and plundered the suburbs of Moscow.

Thus in the late sixteenth century Russia found itself at a crossroads: "It was precisely at this time that the question was decided as to which road Russia would travel – the road through the renewal of feudalism through the 'new edition' of serfdom, or the road of bourgeois development."[9] The "new edition" of serfdom – the "second serfdom" – referred to here has been discussed by a number of historians, particularly in relation to the West. There the transition from feudalism to capitalism was well advanced by the end of the thirteenth century when, faced with labour shortages caused by the plague and the consequent upward pressure on agricultural wages, landlords sought to reimpose limitations on the peasantry, attempting to institute the "second serfdom." The resulting *jacqueries* and urban revolts forced them to abandon such moves, except in lands east of the Elbe, where municipalities were weak and seigneurial power still strong.[10]

Russian attempts to institute a "second" serfdom may, however, be a special case, since there the "first" serfdom was never fully developed. The "nomadic brake" of the Mongol conquest arrested economic developments which had paralleled those of the West. The epicentre of the Russian polity shifted from the southwest to the northeast, from Kiev to Moscow. "The reclamation and colonization of vast unpopulated spaces halted the descent of the Russian peasantry towards permanent servile dependence, which had been well under way during the last centuries of the Kievan state."[11] The exigency of the Livonian war and the general economic crisis led the state to intervene on behalf of the lesser gentry in an attempt to ensure that this class, which through service tenures (*pomest'ia*) provided mounted and armed soldiers, would continue to be economically viable. The rules of the "Forbidden Years," which suspended the right of the peasant to settle his accounts with the landlord and move, were introduced during the last years of the Livonian war. Originally intended as an emergency wartime measure and applied only in selected localities, they became the norm nationwide.[12] Peasants on the estates of military servitors became fully enserfed, with severe penalties for fugitives or those harbouring them.

These measures of enserfment did not go unresisted. It was no accident that the main base during the Troubles for both pretenders claiming to be Tsarevich Dmitry, as well as that of the Bolotnikov rebels, lay in the Komaritsk district, where the peasantry had not been long enserfed, and freedom was still a recent memory. Other peasants fled to the frontier to join military brotherhoods of freemen called Cossacks, who hired themselves out as mercenary bands to the Polish, Hungarian, Imperial, or even the Muscovite government, while at the same time practising profitable extortion from travellers and merchants in the steppe and along the rivers. Another recourse for the destitute was self-sale into limited-service contract slavery (*kabala*), a "stress phenomenon"[13] that, like the adscription of the peasants to the soil, tended to perpetuate itself.

Compounding the social crisis was the dynastic crisis precipitated by Ivan IV, who had worked sedulously to extirpate the collateral line of the Staritsa princes and in a temper tantrum had caused the death of his eldest son. Thus his successor was not the strong and able Ivan Ivanovich, but the simple-minded younger son Fedor (reigned 1584–98). Within a year of Fedor's accession the effective rulership was assumed by his brother-in-law Boris Godunov, who proved to be a very able administrator.[14] Fedor Ivanovich's reign was a time of relative tranquillity. The Tatar invasion of 1591 was effectively repulsed, and a successful war against Sweden concluded with the Peace of Täysinä (1595), in which some of the ground lost in the Livonian war was regained. The truce with Poland on the western front held. The regent, deservedly, took much of the credit for these achievements.

So successful was he as regent that, when Fedor died, Boris was elected tsar. Although his detractors criticized the mechanics of his election, and with the benefit of hindsight denounced him as a usurper, no serious alternative candidate was put forward. His reign, however, was so catastrophic that contemporaries could hardly be blamed for seeing in the harvest failure, famine, plague, and domestic strife the judgment of God. At the outset of his reign the omens were favourable. Patriarch Job, Boris's friend, mobilized the spiritual resources of the church behind this new tsar who, like David, had been chosen not according to birth but by divine will. The boyar families, however, regarded him as an upstart, and he himself was extremely sensitive to any challenge to his legitimacy. While still regent he had come into conflict with the Shuisky princes, and in 1600 the Romanov family felt the weight of his displeasure: they were convicted on fabricated charges of sorcery and sent into an exile which not all of them survived. Fedor Nikitich Romanov, the future Patriarch Filaret and father of the future tsar Michael, was compelled to take monastic vows and was kept in strict confinement for the balance of the reign. It is widely considered that the "resurrection" of Tsarevich Dmitry and the resulting chaos had some connection with the disgrace of the Romanovs: because Boris was not only a usurper but also a shedder of innocent blood, God punished both him and Russia.

Dmitry (born 1582), Fedor's half-brother, had been exiled, together with his maternal relatives, to the principality of Uglich when Fedor ascended the throne, and was kept there under close surveillance. On the afternoon of 15 May 1591 he was found dead in the palace courtyard with his throat slit. An investigatory commission, headed by Prince Vasily Ivanovich Shuisky, was dispatched to Uglich. The findings of the commission showed that the tsarevich had died accidentally, but suspicions of foul play were by no means dispelled. As the new century opened, rumours circulated that the tsarevich was in fact still alive, and was living incognito in Poland. The person who emerged in 1603 as the pretender was probably Grigory (or Grishka) Otrepiev, a monk of the Miracles monastery in the Moscow Kremlin who had served as a personal secretary to Patriarch Job and therefore was well informed about Muscovite political affairs. Otrepiev fled to Poland in the Lenten season of 1601, and there cast off the monastic garb (hence he was referred to frequently as *rasstriga*, the "Renegade Monk"). He became a valet to Prince Adam Wisniowiecki, to whom he revealed himself as the long-lost tsarevich.[15] Subsequently he was introduced at the court of King Sigismund III of Poland (reigned 1587–1632), became a convert to Roman Catholicism, promised marriage to Maryna Mniszech, daughter of the governor of Sandomir, and in October 1604 crossed the Muscovite frontier with an army composed of Cossacks and Polish irregulars. Despite some setbacks, he established himself firmly on Russian soil during the winter of 1604–05. Boris was losing his nerve, and morale in his army was abysmally low. Commanders were saying openly that "it is hard to fight against our lawful sovereign," and draconian penalties against defaulters were needed in order to keep the field army up to strength. The army was less intent on following up its signal victory at Dobrynichi than on inflicting reprisals upon the local civilian population. Either Boris's commanders were criminally irresolute, or they were hedging their bets.

When Boris died on 13 April 1605 a large portion of his realm was in revolt, while his son Fedor Borisovich commanded scant respect. Peter Basmanov, Boris's trusted commander, declared for Dmitry, whose advance on Moscow thereafter was in the nature of a triumphal progress. Fedor and his mother were murdered, and his sister was confined to a convent after, according to some accounts, first having been debauched by the pretender. Her tragic figure, like a Greek chorus, stayed in the background of the terrible events of the next decade.

Dmitry, enthroned in Moscow, treated his Russian backers with studied contempt. Within a few weeks of his accession a conspiracy to dethrone him was headed by Prince Vasily Ivanovich Shuisky, who was arrested, sentenced to be beheaded, and then had his sentence commuted to banishment. Even this milder punishment was remitted, and Shuisky was permitted to return to the capital, where he lost no time in resuming his conspiratorial activities. Dmitry played further into Shuisky's hands by taking a foreign bride, Maryna, who was accompanied by a suite of Poles and Jesuits. The latent Russian xenophobia erupted on the night of 17 May 1606; Dmitry was murdered and Vasily Ivanovich Shuisky (reigned 1606–10) seized the throne.

At first glance the new tsar's credentials were impeccable. Dmitry had been exposed as an impostor and the old ruling line was extinct. Everyone in the genealogy-conscious ruling circles knew that the Shuisky family was descended not only from the great thirteenth-century hero Alexander Nevsky but also from his son, who was older brother to Daniel, the progenitor of the House of Moscow. The family also had a formidable power base not only in its ancestral lands around Suzdal but also in the northwest, around Novgorod and Pskov. Vasily's uncle, Prince Ivan Petrovich, had distinguished himself at the defence of Pskov during the winter of 1581–82 against the Polish king Stefan Bathory. Both he and his kinsfolk had, in the opinion of many, suffered unjustly at the hands of the regent Godunov in 1587, and Vasily himself had later put his life on the line when, shortly after the pretender's entry into the capital, he had denounced the new tsar as a brigand and heretic.

What then was wrong with Shuisky? He is reminiscent of those politicians in modern times who win elections by a landslide but for whom nobody subsequently will admit to having voted. Technically he is acknowledged to have been a lawful tsar, and his legislative acts and grants were recognized as valid by his Romanov successors, yet historians refer to him as Vasily Shuisky, or simply as Shuisky, never according him the courtesy of an ordinal as Vasily IV. Neither in historical literature nor in the consciousness of the Russian people did he become fully legitimate. Perhaps the logic applied to Shuisky was the reverse of that applied to Godunov: according to many, Boris usurped the throne, so things began to go wrong; under Shuisky things went wrong, and therefore he was a usurper.

Historians who look for economic causes rather than divine anger see in the Time of Troubles "a delayed-action political sequel to the economic collapse of the 1580s."[16] No sooner was Shuisky settled on the throne that he was faced with the Bolotnikov rebellion, the first of the "peasant wars" that were to punctuate Russian history over the next two centuries. A runaway elite slave turned freebooter, Bolotnikov acted in the name of the "just tsar" Dmitry, who was alleged to have escaped from his assassins in Moscow. Bolotnikov attracted to his standards a motley force which attempted to arouse the urban poor of the capital against the boyar regime. Initially the movement attracted elements of the provincial gentry, but the latter were eventually to change sides and give Shuisky their grudging support for a few years. One of the main weaknesses of the Bolotnikov rebellion was the failure of the insurgents to produce a Dmitry, until just as the rebels went down to defeat.

The supporters of False Dmitry II were even more ill-assorted. His initial support came from some of the defeated followers of Nicholas Zebrzydowski, who had led an unsuccessful aristocratic rebellion against King Sigismund of Poland. With these and various Russian malcontents, False Dmitry II advanced on Moscow, established his rival capital at Tushino, a village on the northwestern approaches to the capital, and inherited Maryna, the consort of the first pretender. Moscow was under virtual blockade for the next two years, the tsar confined "like a bird in a cage." The Trinity monastery also withstood an epic siege by Polish irregulars, commanded by Jan-Piotr Sapieha and Aleksandr Jozef Lisowski.

During the Time of Troubles, foreign mercenaries were active on both sides. The mercenary market was in a slump with the lull in the Eighty Years' War and the subsequent Dutch truce (1609–21). Hostilities between France and Spain had ended with the Peace of

Vervins (1598), and the Huguenot wars similarly had come to an end. Germany for the moment was uneasily quiescent. *Condottieri* were therefore to be had cheap. Boris had had an élite corps of German mercenaries, who, having fought valiantly against the forces of False Dmitry I at Dobrynichi, were later received into his service. One of these mercenaries, Jacques Margeret,[17] went home after the overthrow of the first False Dmitry, returned to fight under the banner of the second, and shifted over to Polish service in 1610–11. In 1612 he offered his sword to the Russian liberation forces and was quite offended when, not surprisingly, he was turned down. Many of the troops in Swedish service, whose aid was negotiated by Shuisky in 1609, were in fact foreign mercenaries led by Jakob de la Gardie, himself the son of a French immigrant to Sweden. Many of these mercenaries changed sides after the defeat of the Muscovite army at Klushino (24 June 1610). In short, the loyalty of mercenary troops lasted as long as they were regularly paid and their banner on the winning side.

In Poland the royal army was really the sum of the retinues led by the magnates. One of the unfortunate effects of the "golden liberty" enjoyed by the aristocracy was that if a number of them became disaffected with royal policy, or were on the losing side in a double election, they formed a "confederacy" and launched a civil war against the king. Such was the Zebrzydowski *rokosz* which tied the hands of King Sigismund at a time when Muscovy was particularly vulnerable.[18] After Stanislaw Zolkiewski, the crown hetman,[19] defeated the rebels at Guzów (6 July 1607), many of the confederate bands trickled across the Muscovite frontier in search of further employment. Mikolaj Miechowicki and his successor Roman Rozynski, who commanded False Dmitry II's forces, were such displaced military leaders. Sapieha and Lisowski, who led their polyglot bands of freebooters, negotiated for their services with rulers as between equals. A Polish regiment under Colonel Pawel Chmieliewski even fought under Muscovite command in the closing stages of the Troubles.

The dynastic and social crisis in Muscovy exposed it to the attentions of its predatory neighbours, Poland and Sweden, although their capacity to intervene was greatly hampered at first. Poland was bound by the twenty-two-year truce concluded with Muscovy in 1600, and so could send only covert help to Dmitry, while the Polish king's ambitions in Russia met with strenuous disapproval on the part of a substantial party in the Sejm, which was being asked to foot the bill, and then were thwarted by the Zebrzydowski rebellion.

Since Sigismund Vasa, elected king of Poland in 1587, also succeeded to the Swedish kingdom in 1592, there were fears that

Muscovy might have to contend with the combined forces of both crowns. Quite the contrary occurred. In Sweden, Sigismund came into conflict with the nobility and the royal dukes because of his ardent Catholicism and alleged neglect of Swedish interests. In 1599 he was deposed in Sweden although retaining his rule in Poland, and the regency was assumed by his cousin Duke Karl of Södermanland who, however, was prevented by his respect for constitutional niceties from assuming the kingship as Karl IX until 1604.[20] Once he was king, he was in perpetual conflict with the nobility, and became embroiled in the first of a series of wars with Poland over Livonia, suffering a disastrous defeat at Kirkholm (September 1605). He also had to keep a wary eye on Denmark, which at that time still held Skåne and thus commanded both shores of the Sound, and was looking for an opportunity to attack Sweden in the rear. Indeed Christian IV, king of Denmark (reigned 1596–1648) waited until the bulk of Sweden's army was engaged in Russia, before launching the War of Kalmar (1611–13).

Shuisky, hard pressed in Moscow, sought Swedish aid. This, by the Treaty of Vyborg (28 February 1609), Karl was prepared to give, at the price of strategic territorial concessions.[21] The territories in question would threaten Poland's newly acquired possessions in Livonia, so Sigismund, viewing these Russian-Swedish dealings as treachery, no longer felt himself bound by the 1600 truce with Muscovy, which the Polish ambassadors had confirmed with Shuisky's government in 1606. The Polish royal army invaded Muscovy under the personal command of King Sigismund, who appealed to all the Poles already in Russia to rally to his standard at Smolensk. At the same time a relieving column under Shuisky's cousin Skopin, reinforced by Swedish auxiliairies under Jakob de la Gardie, advanced on Moscow. These two factors brought about the collapse of the pretender's camp at Tushino and False Dmitry II's flight to Kaluga.

Skopin entered Moscow in triumph, and it seemed that the Shuisky regime was saved. For about a month Shuisky basked in Skopin's reflected glory, but on 23 April 1610 the young hero collapsed at a christening feast and died two weeks later. It was widely alleged that the tsar's sister-in-law Ekaterina, a daughter of Ivan the Terrible's sinister henchman Maliuta Skuratov, had poisoned him. Her husband, Prince Dmitry Shuisky, was known to be hostile to Skopin, whom he saw as a threat to his own ambitions. If Skopin was indeed murdered, the Shuisky regime had squandered its only valuable asset, who was described by the nineteenth-century historian Soloviev as "the last of the Riurikids enthroned in the hearts of the people."[22] Instead of Skopin, the Muscovite army sent to stem the advance of

Zolkiewski was led by Prince Dmitry, "a commander with a craven heart, encumbered with effeminate things, loving beauty and food, and not the drawing of the bow."[23] The battle of Klushino was lost, and in less than a month Vasily Shuisky was deposed by the very gentry who had so reluctantly come over to his side in the autumn of 1606. In December False Dmitry II was murdered by his Tatar bodyguards. With two key contestants removed, it was time for a realignment of allegiances.

Before Dmitry's death, because of his continued threat, the interim boyar administration in Moscow came to an agreement with Zolkiewski whereby they accepted Sigismund's eldest son, Prince Wladyslaw, as tsar, on condition that he come to Moscow and accept the Orthodox faith. The Muscovites also agreed to accept a Polish garrison to protect them against Dmitry's forces, which were advancing from Kaluga. Zolkiewski left Moscow with what appeared to be a satisfactory agreement, only to arrive at the encampment outside Smolensk and discover that Sigismund was bent on advancing his own claims and had no intention of abiding by the hetman's treaty. For their part, the Moscow boyars agreed to Wladyslaw's candidacy only to counter the threat of False Dmitry II. With the death of the pretender and the patent perfidy of the Polish king, divisions began to appear within the boyar camp. Patriarch Hermogen, who initially had given qualified support to Wladyslaw, now saw him as a threat to the Orthodox faith, and entered into communication with the national liberation forces seeking to rid Russia of all foreign intruders.

During the Troubles the populace in the many localities had vacillated, taking first one side and then the other. The Shuisky regime was unpopular, but so were the depredations of the Polish and Cossack supporters of False Dmitry II. Not infrequently, declarations of support for Moscow simply meant that a given locality was making its own arrangements for self-defence. In 1611 these local defence organizations, which increasingly had corresponded with one another, now coalesced and began to move over to the offensive. The gentry of the southern towns, led by Prokopy Liapunov, advanced on Moscow, having concluded an agreement with the Cossack commanders Prince Dmitry Timofeevich Trubetskoy and Ivan Martynovich Zarutsky. They succeeded in infiltrating the town quarter of Moscow during Holy Week and gave the Poles a stiff fight, confining them to the Kremlin and Kitay-gorod. The First Militia Force, as the movement came to be known, having failed to dislodge the enemy from the city centre, and having destroyed the outlying quarters, formed a siege. But once again gentry and Cossack aspirations, as in the Bolotnikov rebellion, came into conflict; besides, the triumvirate was basically an agreement between one honest man, Liapunov, and two rogues. Members of the gentry contingent went back to their estates, while the Cossacks, influenced by Polish disinformation, contrived the murder of Liapunov. Meanwhile Patriarch Hermogen had been starved to death in a Kremlin dungeon. It seemed that the hopes of liberation from the Polish yoke were shattered.

The struggle was taken up again by the townspeople of Nizhny Novgorod, led by their elected elder Kuzma Minin. They raised funds by exemplary self-sacrifice; recruited, paid, and equipped the Second Militia Force; and appointed Prince Dmitry Mikhailovich Pozharsky to lead it. Minin and Pozharsky's talents admirably complemented each other. The Second Militia Force was organized during the winter of 1611–12, and in March 1612 moved by way of Kostroma to Yaroslavl, where elements of a provisional government were set up. Zarutsky, after an abortive attempt, motivated by jealousy, to assassinate Pozharsky, fled to Mikhailov to cast his lot in with Maryna, widow of both pretenders, and her infant son Ivan Dmitreevich, heir to the residual claims of the Dmitrys. The civil war was thus prolonged for more than a year.

Pozharsky advanced on Moscow and came to a working arrangement with Trubetskoy. The combined forces, having beaten off a Polish relieving column led by Hetman Jan Karol Chodkiewicz, tightened the ring around the Polish garrison, which finally surrendered in October. The following months were taken up with preparations for a full Assembly of the Land to elect a new tsar. The leaders of the Militia Forces had considered seriously the candidacy of a Swedish prince, but when the Assembly finally met, it decided upon Michael Romanov.[24]

The Time of Troubles was a critical turning point in Russian history, when it seemed that all the labours of the House of Moscow would be brought to nothing. It was a furnace in which Russian national consciousness underwent a fiery trial. In many respects it was a shameful epoch, when the natural leaders of society, absorbed by their own selfish interests, were muzzled by "insane silence" (*bezumnoe molchanie*) and were "silent as fishes" while Russia fell prey to domestic strife and foreign depredation. On the other hand, in times of crisis the names of Minin and Pozharsky are invoked with pride, and their statue had occupied a place of honour on the Red Square since 1818. The year 1612 ranks along with 1812 and 1941–45 in the battle honours of the Russian people.

As far as religious and cultural attitudes are concerned, the Troubles reinforced the traditional Russian xenophobia. While Vasily III and Boris Godunov had been looked at askance for their partiality to foreign ways, with False Dmitry I and the machinations of Sigismund III's supporters these trends seemed to have reached their logical conclusion, with Poles and Jesuits strutting around the Kremlin. After the Troubles, Moscow seemed to shut itself off from Western cultural influences even more completely than before. In architecture the "tent" churches, as exemplified by that of the Ascension at Kolomenskoe (1532) ceased to be built. Patriarch Filaret insisted that converts to Orthodoxy from Roman Catholicism be rebaptized. Although foreign soldiers and technicians continued to be hired, they were considered at best a necessary evil, and in 1652 they were segregated to a special ghetto beyond the Yauza river, outside the Moscow city limits. It was not until the annexation of Ukraine (1654), which opened the way to the operation of new influences in the Russian Orthodox community and the marriage in 1671 of Tsar Alexis to a lady reared by a Scottish foster mother, that Russia can be said to have opened up to outside, particularly Western, influences. Even so there was a powerful nativist reaction, exemplified in its extreme form by the Old Believer schism.

The era also brought into relief the problem of legitimacy. Ivan IV had deliberately eliminated the only collateral line to the ruling house, and in his rage had killed his only viable successor. Fedor Ivanovich died chidless, though he did have a daughter, Feodosia, who died in infancy in 1594. Dmitry, whether by accident or design, had been eliminated in 1591. Who then was the legitimate heir? Had the reign of Boris been more fortunate, doubtless a Godunov dynasty would have been established, since his son Fedor Borisovich was a young man of great promise. False Dmitry at first met with favourable response; contemporary apologists drew on Old Testament analogies to Joseph in Egypt and David's succession to Saul, and many commentators offer the opinion that had he been prepared to show even minimal respect for Muscovite customs, he would have remained upon the throne. Shuisky had excellent credentials, but his rule foundered on his manifest personality defects, as well as the disorders of his reign. Princes Wladyslaw of Poland and Karl Filip of Sweden were, though foreign, of the blood royal, and the sentiment was widespread at the 1613 Assembly that "we have had no luck with sovereigns of our own race." Michael Romanov's candidacy was at best shaky, his intellectual talents exiguous, and, in view of what had happened to previous tsars, his reluctance to assume the throne was not entirely feigned. His legitimacy as a ruler was to be challenged repeatedly. Our chronicler, Bussow, could hardly be blamed for thinking that Michael would not be able to hold on to the throne for long. For this reason Muscovite ambassadors were notorious sticklers for correct formularies on treaties and diplomatic documents. Michael began to style himself as the grandson of Ivan IV and, as the Romanov dynasty established itself, the number who were sufficiently lacking in tact to point out that his kinship to the ruling house was based merely on the marriage of his great-aunt Anastasia to Ivan decreased sharply.

Another phenomenon which made its appearance in Russia at this time was "pretenderism" (*samozvanshchina*). Impersonators of actual or would-be rulers were not unusual. Anglo-Saxon readers are familiar with the impostures of Perkin Warbeck and Lambert Simnel in the reign of Henry VII of England, while Pope Clement VIII was quick to draw an analogy between events in Russia and the alleged reappearance of King Sebastian of Portugal.[25] Perhaps a more apposite paradigm might be found in the *falsi Nerones*: during late antiquity, social revolts were led by self-proclaimed reincarnations of Emperor Nero, whom popular imagination depicted as a champion of the oppressed against the depredations of the patrician class. Ivan IV, undoubtedly as bloody a tyrant as Nero, also came to be regarded in the mythology of the people as someone whose took vicarious revenge on the "wicked boyars." It is apparently human nature to experience a certain *Schadenfreude* at the discomfiture of one's social superiors.[26] There was no doubt that Ivan IV had died, but Tsarevich Dmitry, the circumstances of whose demise were shrouded in mystery and suspicion, was an ideal candidate for the role of the "just tsar." The Soviet ethnographer K.V. Chistov even postulated a pre-existing cycle of "socio-utopian legends about returning deliverers."[27] Although this thesis has not stood up to the penetrating analysis of Maureen Perrie,[28] perhaps the Dmitry episode was the start of such a cycle: the False Peter, the proliferation of pretenders in Astrakhan, and the successive reincarnations of Dmitry himself. Through much of Michael's reign (1613–45), the Vasa kings of Poland kept in reserve a number of pretenders who purported to be either Dmitry himself, his posthumous son, or a fictitious son of Vasily Shuisky.

The phenomenon of pretenderism as representative of social justice became a common theme in peasant revolts. Stenka Razin (1670–71) felt it necessary to spread the rumour that Tsar Alexis was marching in person with the rebel troops; Emilian Pugachev, during the 1773–75 uprising, impersonated the late Peter III; and the Decembrists in 1825, for the benefit of the peasant-soldier rank-and-file, maintained that Grand Duke Constantine was the legitimate ruler. In none of these instances did the reality bear any resemblance whatsoever to the myth of the "just tsar."[29] In many lesser revolts it was not unusual for some pretended royal personage to claim to represent a "just" ruler, who wished to render true justice to the people.[30] Bussow is particularly useful in revealing the true content of the social programs of both major reincarnations of Tsarevich Dmitry, and of Bolotnikov. As Maureen Perrie remarks: "Bolotnikov was not a conscious social revolutionary. When he laid siege to Moscow at the end of 1606, he called on the serfs in the capital to kill their masters and seize their wives and estates, and urged the poor to kill and plunder the rich. But these actions were undertaken as a punishment of the traitors to the true Dmitry, and Bolotnikov promised high rank, including that of boyar, to Muscovites who came over to his side. Similarly ... the Second False Dmitry promised to reward the serfs and servants of Shuysky's adherents with their masters' estates and with their daughters if they gave him their support. This was not part of any consistent anti-feudal policy, however; Bussow notes that the pretender also gave land and peasants to princes, boyars and foreign merchants who joined his army."[31] Skrynnikov similarly concludes: "The civil war again produced a vertical division through all orders and groups of Russian society, from the aristocracy at the top to ordinary people at the bottom. The Troubles finally lost any resemblance whatever to 'class warfare' and its highest form – the 'peasant war.'"[32]

"Social bandits," though excoriated by the authorities, frequently become underground heroes commemorated in popular ballads. Such songs about Stenka Razin, for example, are legion; yet no popular songs commemorate Bolotnikov, though they did extol the peasants of the Severian region "who did not wish to serve any lords."[33]

The social conflicts of the period overlapped. The sixteenth century had seen the rise of the service-tenured landholder (*pomeshchik*), who provided the backbone of the Russian cavalry.[34] At the same time the bureaucracy had extended well beyond the royal household stage of government, to the extent that a whole subclass of chancellery officials (*d'iaki*) manned the network of government departments (*prikazy*), and the upper stratum of such officials occupied seats in the Boyar Council.[35] A select number of the service gentry (*dumnye dvoriane*) also obtained places in the council. Yet despite these concessions to the upper strata of military and bureaucratic servitors, there remained considerable jealousy on the part of the rising classes concerning the apparent boyar monopoly of political power. The boyars in turn resented the elevation of any one of their number. Boris Godunov and Vasily Shuisky had both, prior to their elevation to the throne, displayed ability as leaders of the boyar élite; yet when they stepped out of the inner circle inward to the epicentre, they failed. Both were acutely sensitive to any aspersions on the legitimacy of their rulership, since they themselves were aware that they had transgressed the most basic precept of an unspoken and unwritten code.[36] For many, a "boyar tsar" was a contradiction in terms. The gentry were forced to tread a thin line between opposition to the boyar oligarchy and support for forces of social revolution. A number of gentry flocked to the standards of False Dmitry I, to Bolotnikov as the "great voevoda" of False Dmitry II, or to the second pretender himself, only to change sides when it became apparent that anarchy was gaining the upper hand.

Concomitant with the struggle between the greater and lesser feudatories was the rearguard action of the peasantry against enserfment, characterized by some historians as a revolt of the periphery against the centre. The most deadly manifestation of the periphery was Cossackdom; the steppe Cossacks had their origin in the flight of peasants and bondsmen from feudal injustice. Now they were able to wreak terrible vengeance upon the heartland, in the course of which their ranks were swelled by assorted malcontents. Even after Russia had apparently set its house in order by agreeing upon a new tsar and expelling foreign invaders, the Romanov regime had to spend much of its time and effort, both literally and figuratively, putting out fires caused by footloose bands of Cossacks and unpaid irregulars parading around in various liveries.

As if the domestic turbulence were not enough, Muscovy was at this time caught up in the conflict between Poland and Sweden. Russia was the *tertium quid* in the bitter contest between the two branches of the Vasa family. Both were seeking to control the Baltic littoral. Estonia, conquered by the Swedes in 1561, was the base from which they sought to extend into Polish-held Livonia. Conversely Poland, having by Chodkiewicz's victory at Kirkholm (1605) repelled Swedish attempts to obtain Livonia, was casting envious eyes on Estonia. Each was trying to outflank the other by seeking to control Muscovy.

In the case of Poland, two other factors were operative. First, Sigismund III never acknowledged the usurper Karl as the rightful ruler of Sweden.[37] If he could control Muscovy covertly, albeit unsubtly, though False Dmitry I or II or, as after 1609, openly through advancing the claims to the Muscovite throne of either his son Wladyslaw or himself, Sigismund hoped to direct the combined forces of Poland, Lithuania, and Muscovy against Sweden. Second, there was the alluring prospect that the Catholic counter-reformation would bring the schismatic Russians into the true fold. The Union of Brest (1595) had created the Uniate church as a bridge between Rome and the Orthodox communion. False Dmitry, a covert Roman Catholic, had Jesuit chaplains in his entourage. Pope Clement VIII (reigned 1592–1605), to whom Dmitry wrote a grandiloquent letter soliciting his support,[38] was sceptical both about the authenticity and the prospects of the sender. Clement died in 1605 and, after the brief intervening pontificate of Leo XI, was succeeded by Paul V (1605–21), who embraced enthusiastically the cause of Dmitry, and later that of Wladyslaw as the inheritor of Dmitry's claims.

Sweden had intervened in Muscovy initially in order to improve its strategic position on the Baltic. Karl IX had repeatedly pressed offers of aid on Shuisky who, knowing that such aid came at a price, persistently refused. Finally he was in such dire straits that in 1608 he sent Skopin, who negotiated the Treaty of Vyborg. With Swedish help the blockade of Moscow was relieved and the Tushino camp dispersed; but after the defeat at Klushino the Muscovite war chest, which was to have paid the Swedish auxiliaries, was captured by the Poles. In any case with the deposition of Shuisky the Swedes lost their paymaster and therefore had to fend for themselves. They struck northwards and in July 1611 captured the city of Novgorod. De la Gardie then promoted the candidacy of a Swedish prince, either Gustav Adolf or Karl Filip,[39] who was received positively in some Muscovite quarters. In the end the two intervening powers, thwarted in their more grandiose plans, settled for territorial gains that, though modest in extent, were of great strategic importance.

For Russia the Time of Troubles was the most perilous revolutionary situation in the seventeenth century. Had the scheme of Sigismund III or de la Gardie succeeded, Muscovy would have been reduced to a mere appendage of a foreign power, its social structure a shambles. The Bolotnikov rebellion threatened Moscow itself, whereas other uprisings were stemmed at a safe distance from the capital. The urban riots of 1648, the copper riots of 1662, and the revolt of the musketeers in 1682 were provoked by specific grievances, and were of a localized nature. The Old Believer schism, apart from the armed resistance of the Solovetsk monastery (1668–76), for the most part led to non-violent forms of opposition. The failure of these potentially divisive movements allowed the Romanov regime to provide some stability, although it achieved its legitimation simply by holding on to the throne; Michael and his son Alexis reigned for a total of sixty-three years. This factor, rather than the innate abilities of either monarch, strengthened the dynasty against any serious challenge.

Did the Troubles bring about any social or intellectual changes, or broadening of intellectual horizons? At first glance the answer to this question is resoundingly negative. Most of Michael's reign was spent in making up lost ground, and there is some question whether Alexis was a precursor of Peter the Great or merely Ivan the Terrible with a human face. The presence of Poles and Jesuits in the heart of Russia reinforced anti-Western prejudices. The church under the tutelage of Metropolitan Jonas was too obscurantist for Patriarch Filaret, who on his return in 1619 sent the *locum tenens* packing and reversed many of his decisions. Yet Filaret himself was not exactly noted for progressive sentiments. The continued presence of foreign experts was only grudgingly tolerated, and scholars even suspected of being tainted by Western ideas were likely to end their days in monastic confinement. None were sent abroad to study, and the government of Michael tried unsuccessfully to obtain the return of those who had been sent abroad during the reign of Boris Godunov.

The only bright spot in the almost unrelieved gloom is in the realm of historical writing, in which the authors explored what lessons the dreadful events of past years held for Russia, and how these events could be explained other than in terms of divine anger. With the writings of Avraamy Palitsyn, Ivan Timofeev, Prince Semeon Ivanovich Shakhovskoy, Archpriest Terenty, and the anonymous compiler of the *1617 Chronograph* we see the beginnings of historical writing as a humanistic pursuit.[40] The accounts of foreigners who were present in Muscovy during these years admirably complement these annalistic writings. Not the least of these is Bussow's chronicle.

THE CHRONICLER

Conrad Bussow was born at Ilten, near Hanover, in 1552 or 1553, the son of a Lutheran pastor. In 1569, at the age of sixteen or seventeen, he left his father's parsonage to seek his fortune as a soldier. For his time, he had a fairly good education. His chronicle is replete with Latin words and phrases, and he knew his Bible well, both in the Vulgate and the German versions. It is also probable that he used Latin as a common language in conversing with members of the Polish or Swedish aristocracy. From the frequency with which he quotes them, it might not be too fanciful to suggest that he carried Plautus and Josephus in his knapsack.

Perhaps Conrad was intended to follow his father's footsteps into the ministry; the church and the army are, after all, the twin avocations of the rural squirearchy. He was religious in a conventional sense, a conscientious churchgoer whose daughter married a

Lutheran divine. The camp and the battlefield, however, were scarcely conducive to a life of piety; in his chronicle he is apt to use salacious language, though doubtless he is merely reporting accurately the words of others. Loyalty to his current paymaster seems to have sat lightly on his shoulders, and his occasional moral indignation at the perfidy of others seems singularly misplaced. Yet at the same time he has tried to give an honest report. His religious upbringing leads him to frequent reflections on the transient nature of earthly power, and gives him the ability to view the contending parties with equanimity.

Little is known of Bussow's early career, but it is known that he was in Polish service under King Stefan Bathory (reigned 1575–86). Despite having for a while a common ruler in Sigismund Vasa, Poland and Sweden increasingly fell out with each other. With Russia pushed aside in the triangular contest for the Baltic littoral, these other two contestants were now fighting over the spoils. Bussow opted for Swedish service, perhaps out of sympathy for his co-religionist Duke Karl of Södermanland, who also had dynastic ties with Bussow's North German homeland.[41] Some time in the 1590s Bussow established himself in Riga. This city had been under Polish rule since 1581, but had a well-established German burgher community resident there since the thirteenth century. Whom and when he married there we do not know, but later, when in Russia, Bussow is known to have had at least two grown children. He also mentions relatives by marriage in Livonia several times in his chronicle, and his travelling companion in 1606 on a journey from Moscow to Uglich was a merchant whom he had previously known in Riga.

Bussow was well rewarded for his desertion to the Swedes, and enjoyed positions of trust. On the title page of his work he calls himself "Inspector and Intendant" of the lands conquered by Duke Karl in Livonia, and he also commanded Neuhausen and Marienburg at one time or another. Duke Karl had been able to subdue Finland and Estonia, since he had much local support, but Livonia was another matter. Despite initial successes, it became evident that Karl, with his bad strategy and inexperienced commanders, would lose this round in the Baltic contest, especially once the Polish-Lithuanian chancellor Jan Zamoyski landed in force in Livonia in 1601.

Under these circumstances Bussow may have decided that Tsar Boris was the Poles' ablest opponent, as, if we are to believe the allegations of Peer Peerson of Erlesunda (Petreius),[42] by 1599 Bussow had been recruited in Narva by Timofey Vykhodets and a certain Ivanov as an agent in place for Boris, to whom he conspired to hand over the city at an opportune moment, probably in mid-April 1601.

The plot was discovered and some of his co-conspirators were exe-cuted, while Bussow himself was forced to flee to Muscovy. There he was richly rewarded by Boris with estates in the regions of Kaluga, Krapivna, and Rogozhna. Although he took an active part in sub-sequent campaigns, there is no evidence that he held any major command. The estates in question were apparently not service ten-ures but a reward for services already rendered by an agent who had "come in from the cold."

Bussow's role in the Time of Troubles appears to have been that of an observer rather than an active participant. He did serve Boris and False Dmitry I, but in 1606 Shuisky dismissed him and gave him leave to retire to his estates. At the time of the Bolotnikov rebellion, of which he gives the most detailed account of any source, he was living at Kaluga, which for a time was the rebel headquarters, where his house servied as a social centre for the expatriate German community. His son, also named Conrad, was in the rebel ranks among the defenders of Tula, which surrendered in May 1607, and for his pains was exiled to Siberia, whence he returned shortly before his father's death.

The older Bussow seems to have had all the instincts of an inves-tigative reporter. He always seemed to be where the action was. He records personal conversations with False Dmitry's trusted com-mander Peter Basmanov, and with the Polish freebooter Sapieha at the siege of the Trinity monastery. He was on familiar terms with Prince Adam Wisniowiecki, and observed the Bolotnikov rebellion at close quarters. He was also present at the siege and conflagration of Moscow during Holy Week of 1611, and must have guessed that, despite the current disarray of the Muscovites, the cause of the Poles and the candidacy of Wladyslaw were as good as lost. There were scant prospects of employment for an old soldier approaching his sixtieth year and so, instead of accompanying most of his comrades-in-arms to King Sigismund's encampment at Smolensk, he betook himself to Polish-held Riga, where he stayed for a while with his wife's relatives.

Perhaps he thought he would emulate his former comrade Jacques Margeret, who after the fall of False Dmitry I returned to France and, with royal patronage, published what in seventeenth-century terms was a best seller. Bussow, who in Russia had been a prosperous landlord, must have found it galling to live on the charity of his wife's relatives and hoped to recoup his fortunes as an author. In collabo-ration with his son-in-law Martin Beer, either at Riga or Dünamünde, where Beer had obtained a living, Bussow prepared the first recen-sion of his chronicle, entitled the *Summarische Relatio*. He then returned to his native Lower Saxony and in November 1613, from Hanover, sent the manuscript, together with a covering letter (see Appendix One), to Duke Friedrich-Ulrich of Brunswick-Wolfenbüttel (reigned 1613–34). He was evidently in straitened circumstances, because he states in his letter that he could not afford to pay a printer. Thanks to Petreius, whose damaging revelations[43] found their way into print in 1615 but were common knowledge well before then, Bussow was in bad odour with King Gustav Adolf, who happened to be related to the duke. Besides, Friedrich-Ulrich had no time for literary matters, since he was locked in a bitter struggle with the burghers of Brunswick, which in 1616 erupted into open warfare in which the city, with the aid of Dutch mercenaries, asserted its independence from ducal control.

Receiving no response from Friedrich-Ulrich or from the duke's chamberlain Johannes Peparino, to whom he also wrote a begging letter in February 1614 (see Appendix Two), Bussow began to prepare another recension. Since this was done without the "help" of his son-in-law, this time the language is more colourful, and there is far more autobiographical information. There are, however, some signs of his lack of sophistication. We can safely say that Bussow, despite the Slav tint to his name, had no Slav background in his native Lower Saxony, even though Polabian and other dialects are attested to in that region as late as the mid-eighteenth century.[44] Bussow's knowledge of Russian is of the "kitchen" or "camp" variety. When he does try to render Russian, he betrays a total ignorance of the logic or syntax of the language, and sometimes his translations are downright erroneous. His Latin tastes run to what may be termed *Kriegslatein* – Josephus and Plautus; he appears to be relatively innocent of Virgil and Cicero. Even his German style has been characterized as "in many places awkward, even crude and ungrammatical."[45]

Although Bussow was undoubtedly an acute observer, he had one important blind spot. It is amazing that someone could live for ten years in a country without acquiring the slightest insight into, or empathy for, the local culture. In particular, his notions about the Russian Orthodox Church are utterly bizarre. On the other hand the reader has the benefit of his expertise on military affairs. His accounts of battles and sieges are convincing, though he tends to be careless about figures, which are designed to appal or impress rather than to give reliable statistical information. His map, reproduced at the end of this volume (see Appendix Three) is concerned less with Moscow's architectural features than with military objectives, such as fortifications, towers, gates, rivers, and bridges. He is full of praise for his fellow German mercenaries, no matter in whose service, except in the case of those whose treachery might have placed their compatriots in jepoardy (see chapters 13–14). It is possible that in some places he embroidered his tale for literary effect; on the other hand this was a time when all too frequently truth was stranger than fiction.

While Bussow was reworking his text, somehow the original Martin Beer redaction came into the hands of Petreius, who borrowed from it extensively in his account of Muscovy published in Swedish in 1615 and subsequently in German in 1620.[46] Bussow himself was far less fortunate. By 1617 he had completed a second and third recension and had engaged a printer in Lübeck, but died before the book could go to press, and the publication venture was abandoned. Doubtless the fact that Bussow was no longer around to accuse him of literary piracy emboldened Petreius to proceed with his Leipzig publication.

THE CHRONICLE

Even though Bussow's appeal to Duke Friedrich-Ulrich went unheeded, it was fortunate that he sent his manuscript there, since the Brunswick branch of the Guelph family, in sharp contrast to their Hanoverian cousins, were ardent bibliophiles. The ducal library was founded by Duke Julius (reigned 1568–89), who issued the Library Ordinance, gathering together into a central depository at Wolfen-büttel all the libraries of dissolved religious houses. The collection was expanded further by Heinrich Julius (reigned 1589–1613), through later much of it was handed over to the University of Helm-stedt. Bussow's would-be patron Friedrich-Ulrich was the least fortunate of the dukes; he lost control of his capital city, and in the course of the Thirty Years' War forfeited much of the territorial gains of his predecessors. In 1629 he lost the remunerative administrator-ship of the diocese of Halberstadt and title to the newly built cathe-dral. His successor August (reigned 1635–66) made a separate peace with the Emperor and remained neutral for the rest of the war.

Although Duke August was in fact its second founder, the library not inappropriately now bears his name. He put it on a new footing in 1643, housed the collection in a freestanding building, took a personal hand in the cataloguing, and under the terms of his will made the library available to the public. At that time the collection numbered 130,000 volumes, the largest in Europe.[47] In 1690 Duke Anton Ulrich (reigned 1685–1714) appointed as librarian the phi-losopher Gottfried Wilhelm Leibniz, who remained there until his death in 1714. Under his tutelage the first alphabetical catalogue

The rotunda of the Herzog August Library, Wolfenbüttel, designed by Hermann Korb, 1706–10, and demolished in 1887. Herzog August Library, Wolfentbüttel

was compiled, and the famous Rotunda was built.[48] Another celebrated librarian was the playwright Gotthold Ephraim Lessing, who was at Wolfenbüttel from 1770 until his death in 1781.

During the Napoleonic era both branches of the Guelph family were dispossessed in order to make way for the kingdom of Westphalia, ruled by Jerome Bonaparte. The University of Helmstedt was abolished in 1810 and its assets, including the original Wolfenbüttel collection, were transferred to the University of Göttingen. With the Restoration settlement of 1814–15, Göttingen once again belonged to Hanover, so Brunswick reclaimed the former Helmstedt collection for the Wolfenbüttel library, where it has remained ever since.

Bussow himself passed into relative oblivion until the middle of the nineteenth century. Apart from the fact that Petreius pirated much of his material, it was the 1612 recension, of which scholars thought Beer was the principal author, that was used as a source by historians, notably Nikolai Mikhailovich Karamzin (1766–1826), who drew from it extensively in the last three volumes of his *History of the Russian State*, published in 1819. It was his version of the Time of Troubles that provided the plot for Pushkin's play and Mussorgsky's opera, so indirectly two great artistic works owe their origin to Bussow. Karamzin draws on the first six chapters of Bussow's text, especially the parts dealing with Boris's regency, reign, and legacy, which contain references to "craft and cunning," the presumption of predetermined guilt, and the parallelism between the fate of Dmitry and that of Boris's son.[49] Karamzin was using a transcription of the Wolfenbüttel manuscript contained in the codex Guelf 86 Extravagantes; this was the version presented by Bussow to Duke Friedrich-Ulrich (henceforth referred to as Wolfenbüttel I). The transcription had been commissioned by Count Nikolai Petrovich Rumiantsev (1754–1826), and is therefore called the Rumiantsev manuscript. Rumiantsev tentatively suggested that Martin Beer was the author. Karamzin knew that Petreius had lifted much of his material from this source; he was also aware that some eighteenth-century scholars had attributed the authorship of the chronicle to Bussow, but he dismissed this attribution out of hand and came down solidly in favour of Beer. Karamzin's hypothesis was reinforced by Nikolai Gerasimovich Ustrialov (1805–70), who in 1831 included a Russian translation, the first published version in any language, under Beer's name in his anthology *Tales of Contemporaries concerning Dmitry the Pretender*. His translation was based upon the Wolfenbüttel I and Rumiantsev manuscripts.

Other scholars, working from a different recension than that used by Rumiantsev, Karamzin, and Ustrialov, suggested Bussow as the author. Christian Kelch, a native of Pomerania who came to Reval in 1680 and later became a Lutheran pastor in rural Estonia, cites both Petreius and Bussow in his *Liefländische Historia* (Reval, 1695), but has no idea of any connection between the two. His Bussow citations suggest that he had a copy of the 1617 recension before him. Gottlieb Treuer, a professor at the University of Helmstedt early in the eighteenth century, was also acquainted with a later version of the Bussow chronicle. Later in the same century the library of the Imperial Academy of Sciences in St Petersburg acquired a first- or second-hand copy from Johann Christoph Brotze, co-rector of the Riga *gimnazium*. This copy came to be known as the Academy manuscript.[50]

Christoph Schmidt, also known as Phisildek, provides more precise information about the manuscripts in the Wolfenbüttel library. In 1773 he referred to the *Chronicon Moscoviticum*, but also to another manuscript which he calls the *Newe Zeitung aus Moscowiter Landt* and identifies as another version of the same work. Later he cites in full the title page of this manuscript, which leaves us in no doubt that he had before him the version contained in the codex Guelf 125.15 Extravagantes, also known as the Wolfenbüttel II manuscript.[51]

The other main "family" of Bussow codices is that of the Dresden manuscript, a secondary copy of the 1613 redaction, transcribed around 1670 and kept in the Electoral (later Royal) library of Saxony. This manuscript, long regarded as the most authoritative, was destroyed during the Second World War, but not before two notarized nineteenth-century copies had been made. The great bibliographer Friedrich von Adelung (1768–1843) commissioned a copy early in the 1840s, and the Russian Minister of Justice, Count Viktor Nikitich Panin (1801–74), had his copy made in 1851. These copies are known as the Adelung and Panin manuscripts respectively.

Despite these discoveries, the attribution of the chronicle to Martin Beer went virtually unchallenged throughout much of the early nineteenth century. For thirty years Adelung himself, until he came into possession of his copy of the Dresden manuscript, believed in Beer's authorship. In the second volume of his *Critical-Literary Survey of Travellers in Russia*, published posthumously in 1846, Adelung has a sixty-five-page entry reconstructing Bussow's biography from the internal evidence of the chronicle.[52] His son Nicholas, who was his literary executor, included a notation (page 402) indicating that his father had intended to publish a critical edition of Bussow's work, based upon the Academy manuscript.

The torch was then taken up by A.A. Kunik, who in 1849 published a summary of scholarship to date, also drawing on research done independently by the German historian E. Hermann and the Finnish scholar Jakob Grot.[53] In 1851 Kunik edited and published the first full printed text of the chronicle with Bussow's name as the author.[54]

Bussow's "rehabilitation" was now complete. In his eighth volume, first published in 1858, Sergei Mikhailovich Soloviev (1820–79), whose multi-volume *History of Russia from the Earliest Times* superseded the long-unchallenged scholarship of Karamzin, correctly cites Bussow as the author of the chronicle.[55] Bussow also assumes his rightful place in *Notes on the History of the Troubles in the Muscovite State in the Sixteenth and Seventeenth Centuries*, by Sergei Fedorovich Platonov (1860–1933), which first appeared in 1899 and is still considered the classic study on the subject,[56] not entirely superseded by R.G. Skrynnikov's excellent monograph.[57]

Almost exactly a century after the appearance of the Kunik edition of Bussow's chronicle, the Soviet historian Ivan Ivanovich Smirnov (1909–65) published his account of the Bolotnikov rebellion,[58] for which Bussow was, of course, a major source. This led him to bring out a new critical edition of the chronicle itself, complete with Russian translation, and annotations by A.I. Kopanev and M.V. Kukushkina. It appeared in 1961 and was Smirnov's last major work.

Smirnov was labouring under a number of handicaps. His health was failing, and by then the Dresden manuscript had been destroyed, so he was unable to check the Adelung manuscript, which was the basis for his edition, against it for accuracy. The Adelung manuscript is at best a second- or third-hand copy, and it is a truism that the possibilities of scribal error increase with each copying. Although Smirnov did visit Wolfenbüttel while working on his edition, he did not stay there very long, and therefore had to rely upon microfilm copies of materials deposited there. Although the German text (pages 199–327 of the Smirnov edition) is largely based on the Adelung manuscript, variants from the Panin, Academy, and Wolfenbüttel II manuscripts have been included.

The present translation was based on the German text reproduced in Smirnov's Russian edition of 1961, which I have verified against the manuscripts held in the Herzog August Bibliothek. I have paid particular attention to Wolfenbüttel II (125.15 Extravagantes), which in my opinion represents the most authentic of the Bussow manuscripts, being the latest original document compiled during the author's lifetime. In particular I have adhered to the paragraph breaks and emphases contained in this version. Emphases in the manuscript are indicated by the use of large characters, Latin script, or both. In the translation such passages are in boldface type. Where appropriate, I have also incorporated some of the additional information contained in the Academy manuscript, as reproduced in Kunik's German edition of 1851. While this volume was in preparation, a new German edition was to have appeared,[59] but it seems that this project was abandoned in the wake of the dramatic political changes overtaking Germany in 1989.

Chronology

1533   Accession of Ivan IV, aged three.

c. 1552   Conrad Bussow born at Ilten, Lower Saxony.

1552   Russian conquest of Kazan.

1556   Russian conquest of Astrakhan.

1558   Outbreak of Livonian war.

1561   Swedish conquest of Estonia.

1565   Institution of oprichnina.

1569   Bussow embarks upon military career.

1570   Sack of Novgorod by oprichnina.

1571   Moscow sacked by Crimean Tatars.

1572   End of oprichnina.

1575   November. Stefan Bathory elected King of Poland.

1581   Yermak's expedition to Siberia.
Death of Tsarevich Ivan Ivanovich.

1582   15 January. Truce of Yam Zapolsky between Russia and Poland.

1583   Three year truce signed with Sweden on the Pliuss river. Extended in 1586 and 1587.

1584   19 March. Death of Ivan IV. Accession of Tsar Fëdor Ivanovich.

1586   12 December. Death of Stefan Bathory.

1587   27 December. Sigismund III crowned King of Poland.

1589   Job elected first Patriarch of Moscow.

1590–93   War with Sweden. Russia regains Ivangorod, Yama, Koporie, and Karelia.

c. 1590   Introduction of Forbidden Years on nationwide scale.

1591   15 May. Mysterious death of Tsarevich Dmitry at Uglich. Moscow defended against Crimean Tatar invasion.

1592   Sigismund III of Poland also becomes King of Sweden.

1592–1605   Pontificate of Pope Clement VIII.

1595   Peace of Teusen between Russia and Sweden.

1597   Decree on five-year limitation on recovery of fugitive peasants.

1598   7 January. Death of Tsar Fedor Ivanovich. Election of Boris Godunov.

1600   Romanovs convicted of sorcery and exiled. Fedor Nikitich Romanov tonsured as the monk Filaret. First rumours of Pretender in Poland.

1601–02   Partial restoration of peasant departure on St. George's day.

1601–03   Famine in Muscovy.

1603   Khlopko rebellion. False Dmitry declares himself in Poland.

1604   October. False Dmitry invades Muscovy.

1605   21 January. False Dmitry suffers defeat at Dobrynichi.

13 April. Death of Boris Godunov. Fedor Borisovich proclaimed as tsar.

7 May. Basmanov persuades the field army at Kromy to declare for Dmitry.

7 June overthrow of Godunov dynasty. Deposition of Patriarch Job. Ignatius installed in his place.

Polish forces under Hetman Chodkiewicz defeat the Swedes at Kirkholm

Death of Pope Clement VIII. Paul V becomes pope after the brief pontificate of Leo XI.

1606   8 May. Marriage of False Dmitry to Maryna Mniszech.

17 May. Murder of False Dmitry. Vasily Shuisky proclaimed tsar. Patriarch Ignatius deposed, Hermogen installed.

1606–07   Bolotnikov rebellion.

1606–08   Zebrzydowski rebellion in Poland.

1607   March. Fifteen-year limitation for recovery of fugitive peasants.

May. Fall of Tula. End of Bolotnikov rebellion. Conrad Bussow the younger sent into Siberian exile.

1608   July. Establishment of Tushino encampment.

1609   February. Treaty of Vyborg. Shuisky accepts Swedish aid.

September. Overt intervention by Sigismund III.

16 September. Commencement of siege of Smolensk.

1610   March. Fall of Tushino camp. Skopin enters Moscow.
        May. Death of Skopin.
        24 June. Defeat of Shuisky's army by Zolkiewski at
        Tushino.
        17 July. Deposition and forcible tonsure of Vasily Shuisky.
        False Dmitry II slain by Tatar followers.

1610–11 Winter. Organization of First Militia Force.

1611   17 Februrary. Death of Patriarch Hermogen.
        19–20 March. Uprising in Moscow against Poles.
        March–April. Arrival of First Militia Force in Moscow.
        30 June. Council of the Whole Land. Bussow leaves Mus-
        covy for Riga.
        16 July. Novgorod occupied by Swedes.
        1 September. Kuzma Minin elected town elder in Nizhny
        Novgorod.
        Autumn. Organization of Second Militia Force under
        Minin and Pozharsky.
        November. Death of Karl IX of Sweden; accession of Gus-
        tavus II Adolphus (reigned 1611–32).

1611–13 War of Kalmar between Denmark and Sweden.

1612   March-April. Second Militia Force moves from Nizhny
        Novgorod to Yaroslavl.
        3 June. Fall of Smolensk.
        July–August. Forward detachments of Second Militia
        Force advance from Yaroslavl towards Moscow.
        22–24 August. Second Militia Force defeats relieving
        column under Hetman Chodkiewicz.
        October. Bussow composes first recension of chronicle, in
        collaboration with Martin Beer.
        22 October. Kitay-gorod liberated by Second Militia Force.
        26 October. Kremlin reoccupied by Muscovite forces.

1613   20 January. Peace of Knäred between Denmark and
        Sweden.
        21 February. Election of Michael Romanov.
        28 November. Bussow composes letter to Duke Friedrich-
        Ulrich.
        Bussow begins work on second recension.

1614   4 February. Bussow writes to Duke Friedrich-Ulrich's
        chamberlain Johannes Peparino.
        Capture and execution of Zarutsky and the Little Brigand.
        Incarceration of Maryna.

1615   Siege of Pskov by Gustavus Adolphus.
        Petreius publishes in Swedish his *True and unique descrip-
        tion of Russia.*

1617 27 February. Peace of Stolbovo between Russia and Sweden.
Death of Conrad Bussow.
1618 Outbreak of Thirty Years' War.
1 December. Truce of Deulino between Poland and Russia.
1619 June. Filaret returns and is consecrated Patriarch of Moscow.
1620 Petreius publishes in Leipzig the German version of his history.
1622 Death of Xenia Borisovna Godunova.

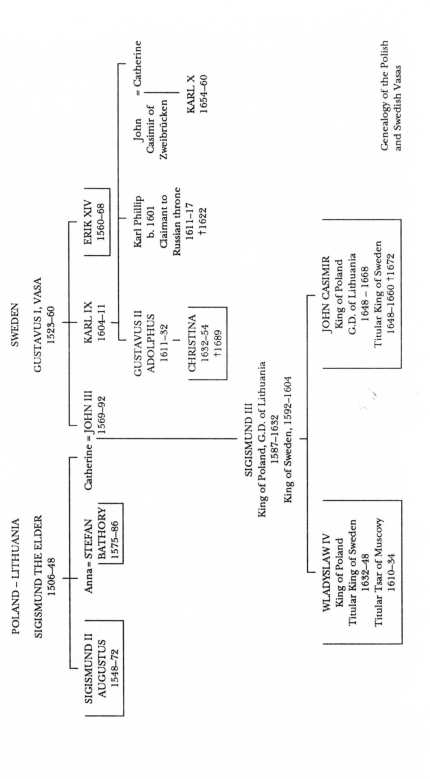

POLAND – LITHUANIA   SWEDEN

SIGISMUND THE ELDER
1506–48

GUSTAVUS I, VASA
1523–60

SIGISMUND II
AUGUSTUS
1548–72

Anna = STEFAN
BATHORY
1575–86

Catherine = JOHN III
1569–92

KARL IX
1604–11

ERIK XIV
1560–68

GUSTAVUS II
ADOLPHUS
1611–32
|
CHRISTINA
1632–54
†1689

SIGISMUND III
King of Poland, G.D. of Lithuania
1587–1632
King of Sweden, 1592–1604

Karl Phillip
b. 1601
Claimant to
Russian throne
1611–17
†1622

John = Catherine
Casimir of
Zweibrücken
|
KARL X
1654–60

WLADYSLAW IV
King of Poland
Titular King of Sweden
1632–48
Titular Tsar of Muscovy
1610–34

JOHN CASIMIR
King of Poland
G.D. of Lithuania
1648 – 1668
Titular King of Sweden
1648–1660 †1672

Genealogy of the Polish
and Swedish Vasas

A. I

Verwirrter Zustand
des Rüßischen Reichs,

unter Regierung derer Czaren Fedor Iwanowiß Boris Gudenov,
und sonderlich derer Demetriorum,
auch Basilii Zuski, und des hierauf erwehlten Königl. Polnisch
Printzen Uladislai
von A°. 1584. biß 1613.

nehmlich bis zum anfang des jetzt glücklich herschenden
Czarischen Hauses,
von Jahr zu Jahren
in einem gar genauen und sehr merckwürdigen
Tage=Buche,
dergleichen particularitäten sonst gar nirgends bishero
beschrieben und bekant, mit fleißiger und aufrichtiger feder
meist gegenwärtig und augenscheinlich aufgezeichnet,
und
der Nachwelt zum Andencken in einem alten authentiquen
MSto nachgelassen, von einem damahls in Moscau wohn-
haften Teutschen,

Herrn CONRAD BUSSO, anfänglich Ihro Königl.
Majt Caroli Hertzogs zu Sudermanland und nachsthin Caroli IX.
oder Intendanten
Königs in Schweden Revisore über die von der Cron Polen
conquêtirte Länder, Städte, und Schlößer in Lieflant,
hernachmahls Inhaber derer güter Fedoroffski, Rogorna,
und Kropivona in Moscau.

Title page of Codex Guelph, Extravagantes 125.15. Herzog August Library,
Wolfenbüttel

The Disturbed State of the Russian Realm

DURING THE YEARS OF THE REIGNS OF
TSARS FEDOR IVANOVICH, BORIS GODUNOV
AND ESPECIALLY THE DMITRYS AND
VASILY SHUISKY, AND ALSO WLADYSLAW,
PRINCE OF THE KINGDOM OF POLAND,
FROM 1584 TO 1613

impartially recorded in a very detailed
journal with such particulars as are not
produced anywhere else, by the living
pen of a German who was residing at the
time in Moscow, namely Conrad Bussow,
sometime inspector and intendant of
His Royal Highness Karl, Duke of
Södermanland and later King Karl IX,
in the lands, towns, and fortresses
in Livonia, conquered from the Crown
of Poland, afterwards proprietor of
the estates of Fedorovskoye, Rogozhna
and Krapivna in Muscovy.

REGISTER
Derer Geschicht vnd Sachen so in diesem Buch be‟ griffen

Caput 1   fol: i

Von Kneeß Pfedor Jwanowitz des Tyrannen Jwan Basilowitz Sohn.

Cap: 2   fol: 3.

Wans Brüder Boriß Pfedrowitz Güdenow, Wie
der zum Regiment kommen.

Cap: 3   fol: 33.

Von desselben Sohn Pfedor Borissowitz

Cap: 4   fol: 36

Von Demetrio primo. Der sich außgab für den
Jüngsten Sohn des Tyrannen Jwan Basilowitz
Darüber Boriß Pfedrowitz, Von dem Reiche ver-
stoßen. Vnd Demetrius noch für außgesandem
Jahre, auch selbst vmbgebracht wurde.

Cap: 5   fol: 52

Wie nach Demetrÿ entödtung, ein graweliche
Passion, mit den Polen gespielet worden.

Cap: 6.   fol: 55.

Waß die Moßcowiter, mit Demetrÿ Vnmaßt
vnd ihrem Vater, dem Wojwoden zu Sandimyr
nach ihres Herrn, des Keysers Demetrÿ todte,

Table of contents from the Wolfenbüttel II manuscript.

tractiret, Vnd die sie endtlich ins Landt verschickt
vnd gefänglich gehalten worden.

Cap: 7.   fol: 60

Wo der Artzdte Demetrius, vnd sein Vietter, der
Herr Peter Pschedrowitz Paschmanoff, vnd auch
die 2135 ausgeschrenckte Polen geblieben, Vnd
von den Miraculen, die sich zu außführung des
Demetrÿ Leiche begeben.

Cap: 8   fol: 65.

Eigentlicher Beweiß, das Demetrius primus
nicht des Tyrannen Sohn, sondern ein frembdling
gewesen.

Cap: 9   fol: 67

Von Kneeß Wassili Iwanowitz Sühskj, der den
Reussen offenbahrte, das Demetrius, nicht der
rechte Zahherr were, vnd damit verursachte, das
Demetrius vnd seine Polen, überfallen vnd vmbgebracht worden.

Cap: 10.   fol: 67

Zueglaichen auch vom, Sigismundo tertio, König in
Polen etc. e wie der Stat Mayts Juß Mittel
kommen. etc.

Cap: 11.   fol: 69.

Von Kneeß Gregori Sachoffskoj Fürto et Figmento
mit etlichem ehe dem Sühskj. vnd ganzem Moßko-
witer Landt, mercklichen Schaden zufüegt.

Cap: 12   fol: 73

Von Ivan Polutnick. Der auß Venedig in Polen
kommen, Vnd mit einer Kriegßmacht Jns Moßko-
witer Landt abgefertiget wird.   Da ehr
          groß &c.

große Einige führete: Vnnd glaubetet von dem, der
Ihn auß Polen geschicket; vnd daß er der rechte De-
metrius were, berichtet hatte;) verlassen würdt.
Item wie dieser Polütnick, sich ergeben müssen;
Vnd wie er endlich vmbs Leben kommen.

Cap: 13 fol: 81

Ein Cosack würdt auß der Belagerung Thula
an den Woywoden Zu Sandimyr, heß, in Polen
abgefertiget. Mit dieser Instruction. Wo der
Jenige; der den Polütnick in Raußlandt gesandt;)
nicht kommen, vnd sie entsetzen wolte, daß sie als-
dann, dem Könige in Polen, wolten alles außtragen
Was sie daselbst in Rußlandt, gewonnen vnd einge-
nommen hätten. Damit sie von Ihrer Mayt. entt-
setzt werden möchten. Herauß dan also wie
auß dem festen Schloba in Weiß Rußlandt, vi-
wer bekommen würdt. Der zugleich gutt Reüsch
vnd Polnisch reden, schreiben vnd lesen konte. Vnd
als einer der Demetrius were; abgerichtet, vnd
in das Moscowiter landt geschickt worden.

Cap: 14 fol: 81

Vom Demetrio secundo, der auß Polen, auß den
Moscowiterschen (Landtzen, ankam, Vnd daß er der
rechte Demetrius were, welchen Suhsky, Erste
vmbkommen wollen;) vorgab. Ihm aber seine
practicken, nicht so glücklich; als dem Demetrio
prime; abgehen wolten. Jedoch er biß ins dritt
Jahr, dem Rußlande, treffliehen Schaden zufügte.
Vnd wie er außgeruget von Teütschen vnd Polen
die bey Ihm waren, sehr gewesen. Hernacher aber
e die Ihr Mayt. auß Polen He, mit ihrem Exer-
citü vnter Schmolensky, in Rußlandt anlangte.

1 *Prince Fedor Ivanovich*

Ivan Vasilievich, the tyrannical Grand Prince of Russia, or of the Muscovite land (as people call it), died on the Sunday after Cantate Sunday[1] in the year 1584 and was survived by two sons, Fedor Ivanovich and Dmitry Ivanovich.[2] The government was transferred to the elder son, Fedor Ivanovich.[3] The younger son and his mother, the tsar's surviving widow Maria Fedorovna Nagaia, were given the principality of Uglich in order to maintain their princely status. This principality is situated ninety versts (which are reckoned five to the German mile)[4] from the capital of Moscow.

Afterwards, however, since Fedor Ivanovich was quite a pious and God-fearing man after the Muscovite manner, and was concerned with his idols rather than with the rulership, and would rather go to St Nicholas and the Most Pure Virgin[5] than spend time with his senators in the council chamber, he held an assembly with his senators, princes and boyars[6] and informed them that the affairs of state were too hard for him to sit in judgment over such a monarchy. They should seek out from among themselves a clever and prudent man to whom they could entrust the burden of the rulership, so that he himself might serve his God so much the better, with less anxiety and distraction.

So Boris Fedorovich Godunov, a noble from a not very distinguished family[7] but a clever and very prudent man, was chosen as regent over the Russian monarchy,[8] and after the ceremonies were concluded, the tsar stood up, took from his neck a great golden chain, placed it around the neck of the chosen man, and said: "Hereby will I, the tsar of all Russia, take from around my neck the burden of the rulership and, Boris Fedorovich, I will place it around your neck. You shall decide all minor matters in my whole land. You must report to me on all great and important matters, on which you shall not decide without my foreknowledge. But I shall still be tsar." After this had occurred, he had him publicly proclaimed as regent.

This Boris Fedorovich exercised his office with such devotion and skill that almost everyone was amazed, and it was still said by all that there was not his equal in Russia, in that he had rectified many injustices, many abuses had been curtailed, and many widows and orphans had obtained justice through him.[9] Since he had thereby earned such praise, the Muscovites said, "If the tsar passes away without issue, and his lord brother, the young Prince Dmitry, also perishes, then there would be nobody in the whole tsardom worthier to become the new tsar than this very regent, to whom there would be no equal in all the land for his wisdom and intelligence."

Because of such opinions, which were brought to his ears by his spies and informers,[10] Boris became covetous and inflamed with desire to become tsar thereafter, but without being noticed and by cunning. He also contrived that his sister, Irina Fedorovna, whom the pious and simple tsar had taken to wife, did not have any issue who would have had to die off before he could become tsar.[11]

He also ordered a continual watch to be placed upon the young prince at Uglich, the tsar's brother Dmitry Ivanovich, to observe his words and childish play, and the tyrannical nature of his father began to be noticed. Thus he used to command his playmates, boys of noble families, to write the names of certain princes and noble lords and to have snowmen made of them, saying: "Let this one be a prince, this one a lord, this one a boyar, etc.," after which he said: "This is how I shall treat them when I am tsar," and with those words he began to knock the head off one snowman, the arm off another, the leg off a third, while the fourth he ran right through, and so on around the circle.[12]

Many lords thus feared that he might resemble his father, the dreaded tyrant, and because of this they wished that he would soon join his father in the grave, especially the regent, whose snow figure the tsarevich had placed first in line, and whose head he had struck off, and who thought, like Herod, according to the proverb: "Better to surprise than be surprised."[13] There could be no delay. The young lord had to have the yellow wiped off his beak[14] lest he should grow up to be a tyrant.

In great secrecy Boris hired two Russians to slit the prince's throat in the playground when he was nine years old, and in this way he cleared his own path to the tsardom. In order that it should not be known by whose command this murder had been committed, the regent also ordered that the two murderers, whom he had tempted previously with much money for this purpose, be killed themselves on their way back to Moscow, so that Tsar Fedor Ivanovich could never find out who his brother's assassins were, even though he had so many of the palace guards and guardians of the young lord impaled, beheaded, or drowned, or caused them to undergo such torture that many innocent people lost their health and their lives, since the true malefactors and murderers had been killed on their homeward journey.[15]

The regent also hired certain incendiaries, who set fire to the capital city of Moscow in many places, so that on either side of the Neglinnaia river some thousand houses were destroyed; this was done so that one grief might drive out another, and that each would think more of his own misfortune than the death of the murdered lord.[16] Thus it happened that the young prince perished in his tender youth and was laid to rest in the earth there at Uglich.

ANNO 1597

In this year the simple-minded Tsar Fedor Ivanovich fell into a deadly sickness, from which he died on the day after Epiphany.[17] But even before his death the state councillors had held an assembly to ask the sick tsar who, when God called His own to him, would succeed to the tsardom, since he was without any children or brothers. The tsaritsa, Irina Fedorovna, the regent's own sister, addressed her husband, saying that he should entrust the sceptre to her brother, the regent, who had hitherto governed the land so well. But he did no such thing, extending the sceptre to the eldest of the Nikitich brothers, of whom there were four.[18] Fedor Nikitich was the closest of all to the crown and the sceptre, but he did not take hold of it, but rather thrust it on his next brother, Alexander, who passed it to Ivan, the third brother, who passed it to a fourth, Michael, who passed it on to yet another prince and lord. Nobody wanted to grasp the sceptre before anyone else, even though each was eager to do so, as will be related later. Since the already dying tsar could not delay the handing over of the sceptre, he said: "Take the sceptre whoever will, for I can no longer hold it." The regent, although nobody had asked him, stretched out his hand over the heads of the Nikitich brothers and other persons (who had allowed themselves to be asked) and took the sceptre himself. At that moment the tsar departed from this life, and on the next day, according to their custom, they laid him to rest in the church alongside the other tsars. He had reigned for twelve years.

11 *Concerning Tsar Boris Fedorovich, and How He Came to Rule*

After the death of Tsar Fedor Ivanovich the magnates began to regret that they had refused for so long to take the sceptre, and were very vexed that the regent had been so swift to grasp it. They began to slander him before the people because of his ignoble ancestry, saying that he was not worthy to become tsar. But this did not help them; he who had grasped the sceptre had a good year, and was finally crowned tsar, even though the lords' stout Muscovite cheeks almost burst in envy. Therefore the regent and his sister Irina, widow of the late tsar, acted very craftily. The tsaritsa secretly summoned most of the hundredmen and fiftymen[1] in the city, bribed them with money, gave them lavish promises, and urged them to persuade the soldiers and citizens under them that, when they should be summoned to elect a tsar, they should not agree to anyone but her brother, the regent, who had hitherto been solicitous for the welfare of his subjects and had also led the country in a manner which could not compare to the manner in which many a former tsar had governed. She said that he would let them enjoy themselves if they would help him attain this end.

The regent himself had also gained the approval of certain high-ranking monks from various monasteries throughout the land; also of widows and orphans, whose long-standing lawsuits he had resolved in their favour during his administration; also of certain boyars, to whom he had advanced money and promised great things if only they would agitate among the common people, so that when they were called together for the election they would give their votes to none other than himself. Without delay they proceeded to fulfil this crafty design.

As long as the weeks of mourning lasted, everything went, as they say, confusedly. The regent ceased to concern himself with administrative tasks, so that none of the courts functioned and no legal matters were attended to.

At the same time there was unrest in all the land, and the situation appeared perilous. On the expiry of the six-week period of mourning (as is their custom), in order that the country should not suffer yet greater evils, all the magnates and crown justices were obliged to summon all the estates of the land to the capital city of Moscow, each man to give his opinion as to which of these great lords, princes, and boyars they should choose to have as their tsar.

When all the estates of the realm had assembled for the election, the regent came out to them. He surrendered to the realm the imperial staff and resigned the administration, pretending that he was very glad now to be relieved of the cares and toils, and that the crown and the sceptre were hateful to him; whereat many of these great personages marvelled, not knowing what was in store for them.[2]

While the regent was strolling around, the princes began to call to each other. One spoke to another, who spoke to a third, saying: "This one is worthy to become tsar." When the assembled boyars were called upon to give their opinion, an old man came forward as spokesman for all the boyars. He knew which way things were going,[3] and so he said: "Princes! My dear lords, this matter is not the concern of our estate alone, but of all the subjects of the realm. Whatever they think good, we will not oppose." Thereupon came all the estates, high and low, in great numbers, and the majority saying: "There are in the country enough noble lords, princes, and boyars, but we do not have a wise and judicious tsar." Since the regent Boris Fedorovich had conducted matters of state in a manner incomparable to anyone since the monarchy had been established, they wanted to have him as tsar and nobody else. Then they began to say that the voice of the people was the voice of God;[4] whoever was chosen by all the people was undoubtedly also chosen by God.

These sentiments were not very gratifying to the ears of the great lords, princes, and boyars, but they had to hold their peace. They sent for the regent, but he refused to come, since he did not wish to become tsar (so skilfully did he know how to conceal his guile), and secretly fled to his sister in the New convent,[5] there to take counsel with her (or so he spread the rumour) as to what he should do, whether to go away to a monastery and become a monk, or do something else.[6]

His loyal supporters then rose to meet the situation. They incited the mob,[7] saying that they should not be so dilatory about the business or the regent would be tonsured and then it would be too late; nor would it be possible to find so wise a lord in the whole of Russia. At this point there arose a great clamour among the common multitude, which began to cry out that the lords should make an end to their deliberations and go out with them to the New convent, and together with them should do all possible to expedite the matter at hand. When all the estates had assembled and unanimously agreed to offer the tsardom to the regent, there came forward the senior and most eminent of the monks and priests, princes and boyars, merchants and courtiers, musketeers and artisans to be received by him. But he sent them word that they should save their breath, since they would not achieve anything. He had served the world and been burdened with the administration of the tsardom long enough. Now he wanted to seek tranquillity. Thereupon all the people began to cry out with a loud voice, so that it echoed to the heavens: "Have pity upon us poor scattered people, who do not have a shepherd, and do not refuse to become our tsar."

Such cries continued until he came out. He thanked those present for the honour which they had wished to bestow upon him, but he counselled them to address themselves to the noble magnates and princes, who had more exalted titles and ancestry than he, and who were also older and more experienced. But they did not wish to hear of anyone else, but persisted all the more. They lay with their faces to the ground, and from time to time arose, crying and begging: "Have pity on us, have pity! Have mercy, Lord, have mercy and be our tsar!" But he went back into the convent, and would not let himself be moved.

Then the crowd as a whole thrust forward a group of boys and young men, who chanted piteously in front of the convent, that he might thereby be moved. "Have pity on us, Lord Boris Fedorovich! Though you are not being merciful to our fathers, at least show mercy to us and be our tsar. If perhaps our elders have done evil against you, and for this reason you will not heed our pleas, nevertheless we ourselves are guiltless. Therefore on our account be tsar and lord to this wretched people. This land is full of lost sheep who have no shepherd; be our shepherd according to the will of God, Who will reward you."[8]

In response to this plea from the young men he once again came out, accompanied by his sister, the dowager tsaritsa, but once again he declined. Then the young men began to address themselves to the tsaritsa, begging her to have pity on the scattered sheep and to persuade her lord brother that he no longer refuse to become tsar.

The tsaritsa did as she was asked. She skilfully began to persuade her brother to allow himself to be moved, and give the poor people a favourable answer.[9] Thereupon he addressed the people, saying: "Since I see that a majority of people from all estates are assembled here, and are incessantly begging me, I conclude from this that it is God's will to have me as lord over Russia. In order, however, that I may better ascertain the will of God, I request that the matter be put off for a few weeks, so that all the land might assemble near Serpukhov in June, for a campaign against the Crimean Tatars. If I then see that the whole land is obedient to me, I shall take it as a sign that all the estates are serious about the election."[10]

In this manner the regent gave many refusals, even though he had long desired to be tsar. Consequently, in June all the land around Serpukhov was summoned to proceed against the Tatars and also to elect the regent as tsar.

About the stipulated time and in the appointed place, there assembled eight hundred thousand men skilled in the use of firearms, swords, bows, and arrows.

There was also drawn up a considerable body of artillery, about a hundred pieces of large calibre (there are quite a few of them in this country, and they are so splendidly large and so fine that it is scarcely to be believed here among the German nation), firing salutes in order to impress the Persian and Tatar embassies, which had arrived there and which were to have audience in the field.[11]

In this manner so much powder was expended, and such splendour and magnificence was shown, that both ambassadors were overawed with the great power of the Muscovites, their weaponry, power, and riches, and they doubtless said **that there was no lord equal to this one in the whole wide world**.[12] In this manner both the ambassadors were escorted back to Moscow, and the newly elected tsar conveyed his thanks to the whole community of the land for its obedience and, coming out onto the open field, gave his consent to be tsar, assuring everybody that, with the help of God, he would care for his subjects in such a manner that they would flourish and prosper. Thereupon all of the multitude wished him good fortune, and the most eminent person from each of the estates conducted him back to Moscow, where the imperial crown was placed upon him on **1 September in the year 1597**,[13] in the Church of St Mary (whom they call *Prechista*, that is to say, the Intercessor),[14] by the Patriarch, who in that country is head of the clerical estate. So in this way the regent of the land received the golden carriage for which he had striven for so long by all kinds of cunning and hostile machinations.

At the end of the coronation ceremony, when the tsar had been crowned and led back out of the church, much gold was scattered among the people. The new tsar also gained the favour of the whole land by releasing the whole country from paying the dues the tsar normally expected on the feast of St Giles,[15] which on the occasion of his coronation he was to have received in double the amount. All widows and orphans, citizens and foreigners, were presented with money and victuals[16] at the order of the tsar.

All prisoners throughout the land were released, and even given gifts. The new tsar vowed that for five years he would not put anyone to death but would punish evildoers with demotion and exile to distant territories.[17] He ordered new courthouses and chancelleries to be built.

He issued new decrees and statutes, and put an end to all heathen, sodomite excesses and sins which had hitherto been prevalent in all the land. He strictly forbade excessive drunkenness and closed public houses and taverns with the earnest threat that he would sooner forgive murder or robbery than leave unpunished the opening of a tavern in contravention of his law for the sale of brandywine, mead, or beer, whether consumed on the premises or elsewhere. Each man might enjoy in his own house what God provided, and could provide for his friend or guest, but could not sell any intoxicating beverage to Muscovites, and whosoever could not support himself without the tankard or the tavern, then let him present a petition and the tsar would give him lands and peasants in order to support himself.[18]

During the reign of the tyrant Ivan Vasilievich, many Germans had been taken prisoner and had been brought from Livonia into the country, and had been settled together in a pleasant place where they lived together about half a mile from the Tsar's Kremlin and were well fed.[19] Many of them had served the tsar in the field, and for this had been well rewarded with good estates. To them he had given freedom to hold religious services in their own houses and, in order that in the future he might have among his subjects wise and capable people, he proposed to show his generosity to all the land and recruit scholars from Germany, England, Spain, France, Italy, and elsewhere to set up schools for instruction in foreign languages. But the monks and priests were against it, and would not give their consent, saying that the country was broad and wide and at present was of uniform faith, customs, and speech. If languages other than the native tongue should appear among the Russians, then there would arise dissensions and wrangling in the land, and internal peace would not hold as it had hitherto.

Although because of the opinions of the monks and priests this good intention had to be laid aside, nevertheless he allowed eighteen noble youths from among the Muscovite children to be selected, six of whom were sent to Lübeck, six to England, and six to France, in order that they might be maintained in the schools there, and also that they might gain facility in foreign languages. But up to now only one has returned to Russia, the one named Dmitry, whom King Karl of Sweden appointed as an interpreter to Lord Pontus de la Gardie.[20] The others have had no desire to return to their country, but have travelled even further afield in the world.[21]

To the Germans and merchants who had been taken as captives for many years from the Livonian cities of Dorpat, Narva, Fellin, and other cities (as has been narrated previously), Boris gave freedom, with permission to travel without let or hindrance within and outside the country, and to trade and move about wherever they wished. He ordered loans to be advanced to them out of the imperial treasury, to some three hundred, to others four hundred rubles, without any interest or charges for the entire time until the loans fell due. Up to this time the loans have not been called, nor has anyone paid them back.

And all this was done to the end that his name should be spread far and wide on account of his praiseworthy and generous acts; but every merchant had to swear an oath that he would not defect, that he would not take anyone with him out of the country without the tsar's express permission, and that he would never think ill of the tsar but, on the contrary, always praise and extol him before all men.

ANNO 1599

In this year Boris received tidings concerning the Swedish duke Gustav, the son of Erik, who in his youth had been sent from Sweden by his lady mother who (because she was only the daughter of a humble knight) feared the Swedes would pursue and kill him.[22] He wandered about the world, and eventually settled at Riga, together with very few servants. Through secret emissaries the tsar invited him into his country, ordering that he be met with pomp on the frontier and given large gifts and presents. He wished to marry him to his only daughter. He placed at his disposal and offered him the use of all his soldiers, whom he could use against his treacherous Swedes (as the Muscovites called them on account of their particular dislike of the Swedish nation, since they had suffered great damage from their numerous wars with the illustrious crown of Sweden),[23] to avenge his wrongs upon them and regain the hereditary throne of his fathers.

But Duke Gustav did not wish to consent to this, replying that **he would sooner perish himself** than subject his country to devastation and deprive thousands of people of their lives. He uttered so many other unseemly sentiments that it must be concluded either that he had overtaxed his brain (for he was a learned man) or that his sufferings had deprived him of his senses. Finally, since nobody wished to make war upon the illustrious realm of Sweden, the tsar withdrew his benevolence and affection towards him, and not only would not give him his daughter but even cast such disfavour upon him, that he was exiled altogether from Moscow to Uglich. There he was maintained in a princely fashion, and he died there during the reign of the third subsequent tsar, Vasily Shuisky.

On his deathbed the duke bitterly reproached his concubine, Mistress Kater (whom he had brought, together with her husband, from Danzig), because she had had so much influence over him that not only could he not abandon her but also he valued her counsels above the benevolence of the tsar, and so she was the first and last cause of all his misfortunes.[24] He was buried at Kashin in the monastery of Dmitry Solunsky[25] on 22 February 1607 by the German pastor, Master Martin Beer of Neustadt.[26]

ANNO 1600

In this year the tsar recruited from Germany certain physicians and apothecaries. One physician, who had arrived with the English ambassadors, was requested from the embassy. He was Hungarian, and was called Christopher Reitlinger, a very experienced man and a good physician, who was also skilled in many languages.[27] The others recruited from Germany were Dr David Vasmar[28] and Dr Heinrich Schroeder from Lübeck, Dr Johannes Hyschlenius from Riga, and Dr Kaspar Fiedler from Regensburg. All of these had doctor's degrees and were learned men. The sixth was called Erasmus Benski,[29] from Prague, and he was a medical student. The tsar retained all of them to care for his body, nor were they permitted to attend anyone else, even the great lords, unless previously they had come before His Majesty to obtain his permission.

These were the salaries paid the physicians. Each had two hundred rubles[30] annual salary. They also received monthly rations,[31] that is, subsistence for themselves and all their servants, sixty cartloads of firewood, four tuns of mead, four barrels of beer, one and a half quarts of aquavit daily, the same amount of vinegar daily,[32] and also a side of bacon every other day. On the occasion of banquets (at which there was splendid food), they were presented with three or four dishes from the tsar's table, even one of which could scarcely be carried by a strong menial. Each month they had twelve rubles, that is, thirty-six reichsthalers and twelve groschen, or sometimes fourteen rubles, that is, thirty-six reichsthalers and thirty-three mariagroschen, to buy fresh food daily. The tsar honoured each of them by giving five horses from his own stable, from which he also gave hay and straw sufficient for the generous upkeep of seven horses. He also gave each a good mount, on which he could ride every morning in summer to the Kremlin and to the apothecary, and also a separate horse to draw his sleigh in winter; also two coach horses for their wives, in order that they might attend divine service, and also a workhorse to draw water.

In addition the tsar gave each of them a splendid estate, with thirty or forty peasants. Whenever the medicine which they prescribed for the tsar proved to be effective, they were also given a good length of damask or velvet for a caftan, or forty fine sables.[33] Whenever they attended a great lord, prince, or boyar at the tsar's command, this also did not go without reward. In this way the doctors were held in high esteem, equal to the greatest princes or boyars. He frequently took counsel with them on most important matters, especially on religious subjects, and finally he requested them to pray for him, that he might attain salvation.

Thus the doctors lacked nothing under this tsar, except that they did not have a church.[34] Accordingly they presented a common petition to build a church in the fashion of their choice in the German settlement, situated about a quarter of a mile outside the city of Moscow. The doctors gave generously towards the building of the church, and not a single German failed to follow suit, and they built such a church to the glory of God that subsequently even the tsar considered this German church more worthy than many of his own churches to receive the remains of the brother of the King of Denmark, Duke Johan. He then ordered a tower to be constructed next to it and three bells to be hung there, to be tolled during the duke's interment and in future on each occasion when one of his people died.

So much money was left over after the building of the church that the German community, in addition to their former old pastors (who had been taken prisoner and brought with all the others from Livonia into Russia), called an additional pastor, Master Woldemar Hulle-mann from Westphalia, and a theological student Martin Beer, from Neustadt,[35] both of whom had arrived in the country that very year for the sake of religious ministry and to give instruction in the school. These men did not spare their labour or strength for the glory of God, and in a short time the music in the church was sung in six, seven, or eight parts. The physicians themselves did not disdain to sing in the choir, and many good people began to weep for joy that the merciful God had permitted them to live to see such a splendid time in Moscow.

At the beginning of his reign, Boris had concluded a treaty with Rudolf, the Holy Roman Emperor, and had sent to His Imperial Majesty incense worth many thousands of rubles, fine black fox furs, sables, marten skins, etc., and had promised ten thousand men annually to defend Christendom against the Turks.[36] In this year the Turkish emperor sent an ambassador to Moscow, to Boris Fedorovich, with valuable presents and gifts, desiring his friendship. But Boris sent all these things back to him, together with his reply, "**Insofar as you are the inveterate enemy of Christendom and of our brother the Holy Roman Emperor, we neither are able nor willing to be your friend, but as long as we live we shall be your enemy, and will do all in our power against you.**" He also sent the Turks a splendid hide of tanned white pigskin made into a large leather pouch, which was encrusted in glistening diamonds[37] and well sewn, but was filled

LIVONIA ca. 1600

with pig manure. The Turkish embassy received this gift with such
esteem that to this day no further embassy has come to Moscow.[38]

He also concluded a perpetual peace with the King of Sweden.[39]
With the Poles he concluded a twenty-one-year truce,[40] and also
entered into negotiations with the Tatars. He also concluded friendly
and neighbourly relations with His Majesty, King Christian of Denmark, and also with His Majesty's brother, Duke Johan, to whom he
wished to betroth his only daughter. But after that good lord had
been six weeks in Muscovy, he died of a burning fever, and was
buried solemnly in the German church, where his remains are to
this day enclosed in a vault near the altar.[41]

And although the church itself was completely burned down by the
soldiers of the second Dmitry (as will be related hereafter), nevertheless the prince's burial place remained intact.[42] All that His Princely
Grace had brought with him from Denmark into Russia, and all that
with which the tsar had honoured him, was sent with the retinue of

His Princely Grace back to the Danish kingdom. He rewarded all the princely servitors, lords, gentry, knights, squires, and all the others who were with him, with splendid honours, to such an extent that not even the meanest stableboy or kitchen menial was forgotten.

ANNO 1601

On 4 October of this year he showed his kindness and benevolence to those who had been driven out of Livonia. For when Duke Karl of Sweden[43] had in this year conquered most of Livonia from the Polish crown, he subjected almost all of Livonia to himself on behalf of the Swedish crown, and compelled the nobles and non-nobles (since they had been left undefended by their lord the King of Poland) to break their oath and swear allegiance to the Swedish crown. The Poles, however, who subsequently took to the field, offered him resistance, winning a few victories before Erlau, Kokenhausen, and other places, recovering and capturing the lost cities and castles, and so fortune turned its back on Karl. So the good[44] people who had previously sworn allegiance to him and to the crown of Sweden did not know where they should live, having to leave their houses and goods behind and flee with their wives and children before the Poles. They wished to seek refuge in the fortresses still belonging to Karl, but since the fortresses of Sesswegen, Marienburg, and Kirrumpä[45] were in a ruined state, they decided not to await the arrival of the embittered Poles.

Accordingly, about thirty-five of them, noble and non-noble, who had lands and peasants of their own, gathered near the fortress of Neuhausen, situated right on the Muscovite frontier.[46] They wished to take refuge from the Poles, but the governor of that fortress, Otto von Vittinghofen, a Livonian nobleman whom Duke Karl had appointed castellan there, refused to receive them, declaring that there was no room to spare for them. Yet several weeks after I, Conrad Bussow, left, having administered this fortress for almost four years at the appointment of His Highness Duke Karl (who had appointed my humble self as one of the intendants of all the lands, fortresses, and cities conquered from the Polish crown), he found plenty of room for the Poles, to whom he betrayed and surrendered the fortress, at the same time violating his oath and duty, which he had sworn to His Princely Grace and the most praiseworthy crown of Sweden, even as previously he had betrayed the oath which he had sworn to the Polish crown.[47]

Wherefore these unfortunate people were reduced to destitution and were greatly distressed, not knowing where they and their families could seek refuge from the Poles. They decided to cross the Muscovite frontier and seek refuge close to the Muscovite Caves monastery,[48] requesting permission to remain there for a short time.

Even though the local abbot granted their requests and pleas, he did not dare delay in informing the tsar in Moscow of this occurrence, with a request to instruct him whether he should suffer them to remain there. He received a reply that not only should he permit them to remain encamped there but he should also express to them the tsar's solicitude, and tell them that the tsar took their misfortunes very much to heart. The tsar also insisted that they be invited in his name to be guests in the monastery and, after they had been entertained, the tsar wished them to come to him in Moscow, since they had lost all their possessions in Livonia and the outcome of the conflict was still uncertain, for the war could last still some considerable time. There he would give them three times the amount of land that they had possessed and lost in Livonia.

When the abbot, in accordance with the tsar's commands, invited them as guests into the monastery and expounded to them the tsar's good wishes with his proposal, they were more distressed than pleased. Since they were free people, they did not wish to fall into perpetual servitude. For this reason they thanked the tsar for his great benevolence, his Christian solicitude, and his generous offer, as well as the lavish hospitality of the abbot, but requested permission to stay a little longer. Thereupon they left the monastery and returned to where they had their encampment.

On the following days they were visited frequently by monks and boyars, who strongly urged them to go to the tsar in Moscow, since he would be so gracious to them, and show them such favour, they said, that they would not be sorry but, on the contrary, they would be gratified all the more. But despite all these importunate urgings, not one of them showed any desire to be persuaded.

Several days later, they were visited by an interpreter from the Monastery of the Caves, a Muscovite who for several years had been captive among the Germans in the Swedish realm, and who had thoroughly learned the German language. He said that he had been shown so much kindness and favour by the Germans who had held him captive that he was very well disposed towards the German nation, and he also felt very friendly towards them in particular. Since the Tsar of Russia had invited them to Moscow, and was making them such kind and generous offers, he urged them in conscience not under any circumstances to reject such great kindness, or persist in their refusal any longer, for in confidence he could not conceal from them that, in the event that they rejected the tsar's kindness, and refused to go to Moscow of their own accord, not one of them would be allowed to return to Livonia but they would be arrested as spies and taken bound hand and foot to Moscow. And if they should be dealt with thus, they should understand that no good would come of it for any of them, and they would be far wiser to declare to the abbot, without delay, that not only would they accept the favour offered by the tsar with profound gratitude and devotion but also they should decide and resolve finally to set off at the earliest opportunity and go to His Majesty the Tsar in Moscow.

The interpreter's words and advice greatly alarmed the good people. They vehemently blamed Otto von Vittinghofen for not having admitted them to the fortress, for if they had all been there to aid the defence, he would never have seen a single Pole in Neuhausen as long as he lived.

These good people were not a little perturbed. One proposed this thing, another that. In Livonia there would have been no place for them under Polish rule, and Duke Karl was no longer in any position to offer them protection, since the Poles had conquered all his fortresses and cities. Therefore whosoever came into Russia would have to stay there for good. Accordingly it would be far worse for them if here, as the interpreter had counselled them privily, they brought upon themselves anger and disfavour; all the more so since they would have ungraciously refused the great favour which had been extended towards them.

Therefore with one accord they decided to choose the lesser of two evils,[49] as the saying goes, and appeared before the abbot, telling him that they were fully prepared to set out for Moscow, to the Tsar of All Russia, provided that they were not held captive there, nor would they or their wives and children be killed. Such a declaration on their part pleased the abbot exceedingly. He gave them much encouragement, saying that they could proceed safely and confidently, for nobody had any evil intentions towards them. He swore by his God and upon the cross that no evil would befall them, but rather great favour and many benefits.

Having thus given their oath to the abbot and kissed the cross, they entered the monastery, albeit sadly. The abbot and the monks received them very graciously, lodged each one with his family in the hospice, and allowed none to pay so much as a penny for their entertainment. The tsar ordered them to be maintained without charge, both in the monastery and also at Pskov, Novgorod, Tver, and all the places on the way. Wine, beer, mead, and also boiled and roasted meats were given to them in such quantity that it would have been sufficient for thrice as many.

Andrei Vasilievich Trubetskoy, who at that time was governor of Pskov, and all the citizens gave them a splendid welcome. Not only were their own names recorded but also those of their wives, children, household servants, and maids. They also recorded who among them was of noble and who of non-noble rank, and what property had belonged to whom in Livonia, and also who was in service with whom or what had been his occupation. This report was sent on ahead to Moscow. The Livonians were kept there altogether eight days, and in general were entertained very well. They were persuaded to sell their horses and put the money in their purses, for the tsar had horses enough to make the journey.

They were provided thereafter with all the drivers and horses they needed, and the servitors, who were poorly clad, were issued with warm fur robes. Thus they set off in the name of God and arrived in Moscow in November of the year 1601.[50] The tsar had vacated a boyar palace close to the Kremlin in order to billet the Germans, and immediately he ordered to be sent there all that was necessary for their housekeeping – wood, fish, meat, salt, butter, cheese, wine, mead, beer, and bread – and even attached a Muscovite to the head of each household as a steward,[51] who could be sent for provisions and other purchases, and to sell or procure or do whatsoever was needed.

On 23 November the tsar sent them some money, to one six rubles, to another nine, and to a third twelve, to some more, to others less, according to the number of people each had with him, to purchase what they needed, and they were also given weekly rations.

On 12 December the new Germans were told to make ready and dress in their best clothes on the following day, when they were to have an audience with the tsar. But most of them excused themselves, saying that they were not worthy to appear before His Majesty in such shabby attire. The tsar sent his reply, saying that this did not make any man unworthy; he wanted to see their persons, not their clothes. Let every man come in the best clothes he had brought with him. He would clothe them in the same manner as his own Germans, who had come to him on account of his reputation, and would provide for them handsomely.

On 13 December the tsar sat with his son in state with all his senators and high boyars, all dressed in diamonds and cloth of gold, adorned with items of finery, great gold chains and handsome jewels, standing and sitting around the tsar and his son in the same audience chamber.

The vaults above and all the four walls and the floor, wherever people walked and wherever they stood, were covered with valuable

Turkish tapestries and[52] carpets. So the new Germans were conducted before His Majesty in due order, the eldest first, then the middle-aged, and then the youngest, all of whom paid their respects in German to the tsar and his son.

The tsar said through his interpreter: "You foreigners from the Holy Roman Empire, you Germans from Livonia and Germans from the Swedish kingdom, all are welcomed by us in our country. We are pleased that you have arrived safe and sound after so long a journey to our capital city of Moscow. Your woes, and the fact that you have had to flee, abandoning your loved ones and forsaking all, we have taken very much to heart. But do not grieve. We shall recompense you threefold for all that you possessed over there. We will make your nobles princes, and your burghers and lesser servicemen nobles. We will also allow your non-German[53] servants and your drivers to be freemen in our country. We will give you sufficient land, peasants, and servants; we shall clothe you in velvet, silk, and brocade, and will fill your empty pockets once again with money. We shall be to you, not a tsar and sovereign, but a father, and you shall be unto us not subjects, but our Germans and sons, for nobody shall have authority over you but we ourselves. We will be your judge if any contentious matters arise among you. You may practise your faith, religion, and observances as freely as in your own country. You shall swear to us by your own God and faith that you will serve us and our son truly, not betray us or go from us out of the country without our permission, or flee or defect to any other sovereign, whether to the Turks, Tatars, Poles, or Swedes. If you hear of any treasonable sentiments against us, you must not conceal them from us. You shall not do any harm to us, whether by sorcery or by poison. If you observe and stand fast by all this, we shall favour and reward you to such an extent that men will speak of it abroad among other nations, especially in the Holy Roman Empire."

Dietloff von Thiesenhausen, a skillful and eloquent Livonian noble, pronounced on behalf of all a short speech of gratitude for the tsar's benevolence and kindness, and under oath undertook on behalf of them all to be faithful and devoted even unto death to their Lord Father, the Tsar of All Russia. The tsar replied: "My dear children, pray to God for us and for our health. As long as we live you shall not want for anything." He grasped his pearl necklace with his fingers, saying: "We would even share this with you."

Thereupon the tsar stretched forth his hand with the staff, and the Germans had to come forward one by one to kiss his hand and that of his son. After that he commanded that they all remain to partake of the midday meal at His Imperial Majesty's table. A long table was brought in directly before the tsar and his son. The more senior were placed at the table in such a manner that the tsar could see their faces, while the others sat with their backs to him. First of all fine wheaten bread and salt were set on the covered table in silver dishes. Noble boyars were commanded to serve and wait upon table. For the first course this large long table was so loaded with so many fine viands and dishes that there was scarcely room for anyone to put down a slice of bread.

This entertainment went on until the evening. There was a great superfluity of all kinds of foreign wine, mead, and beer. The tsar ordered the first courses to be brought to him. He ate from them, saying: "My dear Germans, we have invited you to share the tsar's salt and bread,[54] and to dine with you in person. Therefore, take and enjoy what God has sent." The Germans arose, blessed his food, saying: "**God grant our lord[55] good health and long life.**" As soon as the tsar had taken his first sip, he ordered the name of each man to be called out saying: "**We drink to you all. Accept our toast.**" The boyars plied the Germans with drink, but they observed moderation, since they had been advised by their stewards of the tsar's temperance and his dislike of seeing people flushed with drink. The gracious tsar took note of this and asked with a smile why they were not making merry and drinking each other's health, as was the custom among the Germans. They replied that this was not the suitable place, for here each had to deport himself respectfully, and in the tsar's presence it was befitting to behave with moderation. The tsar replied: "We wish to entertain you, because we have invited you, and all that you have done today has been well done. Drink our health on that; everything is provided, and when you are ready to return to your lodging, horses and carriages are ready and waiting to take you back safely." Then the tsar stood up and had himself conducted within to his consort. He ordered silver casks with golden hoops, containing all manner of costly beverages, to be brought into the palace. He ordered the boyars to entertain the Germans in such a manner that they would not remember how they had got back home, which indeed was what happened to most of them.

On 18 December the Germans were ordered to the chancellery of military appointments.[56] The chancellor divided them into four groups. The first group consisted of the senior and most noble, who were told that the tsar, their father, on the occasion of their arrival had granted each, in addition to his monthly sustenance, fifty rubles in money, a Hungarian robe of cloth of gold, a length of black velvet, and forty fine sables, so that they might clothe themselves in honour of the tsar; and the same amount of money would be given them annually. They would also be given an estate with one hundred fully equipped peasants. All this would be granted them within the next few days.

The second group consisted of men in their thirties and forties. These were given each thirty rubles, a length of red damask, forty sables, a robe of silver thread, and an estate with fifty fully equipped peasants, together with an annual salary of thirty rubles.

The third group consisted of younger nobles and several of the more experienced soldiers. These were given each twenty rubles, a length of ordinary velvet, a piece of red silk to make a robe, forty sables, thirty fully equipped peasants for their estates, and their annual salary was twenty rubles.

A fourth group consisted of younger commoners, and those who had been knights or squires in the retinues of nobles. These were given fifteen rubles, a length of scarlet silk to make a robe, a length of yellow damask to make a robe, a lesser quantity of sables, and each an estate with twenty fully equipped peasants on the holding, and their annual salary was fifteen rubles. Furthermore it was stipulated to them that whenever the tsar required them to fight against his enemies, they were to be ready at all times, as was indeed incumbent upon them for having received such splendid estates and such generous monetary reward. Thus the good kind tsar Boris Fedorovich made so many destitute people noble and rich, turning their sorrow into joy. This therefore was proclaimed far and wide.

ANNO 1602

Emissaries came to Moscow from the city of Lübeck, Master Konrad Germers the burgomaster, Master Heinrich Kerckling, a member of the city council, and Master Johannes Brambach, the town secretary, with a number of townspeople and splendid and valuable presents and gifts. In the name of the whole Hansa they solicited free trade and commerce. They also sought the ancient privileges which they themselves had held, together with permission to reopen the counter[57] which formerly they had there.[58] Having heard their proposal, the tsar explained that he did not wish to deal with the Hansa, because he did not know anything about it, but with the city of Lübeck, with which he was conversant and to which he was inclined always graciously, he wished to have friendship and good neighbourly relations. And in fact he was generous to them, giving them great trading privileges in his country and graciously permitted them once again to trade and open their counter, so that the citizens of Lübeck on this occasion obtained and were granted so much that, regardless of the lamentable war and desolation of the country, the city of Lübeck was to derive considerable revenue.

In short, this Boris tried to rule in such a way that his name would be praised in many lands, that there should be tranquillity in his own land, and that his subjects might live in great security. He ordered the construction and improvement of many fortresses and towns. He had the whole great capital city of Moscow surrounded and fortified with great high walls of quarried stone. At the same time he had the great town and fortress of Smolensk completely surrounded by a wall, twenty-three feet thick and very high, so that the king of Poland's soldiers (when the king, as will be narrated hereafter, besieged Smolensk) could hardly build scaling ladders of length sufficient to reach the battlements.[59] On the Tatar frontiers he had built two strongholds, one of which was called Borisgorod, in his honour, while the other was called Tsargorod; their purpose was to repel and hinder the annual Tatar raids.[60]

But the Lord did not bless his reign, since he had obtained the tsardom by murder and treachery. In the end he brought just retribution upon himself.[61] What he had done was visited in turn upon himself and his dear ones. For what he had done, God rewarded him accordingly. He had attained his possessions and his crown by such violence that he, like Herod, was to live in great anxiety and suspense.

The first to rise up against him was Bogdan Belsky, a godless malefactor and bitter tyrannical enemy of the Germans, who had formerly been a chamberlain to Ivan Vasilievich.[62] Ivan had instructed him and instigated him in many acts of cruelty. The tsar had sent this troublemaker to be governor and master of the works on the Tatar frontier, where he was to complete the construction of Borisgorod. When the stronghold was completed and ready, this evildoer made bold to maintain that he was now tsar in Borisgorod, while Boris Fedorovich was tsar in Moscow. But he did not bear the title for very long, in fact only until the matter came to the attention of Boris Fedorovich through one of the Germans who had been sent with Belsky. He ordered the self-proclaimed tsar of Borisgorod to be brought from there to Moscow in such regalia as befitted not a lord but merely a common mutineer, since he was no better than that.

But since, as has been narrated previously, Tsar Boris had given an oath that he would not shed blood for five years,[63] he had all Belsky's possessions and goods confiscated, and gave his bondsmen manumission, with permission to serve wherever they wished. A Scottish captain, Gabriel by name, was ordered by the tsar to tear out the beard of the pretender tsar in handfuls. Finally he was sent in disgrace to Siberia, which is situated several hundred miles from Moscow, and which in former times had been conquered from the Tatars, so that there he could indulge his unrestrained thirst for power.[64]

Others who were disaffected towards him were the four Nikitich brothers, whom I mentioned earlier, who after the death of Tsar Fedor stood closer to the throne and had been offered the tsar's sceptre, but had refused, whereupon Boris Fedorovich had taken it, even though he had not been called upon to do so, nor had the sceptre been offered to him. They were heartily grieved at the manner in which Bogdan Belsky had been treated. For some time they had held their peace and kept silent, but finally they resolved to proceed in a different fashion, namely to administer poison to Boris and in this manner to destroy him. But they also were unsuccessful, since they were denounced by their own people, and all their dear ones were brought to perdition, and the ringleaders were likewise sent in disgrace several hundred miles distant.[65]

Thereafter Boris was very careful what he ate or drank, and also paid great attention to his personal security. He ordered many thousands of musketeers into the city to guard his person day and night, wherever he went or wherever he was, whether he was in the Kremlin, or on pilgrimage to some monastery, so that the princes and boyars could do nothing against him, whether by poison or by mutiny.

Seeing that he could achieve nothing either by poison or by murder, the devil inspired them with another poison, namely recourse to deceit, and they used for this end a surprising instrument of the devil, and it happened in such a manner that everyone said: **"What Stygian Pluto does not dare attempt will be tried by a renegade monk and a deceitful old woman."**[66] There was a monk whose name was Grishka Otrepiev. Since all the monks were in league with those who wished to betray or rebel against Boris, they persuaded him to go away and, in order to allay suspicion, they claimed that he had fled the monastery. He was instructed to proceed to the Kingdom of Poland, there in great secrecy to seek out a young man similar in age and stature to the young Dmitry who had been murdered at Uglich and, when he could find such a person, persuade him to proclaim himself as Dmitry, saying that when his assassins were prepared to kill him, some devoted people, by the will of God, had taken him away in great secrecy, and another had been killed in his place.

The monk needed no urging. Having arrived at the Polish frontier, on the Dnieper in White Russia (which belongs to the Polish crown), he cast forth his net and landed just the kind of person he wanted, namely a well-born and valiant youth who, as I have heard from some prominent Polish lords, was a natural son of the former Polish king Stefan Bathory. This same monk instructed the young man in all that was needed to fulfil his design.[67] After thorough instruction, he gave him this piece of advice, that he should attempt to enter the service of Prince Adam Wisniowiecki,[68] since he lived in White Russia right on the Muscovite border, and that whenever he had a favourable opportunity he should complain, with mournful countenance and sorrowful words, of his ill fortune, and reveal to the prince that he was the rightful heir of the Muscovite realm and the youngest son of the former tsar, Ivan Vasilievich, and that when he was yet a child, Boris Godunov had tried to kill him, and that had not God hindered his design, and had not some devoted people succeeded in removing him, he would have been murdered.

He should always and everywhere conduct and comport himself as he, Otrepiev, had instructed and taught him. And so that the princes and others would believe him (when in due course he revealed himself to them), the monk also gave him a golden cross given the murdered Dmitry at his baptism as a christening present by his godfather, Prince Ivan Mstislavsky, which had been around his neck when he was killed. On this cross were engraved the names of Dmitry and his godfather.

After the monk had set this stratagem in motion, he returned to Russia and proceeded to the field Cossacks on the Wild Steppe, spreading the rumour among them that the legitimate heir of the Muscovite land, Dmitry Ivanovich (whom the now reigning Boris had wished to destroy at Uglich) was truly alive and held in great honour at the dwelling of Prince Adam Wisniowiecki on the frontier. They should rally to him, and he would later reward them generously if they held true to him. And the monk Grishka Otrepiev who had been sent did not spare any effort to raise a detachment of soldiers.

The youth who had been so instructed was hired as a valet and comported himself well. And so, one day when the prince was stepping into his bath, and he was in attendance in the bathroom, the prince ordered something to be brought to him in the bathroom, but he did not bring it. Whereupon the prince was angry and gave him a slap in the face, berating him as a whoreson. Then the youth made an expression, as if he took all this very much to heart, and wept bitterly in the bathroom, saying to the prince: **"If only you, Prince Adam, knew who I am, you would not have abused me and called me a whoreson, neither would you have borne so heavily**

upon me for such a triviality. But since now I find myself here as your servant, I must bear this with patience."

The prince said: "Who are you? What is your name?" The youth was well rehearsed and he did as he had been instructed, claiming to be the youngest son of Ivan Vasilievich, lately tsar in Moscow, and related in correct order how he had fared in his childhood, and how the now reigning tsar Boris Fedorovich had made an attempt upon his life. He also told how he had escaped, who had aided him, and how long he had maintained himself secretly in White Russia before entering the prince's service. He also showed him the golden cross set with costly jewels, which his godfather had given him as a christening present at his baptism – all according to what the monk Grishka Otrepiev had instructed and taught him. Falling at the prince's feet in the Muscovite fashion, he said: "Prince Adam Wisniowiecki, since it now happens that you have learned who I am, I now place myself in your power. Do with me as you wish, since I wish no longer to live in such abasement. If you will help me regain what is mine, you will receive back everything and more, if God will help me."[69]

Prince Adam was amazed and astounded and, since the young man was courteous, and also clever and modest, and had also shown him the fine cross, he believed his words, being convinced that he truly was the son of the tyrant. He asked forgiveness for the slap in the face and the abusive words, invited him to remain in the bathroom and also bathe himself, and asked him not to emerge until he came back for him.

He went to his wife and ordered her to make preparation throughout the kitchens, cellars, halls, and chambers, to do and prepare everything that they might that very evening entertain and lodge the tsar of Muscovy. This news appeared especially strange to his wife and all his household, namely that the tsar of Russia should visit them at such short notice and so unexpectedly. He had six horses saddled and splendidly caparisoned, assigned to each a groom dressed in fine clothes, had his best carriage prepared as quickly as possible, and had six choice carriage horses hitched to it and kept standing in the courtyard. The servants doubtless thought that the master himself was preparing to go on a journey somewhere.

As soon as everything was ordered according to his satisfaction, he took with him twelve of his servants, went to the bathroom, and honoured with costly garments his erstwhile servant, the young tsar of Russia. He did him ample honour, attended him personally, led him out of the bathroom and presented him with the six riding horses and six attendant grooms, together with the saddles, swords, muskets, and all other appurtenances, and also the princely carriage with the six carriage horses and footmen and other servants to attend his person. He asked if His Majesty would be so gracious as to accept such mean gifts from him, a mere prince, and that if he could do him any other service, he would not spare any labour or effort. Let him not doubt that he should expect all the best from him. The young man bowed deeply and thanked him, promising that if God helped him he would recompense the prince a hundredfold. From that time on he maintained himself in a lordly manner.

Thus it was that a rumour concerning the young man was bruited hither and thither, reaching the ears of Boris Fedorovich, the tsar reigning in Moscow, who had ordered the young Dmitry strangled during his childhood. He was greatly terrified by the news, thinking such a matter not conducive to tranquillity and peace with his enemies the Poles. On account of this, he sent in great secrecy to Prince Adam Wisniowiecki, offering him several Muscovite fortresses and cities situated on the border as his hereditary possession and a large sum of money if only he would surrender the brigand.[70]

As a consequence of this offer from Boris, the prince was even more confirmed in his resolve to cast aside his doubts and believe that the young man truly was the son of the tyrant, since Boris was so intent upon pursuing him. He sent messengers back saying he had no such person with him, and that he had heard nothing about him, nor did he know anything.

But since the extent of Muscovite power and its close proximity caused the prince certain misgivings, and therefore he feared an unexpected attack, he ordered a carriage to be made ready immediately for himself and the young man and, accompanied by a number of outriders, withdrew with them to another town, called Wisniowiec, situated several miles further from the frontier and deeper into the country. There he showed the youth Boris's letter. When he had seen and understood its contents, he wept bitterly, saying: "As God and you will![71] Do with me what you will. I am in your power, and I entrust myself to you."

The prince said that he should have no fear, for he would not betray him. He had travelled with him from his castle to this place, a little further from the frontier, lest he be captured in an unforeseen attack (for it was so close to the frontier) and fall into the hands of his enemies. Here in this town of Wisniowiec he should remain with his servants, while he, the prince, would travel back, and if he heard anything further concerning Boris, he would inform the young man immediately.

If Boris Godunov sent yet another messenger to Prince Adam Wisniowiecki, with yet more generous offers than before, and at the same time dispatched many assassins to shoot the man claiming to be Dmitry, then the prince would see to it that Dmitry was sent on from there to Upper Poland, to the governor of Sandomir, where he would also be accepted as the son of Ivan Vasilievich and would remain unharmed by Boris's assassins.

ANNO 1604

In January Master Johan Thierfeld wrote from German Narva[72] (which is situated in Livonia upon the Muscovite border) to Finland, to the governor of Åbo, informing him, among other things, that there was certain news that Ivan Vasilievich the Tyrant's youngest son, who was reputed to have been murdered, was truly alive and had been with the Cossacks in the Wild Steppe, and was striving to recover his patrimony, on account of which there was much unrest in Russia. The Muscovites seized this emissary on the way, and sent him first to Ivangorod (which is called Russian Narva) and then on to Moscow, but the letters which were found upon him gave Boris very little pleasure.[73]

In the same year and month Tsar Boris sent an emissary to Kazan (which lies 250 German miles beyond Moscow, while Astrakhan is five hundred miles). The name of this emissary was Stepan Stepanovich Godunov, a kinsman of Boris. In the Wild Steppe, through which he was obliged to travel, he was overtaken by the savage Cossacks, whom the devil's agent, the monk Grishka Otrepiev, had set afoot, and who were on the march to besiege the town of Putivl, which is situated within Russia on the White Russian border, in order to seek out their lawful sovereign (for they knew no better) with Prince Adam Wisniowiecki, who was in the vicinity. They beat to death many of the retinue of the tsar's emissary and took some of them prisoner. The emissary himself escaped with great difficulty and was forced to return to Moscow without achieving his mission. Some of the prisoners were set free with instructions to go to Moscow to their unlawful tsar, and give him the news that they would come to Moscow with several thousand men, field Cossacks and Poles, and also bring with them the lawful heir Dmitry.[74]

These and many other missions, which came simultaneously out of White Russia, Poland, and Lithuania, troubled Boris so much that he began to doubt who had been killed when he had given orders for the slaying, whether the young lord Dmitry or some other person in his place. He therefore ordered an inquiry to be made with special diligence, and, having received conclusive evidence that it was the true Dmitry and that none other had been killed in his place, he pondered and realized that all this must be the contrivance and machination of those traitorous princes and boyars.[75]

But if I may interject the truth, it was a punishment from God, to teach Boris that no wisdom can prevail against the Lord God, Who can turn the cunning mind into foolishness. Boris was of the opinion that he had attained the tsardom by his own cunning, without the aid of God, and therefore it was necessary that he recognize that his crafty stratagems would avail him nothing against the Lord God and so, although his intentions had been prudent, not one of them had had a fortunate outcome.

The alliances which he had concluded with great potentates had been of no assistance to him. All his labours and strivings, which had been applied with his great understanding to the betterment of the land, were little heeded. The unprecedented generosity of his alms-giving, which he had given out during the great scarcity which had continued and lasted for several years, had not saved the poor from great famine and plague in his country, for people had died by the thousands.

The famine began in 1601 and lasted until 1604, during which time a cask of rye cost ten or twelve florins, whereas previously such a cask had ordinarily cost no more than twelve or fifteen maria-groschen, and the famine in the land was even more severe than at the siege of Jerusalem, which can be read about in Josephus, when the Jews devoured dogs, cats, rats, and mice, leather from saddles and shoes, and even pigeon manure. On account of the great hunger one noble lady hacked to pieces her own child, whom she boiled, roasted, and then ate. More gruesome tales are not to be found even in Josephus.

But I swear to God that this is the truth. I saw with my own eyes people lying on the streets, eating grass like cattle in summer and hay in winter. Some were already dead, with hay and dung in their mouths, and also (pardon my indelicacy) had swallowed human excrement and hay. It cannot be reckoned how many children were slain, hacked to pieces, and cooked by their parents, parents by their children, guests by their hosts, or hosts by their guests. Human flesh, cut into small pieces and cooked in *pirogi* (that is, baked pasties), was sold in the market as the flesh of other animals and eaten, so that a traveller at this time had to take great care with whom he lodged.

At that time, on account of the fearful scarcity and famine, such dreadful, inhuman, and in some cases unprecedented slayings as these took place, and many dead bodies of people who had perished through hunger were found daily in the streets. All this was reported to Boris. He thought to avert this distress and divine punishment from his treasury, and ordered four great suburbs to be enclosed within the outer wall of the great city, which has a circumference of four German miles. He assembled the poor in the city early each morning, and paid each man one penny, thirty-six of which are equal to one ordinary thaler. Such benevolence prompted all the poor country folk to abandon their homesteads, leave everything behind, and rush with their wives and children to Moscow, where they hoped to receive money. Such a multitude of paupers assembled that more than five hundred thousand pennies were distributed daily (this is equivalent to 13,888 thalers and 32 mariagroschen).[76]

This went on continually, but the scarcity did not abate. Daily, everywhere on the streets, hundreds of corpses were gathered up at the tsar's command and carried away on so many carts, that to behold it (scarcely to be believed)[77] was grisly and horrible. The dead had to be washed carefully by persons especially appointed for the task and wrapped in a white linen shroud; then a pair of red slippers was placed on their feet, and they were carried to the "House of God,"[78] that is, the place where those who have died without the benefit of the sacrament are buried. And on account of the tsar's benevolence in feeding the hungry, or clothing and burying the dead, many thousands of rubles were expended in these four years and the treasury was somewhat exhausted.[79]

In order to make an easy reckoning, and according to information which I obtained from chancellery officials and merchants, in the city of Moscow alone more than five hundred thousand persons[80] died of hunger at the time of the famine, who while they were alive had received subsistence from His Majesty, and who after their death received red slippers and a white shroud and were buried at his expense. This occurred in one city alone. What multitude of people died over this long time from hunger and plague in all the corners of the land in other cities, to be buried at the expense of the treasury! **O, how many hundreds of thousands these must have been!** How many hundreds of thousands a year this all must have cost! **O woe! How God's fearful anger is ignited, and burns over all the land!**[81]

Yet Boris was so blinded and deluded that so many calamities did not move him to humble himself, and he sought all the more to avert this misfortune by means of his rich treasury. And even though God in His benevolence and mercy saw to it that some ships came from the German coastal cities to Russian Narva (which the Russians call Ivangorod), which could have fed some hundreds of thousands of people, Boris could not countenance such a disgrace, that grain from foreign countries should be bought and sold in this country, so rich in grain, and so the ships turned around and put out to sea without selling their grain. Nobody was permitted to buy a single ton of grain, on pain of corporal punishment.

He ordered a survey throughout the land to seek out further stocks of grain, and thus discovered many stacks of grain a hundred or more spans[82] long, which had stood in the fields for fifty years or more without being threshed and were overgrown by trees. He ordered this grain threshed and brought to Moscow, and also sent among the other towns. He also had his granaries opened in all the towns, and many tons were sold at half price. To widows and orphans who were sorely in need but were ashamed to ask, especially those of the German nation, he unsparingly sent several tons of flour to their houses, lest they starve. He also called upon the princes, boyars, and monasteries to take to heart the calamities of the people and make available their grain supplies, selling them at a somewhat lower price than they were currently asking.

But even though all this was done, the devil of avarice, through the will of God, so prompted the Muscovite grain speculators to take advantage of the situation that they persuaded poor people to buy up cheap grain for them from the tsar, boyars, and monasteries, which they afterwards resold at greatly inflated prices. By the time God's anger was appeased and the famine had run its course, many hundreds of thousands had perished through hunger, and Boris had almost completely exhausted his treasury; new horrors and punishments then overtook them, namely war and bloodshed, as will be narrated hereafter.

In July 1604 Freiherr von Logau, the ambassador from the Holy Roman Emperor Matthias[83] came to Russia with a numerous suite. Boris gave orders that in those places through which the embassy passed, no beggar should be seen. He also ordered emergency supplies to be brought to the markets in those towns, lest foreigners notice any scarcity. Since it was necessary to meet the ambassador and receive him ceremoniously half a mile from Moscow, each of the princes, boyars, Germans, Poles, and all other foreigners who had lands and peasants was ordered, on pain of forfeiture of annual salary, to array himself richly and splendidly as possible, in velvet, silk and brocade, wearing his best garments in honour of the tsar, and to come out and meet the Imperial ambassador and to take part in his entry into Moscow. Many an unfortunate person, against his will and desire, had to array himself luxuriously, buying and borrowing from merchants at double the price for such costly items as neither he nor his forebears had ever worn or had had any desire to wear. Whosoever on this occasion was the most splendidly arrayed was the tsar's best servant, receiving an increment to his annual salary and landed possessions. He who did not array himself in such a manner, or in relation to his means arrayed himself poorly, was subjected to abuse and threatened with confiscation of his annual salary and landed possessions, despite the fact that on account of the famine he had been compelled to pawn his precious wardrobe and had scarcely enough to provide for necessities.[84]

All kinds of articles were supplied and ordered for the entertainment of the lord ambassador, and the people went about so splendidly that there was no scarcity to be seen in the streets, only within doors and in the heart. Under threat of corporal punishment no one was to complain to the lord ambassador's suite that there was or ever had been scarcity in the land, but instead was to say, falsely, how cheap things were. By such inordinate pride Boris inevitably drew upon himself the even greater wrath of God, and the sword followed upon famine and plague.

While the famine continued, there were many unusual portents heralding the onset of war. At night there appeared in the sky fearful flashes of light, as if two armies were in combat, from which there was as much brightness and light as if the moon were shining. Meanwhile two moons stood in the sky, and several times three suns. Many unprecedented windstorms arose, as a result of which many of the gables upon the city gates were cast down, as well as the crosses on the churches. Humans and animals gave birth to many monstrosities, fish disappeared from the waters, birds from the air, and beasts from the forest, and whatsoever of these was cooked and brought to the table had no longer its previous natural taste, even though it had been elaborately prepared. Dogs devoured each other, and so did wolves.[85] From whence the sword came,[86] wolves set up so great a howling as no man could have thought possible. Wolves roamed around in such large packs that travellers could not move in small groups. One German goldsmith caught a young eagle and, since he could not hold it alive in captivity, he beat it to death and brought it to Moscow, which was also a novelty, as eagles never appear in those parts. Various breeds of fox, grey, red, and black, ran around Moscow in broad daylight within the walls and were caught. This continued the whole year, but nobody knew whence so many foxes had come. In September of the year 1604 a black fox was killed in close proximity to the Kremlin. One merchant paid ninety rubles for pelts or fur. This is equivalent to three hundred Polish guilders, at the calculation of thirty mariagroschen to one florin.

These and similar signs appeared, but the Muscovites paid no attention to what they portended, like unto the Jews at Jerusalem, who took evil omens for good auguries. The Tatars interpreted these portents thus: in the near future some evil peoples would roam throughout the Muscovite land and attempt to seize the crown – which is exactly what happened. Also since dogs were eating dogs and wolves were eating wolves, this contradicted the old proverb, **"Wolves do not eat each other."** One Tatar explained it thus: the Muscovites would betray each other, tear each other apart, and destroy each other like dogs.

At the same time that these portents occurred, divisions and dissensions appeared in all orders of society, so that one man could expect nothing good of another. The fearful rise in the cost of merchandise, much worse than that practised by the Jews, usury much worse than that exacted by the Turks, and the fleecing of the poor occurred everywhere. For everything that was needed, one had to pay twice what had been paid previously. A friend would not lend money to another without charging interest, which would in the end cost him triple what he had borrowed, for a ruble weekly cost four mariagroschen.[87] If the loan was not repaid within the stipulated time, the security was sold.

The new styles of clothing and the costliness of the cloth from foreign nations, the coarse pretentiousness and false vanity whereby each considered himself more exalted than the others, the gluttony and drunkenness, whoring and villainy, which engulfed everyone high and low in a flood of sin, thus provoking the Lord God to punish, correct and end it with fire, sword, and other calamities: all these were too numerous to describe.

In the same year, 1604, on the second Sunday after Trinity, in clear noonday next to the very Kremlin of Moscow, there appeared alongside the sun a bright and dazzling star, at which even the Russians, who normally pay no attention to portents, were truly amazed.[88] When this happening was reported to the tsar, he immediately summoned a worthy old man, whom he had recruited a few years previously to Moscow from Livonia, and had rewarded with splendid estates, and to whom he was particularly benevolently disposed on account of the devoted service he had rendered. The tsar ordered the imperial chancellor, Afanasy Ivanovich Vlasiev,[89] to ask this old man what he thought concerning these newly appearing stars.

He replied that **the Lord God, by these unusual stars and comets, was warning potentates and great lords**, and that the tsar should keep his eyes open and observe in whom he could place his trust, strongly guard the frontiers of his realm, and carefully defend them against foreign intruders. For in those places where such stars appeared, there commonly arose considerable dissensions. This man was generously and richly rewarded with an increase in his landed possessions, sables, cloth of gold, and money.

Soon afterwards, in September of that same year, there assembled on the Muscovite frontier about six thousand field Cossacks, whom the monk Grishka Otrepiev had recruited in the Wild Steppe, assuring them that **Dmitry, son of the former tsar Ivan Vasilievich, was truly alive**, and was dwelling with Prince Adam Wisniowiecki in White Russia.[90] The monk then commanded him whom he had rehearsed for the part of Dmitry to come to them and in the name of God try his fortune against Boris and lay claim to his hereditary throne, in which venture he and the Cossacks who were with him would aid him by their counsel and by their deeds.

The monk and the Cossacks awaited Dmitry's arrival with great impatience. Meanwhile Dmitry, who was living among the Polish nobles, was becoming quite well known and had received much help and support from many, from Prince Adam and others, and had with him several regiments of Polish cavalry. With these he proceeded to the frontier, where together with the Cossacks he had a force of about eight thousand men. With these Dmitry tried his fortune, demanding of the frontier fortress of Putivl that it surrender to him voluntarily, since it was his hereditary possession. The instrument of the Devil[91] let himself play a major part in this venture. In October the fortress surrendered to Dmitry without resistance, as a result of which his handful of forces was considerably augmented.[92]

When news of this was brought post haste to Boris in Moscow, he was not a little disturbed, knowing very well whence it had come and where it might lead, and, remembering what the old man had said concerning the appearance of the star, began to complain bitterly against the treason and perfidy of the princes and boyars, telling them to their faces that this was their handiwork, through which they sought to overthrow him; nor was he mistaken in this.

He quickly sent letters throughout the entire land, ordering all foreigners, princes, boyars, musketeers, and whosoever was trained in warfare, on pain of death and confiscation of their property, to repair to Moscow by the feast of St Simon and St Jude, 28 October. On the next day he sent out similar proclamations, and on the third day the same, to emphasize that this was a serious matter and that a major crisis was imminent. Accordingly, within the course of a month more than a hundred thousand were assembled.

Boris sent with them his chief commander, Prince Ivan Mstis-lavsky,[93] who had nothing to do with those who were disloyal, to encounter the enemy before Novgorod-Seversk as soon as possible. Those other princes, boyars, and all those who were under obligation to go on campaign but had remained at home, he ordered to be chased out of their estates by his officers to join the forces in the field. He ordered the estates of several of those who had been disobedient to be confiscated, and some were cast into prison, while others were punished with the whip until their skin was so torn that nowhere on their backs was there left a patch of whole skin large enough that the point of a needle might be placed upon it.

Having experienced such severity, none of those obliged to report for campaign wished to be arrested in their homes, and large groups reported daily, so that in November, around Martinmas,[94] about two hundred thousand men were assembled. A notable lord, Peter Fedorovich Basmanov, was closely besieged by Dmitry in Novgorod-Seversk, but he held out valiantly, and heaped great scorn and losses upon the enemy.

Hearing of the approach of a large force, Dmitry abandoned the fortress, proceeded to the open field with great stealth and, when he had the opportunity, attacked with his small force on the blind side (as the saying goes),[95] not far from Novgorod-Seversk, inflicting great damage, though he himself did not derive much benefit from it.[96] Boris's field commander, Prince Mstislavsky, received fifteen body wounds in this battle, and if seven hundred German cavalrymen, who had come from their estates to join in the campaign, had not come to the aid of the Muscovites and relieved them, the outcome would have been bad for the Muscovites. These seven hundred Germans drove Dmitry further back, so that he had to abandon the Severian land and cease his attempts to take Basmanov's fortress.

After Lord Basmanov and the fortress were delivered as a result of this from the enemy, he came to the tsar in Moscow on 15 December, the feast of St Valerian, and his faithful service and valiant conduct caused him to be received in splendour like a prince. The tsar sent the leading princes and boyars of the court to meet him outside the city and greet him on the tsar's behalf. To honour him publicly the tsar lent his own horse and sleigh to fetch him, and so he rode through the whole city of Moscow as far as the Kremlin, and was as splendidly escorted as if he were the tsar himself.

When he appeared before the tsar, he received from the tsar's own hands a golden bowl weighing six pounds and full of ducats, and was told that he was being given this as a warrior on account of his brave and valiant deeds, in token of his sovereign's gracious esteem, and in order that he might serve the tsar as devotedly as he had done hitherto. In addition to this, the tsar ordered that he be given two thousand rubles in cash, that is, 5555 ordinary thalers and 20 mariagroschen, and also assorted silver plate, and made him a great lord in the land, giving him much land with peasants. He promoted him to membership of the boyar duma and placed him very highly. He was greatly loved and esteemed by all.

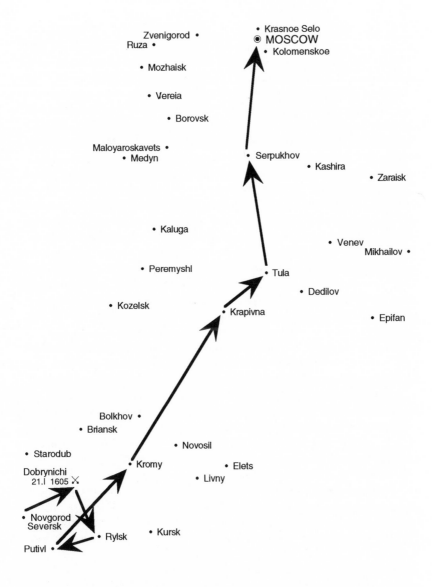

Zvenigorod •
Ruza •

• Krasnoe Selo
◉ MOSCOW
• Kolomenskoe

• Mozhaisk

• Vereia

• Borovsk

Maloyaroskavets •
• Medyn

• Serpukhov
• Kashira

• Zaraisk

• Kaluga

• Venev
Mikhailov •

• Peremyshl
• Tula

• Kozelsk
• Krapivna
• Dedilov

• Epifan

Bolkhov •
• Briansk

• Novosil

• Starodub

Dobrynichi
21.I 1605 ✕

• Kromy
• Elets
• Livny

• Novgorod
Seversk

• Rylsk
• Kursk

Putivl •

ANNO 1605

In January the Muscovites once again set out on campaign with all their forces in order to pursue Dmitry further. They were over two hundred thousand strong,[97] and came on 20 January, the feast of St Fabian and St Sebastian, to Dobrynichi. Dmitry had also gathered with his own forces, and had assembled an army of fifteen thousand. With these, on 20 January, he attacked the whole Muscovite force, set upon it, and beat it so badly that they yielded and were obliged to flee.

He captured all of their artillery, and would this time have been in possession of the field and celebrating his victory if two squadrons of German cavalry, which had been deployed up on the flanks, had not joined battle. Their captains were Walther von Rosen, a noble from Livonia and a fairly elderly man, and Jacques Margeret, a Frenchman.[98] These attacked Dmitry's formations with such force that not only were they unable to pursue the fleeing Muscovites but they were even forced to abandon their captured artillery and flee headlong. The Germans' battle cry was *"Hilff Gott! Hilff Gott!"* God helped them. They boldly pursued Dmitry's fleeing army, fired at the horsemen, and cut down all those they could reach or pursue. When the Muscovites saw the bravery of the Germans, and how they alone were driving the enemy from the field and pushing them back, they regained courage and came in thousands to the aid of the Germans, learning also to call out the German battle cry *"Hilff Gott! Hilff Gott!,"* and the Germans were not a little amused that Dmitry had so quickly inculcated in the Muscovites the ability, in an instant, to appropriate the German language and battle cry so well.

During the flight Dmitry himself was all but laid low. His personal mount was wounded in one shank under him, and he himself scarcely got away. He certainly would have been shot or taken captive had not certain traitors hindered the Germans (who had put Dmitry and his army to flight and were pursuing them) by sending one messenger after another with orders to halt and turn back, since enough blood had been shed, the chief aim had already been attained, and victory was assured. So the Germans turned back, and the Muscovites **(at least those who were not party to the counsel of the godless)** greatly loved and praised them for their valour. The Muscovites also said that the German God was stronger than the Russian God, for the Germans had only been a handful, yet they had all the same assured the victory, whereas the Russians, who numbered more than a hundred thousand against a comparatively insignificant enemy contingent, had been put to flight at the first onslaught and compelled to leave their camp and abandon their artillery.[99]

Dmitry, with the small forces remaining to him at the time of his flight, had no sooner reached Rylsk than, fearing to remain there, he proceeded further in great sorrow and tribulation closer to the frontier, to Putivl. Now he feared that all was lost: he had suffered a great defeat, had lost most of his men, and had with him only a mere four or five thousand Cossacks, who had retired to a hideout[100] called Kromy; he would have no further successes. He therefore should abandon all hope of becoming tsar of Russia, especially since, having captured and occupied the area previously conquered by Dmitry because of this victory, the Russians, who knew nothing of the secret conspiracy of the boyars, were wreaking a dreadful and merciless vengeance upon those poor peasants who had supported Dmitry. In the Komaritsk district, as this same land was called, so many thousands of peasants, with their wives and children, were suspended by one leg from trees and were shot through with bullets and arrows that it was lamentable and piteous to behold.[101]

Even though Dmitry, as has already been narrated, on account of this had almost abandoned hope, and had lost all desire to attain the tsardom, the abominable Satan would not rest content with this, so he drove and enticed the followers of his instrument Grishka Otrepiev, who had betrayed and forgotten his oath to his own tsar, so that his emissaries, also forgetting their oaths to their own tsar, sent privily to Dmitry, saying that, regardless of the fact that he had sustained a defeat (for which the Germans had been responsible), and that he could not hope to succeed with the few forces remaining to him, he nevertheless should not lose hope because of this or retreat further.[102] They would strive and work so that not only the Germans but also the Muscovites who were at hand would gradually be persuaded to come over to his side. He himself should immediately issue letter after letter, earnestly persuading and urging the Russians to take thought and henceforth not offer such stubborn resistance to him, their legitimate tsar, and not cause the shedding of so much innocent blood, but pause and consider the prosperity and welfare of themselves and the whole country, since peace would be more advantageous to them than war (which in the contrary case would not end as quickly as they doubtless supposed), and that they should strive that without further resistance he receive the throne of his fathers in Moscow, whereby they would obtain peace and tranquillity, and he would reward them for this with all kinds of benefits. If they did not do so, then let them beware that their stiff necks would redound all the more to their ruin and destruction than their prosperity and welfare.

Thanks to this deputation and exhortation, Dmitry once again took courage and each day tirelessly sent out letters in which he related all his circumstances: how old he was, how he was to have been murdered, who had rescued him and taken him away, who his godfather was and what he had given him at his christening, how he had been for some time in White Russia and had come to be with the Polish lords, and also how he had spent some time with the Lithuanian Grand Chancellor Leo Sapieha when he had been sent by the king to Boris in the capacity of ambassador, and how he, Dmitry, had with great anguish seen Boris, his betrayer, seated upon the throne of his fathers.

By such missives, which Dmitry sent throughout the communities of the entire land, he contrived that the Muscovites deserted Boris in large numbers and came over to his side, recognizing him as the lawful hereditary sovereign, and rallying to his camp at Putivl. At the same time Boris sent many thousands of rubles from Moscow to the commander in his camp before Dobrynichi to be distributed to the Germans on account of their outstanding fidelity and good conduct, calling upon them henceforth to display similar loyalty. Furthermore he promised them that their annual salaries and estates would be improved and augmented, and that **even if he had nothing left but his shirt,** he would also be prepared to share that with them.

Boris ordered his field commander, with all his forces, to proceed to Kromy and take that nest, and root out Korela, who together with the Cossacks under his command had withdrawn there at the time of the recent battle.[103] Since the field commander, Prince Ivan Mstislavsky, who had received fifteen wounds in the recent battle, had not recovered, Boris appointed another commander, namely Prince Katyrev.[104] This disturbed certain other puffed-up clowns, who considered themselves more suitable for this appointment, to such an extent that they deserted with several thousand men and went over to the enemy.

The two field commanders, Mstislavsky and Katyrev, together with the foreigners applied themselves to the wooden nest of Kromy. The foreigners set fire to it, so that it burned to the ground, and of all the buildings not a timber was left standing. The Cossacks had dug slit trenches all around and within the fortifications. From both sets of trenches they threw up earth, and under the fortifications they made so many loopholes that they could, as the need arose, enter and sally forth in an instant. The Cossacks also built their dwellings in the earth like mice, so that nobody could disturb them with their shots.

From the outer earthwork they ran slit trenches toward the Muscovite redoubts and took cover in them. When the Muscovites came forward to skirmish, or sent men in for an assault, the Cossacks crept forward like mice out of their holes and defended themselves bravely, and if the Muscovites began to get the better of them they quickly scrambled through the loopholes to regain the inner rampart, and there awaited the Muscovite pursuit. But the Muscovites were chilled to the bone and did not want to go in, and lay in siege for three months, wasting much powder and lead and achieving nothing, since there was so much treason among them, and it grew daily. Also, on one occasion five hundred Cossacks, whom Dmitry had dispatched from Putivl to aid them, forced their way through part of the Muscovite encirclement, in broad daylight, with a hundred sleighs laden with provisions before the opposing Muscovites became aware of it.

The commanders informed the tsar in Moscow of the extent of the treason, of the daily desertion of princes and boyars, and of the consequent daily diminution of his army. The enemy were growing more numerous and stronger, and therefore the situation was perilous. It was uncertain who among those that remained could be trusted. Dmitry was receiving reinforcements of Polish cavalry daily, signifying that he was setting out on another campaign to engage them. The commanders further ventured the opinion that, since there was so much treason, there was almost no hope of withstanding the enemy. Boris was so alarmed at all this that he too fell into despair and took his own life by poison.[105]

On the morning of 13 April he was lively and healthy, but at vespertide he was dead, and on the following day he was laid out in the Moscow Kremlin, in the church beside the former tsars. Thus to this unfortunate lord evil was rendered for evil.[106] **Even as he had conceived evil intentions against the legitimate heir** and had ordered him killed, so men rose up against him and his heir throughout his reign. He could not be so fortunate as to die at the hands of his enemy, and so he had to be his own executioner, and make away with himself by poison. **O evil conscience, how timid thou art!**[107] He had occupied the throne of the Muscovite tsardom from 1 September 1597[108] until 13 April 1605.

III *Fedor Borisovich, Son of Boris Fedorovich*

On 16 April the field commander, Prince Mstislavsky, was recalled from active service to Moscow to assist the young tsar in deciding and carrying on the affairs of state and in his place Lord Peter Basmanov was named and dispatched to the army. He was the same man who, as previously narrated, earlier had been knighted by Tsar Boris and very generously rewarded with land, peasants, gold, and silver. Basmanov called upon every man in the whole camp – Germans, Muscovites, Poles, Swedes, Tatars, and Cossacks – duly to swear homage and pledge their allegiance to the young tsar. **They held to their oath as long as a hungry dog keeps a fast**, for within three weeks the same Basmanov had broken his oath and, with many other military commanders and many thousands of Muscovites, almost the entire camp, with the exception of the Germans, had deserted the young tsar and proceeded to Dmitry in Putivl. In the confusion the Germans, together with a few thousand Muscovites, left and returned to Moscow to their lord the young tsar, who was greatly touched by their steadfastness and recompensed and rewarded them generously, also ordering them to be proclaimed to all the populace as the most loyal and constant people.[1]

Dmitry was more than a little pleased at this act of treachery, which freed and opened up all the highways and byways, all the doors and windows, to good fortune. With his freshly recruited army of Poles, Cossacks, and turncoat Muscovites, he set out on campaign, proceeding from Putivl to Kromy and further.

He sent many messengers with letters to the common people in Moscow, urging them to consider betimes and avert ruin and misfortune for themselves and to destroy his enemies the Godunovs, and without any further resistance recognize him as their lawful lord. He assured them that if this occurred, he would be merciful to them. On the other hand he threatened that if they did not do so, but continued to take the side of his enemies, the unlawful possessors of the throne, and continued to support the Godunovs even though they knew that almost the entire army had recognized and accepted him as the lawful ruler, as a result of which he had conquered many fortresses and towns and even from them was facing very little opposition, then naturally their foolishness and perversity would compel him to come to Moscow in arms and this would mean an end to his indulgence. There would be no mercy, even for babes at their mothers' breasts, should it prove necessary for him, Dmitry, to compel them by force to submit and subject themselves to him. The young tsar's relatives, the Godunovs, gave orders for any of these messengers who fell into their hands to be imprisoned, tortured mercilessly, and subjected to an agonizing death.

Finally on 3 June Dmitry sent one prominent boyar with such a letter to the village of Krasnoye Selo, sometimes also called the Tsar's Village,[2] which lies close to Moscow, in which there lived rich merchants and goldsmiths who had friends and relatives in Moscow. In this letter he informed them how many messengers and letters he had sent, one after the other, to the community in the city of Moscow, and how not one had returned to him, for they had all been killed. He did not know whom to blame for this, whether it was the doing of the community or whether the Godunov lords were doing this secretly. He wished to ascertain the truth of the matter, but this boyar would be the last messenger he would send to Krasnoye Selo, where none of the Godunovs was living. If this messenger did not return with good news, then even babes at the breast would be held accountable. If, on the other hand, he returned in good health and bearing a message of submission,[3] then they would be recompensed with great generosity.[4]

The inhabitants met and received the boyar with all deference, as well as the missive with Dmitry's appeal. They quickly gathered together several thousand, conducted the boyar bearing the letter through all of Moscow to the principal church, called the Church of Jerusalem,[5] which is hard by the very Kremlin gates. There they placed him upon the stone platform,[6] summoned the inhabitants of Moscow, proclaimed Dmitry's letter, and heard the boyar's explication. Thereafter they took counsel and exchanged opinions, finally resolving upon the following: All the land, all the princes and boyars had gone over to Dmitry, who was standing with a large army close to the gates. He was encountering no resistance in the field. The city of Moscow had not been provided and garrisoned with soldiers, and all the people had gone over to Dmitry. None of this would have happened had he not been the lawful heir, and so it would be unreasonable to defend themselves and the city against Dmitry any longer for the sake of the Godunovs. These were usurpers who had stolen the throne, who furthermore could neither protect nor defend them but had plunged them and their wives and children into utter ruin and destruction.

Therefore the shortest and most prudent way out of this predicament, if they wished to save themselves, their families, and all the city, was to send a letter of submission to Dmitry by the hand of the boyar on behalf of themselves and their families, to beg forgiveness and offer their surrender. In order that he should receive them more readily into his favour, it would not be imprudent to deprive the Godunovs (who had exiled the young Dmitry in his youth, thereby causing such great ruin to come upon the land) of their power, and place them under arrest.

Meanwhile certain lords and princes, including some boyars still remaining on the side of the young tsar, Boris's son, emerged from the Kremlin and invited the messenger to enter. The common people would not permit this, and demanded that they say what had become of previous messengers and letters, concerning which they demanded information and an accounting. With these words the common multitude rioted, wishing success for the advancing Dmitry and loudly exclaiming: "**God grant that the true sun will once again arise over Russia**. Hitherto we have sat in darkness, but now the true light shines forth."

They praised Dmitry and cursed the Godunovs, and rushed into the Kremlin in a monstrous fashion. They abused and reviled the late Tsar Boris, his son, and those few friends who remained to them, and among so many thousands not one recollected that Boris indeed had done so much good in all the land, in that in the eight years of his rule he had made many great improvements. All this, and the fact that he had maintained the villains during the great famine, was so far forgotten that it was as if he had never done anything praiseworthy. His son, the young tsar, to whom they had only just sworn allegiance, the dowager tsaritsa, his sister, and all who were of the Godunov family were arrested and their houses sacked, while they themselves, their wives, and children were stripped naked and clapped in irons, and being placed on dung carts were carried without cushions or blankets through thick and thin, in rain and foul weather, from Moscow away to captivity in other fortresses some many miles distant from Moscow. Some of them died on the way, the rest of them starved in captivity and so perished. The prophet spoke truly: **The mighty shall be laid low. Those raised in sweetness and comfort shall faint and suffer need.** The young Tsar Fedor Borisovich, his mother, and his sister remained for the time being in Boris's own house, though they were deprived of their high estate and were closely watched and guarded as prisoners.

Now on that 1 June the rude multitude had vented its anger so mercilessly upon the Godunovs that not one ruler remained within the Kremlin. They now bethought themselves to demand yet another potation from the tsar's cellar. They addressed this request to a certain old boyar, Bogdan Belsky, of whom mention has been made earlier, when Boris Godunov banished in disgrace because of his sedition.[7] After Boris's death he re-appeared, had great authority with the common people, and, since more than anyone else he had a grudge against the Godunovs, he was entrusted with the command of the Kremlin on behalf of Dmitry (whose godfather he claimed to be). With very gracious words he refused the request of the common multitude, saying that the tsar's cellar should not be touched, lest it be empty when Dmitry arrived.

He had conceived a great hatred and enmity towards all doctors on account of one Scottish captain, who prior to the arrival of those doctors, for want of anyone better, had been appointed Boris's personal physician, and at Boris's command, as has been narrated previously, had torn out all of this same Belsky's beard. Even though this captain, Doctor Gabriel, was long since dead, the other doctors had to suffer the consequences all the same, for Bogdan Belsky gave a wink to the base multitude and suggested that, since Boris's doctors had so enriched themselves, it was they who should stand a drink, since they had all manner of beverages in their cellars. Furthermore they had been Boris's confidants and advisors, and so they should pay them a call and drink all their liquor, and he, Belsky, would answer for the consequences.

Thereupon they rushed to the doctors' houses, and once they had been given an inch they took a yard and not only drank up the poor doctors' wine but also hankered after their goods and chattels, pilfering everything they could lay their hands upon, so much so that several of the doctors on that day suffered damages amounting to two or three thousand thalers. In addition to this, many other honest folk, who were living outside the city in unfortified settlements and who, in view of the approaching army, had transferred their goods to the doctors' houses, were plundered for no reason and through no fault of their own. Thus, on this occasion, both I and my family suffered not inconsiderable damage, having lost our possessions in such a fashion. Thus on account of the faults of others, as has been previously narrated, many innocent people had to suffer.

On 3 June all the common people of Moscow sent Dmitry a letter of submission, begging forgiveness and mercy, and promising surrender. He should approach in God's name, since all his enemies had been annihilated except for young Fedor Borisovich, his mother, and his sister, but they, too, were well secured, so that he had nothing to fear from them.[8] Dmitry was now at Serpukhov, eighteen miles from Moscow. He answered that he would not come until those who had betrayed him were so utterly exterminated that not one of them could any longer be found. Since most of them had already perished, so now the young Fedor Borisovich and his mother had to be destroyed. Only then would he come and be their gracious sovereign.

This letter was received in Moscow on 10 June. As soon as it was read out, young Tsar Fedor and his mother were quickly strangled in their chambers. The daughter, whom the Most Illustrious Duke Johan of Denmark would have had as his bride if God had preserved his life, was conveyed to the New convent, and was later given to Dmitry to be his concubine. Two coffins were made, in one of which was placed the son, in the other, the mother. The father, who only a few weeks previously had been buried alongside previous tsars, was exhumed, and all three were borne from the Kremlin to the Sretenka, to a humble monastery, where they were buried in the churchyard without choir or tolling of bell, and without any ceremonies, even though normally they bury their dead with very solemn ritual.[9]

Such a piteous end befell Tsar Boris Godunov and his family, which had been so high and mighty, that the like had not been seen since the Russian monarchy had been founded. And he himself was the first cause of the war now raging in Russia, since he had ordered the youthful Dmitry, son of the old tyrant, to be murdered, and had obtained the tsardom by fraud and deceit. **Truly it can be said concerning him what was said about the Roman Pope Boniface VIII, "He came like a wolf, reigned like a lion, and died like a dog."**[10] His son Fedor Borisovich reigned after the father's death for two months less four days, and was never crowned.

IV *The First Dmitry and His Reign*

Now that Dmitry had received sure tidings that his enemies had been completely purged and played out, he advanced from Serpukhov with his army on 16 June of the year 1605, pitched his camp upon a meadow about a mile's distance from the city of Moscow, and remained there five[1] days in order to test the Muscovite population before entering the city. He was convinced that they were well disposed, since they had made their submission to him, expressing their joy at his safe arrival and sending him many valuable presents of gold, silver, precious stones, and pearls, as well as salt and bread and all kinds of liquor (which after the Russian fashion is the fullest and highest token of honour). He then said he would trust them, and promised to forget all that they had done against him and never again call it to mind. He would not be their lord but their father, and would always wish and seek the best for all his beloved subjects.

On 20 June the Muscovite boyars[2] brought out of Moscow to their new tsar beautiful, splendid and valuable garments of cloth of gold, velvet, and silk, sewn with precious jewels and pearls, requesting him to set forth and receive in the name of God the inheritance of his father (to regain which the merciful God had helped him in such a swift and miraculous manner) and enjoy a fortunate, peaceful, and good reign. All was well regulated and set in order. He had nothing more to fear, nor any further cause for anxiety, so he should now rejoice and be glad, since all those who had wished to devour him were under arrest and could no longer bite him.

On this day all the Germans approached him on the meadow, and handed him a petition that it should not be held against them that they had done His Majesty and his army at Dobrynichi any harm, since this was in keeping with their allegiance and honour at the time. They had acted under compulsion; they were serving Boris who was their lord at the time. They were bound by a solemn oath that they would stand by him faithfully, and they could not break this oath without violence to their consciences. But even as they had truly and faithfully served Boris, so now would they also serve him. Dmitry summoned the commanders (most of whom thought that he would be very angry at them), was very gracious to them, and praised them for their steadfastness and loyalty in that, not only at Dobrynichi had they completely routed him and turned him to flight, as a result of which most of his army had been laid low in the snow, but also at Kromy they had not submitted to him as many thousands of the Muscovites had done, remaining loyal to Boris, who was their lord at the time. Furthermore, if they would serve him no better than they had served his enemy, then he would place greater trust in them than in the Muscovites.

He asked who among them was their standard bearer. As the standard bearer approached, he struck him on the head, and said: "You have struck no little fear in me with your banner. You Germans came so close to me that my own mount (which has been brought back here, but has not yet recovered) was gravely wounded under me, yet he managed to carry me from the battlefield. Had you captured me, you would have killed me." They answered with a respectful bow: "It is better that Your Majesty, praise be to God, has remained alive. God be praised for this, and henceforth may He preserve Your Majesty from all harm."

All was made ready for the triumphal entry. Dmitry ordered all the princes and boyars to ride to the right and left of him. In front and behind rode about forty men, each of them arrayed as splendidly as the tsar himself. He sent his scouts ahead with all the Russians to enquire whether everything was in order, and whether there was any secret villainy.

He incessantly sent messengers hither and thither. The tsar was preceded by many Polish horsemen in full armour, twenty men with trumpets and kettledrums in each group. Behind the tsar and boyars rode as many squadrons of Polish horsemen, in the same marching order and with the same joyful music as those who went before. All day, as long as the entry continued, all the bells in the Kremlin pealed, and everything went so magnificently that nothing of the kind could be better. So many thousands of people were seen on that day, so many brave heroes, such great pomp and might, that not a piece of ground could be seen. The roofs of the houses, the belfries and the market stalls were so crowded that from afar they appeared like a swarm of bees.

The spectators were without number in all the streets and alleys as Dmitry passed by. The Muscovites prostrated themselves, and said: "*Da Aspodi, thy Aspodar sdroby!* God keep you our lord safe! May He, Who has preserved you hitherto in such a miraculous fashion, further preserve you in all your ways!" and "*Thy brabda Solniska!* You are the true sun which is shining over Russia." Dmitry replied: "God also grant health to my people! Arise, and pray to God for me." Just as Dmitry was approaching the pontoon bridge to the watergate, there arose a powerful whirlwind, even though otherwise the weather was fine and clear. The wind scattered sand and dust so strongly over the people that they could not keep their eyes open. The Russians were greatly affrighted by this, and according to their custom made the sign of the cross upon their faces and breasts, and said, "*Pomiley nas buch! Pomiley nas buch!* God preserve us from misfortune."[3]

When the entry was completed, each man was conducted to his own lodging, and everything was done according to plan. The lord Bogdan Belsky, with several princes, boyars, and chancellors, came out of the Kremlin to the platform, close to which were assembled all the inhabitants of the city and some nobles and non-nobles from the provinces. He called upon those assembled to thank God for this new lord, and to be faithful to him. He was the true heir and son of Ivan Vasilievich. He took a cross from his bosom with the image of St Nicholas.[4] He himself kissed it, and swore that this belonged to the true son and heir of Ivan Vasilievich. He, Belsky, had concealed it in his bosom until this day, when he would return it to him. Let them love, honour and respect him. Thereupon all the people replied: "O Lord, protect the tsar! God grant him health! O Lord, destroy his enemies!" This wish was fulfilled later, after Dmitry's death, recoiling upon them in a fearful fashion.

On 29 June, a Saturday, Dmitry was crowned in the church of St Mary in accordance with Russian customs and ceremonies, as has been described earlier in the account of Boris's coronation.[5] After the Feast of the Visitation he released his mother from the Trinity monastery (to which Boris had consigned her, ordering her to take the veil as a nun),[6] and had her conducted with great honour by several thousand mounted escorts to Moscow. Dmitry himself came out to greet her, and they encountered each other with great affability and joy. The old tsaritsa knew exactly how to play her part in this comedy, even though she knew very well, and better than thousands of other people, the truth of the matter, for thanks to this son she could once again resume her dignity and imperial rank. Dismounting, he accompanied her carriage for some distance on foot, the sight of which drew tears from the eyes of the common people, seeing how marvelously God had wrought His good works among the children of men. Thereupon he remounted, went ahead with his princes and boyars, and personally ordered everything in the convent where his mother was lodged. In the Kremlin, at the Jerusalem Gates, opposite the monastery of St Cyril,[7] he ordered fine new apartments to be built, and these he designated as his mother's convent. He entertained her in such a manner that there was no difference between her table and his. He visited her daily, and showed her such love and respect that it is said that thousands of people swore that he was truly the son of her body.

He sat daily with his boyars in the council chamber, demanding resolution of many matters of state, attentively following each speech, and after each had at length expounded his own opinion, said with a smile: "You have taken counsel for so many hours and so racked your brains, and have nevertheless not reached any conclusion. Here is how it should be." Impromptu he was able to find a better solution than all his advisers, whereat many marvelled. Being a good orator, he sometimes introduced into his speech subtle analogies and memorable histories of events which had occurred among all imaginable nations, which he had himself experienced and seen abroad, so that all listened to him with keenness and amazement. Frequently he rebuked (albeit courteously) his exalted magnates for their ignorance, in that they were uneducated and ignorant men, who had not seen, heard, or learned anything except what appeared to them, from their own point of view, good and just. He proposed to allow them to travel to foreign countries to gain experience wherever they wished, to gain some learning, by means of which they might become more accomplished, proper, and skilled people.

He ordered it to be proclaimed to all the people that he personally would hold audience twice a week, on Wednesdays and Saturdays, with his subjects on the gallery, that is, the balcony before his apartments, so that his people would not have to spend so much time in litigation as had been the case previously.[8] He also issued strict orders throughout all the chancelleries, courts, and offices that judges and officials should resolve matters without gifts (that is, bribes), and that they should help each man find justice without delay. He gave both Russians and foreigners permission to pursue their own livelihoods according to their own skill and capabilities, as a consequence of which everything in the land was seen to blossom and scarcity began to disappear.

He kept a joyful table. His musicians, singers, and instrumentalists had to make themselves boldly heard. He discontinued many awkward Muscovite customs and ceremonies at table, namely that the tsar must incessantly make the sign of the cross and have himself sprinkled with holy water. This shocked the Muscovites who were true to their customs, and gave rise to suspicion and doubt towards the new tsar. They drooped their heads as if they had lice behind the ears.

He did not rest after dinner, as previous tsars had done, and which is the accepted custom among the Muscovites, but set out to walk around the Kremlin, visiting the treasury, the apothecary's shop, or the jeweller's, sometimes alone, or sometimes with one or two companions. At other times he went silently about his apartments, so that his guards and household servants did not know where he was, and they would search for him at length throughout the Kremlin until they found him, which was a practice unheard of among previous tsars, for eminent Muscovites could not go from one room to another without being conducted by a crowd of princes, who virtually carried them. Whenever he went on pilgrimage, he never went by carriage but always on horseback. He ordered not the most placid but the most spirited horse, nor did he permit, as had hitherto been the custom among the tsars, that two boyars should place a mounting block for him, but instead himself seized the bridle and himself grasped the saddle, so that he was mounted in an instant. He so handled his argamaks[9] and sat so bravely on a horse like a hero warrior that none of his trainers or other lords or soldiers could compare with him. He was so keen on hunting, riding, and coursing that he had to have the fairest falcons and the best dogs for hunting and tracking, as well as the best English hounds for bear baiting. On one occasion at Taininskoe,[10] he himself, in the open field, warded off a huge bear single-handed and ordered the bear to be set loose, against the advice of his princes and boyars. He attacked it on horseback and killed it.

He ordered a large quantity of mortars and cannon to be cast, even though there were in Moscow a great number of powerful weapons and magnificent, fine, and great cannon, which it is difficult for those who have not seen them to believe. In winter he moved the heavy artillery to Elets,[11] which is situated on the Tatar frontier, intending during the following summer to move against the Tatars and the Turks who were there. But as soon as word of his plans had reached the Tatar frontier and the Tatar tsar (as they call him) had heard of this, he abandoned his principal city of Azov and moved off into the steppe. For himself and his tsaritsa Dmitry built new and magnificent apartments within the Kremlin.[12]

By his eyes, ears, hands, and feet it was apparent that he was quite another Hector[13] when compared to his predecessors, and that he had been educated in a good school, having seen and experienced much. In September 1605 he recalled the love, loyalty, and affection shown to him by the governor of Sandomir in Poland, and also his promise of the governor's daughter, Maryna Yurievna.[14]

He therefore sent his imperial chancellor Afanasy Ivanovich Vlasiev[15] with great gifts – gold chains, rings, gold, and money worth more than two hundred thousand guilders – to the governor of Sandomir, and ordered it to be bestowed on his betrothed and her father, to pay his respects to them both and to ask for her hand. He was also to conclude a solemn alliance and contract between Dmitry and the Polish king, Lord Sigismund III, with the agreement, knowledge, and approval of all the estates.

The Russians were especially displeased at this. They had noticed through many previous instances that they had been cozened and scandalously betrayed, and their opinion was greatly confirmed by the fact that he was disregarding the daughters of the magnates of his own nationality and was about to marry a pagan (as they called other nations), and they eventually even came to the conclusion that he was not a Russian but a Pole.

The three brothers of the Shuisky family conspired secretly with monks and priests from the whole land, and once more worked fantastic plans to get rid of this lord. When the distrust of the Russians became evident, Dmitry resolved no longer to rely upon them as he had done before, but gathered around himself a personal bodyguard composed exclusively of Germans living in Russia.

ANNO 1606

In January he appointed three captains: the first was a Frenchman who, however, was fluent in German, a pious and prudent man called Jacques Margeret[16], under whose command were a hundred bodyguards. They were to carry halberds upon which the tsar's arms were engraved in gold. The shafts were covered in red velvet and inlaid with silver; they had gilded nails and were wound about with silver wire, and from them hung various pennants of silk, sewn with gold and silver thread. They received such quarterly remuneration that most could order themselves velvet cloaks with golden laces and expensive raiment.

The second captain was called Matthias Knudson, a Livonian from Kurland, who was put in charge of a hundred halberdiers. The tsar's emblem was also engraved on both sides of their halberds. Their caftans were dark violet with scarlet cord trim, their sleeves were red, and their hose and jerkins made of damask and ermine.

The third captain was a Scotsman called Albert Wandmann but nicknamed Pan Skotnicki because he had spent some considerable time in Poland.[17] He also was in charge of a hundred halberdiers, whose halberds were designed in the same manner as those of the other hundreds. The difference between these and the others was that their hose and jerkins were of green damask with ermine.

Half of the bodyguard was to watch over the tsar for one day and one night, the other half the succeeding day and night. This gave rise to great discontent, especially among the Muscovite magnates, who said among themselves: "See, our lord is so preoccupied with this guard, that he disregards us. How will it be when he receives the Polish damsel with so many Poles, Germans, and Cossacks?" **There was danger in delay**[18], thought Prince Vasily Shuisky, the eldest of the three Shuisky brothers, especially when Dmitry ordered a survey to be made of the monasteries, to reckon their revenues, to make productive those lands which were heavy with useless and idle monks,[19] and to confiscate the rest, in order to support soldiers who were to fight against the Turks and Tatars, the enemies of Christendom.[20] Thus some clergy who lived in the neighborhood of the Chertolsk and Arbat streets,[21] close to the tsar's Kremlin, were evicted from their houses to make room for the Germans, so that in an emergency, whether by day or night, they could come more quickly to the tsar's aid.

Together with all the inhabitants of Moscow, Shuisky organized all kinds of conspiracies to exterminate and kill Dmitry and all his followers before the foreigners arrived. When by the will of God this diabolical design was discovered, many priests and musketeers were arrested and subjected to torture, and all of them testified that Shuisky was plotting treason. The priests had to undergo torture, and the musketeers were handed over to their comrades to be killed in whatsoever manner they saw fit, and Dmitry declared that whosoever among them first raised his hand against those traitors would be considered innocent of this conspiracy. Then the musketeers set upon the guilty like dogs, in order to show their innocence, and they so tore them apart with their teeth, that it was impossible to determine to which part of the body the pieces belonged.[22]

He also ordered the ringleader[23] of the conspiracy, Prince Vasily Shuisky, to be cast into prison, first delivering him to the torturer[24] to be subjected to the lash upon the rack, before being condemned to death. They brought him to the place of execution, between the Kremlin and the stone market stalls, where he was sentenced. His crime and the due sentence were read out, and the executioner had undressed him and placed his head upon the block in order to sever it with the axe when a German called Martin Sybelski, an unbaptized Mameluke[25] from Prussia, who had the tsar's cap in his hand, rushed from the Kremlin bearing a message from the tsar. He signalled and cried out to the executioner to hold his hand, for the tsar had spared the lives of many traitors and wished also to pardon this one, since he was of so noble a family, and also because his Lady Mother had interceded for him.[26]

What great misfortune resulted from this untimely clemency will be related later in its proper place. Dmitry would have done better to have executed this convicted swindler and traitor rather than pardon him and stay the sword whereby he was to have avenged such evil, and thus he would have prevented much greater harm, misfortune, grief, and misery. Dmitry considered that he had shown by his treatment of this prince that he was sufficiently in earnest, and had set such an example that it would serve as a deterrent to other conspirators, who would not embark upon a like enterprise. Therefore he fell into complacency and lived without fear.

For some time the traitorous princes and boyars held themselves respectfully in seclusion, as if all had been lost, so that Dmitry would feel all the more secure and not contemplate any more evil against them. They accompanied him to the field for hunting and other sports, behaving in a joyful and contented manner, but stored up malice in their hearts.

Six miles from the city of Moscow lies a great monastery called Vyazoma.[27] There on Shrove Tuesday Dmitry ordered a snow rampart to be built, to instruct his princes and boyars how to defend, besiege, assault, and capture a fortress. He took with him his German bodyguard, two troops of Polish horsemen, and all the princes and boyars in attendance at court. He placed the horsemen in a field not far from the monastery. He placed the princes and boyars in the snow fortress, appointing one of them as their commander and voevoda, so that with them he could defend the fortress. He himself wished to attack and assault it together with his Germans. The only weapons on either side were to be snowballs. The Russians were to defend themselves with snowballs and he wished to use the same weapons to go on to the attack and storm the fortress to see whether he could succeed in capturing the fortress from them, or whether they would be able to repel them. The Germans had the advantage in that they had concealed hard objects inside their snowballs, which inflicted many black eyes upon the Russians.

The tsar himself led the attack, and captured the fortress with his Germans and took the princes and boyars captive. He himself overpowered the commander, bound him, and said: "God grant that at some future time I shall also thus capture Azov in the Tatar Tsardom,[28] and so also will I take captive the Tatar khan even as now I have taken you prisoner." He ordered this amusement to recommence, and ordered up wine, mead, and beer so that they could drink one another's health. At this time a certain boyar approached and warned him, saying that he should break off this game. Many of the princes and boyars had received black eyes because of the hard objects in the Germans' snowballs, and were speaking very evil words. He should also remember that there were many traitors among them, and that each prince and boyar was carrying a sharp dagger, while he and his Germans had cast aside their upper and lower weapons and were attacking only with snowballs. Therefore some kind of misfortune could easily occur.

The tsar took this warning seriously, called off the game and returned to Moscow, where he quickly found out that the boyars had been plotting treason. They had intended to murder both him and his Germans simultaneously as soon as the second assault began, justifying this deed by saying that Dmitry and the Germans and the Poles who were with him intended to slaughter and destroy all the princes and boyars on the field, whereas the brave hero had not at any time contemplated such an evil deed.

At that time Dmitry received the pleasing news that his bride was on the way from Poland to Russia. Therefore he sent to her on the frontier fifteen thousand rubles for her expenses and also wrote to the gentry of Smolensk, which is the first fortress from the Polish frontier, instructing them to be prepared to receive his bride and all who were accompanying her in a fitting manner, to entertain them in a royal fashion, and escort them to Dorogobuzh. The inhabitants of Dorogobuzh were to do likewise, as also the inhabitants of Viazma, Tsarevo-Zaimischche, and Mozhaisk. They were also to see to it that nobody lacked for anything, and that each of these guests was received with as much reverence as if he himself were coming in person. From the frontier to Smolensk and to the Moscow Kremlin all the highways and byways were cleaned, bridges were placed even over the most insignificant streams, and the streets were swept so clean, that such cleanliness could not be found in any house or courtyard.

The bride celebrated Easter with her father, brothers, and other relatives who were to accompany her to the citadel of Mozhaisk, eighteen miles from Moscow. Dmitry secretly came out from Moscow at night with several of his followers and appeared among his dear guests somewhat earlier than they had expected him. He remained with them altogether two whole days, and then returned and prepared everything that was needed for their entry. On the fourth day after our glorious Easter (this fell on 24 April)[29] the father of the bride, the governor of Sandomir, came on ahead to Moscow with a small escort and was solemnly received by the princes and boyars and also some of the musketeers.

On the eighth day thereafter, on the feast of ss Philip and James, 1 May, the tsar's bride, Maryna Yurievna, arrived. The tsar sent all his courtiers, princes, boyars, Germans, Poles, Cossacks, Tatars, and musketeers to meet her, about a hundred thousand altogether, magnificently dressed and groomed. He himself dressed up and rode back and forth with only two companions, placing his people right and left according to his disposition, and then returned to the Kremlin. He sent his bride twelve riding horses with expensive blankets, and also saddles, covered with hides of lynxes and leopards, with gilded silver stirrups, the bridles adorned with golden bits. By each horse there was a Muscovite in livery who was to lead it. A great Muscovite carriage was also sent ahead, with red velvet interior. The cushions inside were of cloth of gold inlaid with pearls. Twelve snow-white horses were harnessed to the carriage, and twelve riding horses were sent ahead of the carriage.

Prince Mstislavsky was sent out to the field on behalf of the tsar to pronounce the welcome and receive the bride and her brothers, her brothers-in-law, and all the suite, and he fulfilled the tsar's commission with diligence, after which he ordered the aforementioned twelve riding horses and carriage with twelve horses to be presented to the bride, with the plea that she should not reject this gift sent by her gracious bridegroom. When she arose to accept, the most noble magnates lifted her up by the hand with great reverence, and conducted her to the tsar's carriage.

Ahead of her on foot went three hundred haiduks[30] whom she had brought with her from Poland, with their own shawms and drums. Behind them followed, in full armour, Dmitry's veteran Polish cavalry, which had served him in his campaigns, ten men in each rank, accompanied by their own drums and kettledrums, and behind them the twelve riding horses which had been presented to the bride. The tsar's bride followed, and on each side of her carriage there rode a hundred lancers and two hundred German halberdiers marched alongside her carriage on foot.

Behind the carriage rode the noble Muscovite magnates, with the brothers and brothers-in-law of the bride, followed by the riding horses that the bride had brought from Poland, adorned with great splendour, led by two horsemen, and then the carriage in which the bride had travelled from Poland to Russia. This was drawn by eight dappled grey horses, with manes and tails dyed red. Next came the chief lady-in-waiting, Lady Kazanowska, in her own carriage, drawn by six fine reddish horses. Next came all the ladies in thirteen carriages. Then came the cavalry which had arrived from Poland, in full armour, with drums, kettledrums and shawms, followed by the Russian cavalry with drums of greater diameter than any other drums or kettledrums,[31] and then came the Polish gun carriages, vehicles, and all the baggage train. At the outer, middle, and inner city gates stood Muscovite musicians, who produced a clamorous noise with their trumpets and drums.[32]

Between the Nikitsk Gates and the gates near the Lion Bridge, at the entry of the tsar's bride there arose a fearful stormy wind, such as had risen at the entry of Dmitry (as has been related earlier), and many interpreted it as an **evil omen.**[33] This was a sad day for many Muscovites, in that so many foreign guests had appeared, and they were greatly amazed at all these armed horsemen and asked those Germans who lived with them in their country whether it was the custom in their country to attend a wedding with armour and weapons. They suspected danger, especially when they saw that five or six muskets protruded among other things, from the Polish battle wagons.

The old Shuisky and many other boyars had already set in motion the rumour that this Dmitry was not the true Dmitry. And when the common multitude further observed that Dmitry was about to ally himself with the Poles, that he favoured Germans and gave them preference, and that the Poles had arrived so well armed, all this reinforced the suspicion sown among them by Shuisky. They complained to each other about their situation, namely that this change of rule[34] had brought them no benefit, since previously they had had a gracious sovereign and had lived in peace and prosperity. But now, under this ruler, everything threatened danger. This Polish tsar with his Poles and Germans would destroy all the Muscovites,[35] who could not survive.

When these bitter complaints of the Russians reached Shuisky (whom Dmitry had delivered to the executioner the preceding autumn because of his treason but had pardoned, to his own ruin), he secretly gathered together in his house the hundredmen and fiftymen[36] of the city, together with certain boyars and merchants, and told them there that they could plainly see what great danger threatened all Moscow from the tsar and all the foreigners (of whom already too many had been admitted). What Shuisky had long foretold was now before their very eyes, but when he had tried to do something about it, it had almost cost him his head, while the Muscovite community had sat still and done nothing.

Now, of course, they were well aware what to expect, and what was going on, namely that all the Russians would perish or become subject to the Poles. So therefore this was not the true Dmitry, but a Pole, who had come to the tsardom to be a ruler. His acceptance throughout the land had occurred simply out of the desire to overthrow Boris, which could not have been achieved by any other stratagem. Yet they held on to the hope that this young hero would maintain their God, their faith, and the Muscovites themselves. Things, however, had turned out differently. He loved foreigners more than his own Russian people. He spurned their gods and was defiling their churches, in that he let the unclean Poles enter the churches with their dogs, into the sanctuaries of St Nicholas and the Immaculate Virgin. He had evicted the clergy from their houses to make way for the Latins (by which he meant the Germans, though Latin generally means non-German). He was marrying a pagan Polish woman, and would naturally soon do some mischief, if the Muscovites did not prevent it in time.

In the name of the Christian faith he, Shuisky, was once again prepared to do something if truly they would assist him and actively support him. Let every hundredman and fiftyman secretly inform the men under their command that this Dmitry is not the legitimate ruler. Moreover, he and the Poles have no good feelings towards the Russians. Therefore he should be checked, and to this end neighbours should take counsel to forestall this evil.

The Muscovite population was almost a hundred thousand, while Dmitry and his Poles had only five thousand. Besides, the Poles were not all dwelling in one place but were scattered in various localities, so that if the situation became menacing, then the day should be set and they should be set upon early in the morning while still asleep, before they could seize arms, and so the Muscovites might eradicate and destroy the tsar together with his Poles. Let them all gather together in confidence and secretly inform him, Shuisky, as to what they had resolved, and if the common multitude was inclined to support this measure, then it should be carried out without delay.

The common multitude, which in any case is easily inclined to uproar, soon consented. It was explained to them that in order to purge the Christian city and the Moscow Kremlin of unbelievers, they should adhere to Shuisky and his supporters on the most opportune day to undertake the deed. It was resolved and communicated to them that upon an agreed sign, when they heard the tocsin sound in the morning, each man should hasten out of his house to the Kremlin with the cry: "The Poles wish to kill Tsar Dmitry!" and gain access to the tsar on the pretext that they wished to help him and save him from the Poles. Amid the uproar which they themselves had created, they should kill and make an end of him, after which they should hasten from the Kremlin and massacre the Poles in their houses, on the doors of which that night there should be placed a sign in Russian letters, so that the Russians could distinguish them. The Germans living locally would be spared, since they had always been loyal to the country.

Thus the bell had tolled for Dmitry and the Poles, though both he and they felt very secure. Even though many had informed Dmitry of the danger, he did not investigate, thinking that he had enough force at his disposal to deal with the Russians, who would not in any case dare to attempt anything. He did not consider how the lodgings of the Poles were far removed from the Kremlin and separated from each other. This he realized later with the onset of the tumult and his own pitiful fate, when it was too late to do anything about it.

On 8 May the imperial marriage between Dmitry and the Polish maiden Maryna Yurievna took place. Soon thereafter she was crowned as Tsaritsa of All Russia. At this wedding and coronation there arose a significant dispute between the tsar and the Russian lords over the matter of dress. The tsar and the Polish magnates wanted the bride, when they conducted her into the church, to be in Polish dress, to which she had been accustomed since her youth, for she could not get used to foreign dress. The Muscovites desired that both she and the tsar should be dressed at the wedding in the Russian fashion, in accordance with the customs of the land. After a lengthy dispute the tsar said: "Very well, I shall not alter the customs of my land, and will concede the wishes of my senators, so that they shall not have cause to complain that I wish to introduce many changes and innovations. It is only a matter of a single day." He bade his bride to put on Russian dress, to which she in the end consented. Then they arrayed the bride in very costly imperial vestments, in which they conducted her to the church of St Mary and wedded her to Dmitry.[37]

On the following day, 9 May, Dmitry ordered new Polish garments to be brought to his consort, with the request that she wear them out of respect to him, since yesterday had been the day of the Russian magnates, and he had wished to humour the whole land, so now this day and the days to come would be his. He would govern and behave as he pleased, and not as the Muscovites dictated. From that day the tsaritsa was dressed in the Polish fashion.

The days of the wedding festivities were celebrated splendidly and joyfully with food, drink, singing, and acrobatics. There were not only all imaginable kinds of musical instruments playing but also an excellent choir with thirty-two voices, as fine as any potentate might desire, which Dmitry had summoned from Poland. The Poles became so intoxicated at these celebrations that when they were conveyed back to their lodgings they behaved with great insolence. Any Muscovites they met in the streets they thrust at with their sabres. They pulled the wives of great lords, princes, and boyars out of their carriages and treated them disrespectfully, which the Muscovites silently observed, thinking their own thoughts.

On Saturday, 10 May, on the third day of the marriage, the tsar ordered everything to be prepared in the kitchen according to the Polish fashion, and among other dishes he ordered baked and roasted veal.[38] When the Russian cooks saw this and related it to all, the Russians grew very suspicious of the tsar, and said that truly he was a Pole and not a Muscovite, since the Muscovites consider veal to be unclean and not to be eaten.[39] They suffered this in silence, awaiting the opportune moment. On the same day, 10 May, with Dmitry's permission an Evangelical Lutheran sermon was heard in the Moscow Kremlin for the first time, preached by Martin Beer of Neustadt, since the doctors, captains and other Germans who had to attend the tsar were too far away from the church in the German suburb.[40]

On 12 May it was rumoured openly among the people that the tsar was a pagan. He no longer went to church as diligently as before, he lived by adhering in all things to foreign ceremonies and customs, **ate unclean food, went to church without cleansing himself, did not revere the icon of St Nicholas,** and although from the first day of his marriage a bath had been prepared for him every morning, neither he nor his pagan consort had taken a bath.[41] It therefore followed that he was not a Muscovite, and consequently could not be the true Dmitry. How all this would end, nobody yet knew. So they talked openly in the marketplace, and some of the halberdiers heard this, seized one such rascal and hauled him before the tsar in the Kremlin, also reporting that they had heard similar talk all throughout the marketplace.

Although Dmitry ordered all his guard to be summoned and to be on the alert day and night, and also ordered the person with the loose tongue who had been arrested to be interrogated, the traitorous boyars made light of the rascal, persuading the tsar that the wretched man was drunk and besotted and therefore did not know what he was saying, and that furthermore he was not very bright even when he was sober. Therefore the tsar should not pay any attention to such empty chatter, nor believe each and every tell-tale. He now had enough power to deal with all his enemies should they attempt anything against him. However, things were not quite as his Germans made them out to be.

Thereby the tsar became so confident that he did not heed any warning, and although on 13, 14, and 15[42] May treason was openly and bluntly spoken about and heard, and was reported to him by his captains, he did not attach any particular significance to it. He heard out the denunciations, put the letters aside, and said that no harm would come of it, and that fifty men should stand guard day and night as previously ordered and that the remainder should stay in their quarters awaiting their turn.

But, as the proverb says, "**Danger comes more quickly when it is ignored, and it happens straight away when it is expected in a year**,"[43] and, as St Paul says, "For when people speak peace and tranquillity, it is then that destruction will come upon them" (I Thessalonians, 5). So it happened with this secure Dmitry, whom the traitors seized when he least expected it, for he paid no attention either to miraculous signs or truthful reports. On the night of 16 May there occurred such a fearful snowfall and an unprecedented frost that all the crops in the field froze, which boded no good.

On 17 May the crafty Russians carried into execution their diabolical plan, which they had been hatching for a whole year.[44] At the third hour of the morning, after the tsar and the Polish lords had gone to bed and were sleeping off their revelries, they were rudely awakened from their sleep. In an instant the alarm sounded from all the churches, of which there are about three thousand in all of Moscow, and in each belfry there are at least five or six bells, and even ten or twelve in some of the more important ones. Whereupon from every corner there rushed crowds consisting of hundreds of thousands of men, some with clubs, others with muskets, many with naked swords, spears or whatever came to hand. Fury placed arms into their hands.[45] They all rushed to the Kremlin, crying: "**Who is trying to kill the tsar? Who is trying to kill the tsar?**" The princes and boyars replied: "The Poles." When Dmitry, lying in his bed, heard this fearful alarm and incredible noise, he was alarmed in no small measure and sent his true knight, Peter Fedorovich Basmanov, to ascertain what was happening, and the princes and boyars who were on duty in the outer apartments replied that they knew nothing; perhaps there was a fire somewhere.

The alarm was accentuated by such a fearful clamour on the streets that it could be heard even in the tsar's apartments. Then the tsar sent Lord Basmanov a second time to find out what was going on, whether or not there was a fire, and where it was burning, and himself arose and dressed. Lord Basmanov, seeing outside, within the Kremlin, a countless number of Russians with spears and pikes, was greatly dismayed, and demanded to know what they were doing there, and what was the cause of this alarm. The common multitude replied that he should fuck his mother and go summon the false tsar, since they wished to have words with him. Lord Basmanov now realized treason was afoot. He tore at his hair, and ordered the German halberdiers to hold their weapons at the ready and not admit anyone. Full of grief he returned to the tsar and said, "O woe! You my sovereign are at fault.[46] There is great treachery afoot, the whole community is assembled and is coming to get you. Until now you have not believed what your loyal Germans were telling you almost daily."

Even as Basmanov was conversing with the tsar, there came a boyar, who pushed his way past the halberdiers into the bedchamber and spoke impudently to the tsar, like an insolent traitor and villain. "**Are you not yet awake, untimely tsar? Why do you not come out and give an accounting to your people?**" The loyal Basmanov seized the tsar's halberd and struck the treacherous boyar right there in the chamber, and severed his head from his body. The tsar emerged into the outer apartment and seized the halberd from the hand of Wilhelm Schwartzkopf,[47] a Livonian born in Kurland, proceeded to the next room towards the spearmen, and said, "*Ya tabe ne Boris budu.* You will not find a Boris Godunov in me." Then some people fired at him and his bodyguards, and he was forced to retreat. Lord Basmanov came out onto the balcony, where most of the boyars were standing, and earnestly entreated them to consider carefully what they were about to do, that they forsake such evil deeds and behave in a fitting manner. Tatishchev, a prominent lord, answered him abusively, and said: "You son of a whore, go fuck your mother! Why do I waste time talking to you? You son of a whore! Go fuck your mother and your emperor too!"[48] He seized his long dagger (such as the Russians are accustomed to wear beneath their long robes) and buried it in Basmanov's heart, so that he immediately fell dead on the spot. The other boyars took him and threw him from the balcony, which was ten spans from the ground.[49]

Thus a brave hero, a loyal friend to all the Germans, lost his life for the sake of his tsar. When the common multitude saw that he was dead, he whose bravery and prudence was respected by all, the bloodthirsty hounds were emboldened to attack the bodyguards in force, demanding the surrender of the brigand.[50] The guards advanced with their halberds lowered, but it would have been a bad joke to have rushed into such a hot oven. The mob tore planks from the walls of the guardhouse and overpowered the fifty halberdiers, taking away their weapons. The tsar fled before them to the outer apartments, which were bolted shut, with fifteen Germans who stood before the door with their halberds at the ready. The greatly terrified Dmitry threw his halberd into the room, tore his hair, and without a word left the Germans and went into his bedchamber. The Russians immediately shot through the door at the Germans, so that they were forced to stand aside. Finally the Russians broke through the door, which they had chopped in two with axes, so that each German wished he could trade his halberd for a good axe or musket. They said among themselves: "If all three hundred of our men were here together and we had good muskets, we would be able with the help of God to earn fame and honour by saving our tsar and ourselves. Now we are about to perish with him, since these weapons are only for show, and not for action. O woe! Our poor wives, children and good friends probably already are dead. O woe, woe that the tsar would never credit our reports. Now he will perish, along with all of us Germans!"

Then they rushed into the next room and made it fast, but they did not find the tsar there. He had left his apartments by a secret passage, fled past the tsaritsa's apartments into a stone-built hall, where for fear he leaped through a window fifteen spans from the ground onto a hillock, and would have been safe had he not broken his leg. The Russians went through the tsar's apartments, disarmed the bodyguards, placed a guard over them, and did not allow them to go any further than the guardhouse. They asked them where the tsar had gone, plundered the tsar's apartments, and stole splendid valuables from his chambers. The princes and boyars forced their way into the apartments of the tsaritsa and her ladies, who were already half dead through fear and trepidation.

The tsaritsa, who was short in stature, hid under the skirts of her chief lady-in-waiting, who was a portly matron. The rude princes and boyars (it would be better to call them boors and crude peasants) demanded of the chief lady-in-waiting and maids: "Where is the tsar, and tsaritsa?" They replied: "You ought to know where you have left the tsar; we are not his guardians." Then the Russians said: "You shameless whores, where have you hidden the Polish harlot, your tsaritsa?" The chief lady-in-waiting asked what they wanted of her. They replied with all kinds of unseemly words in their crude Muscovite speech saying: "We would all like to fuck you, one from the front, another from the rear. We have heard that your Polish whores are good for more than one trick, neither can one man suffice for them." And thereafter they bared their horse-like private parts (O Sodom!) before all the assembled womenfolk saying: "See, you whores, see that we are much more potent than your Poles. Try us!"[51] They seduced and led astray all the maidens. One prince ordered one of them to be taken to his house, another ordered another to be taken to his, as they had done with the daughters of the Polish magnates. And within the space of a year many who had been virgins became mothers.[52] The chief lady-in-waiting, under whose skirts the tsaritsa remained hidden, was an elderly stout matron, and so she preserved her honour along with that of the tsaritsa, but they abused her all the same, calling her a double whore, and demanded that she tell them the whereabouts of the tsaritsa. She replied: "This very morning, at the first hour, we conducted her to the house of her father, the governor of Sandomir, and she is still there."

At the same time the musketeers guarding the Chertolsk Gates noticed that the tsar, who had broken his leg, was lying upon a dunghill, and heard him groaning and crying out. They went to him, helped him up, and were about to carry him back to his apartments. But as soon as the common multitude saw this and told the boyars, who were outside the women's quarters and within, they turned away from the chief lady-in-waiting and the tsaritsa and ran down the stairs. The musketeers would have resolved to defend the tsar, as he was promising them many things if they would rescue him, and had already shot and killed one or two of the boyars, but they were quickly overpowered, for they could do nothing more. Many princes and boyars seized the injured man, the tsar, who was broken by the fall and suffering, and they so dealt with him that he could have echoed the words of the prisoners in Plautus's comedy *The Captives*:

"What great injustice, to be betrayed and slaughtered at the same time!"[53]

The princes and boyars carried him back to his apartments, which had before been so richly adorned but were now so hideously destroyed and plundered. In the antechamber there stood a number of his halberdiers, closely guarded and disarmed, who looked upon him so sorrowfully that tears flowed down their cheeks. One of them stretched forth his hand, but was speechless. But it can be imagined quite well what his thoughts were at the time. Dear God, Who knows all hearts, only knows that he called to mind the frequent warnings of the Germans, and how they had so faithfully warned him through their captains.

A certain nobleman, a halberdier called Wilhelm Fuerstenberg, who hailed from Livonia, pushed into the apartments along with the Russians in order to ascertain the tsar's fate, but when he was at the tsar's side he was struck down with a lance by one of the boyars. Then the Russians said: "See what faithful hounds the Germans are. Even now they will not abandon their tsar; let us slay them all." But some of them disagreed, neither did the great lords, the princes and boyars, permit or allow it.

In that apartment they subjected poor Dmitry to a parody of the Passion, treating him almost as cruelly as the Jews did Our Lord Christ. Some plucked at and pulled him from behind and others in front, they tore his imperial robes from him and placed upon him the dirty caftan of a pie seller, while one said to another: "Behold the tsar of all Russia! See what kind of a Tsar of all the Russians is that."[54] while another said: "I have such a tsar at home, in my stable," and a third: "I would like to fuck this tsar," while a fourth struck him on the face, saying: "You, son of a whore, say who are you? Who is your father? Where is your home?" He answered: "All of you know that I am your crowned tsar and the son of Ivan Vasilievich. Ask my mother in the convent, or bring me to the platform on the Red Square and permit me to speak." Then a merchant named Miulnik sprang forward with his musket, and said: "It is not permitted for a heretic to justify himself; thus shall I bless this Polish minstrel!" With these words he shot him through.

The old traitor Shuisky moved up and down the Kremlin without any hindrance, crying to the people that they should do away with the brigand. Then each man wanted to make his way into the apartment and make mock of Dmitry now that he had been shot through, but there was no more room there, so many of them stood outside, saying: "What news of the Polish minstrel?"[55] and the others replied: "He has admitted that he is not the true Dmitry" (which he had not done), "but has said that he is the son of Ivan Vasilievich."

Then they all together cried: "Crucify!" and beat him to death, not letting him live. The boyars and princes drew their swords and daggers. One thrust at him through the head in front, another struck him in the same place from behind, so that a piece fell out of his head three fingers in breadth and hung down only held by the skin, a third struck him in the arm, a fourth just above the legs, and a fifth stabbed right through his body. The others dragged him by the feet out of the apartment by the same staircase on which his faithful knight Peter Basmanov had been stabbed and thrown below (as has been related earlier), and from there they threw him down and said: **"You were good brothers in life, you may now keep each other company in death."**

So lay below in the dirt the proud and brave hero who the day before had sat in such great honour, and the fame of whose bravery had spread throughout the world. Thus the celebration on the ninth day after the marrriage turned into heartfelt grief for the bride, the groom, and all the wedding guests. Thus should man and beast beware of attending Muscovite and Parisian[56] weddings. Dmitry reigned for eleven months less three days.

---

v *What Befell the Governor of Sandomir and the Poles after the Tsar's Murder*

The house where the lord governor of Sandomir was staying with his servants and haiduks, situated in the Kremlin next to the tsar's apartments and the patriarch's palace, was surrounded by many thousands of Muscovites. They also brought several cannon up to the gates, so that not even a dog, let alone a man, dared pass. As long as the disorder continued, the governor was not able to rescue his son-in-law, the tsar, but was prepared to defend himself if the Muscovites were to attack him. All the musicians, singers, and instrumentalists – boys, youths, and grown men – who had been lodged in the monastic houses within the Kremlin were killed immediately after the tsar and Basmanov, a hundred innocent, skilled, and honourable people.

After them it was the turn of the Poles in the Kitay-gorod and the White City to suffer. Some had crouched and hidden under the roofs, others under ruined walls and in cellars, some in straw and some in dungheaps. Some had only just sprung from their beds and were clad only in their shirts, but they were found all the same. Some were clubbed to death, while others had their necks severed with swords. Women and virgins were taken prisoner.

The tsaritsa's brother, the Pan Starosta, with his followers and the Polish nobles who were at hand, valiantly held out in the Wallachian House close to the foundry, and this forced many Muscovites to leap from their saddles and dive for cover.[1]

At the same time the tsaritsa's brother-in-law and the Polish ambassadors gave a good account of themselves. They were lodged in the house where the brother of His Royal Highness the King of Denmark's brother, the Most Illustrious Duke Johan of blessed memory, had died. There were about seven hundred men there, and they threatened to set fire to the city by setting their own house alight, after which they would mount up and fight to the last man unless the Russians solemnly swore to spare their lives. Dmitry's veteran Polish cavalry conducted themselves likewise in their quarters. They held out so valiantly that not even a single Muscovite was able to come to grips with them. The Muscovites trained artillery upon the house and threatened to raze it to the ground if they would not surrender willingly, and even fired two rounds at the house of the tsaritsa's brother.

Then the Poles parleyed, on condition that the Muscovites swore to protect their lives and property. The Muscovites swore by St Nicholas and on the crucifix, but the Poles did not trust them and demanded that the great lords come.

Then the old traitor Shuisky came with his fellow conspirators, and swore that they would do the Poles no harm, but that they should remain peacefully within their houses for several days and not go out among the people, since the inhabitants were very incensed against the Poles on account of the violence and arrogance they had shown to Muscovite women and children. The same mercy was shown to the other Poles concentrated in the large houses. But those who were only in small houses, containing, for example, only eight, ten, or twelve persons, were all massacred like dogs, without any mercy.

Several Poles were able to leap onto their horses and get away from Moscow, hoping to find refuge in the German Suburb with the Germans who resided there. But on the way they met at large renegade Germans who had escaped the gallows and wheel in Livonia and Germany, had come to Russia and changed their religion, having become Mamelukes[2] and blasphemers of Christ, for which reason not even Dmitry had considered them worthy to be in his guard, saying that since they could not remain faithful to God, who had given them body and soul, how then could they remain faithful to him? For this reason they were deadly enemies of Dmitry and his Poles, and were even more incensed against them than were the Muscovites. The wretched Poles had thus escaped the claws of the bear, only to fall into the lion's mouth. These double apostates took their horses and stripped them of their clothes, beat them to death, and threw them into the Yauza stream.

The diabolical riot of murder and homicide lasted from the third to the tenth hour of the day, and 2,135 Poles were either killed or robbed. Among them were many worthy apprentices, German jewellers, and merchants from Augsburg, who had with them much goods and gold. They were all stripped bare, thrown out like carrion into the streets, so that the dogs gnawed at them and the Russian quacks hacked the fat from their bodies, and so they lay for three days under the open sky, until on the third day after the murder Shuisky ordered them to be removed for burial in the cemetery.[3]

This day, 17 May, will be remembered as long as the world endures. It was a piteous and terrible day. On this day the foreigners suffered such fear and terror that it should not be narrated; still less can it be believed by those who read or hear of it. For six hours continuously nothing could be heard but the tocsin, shots, blows, people running and fleeing, and the Muscovites shouting and screaming: "Slay, slay the whoresons,"[4] nor was there any compassion among the tyrannical Russians for the Poles; no pleas, no tears, no appeals were of any avail.

One well-born and worthy nobleman had just leaped out of bed in his shirt and burrowed under the sand in his cellar, taking with him a purse containing a hundred ducats. The Russians found him as they were searching to see whether the Poles had hidden anything. He willingly gave them the hundred ducats, and asked them to spare his life and take him prisoner, saying that he had not offended anyone, neither the tsar nor any of the magnates, and that if they would only feed him, he had enough wealth in Poland to reimburse them, only let them take him to the Kremlin, to the magnates, and he would answer for himself.

How distressed this worthy man was, how deeply he sighed as he saw his servants so cruelly butchered outside his door, as he himself was led through their corpses, I myself saw with my own eyes.

Another Muscovite emerged from a nearby street, and as soon as he saw the Polish nobleman bound fast, he cried: "Slay the whoreson!" The victim bowed almost to the ground in front of the assassin, and pleaded in such a way that even a stone in the ground would be moved, pleading for the sake of God that his life be preserved. Since this was to no avail, he pleaded in Christ's name, and then in the name of St Nicholas and the Immaculate Pure Virgin Mary, but these prayers were equally to no avail. The murderer lunged at him, but the victim tore himself away from those who were leading him, sprang back, and bowed as low as he could before them, saying: "Oh, you Muscovites! You call yourselves Christians? Where is your Christian compassion and charity? Spare me on account of your Christian faith, and for the sake of my wife and children, whom I have left behind in Poland." But his pleas and imprecations were in vain. The murderer inflicted such a deep wound, a span long, in his shoulder, that blood spurted on all sides.

The worthy man ran, still hoping to save his life, but on account of this commotion yet more murderers came into this street, and they so hacked him with their swords that he fell to the ground and rendered up his spirit in a piteous fashion. Then the ruffians quarrelled amongst themselves over who should have his bloodstained shirt and garments. Thus this wretched nobleman lost not only his wealth, clothes, gold, silver, servants, horses, weapons, and pistols, but also his life, which was cause of grief for his dear ones in Poland, as it was for many hundreds of other wives, children, brothers, kinsmen, and friends, all of whom lost their dear ones.

For all the foreigners this was a day of unhappiness, misfortune, and grief. The foreigners' loss was the local inhabitants' gain. One ruffian assembled in his house, as his booty, velvet and silk garments, sables and fox furs, gold chains and rings, tapestries, gold, and silver such as his ancestors had never had. On that day inordinate boasting and bragging was heard. They said among themselves: "**Our Muscovite community is very powerful, all the world cannot restrain us.** Who can count our nation? All must bow down before us." Yes, **my dear Muscovites, when there are a hundred of you against one unarmed man**, then you are redoubtable heroes, and when you attack men who are asleep, then you will not fare badly, so long as there are a hundred thousand of you!

At the end of ten hours the tragedy came to an end, and peace was concluded with those Poles who still remained alive. Throughout all Moscow it became quiet, and the Russians received a breathing space like unto that when the tumult and the sighing of stormy winds and the high rearing waves yield to fair, tranquil, and bright weather. At such a time mariners are more joyful than they were before the stormy winds, since they have survived. Even such a joy was there among us when we heard that there was to be an end to the slaughter and killing, and that so many hundreds of thousands had managed to stay alive in all the disorders and commotion.

How the Muscovites Dealt with the Tsaritsa and her Father

After the tumult had died down, the traitorous band of princes and boyars gathered in front of the tsaritsa's apartments, and let it be known to her that although they were well aware that she was the daughter of an important man, nevertheless she herself was even more aware of the identity of that impostor and brigand who had claimed to be Dmitry and heir to the Russian tsardom, since she had been acquainted with him even in Poland. If she wanted them to set her free, in order that she might go to her father, then she must surrender everything that the brigand had stolen from the treasury and either sent to Poland or had given her here.

She handed over to them, not only her own clothes and ornaments, precious stones and all that she had with her, but also took off the very dress she was wearing and stood before them clad only in a nightgown, and she begged them to take it all and let her go in peace to her father and she would reimburse them for all that she and her people had consumed.

The Russians answered that it was not a question of what she had consumed, but that she should return the forty thousand and fifteen thousand rubles coin[1] that the brigand had sent her, together with the other precious objects and ornaments, and only then, and not before, would she be permitted to proceed to her father.

The tsaritsa replied that all this, and as much again of her own money, she had disbursed along the way out of honour for the Muscovites and their sovereign, and whatever had remained with her here in her apartments they had already taken and received back.[2]

She further entreated that one of her father's servants be permitted access to her, and then she and her father together would hand over whatsoever they could, and the rest would be sent on from Poland as soon as they let her out of Russia. Then one of her father's servants was allowed in and out to carry messages. The father begged that the magnates should come to him, and he addressed them thus, saying: "My lords! You do not wish to permit my daughter to come to me unless she hands over to you the 55,000 rubles which Dmitry, your tsar, sent to her to prepare for the journey in a manner befitting both him and the realm. The equipment for my daughter and myself cost at least as much again. Now you have already taken all this back, slaughtered and plundered our people, and still you have the audacity to demand yet more money from us. I have here with me," he said, "money for my personal expenses which I honestly drew from my treasury in Poland. Here they are – sixty thousand reichs-thalers and twenty thousand Polish silver pieces. If you will free me, my daughter and all our remaining people, I will give you all this and send the balance later."

The Russians replied: "It is yet too early to release you and your people. If you want your daughter to be with you, then pay eighty thousand thalers into our treasury, and we will permit her to come." The poor man said: "What are you doing to me? I will not abandon my daughter, but as for the rest, let it be unto me as the Lord God wills. Here is the money. Bring my daughter to me, together with her chief lady-in-waiting and the rest of her ladies."

After this the tsaritsa and her chief lady-in-waiting were permitted as far as the gates of her father's lodging, but were denied entry until the father had sent the eighty thousand thalers past the gate. They took the money and allowed the tsaritsa to go to her father. With bitter tears and heavy sighs he addressed the Muscovites: "**You have not dealt with us like honest men.** You say that my late son-in-law was not Dmitry, the son of Ivan Vasilievich, yet even so you received him a year ago when he came into your land out of Poland with only a few followers.

You abandoned your Boris by the thousands, came over to him, received him and recognized him as your rightful heir and lord, for which cause we Poles had good reason to believe that he was the true and lawful sovereign.

On this account you deprived Fedor Borisovich Godunov of his life, and eradicated the stem of the Godunovs. You crowned Dmitry as your sovereign, and even thanked us through your official ambassadors for having received and entertained him so honourably and having helped him to his feet. The document to which you have all borne witness by setting your hands and affixing your seals states that he is the lawful sovereign heir to the Muscovite land, and in it you requested our permission to have our beloved daughter as his wife and to send her to him. This document is deposited with us in Poland, so you cannot deny any of this.

We withheld our consent to the marriage, so it was through your princes and boyars that he pressed his suit and conveyed his proposals to her. We did not wish to give our permission without first obtaining the consent of your realm, and also evidence that he was the true heir to the throne. This you sent to us in Poland, and it remains to this day with His Royal Highness. The same testimony was given by your ambassadors in the presence of our king in Poland. How do you dare say now that he was not so? How in all conscience can you say that we Poles deceived you? We, being honourable people, relied too much upon your words, your documents and your seals; yea, and also upon your oaths and cross-kissing. You deceived us, not we you.

We came to you as friends, and you treated us as bitterest enemies. We lived among you without guile, as can be witnessed by the fact that we did not all lodge together in one group but lived scattered about, some here, some there, one here on this street, another there on that street, and so forth, which we would not have done, had we had any evil intention towards you Russians.

You lay in wait for us like assassins, you greeted us with your lips but cursed us in your hearts, as can now, God have mercy, be seen with our own eyes, and by the hundreds of forsaken widows and orphans in Poland, bereaved parents and kinsmen, who were made so by these murders, and who will ceaselessly lament, sighing day and night, the voice of their complaint ascending to God in heaven. **How will you answer before eternity for such evil deeds and fearful slaughter?** Even if my late son-in-law was not the legitimate sovereign and heir to the throne – and we can prove the opposite from your letters and documents – wherein lies the guilt of the hundred innocent musicians? In what way have the jewellers and merchants sinned against you, who took nothing from you but brought fine wares? What harm have these innocent people done you, including women and virgins, whom you have dishonoured and detained in your houses?

If we had felt any enmity towards you, we would have come not with three or four thousand men but with eleven hundred thousand, and would have brought with us a significant force. We came to you in friendship, to attend a wedding, but our people were to be devoured to death among you, their souls were to perish, and all they had was plundered. Do you really think that God in heaven let this slaughter committed by you and your men go unpunished? Oh no, no, the innocent blood will cry out to God. The cry of bereaved widows, orphans, and friends will not cease until the Lord looks down and sees, judges and punishes, of that you can be sure. If you wish to devour and destroy us utterly, you are free to do so. God will be the judge between us. We rely upon God with a clear conscience, but we have never had any evil intention towards you."

The Muscovite princes and boyars replied: "You, lord governor, are not at fault, neither are we, the princes and boyars, at fault, but it is your arrogant Poles that are to blame, who insulted Russian women and children, have done much violence in the streets, and have beaten, abused, and threatened to kill the Russians and thereby stirred up all the inhabitants of the city. Who can oppose hundreds upon thousands, once they have been set in motion? This is the first point. Secondly, your slain son-in-law himself committed many faults, which led to his destruction. He disregarded our customs, usages, and religious services, and even our own persons. He preferred any foreigner to us, despite all his promises and oath. For behold, the Muscovite land is our land, we entrusted it to him, he ought to have been grateful and mindful to what honour and what greatness we had raised him. He ought to have held persons of our nation in higher esteem than any foreigner, then all the world would without a doubt have counted him for Dmitry, even though he was not. He knew very well that he was not Dmitry, and the reason why we accepted him was that we wanted to overthrow Boris. We hoped that with his help we would make things better for ourselves, but we were cruelly mistaken for, on the contrary, things got worse. He ate veal, behaved like a pagan, and finally forced us to do that which was not pleasing to us, and therefore we struck first, and even if he had not been struck down, we would still now strangle him. As for the innocent musicians and the other people who lost their lives, we ourselves wish that they were still alive, but we cannot do anything about that. All this happened during the rioting of an enraged people, and in such circumstances it is impossible to withstand hundreds of thousands of people, let alone to dissuade them. Your daughter's ladies-in-waiting came to no harm, they are with our wives and daughters and are even better cared for than your own daughter, but, if you wish, they can be brought to you at any time. If you will give us your oath, that neither you nor your family, nor anybody on your behalf, will rise up against us, nor bear malice against us or our realm for these wrongs – this is the first condition – secondly, that you will strive to the end that your king will not have any quarrel with us over the killing of his people during the course of the riot; thirdly, that you will send us the balance of the fifty-five thousand rubles, together with everything that you know Dmitry sent your daughter and which we did not find in her treasury – if you will give us this oath, then you will be released. If not, we have such a sufficiency of prisons that, even though you were twice as many, we should be quite capable of locking you up. Think about it."

The governor answered: "All that which my late son-in-law sent to my beloved daughter as his dear betrothed, she brought here with her, and that, together with all I gave her as a dowry, has all been plundered, and she was brought to me here clad only in her nightgown.

You know better than we where everything was concealed, or what became of it at the time of the disorders, when you princes and boyars separated her from her ladies in waiting. We are therefore not a little amazed at your godless demands, since you have robbed us of everything and, having robbed us, dare to demand yet more.

Of the eighty thousand thalers which we, out of compassion for our daughter, were compelled to give to you, you do not have the right to a single penny. This was property earned honestly by the sweat of our brow, and there does not remain a single mite[3] in our treasury that we can pay out.

For the godless violence and unprecedented wrongs which we and our dear ones have suffered at your hands, we swear that we will not bear malice, and will keep our oath, neither will we allow our families to seek vengeance, but will refer it all to Him who has said: '**Vengeance is mine, I will repay**.'[4] May He indeed judge and avenge! I cannot give any undertakings on behalf of His Majesty the King of Poland, my gracious sovereign and king, not knowing whether I can fulfil them. Most of the victims were subjects of His Royal Majesty, and he will take their deaths very much to heart when he learns how inhumanly they were treated. His Royal Highness is my liege sovereign, and so it is not befitting for me to make undertakings on his behalf; do not ask of me the impossible."

The Muscovites answered: "Since you will not or cannot fulfil our conditions, you and your Poles must remain with us under guard while we see how things go between us and your king, and until you replace what is missing from our treasury, and also all that was paid out during the war against your son-in-law. If these demands are not satisfied, you will remain here in our power."

The Governor said: "*Let it be with me as the Lord wills.* Everything, both my cross and my good fortune, come from Him. I shall endure patiently all that He assigns me. The limit to which you can harm me has already been set. Do to me all that God has willed me to suffer and that He will allow you to inflict. You cannot do any more, either to me or my dear ones."[5]

Thereafter, at the end of May, they were all sent out of Moscow, except for the king's ambassadors. Some were cast into prison at Yaroslavl. The lord governor and the tsaritsa, together with her brother and relatives, were also confined together at Yaroslavl in a single house, and there were guarded day and night, so that nobody could or dared go in to them or come out from them unless the Muscovites permitted it. Some of the Poles were transferred to Rostov, some to Galich, a few to Kostroma, Beloozero,[6] Kargopol, and Vologda.[7] Orders were given to maintain them there on bread and water. The Polish magnates were compelled to sell at half price their silver ornaments and all that remained to them after the riots. With that they maintained themselves until the Lord God willed that the second Dmitry rescue them in a miraculous fashion.

VII *What Happened to the Murdered Dmitry and His Champion Lord Peter Fedorovich Basmanov, and Also to the 2,135 Poles, Who Willed That the Second Dmitry Should Rescue Them in a Miraculous Fashion, and the Miracles Which Occurred When They Brought Dmitry's Corpse*

Earlier it was related how Lord Basmanov was stabbed and thrown down from the gallery, then how the Russians for six whole hours had sounded the alarm from all the bells, had run riot, how many Poles they killed, and so on. Now is related what they did with the corpses.

The bodies of the Poles were to lie two whole days and nights in the streets, then they were collected. They lay stark naked to be gnawed by the dogs, and the quacks had begun to hack the fat from them. Then the magnates and boyars ordered the carters to come and collect the bodies from all the streets, take them away, and cast them into a charnel house. Their end did not correspond in any way to their beginning. Their beginning was too brilliant but their end was utterly pitiful, lamentable, and wretched.

The bodies of Dmitry and his loyal champion Basmanov were placed ignominiously on view in the Kremlin until Vespertide, and shortly after the riot had ended they were stripped naked. They attached a bast to the tsar's privy parts[1] and another bast around both his feet, and they tied a cord of bast around both of Basmanov's feet; they dragged them both out of the Kremlin by the Jerusalem Gate and left them lying in the midst of the marketplace near the stalls. Then they brought a table and a bench. The tsar was placed on the table, and Basmanov next to him on the bench in front of the table, so that the tsar's feet lay on Basmanov's breast.

A boyar came out of the Kremlin with a mask and a bagpipe, and laid the mask on the tsar's stomach next to his privy parts,[2] but placed the pipe in his mouth, and laid the sack of the bagpipe on his chest.[3] Then he said: "You son of a whore and betrayer of the land, you forced us for so long to pipe for you, now you can give us a tune."

Other boyars and merchants who came to gaze on him beat the body with whips, saying: "O you friend of the Germans! What great harm have you done unto the homeland![4] How you have squandered and emptied the treasury!" The Muscovite women, most of them from the common people, spoke about his private member and about his tsaritsa in a manner which it is not befitting to write.

Prince Ivan Golitsyn, Lord Basmanov's half brother, had earned such favour from the other princes and boyars that he could take his brother away and have him buried, and he was interred on 18 May in his brother's church, which is close to the English courtyard. Tsar Dmitry was to lie in the aforementioned place for three days and three nights, and was exposed to the fearful mockery of all the Russians.

CONCERNING THE WONDROUS PORTENTS
WHICH TOOK PLACE AROUND THE BODY
OF DMITRY

1 On the third night, on both sides of the table, there appeared fires from the ground. When the guard approached they disappeared, but as he went away they flared up again, which caused such wonderment among the guards that they reported it to the great lords, who themselves came thither, waited there, and saw it for themselves, and therefore gave the order that the body be conveyed early in the morning to the charnel house outside the Serpukhov Gates and be left there.

2 When they took the body away, a fearful wind arose, not throughout the entire city, but only in those places where they were carrying the deceased, and it tore the gable from the tower of the Kulisha Gate as they were carrying the body through it.

3 The Bolvanovsk Gates,[5] which are the last in the outer wall, with three towers, the middle one higher than the two flanking it, were torn by the wind from their foundations, together with part of the surrounding wooden wall, and were thrown back as far as the Yauza Gates.

4 The fourth portent occurred in the charnel house, where they cast Dmitry in with the other corpses. In the morning he was found

outside the doors, which had been locked, and two doves sat on his corpse. When anyone tried to approach him, the doves flew away, and when the person went away, the doves returned. And although once again at the order of the great lords the body was cast into a ditch, and earth heaped upon it, he continued to lie there only until 27 May.

5 At that time the body was discovered in another churchyard, situated far away from that other cemetery.

The whole city was not a little terrified, both the upper and the lower orders, and they marvelled greatly at the strange things that had happened with this dead body. Some said that he could not have been a wondrous hero, since his body would not remain in the ground. Others said that he was the Devil himself, since he was still playing his tricks upon Christians. Yet others said that he was a sorcerer, and had learned his art from the savage Lapps, for they could allow themselves to be killed and yet come to life again, and that he, too, had learned this diabolical art.

Therefore, his body should be thrown into the fire, and he should be burned to ashes.[6] This was done on 28 May, and the ashes were scattered to the wind, so that nothing remained. And although the Poles on the first day of the riot had spread the rumour that the murdered man was not Dmitry but a German who resembled him, all these were only tales and inventions to spring upon the Russians yet another novelty, as will be told later concerning the second Dmitry.

I knew him very well while he was still alive, and I saw him after he was murdered. It was of course the same man who had sat upon the throne, had reigned, had celebrated his marriage, etc. He was killed, he stayed dead, he was burned to ashes and dust, and he will be seen no more on this earth. And no matter how many Dmitrys might appear after him, they will all be impostors and deceivers, and will not reach that worthiness which the dead man attained.

The late sovereign had a heroic and manly spirit, and displayed many splendid virtues, but he also had his failings, namely over-confidence and vanity, because of which, without a doubt, God visited such punishments upon him. His over-confidence was so great that he even became scornful of those who told him of the Muscovites' treachery, in that they wished to kill him along with his Poles. His vainglory increased daily, and also that of his tsaritsa, and it showed not only in that he exceeded all former tsars in his luxury and ostentation, but he also commanded that he be styled "tsar of tsars."

His halberdiers and bodyguards not only had to bow to the waist and kneel as the tsar and tsaritsa approached, but they also had to genuflect, which is not done frequently by people even for the All-merciful God, Who alone is entitled to such reverence. Even so, He who speaks in the Book of the Prophet Isaiah, chapter 45, "I will humble the glorious upon earth,"[7] overthrew and destroyed him.

This unseemly haughtiness was often recalled later by his widowed tsaritsa in her imprisonment, and in her heart she was greatly troubled that she was never wholeheartedly grateful to the Lord God for such favour, that he had raised her, the daughter of a mere governor, to a marriage of such state, and had made her worthy to become the empress of such a great realm. She would say that she and her late husband had been so proud in their estate, and that they had sinned grievously against the Lord God, for which reason He so swiftly and so immediately had inflicted upon them such a fearful retribution. She therefore vowed that if God again helped her in her afflictions, never again would she display such haughtiness. May God bring this about, and have mercy upon her, and deliver her in the name of the Saviour from all the griefs and misfortunes in which I later, in 1611, left her in the city of Kaluga, as I set off for the encampment of His Royal Highness the King of Poland at Smolensk. Amen! Amen! Amen!

Into this tragic mirror all rulers and sovereigns would do well to look, and if any such tendencies begin to appear in themselves, they should correct them in good time, so as not to give the Good God cause to visit such wrath upon them, for it is said: "What has happened to one can happen to many; similar causes have similar effects."[8]

First, all great leaders and rulers should be well aware that their estate is hateful to the Devil, and that whatever he cannot do for himself, he achieves through his instruments, traitors and rebels. Therefore they should not live so degenerately and carelessly, or pass the time in such an unbefitting fashion as is, alas, seen in many, as if there were not on earth any Devil or evildoers. Ah no, no! Devils are everywhere at large and will stop at nothing, especially since they know their time is short. They try by every means to disrupt and overturn the God-established order in the government of realms, in ecclesiastical affairs and the economy. Few reliable people are to be found, "The just have fled," saith the Prophet. Therefore all rulers should cast their eyes up to the heavens, and sincerely pray that God and His angels Raphael, Michael, Gabriel, and others not abandon them in their ways and paths, nor allow the loathsome Devil and his agents to approach them, but should shield them from all misfortune and grant them happiness and blessedness in their rule.

Second, even though God is gracious, and allows rulers as His emissaries and representatives to be in authority and have lordship over others, they should all the same behave with moderation therein and avoid unseemly arrogance, neither accepting honours which are due to the Lord God alone, nor compelling their subjects to render them to their ruler. **God cannot and will not tolerate this for a moment. He does not concede this honour to another**, and will not delay in humiliating such proud people.

As the poet says: "**Every lofty thing can be entrusted safely to God's care.**"[9] So many examples confirm this dictum: Nebuchadnezzar, Pausanias, Croesus, Pompey, Dionysius, Herod, Agrippa, etc., as well as that brave hero Dmitry of Russia, with whom the Lord played His harsh game: "He hath put down the mighty from their seat."[10] For it is said: "What stands high does not endure for very long."[11] He who exalts himself will soon be humbled, as Sirach says in his tenth chapter: "Pride is the origin of all sin, and he who is possessed by it shall spew forth abominations." God always shames the proud, and in the end overthrows them. Therefore for rulers and all other persons in high authority there is no more befitting and laudable aim than to cultivate inner humility and constantly remind themselves of the wise words Simonides uttered to Pausanias: "Remember that thou art a mortal man."[12] Then unseeming vainglory will not find any place in him.

Third, rulers and those in authority should not show untimely kindness and mercy towards open and blatant evildoers, so as not to give rise to even greater misfortune and harm, and also so as not to become an accomplice in the sins of others. God has commanded them not to look the other way from sinners but to expel the evil ones from Israel. Their eyes should not be indulgent towards evil, for then evildoers will prosper. They are servants and avengers, empowered to punish those who do evil; nor should they wear their swords listlessly or just for show, still less should they gird themselves instead with a light foxtail and lightly belabour evildoers, for by such leniency towards bad people they will open the door and windows to more sin. Thereby they will anger the Lord God, and He will take the sword away from them and give it to another, handing him over first to the evildoers and then to others to be punished on account of his folly, which is what in deed and in truth happened to the brave hero Dmitry. He spared the life of the traitor Vasily Ivanovich Shuisky, who had his head on the block and was about to be executed, and who was the true leader, agitator, and instigator of all that clique of traitors; nor was he chastened by this untimely mercy but became even worse, since, as has been narrated previously, he stirred up the whole population to such fearful unrest and slaughter that the tsar, who only shortly beforehand had spared his life, now, along with thousands of others, lost his own life, and all that he had. Truly it might be said that Shuisky "hanged his redeemer on the tree."[13] If Dmitry had drawn his sword against the traitor and rebel Shuisky and had given vent to his anger without mercy, as King David did against the rebel Seth, then all this fearful murder, grief, and misfortune would not have befallen him and all his dear ones, all of which happened and followed from such an untimely act of mercy, and continues until this day. God only knows when it will end.

I will not attempt to say how Dmitry will excuse himself before God on judgment day and be asked to account for his and other deaths which occurred by reason of his connivance and negligence in visiting punishment. If Klaus the Fool had lived to see these events in Muscovy, he would have given a similar verdict to the one he gave before, namely that Dmitry was responsible not only for the loss of his own life but also for the lives of all those who are even now perishing in Russia, since the original cause of all this bloodbath and the warfare which proceeded from it was simply his carelessness, and the fact that he did not deprive the traitor Shuisky of his head.

Therefore let all powerful rulers and lords reflect upon the pitiful end of this Dmitry, and heed God's command to root the evil ones out of Israel, following the example of David, who says in Psalm 101: "Day by day I will destroy all the ungodly that are in the land, that I may root out the evildoers from the city of the Lord."[14] Further let me cite the example of Stefan Bathory, King of Poland, who did not wish to hear when he was urged to spare the lives of convicted traitors but said: "Dead dogs don't bite"[15] and again: "Let justice be done even though the world perish"[16] and gave the command for them to be executed. For it is always the case **that if a person once commit a foul deed, he will not stop at that**, but will commit thereafter a graver and more serious offence. Therefore rulers should be vigilant that there may be peace and a quiet conscience, for then they shall not be accomplices in the sins of others.

VIII *True Evidence That This Dmitry Was Not the Son of the Tyrant Ivan Vasilievich but an Alien*

As for Dmitry himself, people had various opinions about him. Some believe that he was the legitimate heir to the Russian throne, but most people said that he was a foreigner, so I have taken considerable pains to set forth the genuine and factual truth.

On one occasion, Lord Basmanov, who was Dmitry's most loyal servant, and laid down his life for him, as has been narrated earlier, invited me to his house. Since he was very favourably disposed and friendly towards me, I asked him frankly, but in strict secrecy, and persuaded him to reveal to me in confidence the truth concerning our gracious lord. Was he the legitimate heir or not? He then said to me the following in confidence: "You Germans have in him a father and a brother. He loves you, and has exalted you higher than any previous tsar, and I know that you are loyal to him. Pray for him, that God preserve him, and I shall do so with you. Although he is not the son of Ivan Vasilievich, he is still our sovereign. We have recognized him and sworn allegiance to him, and we will never find a better sovereign in Russia."

Furthermore a certain apothecary, who had served continuously for forty years, first the Tyrant, then his son Fedor Ivanovich, then Boris Godunov, and now this Dmitry, and every day in the Kremlin had seen and known Tsarevich Dmitry as a child, similarly told me in confidence, and solemnly affirmed, that this Dmitry was not genuine, but that the true tsarevich greatly resembled his mother, Maria Fedorovna Nagaia.

I received similar testimony from a certain noblewoman, who had several years previously been brought captive from Livonia, but in 1611 was released and, God be praised, had returned to her own people. She had been a midwife at the lying-in of Dmitry's mother, and had witnessed the birth and the rearing of the imperial infant,[1] and had served day and night in the palace.

After this murder I went together with a certain German merchant, Berndt Hoper, a native of the city of Riga, from Moscow to the city of Uglich, but shortly before we reached Uglich we met a Muscovite who was 105 years old, and had been one of the guards[2] in the palace while the young Dmitry was there. We spoke with him concerning the murdered Dmitry, and after a long conversation he revealed to us in confidence what he thought about the murdered sovereign, whether or not he was the son of the old tsar, and we further promised not to reveal it to anybody.

He stood up, crossed himself three times in the name of St Nicholas and said: "This murdered sovereign was a brave hero, and in one year he struck fear into our hostile neighbours, and our Muscovites did us a disservice when they killed him, for they had acknowledged him, placed him on the throne, and had sworn allegiance to him. Even if he did violate some of our customs and usages, this could have been rectified by some other means. He was a prudent sovereign, but he was not the son of Ivan the Terrible. The true tsarevich was killed seventeen years ago in Uglich and is long since decomposed. I saw him lying dead in the playground. God forgive the princes and boyars who overthrew[3] Boris Fedorovich Godunov and put this one in his place. Now they have devoured both of them, and what this will mean for us and all the land, only time will tell."

Many Poles told me that he was an illegitimate son of the late King of Poland, Stefan Bathory. The general besieging the Trinity monastery, whose name was Jan Piotr Pawel Sapieha, was sitting at table with all his officers and boasting of the valour of the Poles, saying that they were not inferior, but superior to the Romans.[4] Among other things, he said: "Three years ago we Poles placed upon the Muscovite throne a sovereign who was to be called Dmitry, the son of the Tyrant, despite the fact that he was not. Now for a second time we have brought hither a sovereign and have conquered almost half the country, and he also shall and must be called Dmitry, even if this drives the Russians out of their minds. This we will do with our troops and with the power of our hand."[5] This I heard with my own ears.[6]

Not one of the noble princes or boyars was favourably disposed to the young Dmitry at Uglich, on account of his cruel disposition, which began to appear in him even in his childish years.[7] Neither can the secret abduction of the young sovereign have been the work of the common people. The Muscovites, especially the nobility, would much rather let their children die any kind of death than allow them to leave the country for other lands; in fact the tsar had to compel them to let them go. They consider their land to be the only Christian land under the sun. They consider all other lands to be pagan, in which people are not baptized, do not know God, do not know how they ought to pray to or serve God, and therefore they assert that their children would perish eternally were they to die in such a foreign country. On the other hand, if they die in their own country, they are assured of going to heaven. Therefore if the Muscovites were not fearful of going to other nations, then they and their wives and children could save themselves and their possessions during this time of protracted war, but they do not choose to do so, and therefore they have lost all that their god St Nicholas has given them.

Therefore this Dmitry was not the son of the old tsar Ivan the Tyrant, but a foreigner, and the Muscovites acknowledged him because they wanted to overthrow Boris Fedorovich Godunov (whom, on account of his great vigilance, they could not otherwise have overthrown), on account of whom they in their thousands deserted him and rallied to this Dmitry, under whom they hoped to improve their situation.[8]

Concerning Prince Vasily Shuisky and the Second Dmitry, Who Sought to Overthrow Shuisky, and Claimed to Be the Escaped Dmitry; also Concerning Sigismund III, King of Poland, How He Intervened, and How His Son, His Royal Highness Prince Wladyslaw, Was Offered the Muscovite Land and Throne

In the same year 1606, on 24 May,[1] which was the eighth day after the betrayal and murder, Prince Vasily Shuisky (the very one who the previous spring was in the hands of the executioner, had been undressed by the executioner's assistants, and had laid his head upon the block, for there, at the place for public executions he was to have been prevented by the axe from any further treasons), without the knowledge or the consent of the Assembly of the Land, but only by the will of the Muscovites, as many as could be considered his accomplices in the murders and treasons, all those merchants, piemen, cobblers,[2] and a few princes and boyars who happened to be present, was crowned as tsar by the patriarch, bishops, and priests, and the whole city swore allegiance to him, both local inhabitants and foreigners.[3] Immediately afterwards, several nobles and chancellors who happened to be in Moscow were sent around the country to administer the oath of allegiance to all the common people and nobility in all the cities and communities.

Having become tsar, Shuisky's first action was to send an embassy to the Polish king, and he accused His Royal Majesty of not observing the truce which he had concluded during his time, and coupled this with a request that he desist from attacks on the borderlands and maintain good neighbourly relations. At the same time he sent the king all kinds of magnificent presents and tokens of esteem and, covering his traces, informed His Royal Highness that his subjects, followers of the governor of Sandomir, had made mockery of the inhabitants of Moscow and had thus created a riot, in the course of which a number of Poles had been killed, but that no evil had befallen the Polish ambassador since he, Shuisky, had personally given him his protection and would soon send him back in perfect health. King Sigismund III also sent his greetings to the new tsar, Shuisky, and recalled the ambassador whom he had sent Dmitry.

Concerning those who had been slain, His Royal Highness replied that the Poles were a free people, that they could go and serve where and whom they pleased, that they had gone with the governor of Sandomir and his daughter of their own free will to attend the wedding, and if they had done some mischief there, and in their turn had suffered because of it, then that was none of the king's concern, and therefore he would in no wise pay attention to it, but he also had no control over the actions of the relatives of those who were slain. They, the Polish nobles, were free people, and if they wished to seek vengeance, His Majesty was powerless to forbid it.

He had no need of the gifts which had been sent, and he returned them, demanding only the return of his ambassador, who shortly thereafter was allowed to leave.[4]

Shuisky had all the other Poles imprisoned in various parts of the country, and thus cleansed the Christian city of Moscow of the presence of pagans (as they call all foreigners), so that there remained (presumably)[5] only true Christians and pious folk.

On 23 June, since he did not trust them, he expelled from Moscow four medical doctors whom Dmitry's Poles and the followers of the governor of Sandomir often consulted. A fifth doctor, David Vasmar from Lübeck,[6] who lived alone and had no personal dealings with these Poles, was retained by Shuisky as his personal physician.

Since at that time the fable of Dmitry's escape had become widespread, the Muscovites were greatly perplexed in their minds on account of these tidings and soon did not know what or whom to believe.

Shuisky, to whom this matter was more vital than to anyone else, wished to awaken the Muscovites from their dreams. So, on 30 June, he sent orders to Uglich to exhume the corpse of the real Dmitry, which had lain in the earth for seventeen years and was by now decomposed, and bring it to Moscow and lay it to rest in the church where the previous tsars lie.

All this was carried out for this aim and purpose, namely that the simple people would realize and see how greatly they had been deceived by Dmitry, and that now they were about to let themselves be deceived by a second Dmitry. And in order that this foolish trick might appear the better, Shuisky ordered a new coffin to be made, a priest's nine-year-old son to be killed and dressed up in costly grave clothes, then to be placed within the coffin and brought to Moscow. He himself, together with his princes, boyars, monks, and priests, came out with crosses and banners to meet the royal corpse and ordered it to be carried in a splendid procession to the church of the dead tsars.

He ordered it to be announced to the populace that Prince Dmitry, innocently slain in his youth, was now a great saint with God. Although he had lain in the earth for seventeen years, yet his body was as fresh as though he had only died yesterday. The nuts which he had held in his hands on the playground when he had died also had not perished or been consumed, nor were his clothes at all soiled, and even the coffin had not been rotted by the soil but looked just like new. Whosoever wished to view him could go to the church of the tsars, where he was laid out. The church would always be open, so that anyone could go there and look upon him. Shuisky bribed a number of healthy persons to pretend to be sick. One was to crawl on all fours and reach out to the body of St Dmitry. Another was led in, pretending to be blind as a post, who in fact had perfectly good eyes and could see very well, and he had to pray to St Dmitry for healing. Both of them were healed. The lame man stood up and walked around, the blind man recovered his sight, and both said that St Dmitry had helped them. So the simple people believed, and there was such dreadful and fearful sacrilege around the corpse that the Lord God on this account became enraged, so that when another who pretended to be blind came and said he wished to recover his sight from St Dmitry, he was himself struck blind right there in the church.

Another who pretended to be sick and had himself carried to St Dmitry to implore his aid was also punished by God, and was destined to drop dead in the church. When this foolery was carried to such extremes that even children began to remark that this was simply a trick and deception, Shuisky ordered the church closed and nobody else admitted, saying that the coming of too many people had disturbed St Dmitry. He was angry at them, so he must be left in peace for a while, and to this end he should not be molested until he was in a better mood.[7]

XI *How Prince Grigory Shakhovskoy by Theft and Falsehood Brought Great Harm to Tsar Shuisky*

At the time of the rioting when Tsar Dmitry was killed, a certain prominent prince, whose name was Grigory Shakhovskoy, stole the golden state seal and fled in the direction of the border fortress of Putivl, taking with him two Poles in Russian dress. Near Serpukhov he crossed the river Oka, gave the ferryman who carried him across a tip of six Polish guilders, and asked him whether he knew who they were. The ferryman said: "No, my lord, I do not know you." The prince said: "My good man, be silent and tell no man that you have just ferried across **Dmitry, tsar of all the Russias**." He showed the simple good man one of the Poles, and said: "See, that is the young hero whom the Muscovites wished to slay, but, praise and thanks be to God, he has survived. We are making for Poland, and we will bring from there a band of soldiers. He will make you a great man, if God will help us to return hither. Meanwhile, be content with this small gift."

The prince repeated a similar falsehood in the city of Serpukhov, deceiving a certain German widow as they sat at table. He gave her a handful of gold and said: "Here, German woman,[1] be content with this, prepare some good mead and brandywine. We, God willing, shall return with a great armed force, but you Germans will not come to any harm." The woman asked: "My lord, what kind of people are you? What are you talking about?" The prince replied: "I am a prince from Moscow, and I tell you that he who is eating and drinking with you at this moment is Tsar Dmitry, whom the Muscovites at the time of their rioting wished to kill, but with the help of God he secretly escaped and in his place left another whom they seized and killed. We shall soon return to you."

Thereupon they rode swiftly from one city to another, until they reached Putivl, repeating the same story in every inn, namely that Dmitry had not been slain but had survived, as a result of which the whole land, from Moscow to the Polish border, believed that Dmitry truly had escaped and was still alive. Rumours of this reached Moscow, and because of this strange and wondrous sentiments were stirred up.[2]

At Putivl the two Poles took leave of Prince Grigory Shakhovskoy and departed directly for Poland, to the wife of the governor of

Sandomir, to whom they gave an account of the fearful conflict which had occurred in Moscow, and told how a certain prince called Grigory Shakhovskoy had secretly brought them from Moscow, and had conducted them throughout the entire country to Putivl, and that this prince intended and had sworn to avenge Tsar Dmitry's death in such a manner that his countrymen would talk about it as long as Russia endured. He was also about to send letters to Poland, pretending that Dmitry, his lord, had reached Poland and was living there, and that they should write thence to Putivl as if Dmitry were replying.

Prince Shakhovskoy assembled all the burghers and community of Putivl and told them how the Muscovites had tried to settle accounts with Dmitry, but that he had secretly escaped, even though they had killed all his Poles, and that he had reached Poland and had arrived at the house of his Polish mother-in-law, the chatelaine of Sandomir, and wished to assemble a new armed force so that he might return to Russia as soon as possible and take revenge upon his perfidious Muscovites. He had ordered him (announcing his royal favour) to persuade them by all means to remain loyal to Dmitry and help him take revenge upon the Muscovites for such humiliation. He would so repay these disloyal hounds that one generation would speak of it unto another.[3]

The inhabitants of Putivl thereupon sent to the Wild Steppe and quickly recruited several thousand field Cossacks, and also called upon all the princes and boyars who lived in the region of Putivl, who also numbered several thousand. When the latter had joined up with the Cossacks, they were placed under a commander called Istoma Pashkov. They were to advance further in Dmitry's name, once again to capture fortresses and cities which had forsaken Dmitry at the time of the Moscow uprising. But they, acknowledging that Dmitry had not been killed but had secretly escaped, was still alive, and was equipping his army, voluntarily surrendered without any resistance, right up to Moscow, and once again swore allegiance to Dmitry, being very displeased at those who were to blame for the dissension[4] and fearful murders in Moscow.

The new tsar, the regicide Shuisky, was alarmed in no small measure at these tidings and quickly called the whole country to arms. And in order that they should report for duty as soon and as quickly as possible, without delay, he devised a falsehood and said that the Crimean Tatars with an army of fifty thousand men had invaded the country and that they had already taken captive many thousands of Muscovites, had carried them off to Tatary, and were raging strongly about the country. Therefore it was necessary to travel swiftly, day or night, to Moscow in order to offer resistance to the Tatars.

In August of the same year the regicide Shuisky's army approached Elets,[5] but they discovered there not the Tatars at all but their own countrymen, princes, boyars, and Cossacks, who were fighting for Dmitry, and these so defeated and exerted such pressure upon them that they were forced to retreat to Moscow.

The supporters of Putivl badly mistreated those who fell prisoner into their hands, who had to swallow biting sarcasm, as their captors said: "You whoresons of Muscovites and your Furrier (so they nicknamed the regicide Shuisky)[6] tried to kill the sovereign, slay his followers and slake your thirst with the tsar's blood. You rogues, drink water and eat pancakes[7] as is your custom. Our tsar will know sufficiently how to avenge this slaughter when he comes with his newly formed armies out of Poland."

Some prisoners were set free, first having been scourged severely, half to death, and they were sent back to Moscow, where they were also badly received by their comrades-in-arms for the news they brought, which was displeasing to Shuisky and his supporters. They were thrown into prison, where they died and rotted.

Shuisky ordered it to be announced to Moscow what great evil the Poles and their fabricated Dmitry had caused Russia, how the treasury had been exhausted, how much Christian blood had been shed, and how, thanks to Dmitry, the unfortunate tsar, Boris Fedorovich Godunov, had perished, together with his son and wife.

Now the traitors to the country were spreading the rumour that Dmitry had fled and had not been killed, but even if this were true (which assuredly it was not), all the same he was not Dmitry, the son of Ivan Vasilievich, but a deceiver, whom they would not wish to acknowledge, lest he introduce a pagan faith into the country. And in order that the people might be moved with Christian compassion, he ordered that the three corpses of Boris, his son, and his consort (which had lain buried for a year and a quarter in a beggarly monastery) be exhumed and carried to the Trinity monastery, to be buried there in royal fashion.

Boris's body was borne by twenty monks, his son Fedor Borisovich by twenty boyars, and Boris's wife Irina Fedorovna[8] also by twenty boyars, and behind these three bodies, on foot, proceeded all the monks, nuns, priests, princes, and boyars, right up to the Trinity Gates of the Kremlin. There they mounted up, ordered the bodies to be placed on sleds, and they escorted them to the Trinity monastery, which is situated twelve miles from the city of Moscow. This monastery is very powerful. Not one lord in all the land dies without making a rich bequest to it. When the country is at war, this monastery must provide the tsar with twenty thousand armed cavalrymen.

The daughter of Boris Fedorovich, who alone remained among the living, and whom Duke Johan, brother of the King of Denmark, who was remembered for his great praiseworthiness and Christian humility, was to have had as his bride (as has been related earlier), followed after these three bodies in a litter hung with curtains, calling and crying out: "**O woe is me, poor abandoned orphan!** The pretender, who called himself Dmitry, was in fact only an impostor. He killed my beloved father, my beloved mother and also my beloved brother, and has devoured all our stem, and now he too has been slain. During his lifetime, and also after his death, he has brought so much grief upon this whole land. **May God judge him! May God condemn him!**" **etc.** Now many wept and regretted him, saying that it would be better were he still alive and still reigning, even though this godless people had deliberately slain and destroyed him, together with his whole family. As the saying goes: Do not discard the old friend until you have proven the new.[9]

The aforesaid Putivl commander, Istoma Pashkov, advanced in August of that year with the forces he had available closer to Moscow, reached Kolomenskoe, and once again brought into subjection and allegiance to the second Dmitry many fortresses, cities, and small towns, without any resistance. At Michaelmas he came even closer to Moscow and pitched his camp at Kotly, which is about a mile and a quarter from Moscow. In the name of his lord Dmitry he demanded the surrender of the city and the extradition of the three Shuisky brothers as the instigators of the riots and fearful slaughter that had occurred. At that time many inhabitants of Moscow, both native and foreign, considered all was lost, and began secretly to leave the city to join the enemy.

XII *Concerning Ivan Isaevich Bolotnikov, Who Came to Poland from Venice, and How in Poland a Certain Person, Who Allowed Himself to Be Addressed as Dmitry Tsar of Russia, Sent Him into Russia to Wage War*

Shortly after Martinmas there came to aid the Putivl commander Istoma Pashkov, by way of the Komaritsk district to Kaluga, and further in the direction of Moscow to Kotly, a very experienced warrior, named Ivan Isaevich Bolotnikov.[1] He brought every locality through which he passed back to its allegiance to Dmitry, who was about to arrive, and by this means he progressively increased his army.

This Bolotnikov was a Muscovite by birth, but in his youth he had been taken prisoner in the Wild Steppe by the Tatars, with whom the Muscovites have to contend every year, and was sold to Turkey, where he was chained to the galleys, and for several years had to fulfil hard and menial tasks, until finally he was freed by the German ships, who defeated the Turks by sea, and was brought to Venice, whence he proceeded by way of Germany and Poland, where he learned of the wondrous changes which had occurred in his native land during his absence.

As soon as he had heard that his lord, Tsar Dmitry, had escaped from the hands of his Muscovite assassins, had arrived in Poland, and was said to be now at the house of the governor of Sandomir, he immediately went to him. As soon as he who claimed to be Dmitry had examined him, had asked who he was, whence he had come and what his intentions were, and had satisfied himself from his replies that he was an experienced warrior, he asked him whether he was willing to serve against his murderous countrymen and perfidious evildoers.

When he replied that he was prepared at any time to sacrifice his life for his legitimate sovereign, the pretended Dmitry said to him: "I cannot give you very much at present. Here are thirty ducats, a sabre, and a felt cloak. Be content with this for the present. Proceed with this letter to Prince Grigory Shakhovskoy at Putivl. He will give you sufficient money from my treasury, and will appoint you general and field commander over several thousand troops. You will advance with them in my place, and if God is merciful towards you, you will

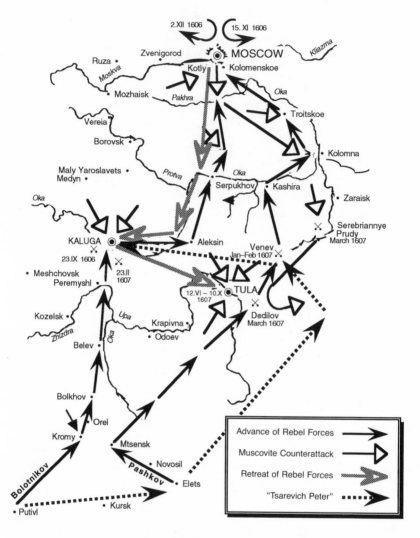

2.XII 1606   15. XI 1606

MOSCOW

Kliazma

Ruza •   Zvenigorod •

Moskva

Kotly   • Kolomenskoe

• Mozhaisk   *Pakhra*   *Oka*

• Troitskoe

Vereia •

Borovsk •

• Kolomna

Maly Yaroslavets •   *Protva*   *Oka*
Medyn •

Serpukhov   • Kashira

Oka   • Zaraisk

× Serebriannye
Prudy
March 1607

KALUGA ●   • Aleksin   Venev
×   Jan–Feb 1607 ×
23.IX 1606   ×

• Meshchovsk   23.II
Peremyshl •   1607

12.VI – 10.X ● TULA
1607   ×

Kozelsk •   *Upa*   Dedilov
Krapivna •   March 1607
• Odoev

Zhizdra   *Oka*
Belev •

Bolkhov •

• Orel

Kromy •

Mtsensk

• Novosil

Pashkov

Bolotnikov   • Elets

• Putivl   • Kursk

Advance of Rebel Forces	⟶
Muscovite Counterattack	⟶
Retreat of Rebel Forces	⟹
"Tsarevich Peter"	▪▪▶

THE BOLOTNIKOV REBELLION
1606 – 07

measure forces against my perfidious subjects. Say that you have seen me and have spoken with me here in Poland, and that I am such as you now see with your own eyes, and that you have received this letter from my own hands."

With this letter and these tidings Bolotnikov immediately set off for Putivl, where he was received very graciously and made welcome, and all of this prompted and inclined the inhabitants of Putivl to believe that Dmitry had indeed escaped, as Prince Grigory also had told them earlier, and was still alive. They struggled yet more valiantly against the oathbreakers, shed their blood, and sacrificed their goods and possessions for his sake, even though this was not the true Dmitry but yet another false one fabricated by the Poles.[2]

On the basis of this letter and these tidings, Bolotnikov was appointed Great Voevoda, that is, the senior commander, and was sent with twelve thousand armed men by way of the Komaritsk district to Istoma Pashkov before Moscow, which he quickly besieged, and would even have obtained the surrender of the city had he not been prevented by disagreements arising between his commanders. This occurred because, having arrived before Moscow, Bolotnikov, as senior general directly appointed by Dmitry, wished to occupy the most comfortable quarters for himself and be more highly regarded and esteemed than Pashkov, since the latter had merely been appointed commander by Shakhovskoy while he, Bolotnikov, had been named and appointed as senior commander by the supposed tsar himself. Therefore Pashkov had to evacuate the quarters he had occupied and yield to Bolotnikov and his soldiers.

This dishonour and shame angered Istoma in no small measure, so that he in turn thought to deceive Bolotnikov and for this reason secretly entered into negotiations with the Muscovite enemy, Tsar Shuisky. He obtained from him large gifts of gold and silver, and told him that up to now not a single soul in Putivl had seen Dmitry, nor did they know any more about him than Prince Grigory Shakhovskoy had told them, namely that he had not been killed, but had secretly fled and was hiding in Poland, etc. Apart from this, Pashkov repeated all that Bolotnikov had communicated, that he had not only seen and spoken with Dmitry in Poland but also that he himself had been appointed his chief commander and deputy. Whether it was true that Dmitry had fled and was now in Poland, and had sent this Bolotnikov, appointing him as his deputy, or whether the Poles and Shakhovskoy had simply fabricated this new Dmitry, he was not in a position to know, but, as had been stated, until now nobody in Muscovy had seen this Dmitry.

Then the community of the city of Moscow sent this demand into Bolotnikov's camp: if this Dmitry who was formerly in Moscow was alive, and was somewhere in the camp or in some other place, then Bolotnikov should either show or send for him, so that they might see him with their own eyes. If this should come about, then they would make their peace with Dmitry, beg his forgiveness and favour, and surrender to him without resistance.

Bolotnikov replied that Dmitry was truly alive in Poland and would soon arrive. He also said: "I was with him, and he himself appointed me chief commander in his place and sent me to Putivl with written instructions." The Muscovites said: "This was undoubtedly someone else, since we killed this Dmitry," and urged Bolotnikov to cease the shedding of innocent blood and give himself up to Tsar Shuisky, who would make him a great man. Bolotnikov replied: "I have given a solemn oath to my lord that I shall not spare my life on his behalf, and I will remain true to this oath. Do as you see fit. If you do not surrender of your own free will, I and my lord will do as we see fit and will soon visit ourselves upon you."

After this conversation Bolotnikov quickly dispatched a messenger to Prince Grigory Shakhovskoy with news of the Muscovites' demands, and with the request to send to Tsar Dmitry in Poland as quickly as possible, urging him not to delay but to return to Russia with all speed and show himself in Bolotnikov's camp, since he had so persuaded the Muscovites that they were fully resolved, as soon as they saw him in person once again, to submit to him, beg his pardon and favour, and surrender without any resistance, so therefore Dmitry had no need to hire any more troops to bring them with him, but only to come himself and hasten thither, since it was only a matter of them seeing him with their own eyes. Then everything would be resolved, since the inhabitants of Moscow would quickly seize his traitors by the head and deliver them unto him.

Prince Grigory did not delay for a moment but wrote quickly and sent into Poland, but he who had conspired with him to impersonate Dmitry and take his place now decided not to take part in this deception, nor did he want to become Dmitry but wished to remain a simple nobleman in Poland and let whoever wished make a bid for Muscovy. Since no Dmitry had appeared before them, the Muscovites took courage and daily made sorties, bravely engaging in skirmishes.

On 2 December, hearing from informers that the enemy was preparing to make a sortie in greater strength than before, Bolotnikov sent information concerning this to Istoma Pashkov, telling him to advance with his forces in order to stiffen resistance to the enemy. But when the enemy ventured out of Moscow with a hundred thousand men, and Bolotnikov was still hoping that Istoma Pashkov, having under his command forty thousand men, would give him loyal support, Pashkov did in fact appear, giving the impression that he seriously intended to engage the enemy. Bolotnikov boldly decided to offer battle, having sixty thousand soldiers at his disposal, hoping that Pashkov would engage the enemy on the other flank.

But the poor loyal hero was shamefully betrayed, for his comrade-in-arms Istoma Pashkov not only failed to give him support but also on the field of battle went over to the enemy with several thousand of the forces he had with him and gave the enemy considerable assistance, even attacking Bolotnikov himself, as a result of which Bolotnikov's army was so thinned out that it had to seek refuge in flight, leaving all of its encampment to be plundered by the enemy with all that was in it.

Ten thousand of his Cossack followers were surrounded so completely by the enemy that, being unable to break out, they surrendered.[3] About eighteen miles from Moscow there is a small town called Serpukhov, and it was there that Bolotnikov rallied his survivors and asked the local inhabitants whether they had enough supplies to sustain him and his soldiers for some considerable time, for then they would remain with them, awaiting Dmitry's arrival. If not, they would leave them and move on further. The inhabitants of Serpukhov replied that they had only supplies to feed themselves and their families for a short time, with nothing to spare for him and his troops.

It was dangerous for Bolotnikov to remain there much longer, since the enemy was fast approaching, so he moved on to Kaluga, the nearest town with a citadel.[4] There he and the people who still remained with him were made welcome, and the inhabitants said that they had enough provisions for a long time, not only for themselves and their families but also for him and all his men.

Since, however, this town and this citadel were not fortified, Bolotnikov ordered moats to be dug on both sides of the stockade and palisades, which already existed, both inside and outside, and the earth which had been excavated was piled against the palisades, so that it was possible to use them as breastworks. But the enemy advanced relentlessly from Moscow and besieged Bolotnikov on 20 December 1606 in the city of Kaluga (where I also happened to be, for one of my estates was in that locality, so I had to remain there). This siege lasted until 26 May 1607.

Meanwhile no Dmitry had appeared to relieve us from the siege. There was nobody in Poland who wanted to risk his life and become Dmitry. When Prince Shakhovskoy now saw that nobody in Poland wanted to undertake this, he thought up a new stratagem to vex the Muscovites, even though no Dmitry had come out of Poland. He had heard from the field Cossacks that the pious, foolish Tsar Fedor Ivanovich, whose wife had been the sister of Boris Fedorovich Godunov, had left behind a son called Peter, against whose life Boris had also made an attempt. This prince, Peter Fedorovich, lived on the Wild Steppe and was about to come to his kinsman Dmitry to ask for the opportunity to live in a princely manner when Dmitry was killed (or, as some say, ran away). Prince Shakhovskoy had sent to this prince, Peter Fedorovich, in the name of Dmitry, calling upon him to spare no effort to recruit as many Cossacks as possible and come with them to Putivl and regain his homeland, holding it until his cousin Dmitry himself arrived from Poland with a newly recruited army and smothered his enemies, after which he, Prince Peter, would be rewarded and given the best principality. In response, Peter gathered together ten thousand men and came with them to Putivl with all possible speed, in the hope of bringing aid to his cousin.[5]

Prince Shakhovskoy travelled with him in person, and they appeared at Tula, which is an excellent fortress. Shakhovskoy's intentions were that, if the Lord God gave them good fortune, and the Muscovites could be convinced, and if nobody out of Poland appeared to lay claim to the country and pose as Dmitry, then this Peter could be tsar, since he was the true born son of Fedor Ivanovich and therefore the lawful heir to the realm. But in the meantime everything had to be done in the name of Dmitry, who in fact had died.

In that year the illustrious Duke Karl sent an embassy from Sweden to Tsar Shuisky in Moscow in order to warn him of the danger, urging upon him extreme caution and informing him that it was not unknown to His Illustrious Highness what plots were being hatched in Poland at the king's court and at the papal curia in Rome, since they had daily intelligence from both quarters. Since His Princely Highness suspected that an assault was being prepared upon the possessions of his neighbour Shuisky (and of course Karl's own possessions were also in danger), therefore not only did he wish to give a friendly warning to his beloved neighbour but also promised that, if he so wished, he would send ten thousand of his best men, either Swedes or Germans, to the borders at Narva or Novgorod for the benefit of the Muscovite land, so that he could hire them if he wished.

Shuisky scarcely needed any such warning, advice or services, and replied to His Princely Highness that hitherto Russia had been able to defend itself against its enemies by the power of its own inhabitants and had never needed the power of its neighbours, and presumably could continue to defend itself in the same fashion. But matters quickly turned out quite otherwise, since Shuisky and all the inhabitants of the land were unable to defend their country or drive the enemy from their soil and they dearly wished to take advantage of the aid offered by His Princely Highness, but now it was not so easy to obtain it as it had been previously, and they had to go to great expense and effort before they received the services of Jakob de la Gardie for their country.[6] In this manner Shuisky came to understand what is so rightly said: "**When you make an offer to a rogue, you must first open the bag.**"[7]

At that time a certain frivolous man called Friedrich Fiedler, a native of Königsberg in Prussia, approached Tsar Shuisky and proposed, for the benefit of the tsar and the whole Russian land, to go and poison the enemy Ivan Bolotnikov, provided that the tsar would give him a good estate and a certain sum of money. Shuisky promised him an initial payment of one thousand Polish florins and a good horse in order to consummate this deed, and with these he should proceed to Bolotnikov, and if he did as he promised, he would be granted a patrimony[8] with a hundred peasants and an annual salary of three hundred florins.

But since this Fiedler was a very frivolous man, and his craftiness was known to all, Shuisky did not wish to rely upon him until he, before he was to receive anything, had sworn an oath and most strenuously had obliged himself to fulfil his promises, which the frivolous knave did, swearing such an oath as made the hair rise on the heads of all that were present. He took the money and set off for the enemy, but he showed him the poison openly, saying that he had been sent by Shuisky to poison him, but since now he did not intend to do so, he would now hand the poison over to him, and he could do with it what he pleased.

For this he received a rich reward from Bolotnikov, but at the same time he hung his soul upon a hedge for the Devil to take whenever he pleased. With this trickery he earned a bad reputation for all the Germans in the land, and did not receive any good fortune or happiness from this Judas money, for many of us can truly relate that, together with this, he lost all his other possessions. His face became fearfully disfigured and happiness fled from him entirely. Later, when the city of Tula fell, he was captured by Shuisky and sent in disgrace to Siberia, together with fifty-two other Germans (among whom, to my great grief, was one of my sons), because when the fortress of Tula was besieged, they were within, on the side of the second Dmitry. May God have mercy upon them all, upon which I urge them to rely in the name of Christ. Amen! Amen!

Siberia had been conquered some time previously from the Siberian Tatars. This land is very desolate, but several years ago they built a number of fortresses to prevent the Tatars and Turks from approaching Russia from that quarter. It is about eight hundred miles from Moscow, but in Moscow some say that it is altogether nine hundred.

The oath ran as follows: "I, Friedrich Fiedler, swear by all the saints, the Ever-glorious Trinity, God the Eternal Father, God the Eternal Son and God the Eternal Holy Ghost, that I shall destroy by poison Ivan Bolotnikov, the enemy of Shuisky and the Russian land. If I do not perform this deed, and through guile deceive my sovereign Shuisky, then may I be deprived of the heavenly kingdom for all eternity, and may the Eternal God the Father forever cease to have mercy upon me. May the precious intercession for me of Jesus Christ the Son of God, my Saviour, forever be in vain and of no account. May the Holy Ghost deprive me of all power and strength and forever refuse to grant me His peace. May the holy angels, who protect me and all Christians forever, be far from me. May the sacraments created for my benefit and that of all people be harmful to me. May I sink alive into the earth. May food and drink not strengthen but poison me, and may the Devil take my body and soul for eternal torment and suffering. If even in my thoughts I should say, 'Let me take my lord's money, but deceive him and in no wise do what I have promised to do,' and I go to my confessor and ask him to absolve me of this sin, then let no servant of God on this earth have power to cleanse me from such a sin, if I do not fulfil what I have promised to do. But I shall fulfil everything without guile, deception, or cunning, and with this poison I shall kill and destroy Ivan Bolotnikov. So may God and this Holy Gospel truly aid me."

O such is the inexhaustible goodness of God and his long-suffering, to behold such fearful, vain, and presumptuous servants of the Devil, who are obstinate in their sins. It is a wonder that the earth did not open and swallow up this evildoer, along with all of us who witnessed this.

In the year 1607, on 13 May,[9] Prince Peter Fedorovich sent his armed forces out of Tula[10] in order to relieve the followers of his cousin Dmitry, whom the enemy Shuisky had for so long besieged in Kaluga. The Muscovites who were besieging Kaluga sent several thousand men against them, and they met at the Pchelna river. The Muscovites were put to flight and were forced to return to their camp before Kaluga with heavy losses and great consternation. Very early the next morning Bolotnikov made a sortie out of Kaluga, falling upon their trenches and keeping them so occupied that they abandoned the trenches and everything that was in them, including their heavy artillery, powder, shot, and provisions, and in great fear and trepidation fled to Moscow, completely abandoning the battlefield.

Now that Bolotnikov and the troops who were with him had been relieved, he went to Tula to Prince Peter Fedorovich. But Shuisky once again took heart, collected his scattered forces and sent them outside Serpukhov, intending to besiege Tula, where those leaders were who were the instigators of everything and from whom originated all these ills. When they had received intelligence of this, Prince Peter, Prince Shakhovskoy, and Ivan Bolotnikov made ready to send a force to intercept the enemy outside Serpukhov, where they fought a fierce battle, and the Muscovites would have been driven from the field had a certain commander named Teletin, together with the four thousand people he had with him, not betrayed the Tula troops, encouraged the hard pressed, and urged them on to fight bravely against their brothers, on account of which the Tula forces were seized with such terror that they threw themselves into headlong flight back to Tula.[11] There they rested for a while and gathered reinforcements as much as they could in the little time they had, so that when Shuisky's forces approached the fortress of Tula they took courage yet again and resolved to meet him with all their forces. But Shuisky had levied throughout the land as many as yet another hundred thousand men, while those who ventured out of Tula were much weaker, and therefore they were compelled to take refuge in the fortress yet again.

In June Shuisky besieged them so tightly in the fortress that nobody could get in or out. On the Upa river the enemy had built a dam a half mile from the city, and the water rose up so high that the whole city was under water so that it was necessary to go about in rafts. Since all access routes were cut off, there was an unheard-of rise in prices and famine. The inhabitants ate dogs, cats, carrion on the streets, horses, oxen, and cowhides. A cask of rye cost a hundred Polish florins, a spoonful of salt half a thaler, nor was there any beer available,[12] so many died of hunger and exhaustion.

Bolotnikov wrote, and often sent messengers to his sovereign in Poland, who had sent him into Russia, with requests for aid, but he did not appear and left him in the lurch. The Cossacks and all the inhabitants of Tula were greatly incensed at Bolotnikov and Shakhovskoy, wishing to arrest them and deliver them to the enemy, Shuisky, since they had put forth such a fantastic tale in assuring them that Dmitry was still alive.

Bolotnikov said: "When I arrived in Poland from Venice, a certain young man, aged about twenty-four or twenty-five, called me to him and told me that he was Dmitry, that he had escaped from the rioting and murder, and that in his place a certain German who was dressed in his clothes had been killed. He took an oath from me that I would serve him faithfully. I have done so up to now and will continue to do so as long as I live. Whether he is genuine or not, I cannot say, for I never saw him upon the throne of Moscow. According to reports, he is in appearance exactly like him who sat upon the throne."

They placed Prince Grigory Shakhovskoy under arrest, because he had said that Dmitry had left Moscow in his company, saying that they would not free him until Dmitry came to release him. If he did not come, then they would deliver him to the enemy, Shuisky, as a deceiver and as the initiator of this war and bloodshed.

Finally Bolotnikov sent out of the besieged city a certain Pole, Ivan Martynovich Zarutsky,[13] to find out what had happened to the sovereign to whom Bolotnikov had sworn allegiance in Poland. Was he on his way, and what was his situation? Zarutsky reached Starodub, not daring to go further. He remained there, and did not bring back any tidings.

XIII– *Concerning a Certain Cossack Sent to Poland*
XIV *to Urge Dmitry to Make Haste, or to Commit*
     Everything to the King in Poland, and How
     a Certain Man from Shklov Claimed to Be
     Dmitry and Came into Russia

Bolotnikov and Prince Grigory Shakhovskoy had ordered a certain Cossack to cross the river with letters and reach Poland. Pointing out and complaining of their desperate situation, they stipulated that if none of the followers of the governor of Sandomir was prepared to claim to be Dmitry and come to their relief, then they should present and commit all the towns and fortresses that they had received on behalf of Dmitry and which were presently under their control to His Royal Majesty in Poland that they might be relieved by His Majesty and not fall into the power of the Muscovites.

Having received this letter, the followers of the governor of San-domir devised means to find someone who would claim to be Dmitry, and they found living with a certain White Russian priest at Shklov, which was under the rule of the Polish crown, a certain schoolmaster of Shklov, who was by birth a Muscovite but had long lived in White Russia and knew how to speak, read, and write well in both the Muscovite and Polish languages. He was called Ivan, and he was a crafty youth, so they negotiated with him, until at last he consented to be Dmitry. They tutored him and sent him towards Putivl together with Lord Miechowicki. There he was recognized as Dmitry, acknowl-edged and honoured, which caused great joy among those who were Dmitry's supporters.

This new Dmitry set out around St James' Day [25 July] from Putivl for Novgorod Seversk, and then further on to Starodub, in the company of two people, Grigory Kashnets[1] and a scribe by the name of Alexius, not claiming to be the tsar, however, but saying that he was Nagoy, the tsar's kinsman. The tsar was not far off, but was with Lord Miechowicki and many thousands of cavalrymen. They should rejoice greatly at this, for he would reward them richly for their steadfastness and grant them many privileges.

But when it appeared that Miechowicki was longer in coming than they had been told, the inhabitants of Starodub on this account took the scribe Alexius, together with Grigory Kashnets and he who pre-tended to be a Nagoy but was in fact the second Dmitry, and brought all three to be tortured. They stripped the scribe, and the torturer laid about his back, telling him he would not be spared until he revealed where Tsar Dmitry was and whether he was alive. Where was he, and why was he so long in coming? The poor chancellor was not used to such treatment,[2] and decided to do as St Nicholas[3] willed, and told them that this Nagoy was Dmitry, not a Nagoy, as he was pretending to be. He then said that if they released him, he would then show them where the tsar was.

After the torturer had released him, he said to the populace: "Oh, you fools, how dare you treat me so in the name of your lord? Do you not know him? He is standing there and sees how you are treating me. That is he, who pretends to be Nagoy. Seize him; if you want to set upon him along with us, then you can do so. For he did not wish to reveal himself until he had proven your loyalty and whether you would rejoice at his coming."

When the inhabitants of Starodub had heard these words, these poor ignorant people fell at his feet, and each said on his own behalf: "I am guilty, O sovereign,[4] before you, and am ready to sacrifice my life on your behalf, and struggle against your enemies." Then they conducted him with great honour into the fortress, into the royal apartments, and acknowledged the second Dmitry, showing him honour as the true Dmitry.[5]

When Ivan Martynovich Zarutsky (who, as has been narrated earlier, had been sent from Tula to Dmitry, and who had delayed for so long in Starodub) heard of this, he greatly rejoiced at Dmitry's arrival and made haste to deliver to him the letters, but at first glance he realized that this was not the former Dmitry. He did not betray this to the people, but on the contrary honoured him as the true tsar as though he were truly obliged to do so, even though he had never set eyes on him before. This great reverence shown by Zarutsky convinced the inhabitants of Starodub still more that this was indeed the first Dmitry.

On the same day Miechowicki, with several troops of Polish cavalry, arrived at Starodub. Dmitry ordered him to proceed immediately to Kozelsk and relieve the siege of the town. He also said that he would soon follow Miechowicki to relieve Tula and Kaluga (where I was myself at the time under siege).

This Dmitry, on the same day, subjected the inhabitants of Starodub to yet a greater proof of loyalty. He ordered Ivan Zarutsky to mount with his spear couched and go outside the gates. Dmitry would then pursue him and they would joust and charge at each other. Zarutsky would attack him boldly with his spear and ruffle up his garments a little, and he would fall down as though he had been struck with great force. When this had taken place, Zarutsky was to ride back to his lodging and conceal himself there. If the inhabitants of Starodub wished to take vengeance upon Zarutsky, then it would be clear to Dmitry that they were loyal to him as their tsar, and of course he would not allow any harm to come to Zarutsky.

Zarutsky did as he was bidden. Dmitry fell from his horse and pretended to be half dead. When the inhabitants of Starodub saw this, they cried out that the traitor[6] Zarutsky must be arrested. They seized him at the gates, beat him soundly with clubs, brought him bound to Dmitry, and asked what was to be done with him. When Dmitry saw how eagerly the people had pursued Zarutsky, he laughed, and said: "I thank you, Christian folk. Now I am doubly sure that you are loyal to me. I simply wanted to prove your loyalty, and to this end I persuaded Zarutsky to play the part." They were amazed at his guile and smiled, but Zarutsky had to bear the brunt of this crude stratagem.

Miechowicki chased the Muscovites away from Kozelsk and remained there awaiting his lord's arrival. On 1 August Dmitry followed him with the intention of relieving Tula. But when he had heard that Shuisky was urging the three towns of Bolkhov, Belev, and Likhvin to change sides and, when the second Dmitry came there, to seize him and hand him over, he retreated to Samov. All the same Shuisky achieved some success, since the three aforementioned towns forsook Dmitry and surrendered to Shuisky. Dmitry himself would have been captured, had he not moved so quickly. The defection of the three towns hindered the relief of the besieged in Tula but, though the flooding and famine put them under severe pressure, they refused to surrender, hoping that the water would subside and they would have the opportunity to make a sortie and with luck break through the hostile army, and so be able to retreat.

There came a sorcerer monk who proposed to Tsarevich Peter and Bolotnikov that for a hundred rubles he would venture into the water and break up the dam, so that the water might subside. After the monk had been promised the money, he immediately stripped naked, plunged into the water, and from the water there arose great turbulence and commotion, as though there were many devils below. The monk was gone for more than an hour, so that everyone thought that he had gone to the Devil, but he returned, though his face and body were so severely scratched that he was scarcely recognizable. When asked where he had been so long, he replied: "Do not be surprised that I was away for so long, I had plenty to do. Shuisky has built this dam and blocked up the Upa with the aid of twelve thousand devils, with whom I had to contend, as can be seen from the marks on my body. I was able to win over half, that is six thousand, but the other six thousand were too powerful for me. I was not able to overcome them, and they are defending the dam strongly."

Since Dmitry had not arrived, and the besieged in Tula had lost hope, and the people through weakness could hardly walk or stand in their houses and lodgings, Prince Peter and Bolotnikov began to parley with Shuisky, declaring to him that if he would spare their lives they would surrender to him, together with the fortress. If he would not agree, then they would hold out as they had hitherto, even if they had to devour each other.

Shuisky was amazed at this, and said: "Even though I swore not to spare a single man in Tula, I will abate my anger and disfavour on account of their bravery. Since they have so firmly observed the oath which they swore to the brigand, I will grant them their lives if they will serve me as truly as they have served him." To this he kissed the cross and sent word that they would all be pardoned. Accordingly they surrendered to Shuisky the fortress of Tula, on the feast of St Simon and St Jude,[7] 1607.

Bolotnikov rode through the postern of the rear gate, where the water was not so deep, to Shuisky's pavilion, drew his sabre, laid it on his neck, prostrated himself, and said: "I have held true to my oath which I gave in Poland to him who called himself Dmitry. Whether he is so or not, that I cannot know, since I have never seen him before. I have served him faithfully, but he has abandoned me. Now I am here in your hand and your power. If you wish to kill me, here is my sabre at the ready, but if, on the other hand, you will have mercy upon me according to your promise and your kissing of the cross, I will serve you as truly as hitherto I have served him by whom I am abandoned."

Shuisky commanded him to rise, saying that he would observe all he had promised, and to which he had sworn. Then all the people, except the local inhabitants, came out of the fortress, and Shuisky once again occupied it with his own men. He sent Bolotnikov and Prince Peter with the fifty-two Germans who were with him in Tula, among whom was one of my own sons, Conrad, under guard to Moscow. The Germans were permitted to go to their own people, but Prince Peter and Bolotnikov were kept under guard there for some time, so that nobody could go in to see them, nor could they go out anywhere, and Shuisky observed the oath which he had given both of them in the manner in which people of his kind usually keep their oaths. He had Prince Peter, who perhaps, and according to people who have good information about the matter, was of the royal stem, hanged upon a gallows in the city of Moscow. He had Bolotnikov sent from there to Kargopol, ordered him kept in a tower there for some time, and finally had his eyes gouged out and then he was drowned.[8]

As soon as Shuisky became aware that the second Dmitry was advancing, he ceased to trust the fifty-two Germans, and therefore ordered that they be sent away from Moscow and deported, as has been mentioned before, to the wasteland of Siberia, to the desolate Siberian lands which, as has been narrated earlier, had earlier been conquered from the Tatars and were situated about eight hundred miles from Moscow. There they were to live among barbarian peoples and wild beasts, feeding only upon fish and meat, without any bread. May the just God mercifully grant them ways and means, and once again set them free to return, in the name of Jesus Christ. Amen! Amen! Amen![9]

As for Prince Grigory Shakhovskoy who, as has been related earlier, was the instigator and originator of all this war, and had incited the inhabitants of Tula by telling them and affirming that Dmitry had not been killed but had left Moscow with him and had set off for

Poland, to the wife of the governor of Sandomir, the proverb held true: "The greater the scoundrel, the better his luck."[10] He was able to turn his imprisonment to good account. The Cossacks and towns-people had thrown him into the tower because no Dmitry had come to relieve them, as he had falsely assured them. But when Shuisky ordered that all prisoners in Tula be set free, this prince regained his freedom and told Shuisky that the soldiers had shut him up in the tower because they had suspected that he wished to leave the fortress and make his submission to him. He was believed, and so the original instigator of all the troubles was set at liberty and soon after went over to the second Dmitry, becoming his chief commander and most trusted counsellor.

After this victory Shuisky set out on a pilgrimage. In the filthy and rainy spring weather he travelled from Moscow to the Trinity monastery, and there he offered thanks to the god Sergius[11] for his grace and intercession, in that he had delivered his enemies into his hands, and prayed that in the future he would grant him victory over the remainder of the rebels in Kaluga and Kozelsk, and also over him who in Samov was claiming to be the first Dmitry. He also made a vow to the God Sergius that, if he would continue to stand by him, he would donate to the Trinity monastery to build a shrine in his honour.

He dismissed all the troops who had been with him in Tula to their estates so that they might have furlough and also allow their servitors and horses to rest until the winter freeze-up. Those who were blockading the inhabitants of Kaluga were to remain in place, while those who were in the borderland outposts were to remain there and render service. Shuisky sent a certain boyar named Georgy Bezzubtsev, who had just endured the siege of Tula and previously had been under siege in Kaluga, to the inhabitants of Kaluga, urging them to surrender the fortress voluntarily. He promised that the tsar would pardon them, as he had pardoned the inhabitants of Tula, if they surrendered to him of their own free will. But the inhabitants of Kaluga sent word to Shuisky that they had no intention of sur-rendering, for their lord, the true Dmitry, was still alive and was at hand, and that even though because of treachery he had been obliged to retreat for a while, he had not fled altogether but would soon reappear. Meanwhile the inhabitants of Kaluga made continual sor-ties against the Muscovite encampments, which were blocking the roads, preventing reinforcements from reaching them and inflicting heavy damage.

Shuisky was greatly angered at the inhabitants of Kaluga for their insolent reply. He greatly wished to invest the city more tightly and attack, so as to reduce it, but, as has been related, his army was dispersed until the winter freeze-up and therefore he had to leave things as they were. Nevertheless, in order to strengthen the encampment close to Kaluga, and in order to engage the inhabitants of Kaluga with greater success, he sent around to the prisons where the Cossacks were confined. He had captured them in the battle with Bolotnikov on 2 December of the previous year 1606, as has been related earlier, and he now sent them word that if they would swear allegiance to him and fight against his enemies he would set them free, give them money, and supply them with the necessary weapons.

The Cossacks agreed, gave thanks to God for their deliverance from prison, and four thousand men swore allegiance to Shuisky. So in November 1607 they were sent to aid the army before Kaluga with many barrels of powder, so as to take and reduce Kaluga by frontal assault. But God so ordained that in the encampment dissensions arose between the boyars and these Cossacks, as a result of which the Cossacks mutinied, so the boyars, who were weaker than the Cossacks, slipped away, abandoning the encampment and all their provisions, and fled to Moscow.

On the next day the Cossacks approached the town of Kaluga and asked to be admitted, since they too were Dmitry's followers. Then they related how, that previous night, they had so terrified the Muscovites that they abandoned their encampment and fled to Moscow, and that in the encampment there were many barrels of powder and provisions, and that they should send some men to carry it into the town.[12]

The governor Skotnicki, to whom the town had been entrusted, did not trust the Cossacks, nor would he admit any of them into his presence, for which reason they bypassed the town behind the fortress and over the river Oka, saying they would move on and seek Lord Dmitry. When the inhabitants of Kaluga saw this happening, they sent out to the Muscovite camp and found everything to be just as the Cossacks had told them. Realizing therefore that the Cossacks were on Dmitry's side, they sent after them post haste, telling them to turn back and they would be admitted. But since they had previously been refused entry, the Cossacks did not wish to return, though they sent a hundred men to remain with them there.

The inhabitants of Kaluga sent out to the Muscovite camp, brought all that was in it, and easily held out until the second Dmitry (whom they took to be the first Dmitry) came to them. They then swore allegiance to him and remained faithful to him unto death, as will subsequently be related.[13] Shuisky once again took the field with his

army, and around Christmas of this year sent it to Bolkhov, in order
to expel Dmitry from Samov.

ANNO 1608

Shortly after the New Year there was such a snowfall that the enemy
could not undertake very much against their opponents on the battlefield during this winter, but all the same they clashed with each other
while out foraging. Whoever was the stronger made off with the
booty.

Knowing that Shuisky had replenished his forces and was once
again preparing to advance, in January of that same year Dmitry
sent into Poland for more cavalry, and thence there came to him
Samuel Tyszkiewicz with seven thousand lancers, and Aleksandr
Jozef Lisowski[14] with seven hundred lancers.

When these Poles arrived, Dmitry advanced with all his forces to
Briansk and besieged it. Shuisky had with him a certain German
named Hans Borck,[15] who at one time had been taken prisoner in
Livonia. Shuisky sent him with a hundred German cavalrymen to
Briansk. During the previous winter he had deserted Shuisky for
Dmitry's band in Kaluga, but had subsequently left his patron in the
lurch and gone over once again to the side of Shuisky, who richly
rewarded him for the intelligence he brought. He did not stay long
with Shuisky, but once more deserted to the side of the second
Dmitry, who would have rewarded this traitor for his services had he
not been dissuaded by the Polish lords. Not having remained a year
in Dmitry's service, he was about to surrender to Shuisky the fortress
of Tula, which had yet again made its submission to Dmitry, but then
he became aware that his treasonable dealings had been noticed and
so he hurriedly fled to Moscow, to Shuisky, who once again joyfully
received him and, as before, rewarded him for his intended treachery
at Tula.[16]

With him there was yet another perfidious knave by the name of
Tonnies von Wissen, also a former Livonian prisoner. These two were
responsible for the death of one of the most prominent and pious
Russian lords, Ivan Ivanovich Nagoy,[17] whom they left in the lurch
on the road during the flight from Tula, as a result of which their
pursuers caught up to him, captured him, and he was drowned by
the second Dmitry at Kaluga.

**From Poland to Dmitry's camp before Briansk there came Prince
Adam Wisniowiecki**, at that time my especially well-disposed lord
and great friend, with two hundred lancers, and Prince Roman
Rozynski with four thousand lancers. When Dmitry's forces were so

increased, he lifted the siege of Briansk and proceeded to Orel, which is quite close to the town of Bolkhov, where Shuisky's army was situated. Dmitry's chief or senior military commander was Miechowicki. He was expelled by Roman Rozynski, who was installed as chief or senior commander.[18]

In April they moved closer to Bolkhov, on account of which the Muscovites took fright, and many of them decided that, since so many thousands of Poles were arriving, this must truly be the first Dmitry. Then many princes, boyars, and Germans came to him, to whom he immediately gave many lands and peasants, more than they had held hitherto, and for this reason they remained constantly on his side, even though they could very well see that he was not the first Dmitry, but somebody else.

Dmitry ordered it to be announced everywhere that wherever there were possessions of boyars and princes who had deserted to Shuisky, their servitors might come and swear allegiance to him and receive their masters' estates, and if any of the masters' daughters were left behind, then the servitors could take them as their wives and serve him. In this way many lowly servitors became nobles, and also rich and powerful, while their masters in Moscow were forced to go hungry.

On 17 April the German commanders from Shuisky's camp (Colonel Barthold Lamsdorff, an inexperienced young lad, who had more than once tried to seek his fortune in foreign lands and in Livonia and Moscow had earned fame over the beer tankards; Lieutenant Joachim Bergk; and Ensign Jurgen von Ahlden), all of them disreputable men, but well acquainted with the Muscovite style of swindling, sent two of their comrades, Arndt Kuddelin and Lubert von der Heyde, from their ranks to offer their loyal and devoted service, and further to tell him that he should advance and when battle was joined they would come over with standards unfurled. They did not care that they had sworn allegiance to Shuisky and had served him for more than a year, that they had received pay from him, and they knew very well that this was not the first Dmitry but someone quite different.

They compelled the remaining cavalrymen under their command to agree to this, and also surrender, leaving their wives and children in Moscow to their fate. And surely, if their treacherous design had succeeded as they had wished, Shuisky would not have left a single German infant alive in the cradle. But the all-merciful God had his way, depriving the feckless commanders of their reason and sense, so that daily they became blind drunk and forgot what they had promised Dmitry.

On 23 April, St Gregory's Day,[19] Dmitry's army appeared near Kaminsk.[20] The Muscovites also took to the field and battle was joined. Then the Germans were ordered to come forward and engage the Poles. But the commanders on that occasion were so steadfast that they forgot the treason they had proposed and bravely attacked the Poles, slaying four hundred men. Dmitry and his commander Roman Rozynski were sorely angered at them. He ordered the German renegades to be sought out, and he would have hanged them had they been found soon enough, but they had hidden and did not dare advance. So it was proclaimed and ordered throughout the camp that the next day they encountered the enemy, no quarter was to be given to any German.

On 24 April, the fourth Sunday after Easter,[21] the second Dmitry once again attacked the Muscovites before Bolkhov with all his forces. His lancers engaged the largest regiment and put it to flight. The perjurer Lamsdorff and his officers ordered his cavalrymen to the rear and were prepared, according to their agreement, to go over to Dmitry with their standards unfurled. Many honest people, who were unaware of this treachery, addressed their colonel, saying: "We are well aware what is going on here. We shall not remain. The Russians are fleeing and the Poles are surrounding us. What are you officers thinking about?"

Lamsdorff berated as scoundrels all those who would not remain with the banner. Then some said: "You can call us scoundrels ten times over, but we will not stay, for we will all be slaughtered. Even though you wish to surrender, our wives and children are too dear to us to allow them to perish through our surrender. We want no part of any trickery." Then they rode off to Moscow together with the Muscovites.

The Zaporozhian Cossacks quickly surrounded the armoured perjurer Lamsdorff and all who remained with him, and at the order of the chief commander Rozynski slaughtered them all, to the number of two hundred, leaving their wives and children widows and orphans, for which the Colonel Lamsdorff will never atone throughout eternity, for the tears of the poor widows and orphans whose husbands and fathers he so basely betrayed and sacrificed will weigh him down into the deepest pit of hell.

If through the permission of God this had not happened and they had remained alive and gone over to Dmitry, this would have led to an even greater tribulation, since Shuisky would not have left a single German alive in Moscow; but since they were slain on the battlefield, even the Russians mourned them as men who had been slain and had perished on their behalf at the hand of the enemy, so the widows retained all of their husbands' estates. Lamsdorff and his fellow conspirators planned this treason and defection only in order to receive from Dmitry and the Poles greater favour and esteem, even at the cost of the lives of the others' wives and children. But the just God would not allow it and straight away gave him his just reward, to which will be added the torments of hell, on account of the innocent lives lost on his account.

Shuisky's army retreated, and on Ascension Day returned to Moscow in such terror that the hands and feet of the Muscovites became powerless, and they would doubtless have surrendered had Dmitry pursued the fugitives quickly. The common rabble said among themselves that if he was not Dmitry, then the princes and boyars, who had gone over to him in droves, would have returned, so without a doubt he was the true Dmitry. They soon speculated how they would justify themselves when he besieged the city, namely that it was not they but the princes and boyars who had killed his people and had expelled him. They themselves knew nothing about it. Another said: "I have heard that he is so clever that he can see by looking into a man's eyes whether he is guilty or not." One bone merchant was greatly alarmed at that, saying: "Woe is me, I will not dare look him in the face, since with this knife I cut up five of his Poles." Such fear and trembling arose at this time among the Muscovites.

On 1 June the second Dmitry approached the village of Taininskoe with all his forces, intended for the siege of Moscow. He reconnoitred the territory in order to determine which place was the most suitable to clear and upon which to pitch his camp. In the same month Jan Piotr Pawel Sapieha came to him with seven thousand lancers from Lithuania. Shuisky had leaguers placed outside Moscow beneath the walls, placed all his army within them and appointed Prince Mikhail Skopin as commander. But on 24 June, on St John's Eve, they were ignominiously surprised by Dmitry and so rudely awakened from their sleep that many continued to lie down and have not arisen to this very day.[22] Shuisky was so greatly alarmed at this that he even ordered the great cannons to be placed on the wall, since he feared that the Poles were intending an immediate assault and would storm the city. Had the Poles done as they ought, on this occasion they would easily have captured and occupied Moscow. Dmitry, on the other hand, was hoping that the Muscovites would surrender without a struggle, and therefore he did not wish to destroy the great city or set it on fire, and even though the Poles against his wishes returned to the attack, he restrained them, addressing these words to them:

"If you wish to destroy the capital, and thereby burn and destroy my treasure, with what then shall I reward you afterwards?"

But even if Dmitry had been in earnest, it would have been much, much better to have destroyed the city than to have subjected half the country to devastation. The country could soon have built a new city, or have rebuilt Moscow, but the city of Moscow could never restore or rebuild all the cities, towns, and villages that were destroyed. For this advice was not given to him by his friends, but by his bitterest enemies.

On the feast of St Peter and St Paul, which in the year 1608 was on 29 June, Dmitry constructed a great encampment at Tushino, twelve versts[23] from Moscow, and remained there until 29 December 1609, and during that time there were many hard fought skirmishes between the encampment and the city, and on both sides many were killed.

Earlier it was related how the consort and widow of the first Tsar Dmitry, Maryna Yurievna, together with her father, the governor of Sandomir, and also Lord Stadnicki and other Polish magnates and all their families were conveyed from Moscow and imprisoned at Yaroslavl and Rostov. Now that the second Dmitry was so well established, had gained victory, and was besieging Moscow, Shuisky feared that he would send to these places to liberate and carry off the tsaritsa, together with all who were with her. Therefore he dispatched several thousand men to go there in secret and bring them once again to Moscow.

Fearing at the same time (for Dmitry with a great multitude of Poles, Cossacks, Tatars, Muscovites, and other nationalities stood so close to Moscow) that the second Dmitry's Poles, who were in the encampment before the wall of Moscow, might enter into a conspiracy with the Poles of the first Dmitry, who would be in Moscow with the tsaritsa, Shuisky proposed to the tsaritsa's father and the other Poles to let them go home to the Polish kingdom if they would give an oath not to go to the enemy and would never again do any harm to Russia. The Poles eagerly complied, thanking God that they were delivered out of the hands of their assassins. On St James' Day of the aforementioned year [25 July 1608] they were led out of Moscow by a long detour, lest they fall into the hands of the enemy along the other route and not reach their own country.

When all this became known to the second Dmitry, he detailed off several thousand men with orders to move quickly and intercept the tsaritsa and her companions along the way. When they encountered each other, the Muscovites turned to flight, except the commanders who were with the tsaritsa. And so the soldiers sent by the second Dmitry brought the tsaritsa, together with her father and all the Poles who were with them, safe and sound to the Tushino encampment before Moscow.

But the tsaritsa, her father, and all the Poles who were with them were more delighted than alarmed, since they were quite convinced that this was truly her lawful husband whom she had married in Moscow. The soldiers who were sent after her were under orders, on pain of death, not to tell her otherwise.

When Dmitry received tidings that the people he had sent had captured the tsaritsa without any resistance on the part of the Muscovites, and that she was on her way to the encampment, he rejoiced and was glad and ordered a salute to be fired several times from the great cannon, and all the soldiers in the whole encampment were similarly to fire salutes from their muskets and other weapons three or four times.

On the road, about eighteen miles from the encampment, while the tsaritsa was rejoicing and singing, a certain young Pole plucked up his nerve and approached the carriage, saying: "Maryna Yurievna, most gracious lady, you are very happy. It would be appropriate for you to rejoice and sing if you were to meet with your lawful husband, but this is not the Dmitry who was your lord, but another." Things turned out badly for him, and it would have been better for him to have remained silent and let matters take their course, for the tsaritsa was so disturbed at these tidings that her happiness and singing turned into sadness and weeping, while the Polish lord, whom Dmitry had sent with his soldiers after her, noticed that she was downcast and not so happy as she had been, and therefore asked why she was so silent and weeping, when in truth she ought to be all the more glad now that she was approaching her lord. She answered him: "That is true, my lord, but I have heard differently." After persistent questioning, she could not keep silent as to who had spoken to her concerning this matter. And when the nobleman, who admitted to his conversation with the tsaritsa, declared also that he was not the only one who had spoken of it but that it was common knowledge throughout the camp, the lord ordered him to be bound hand and foot and carried off to Dmitry's encampment, where Dmitry without trial ordered him to be impaled alive, which would not have happened had he been able to hold his tongue. Thus it is rightly said: "**Loose tongues crucify many who, had they remained silent, could have lived in peace and tranquillity.**"[24]

And even though the tsaritsa was well aware that she had been fed on false hopes, she was obliged all the same to feign great joy, which she did not feel in her heart, so that nobody should be aware of the charade. However, she did not proceed directly to Dmitry's encampment but ordered a separate camp to be pitched about a quarter of a mile apart for herself and all her suite, while she and Dmitry exchanged messages. Finally it was decided that the tsaritsa's father should return to Poland, while she herself would remain in the encampment of her "husband" Dmitry.[25] But they were to abstain from marital intercourse until Dmitry had conquered the Muscovite throne and was seated upon it. Dmitry had to swear to this before God, after which he joyfully went to meet the tsaritsa. They both knew excellently how to play their part and bade each other welcome lovingly and cordially, with much weeping and tears.

On that day, thanks to this masquerade, many good people with perfectly good eyesight were overcome with total blindness. Before all the people she accorded Dmitry suitable respect, as if he were indeed her beloved spouse and sovereign, and he did likewise for her. News of this spread throughout the country, and many therefore decided that he was the true Dmitry.[26] On this account a multitude of princes and boyars came to him from all over to the encampment and swore allegiance to him.

Shuisky, seeing that God was not sending him any good fortune, turned to the Devil and his instruments and resorted to all kinds of sorcery, gathering together all the agents of the Devil, the necromancers, as many as could be sought out throughout the land, so that whatever the one could not do, the other could.

He ordered many pregnant women cut open and their offspring taken from their bodies, and he also ordered healthy horses shot and their hearts cut out, which these sorcerers used so that if such or such a heart was buried or interred somewhere, then Shuisky's forces would be victorious if Dmitry's forces crossed this ground; if the Muscovites themselves crossed this ground, they would be overcome by the Poles.

Many great lords came over from Moscow to the second Dmitry, among them one prominent prince named Vasily Mosalsky, though several days later, as soon as he became aware that this was not the former Dmitry but another, he and many other boyars returned to Moscow and declared to all the people that this was not the first Dmitry but a new brigand and deceiver. When the Muscovites became aware of this, they said one to another: "If this is so, we will look on this matter in a different light, and the brigand and his Poles shall not receive the city, even though we, our wives and our children have to sacrifice our lives."

Together with their tsar, Shuisky, they resolved to send to the Swedish kingdom and request mercenaries from other nations. **To**

this end the prominent lord Prince Mikhail Skopin was sent. The Muscovites strove harder and tried to gain success in this matter, when two drunken rascals and traitors, who had fled from the second Dmitry and deserted to Moscow after the arrival of the aforesaid Mosalsky, mounted the platform on the Red Square and solemnly swore that this man was not the former and true Dmitry but someone else. These lads knew very well how to speak the Muscovite language. One, a Livonian, was called Hans Schneider, while the other was a High German from Austria called Johann Heinrich Carles. The latter had at one time been captured by the Turks in Hungary, had himself circumcised for money and accepted the Turkish faith, and then fled from the Turks into Germany and thence to Moscow, where in order to gain further advantage he had been rebaptized. In order to become noble and rich, he had to renounce his Lord God, in whose name he had been baptized and in whom he had believed in his youth and, what is dishonourable and ought to be punished with death,[27] he spat over his shoulder for a third time and kissed and prayed to the Muscovite god St Nicholas. In Russia this man went no less than three times from one lord to another, first to Dmitry, and then to Shuisky. But the Muscovites hung on every word spoken by this double-dealing Christian and Mameluke, believing everything he said.

When Dmitry realized the Muscovites were not about to surrender voluntarily, he sent Lord Sapieha with fifteen thousand men to the Trinity monastery to besiege it, and from that side to block and cut off the supply line to Moscow. Sapieha remained before this monastery for as long as Dmitry remained before Moscow, neither could he take it, as Dmitry was not able to take Moscow. This monastery lies twelve miles outside Moscow, and thither, to keep Sapieha company, Shuisky sent from Moscow as many cavalrymen as he could recruit, namely thirty thousand men, under the command of his brother Ivan Ivanovich Shuisky.

As soon as Sapieha had received intelligence to this effect, he made ready, intercepted the Muscovites, and the two forces clashed at Vozdvizhenskoe. They fought bravely against each other, and twice Sapieha was put to flight, and for that matter the Poles began to dig in their spurs and their hearts began to tremble. Lord Sapieha spoke bravely to them and put fresh heart into them. "My dear lords," he said, "if we turn to flight, all will be lost, and not one of us will be saved. Poland is very far from here. It would be better to die honourably, like knights, than let yourselves be killed like cowardly whores. Let every man, in the name of God, do his best, and I will be the first in action. Let him for whom honour is precious follow after me. On the third assault God will give us good fortune and deliver the enemy into our hands." Following this, they attacked the enemy for the third time, killing several thousand Muscovites, so that they were obliged to retreat towards Moscow and abandon the field. On this occasion Shuisky's cavalry was so depleted that he could in no wise dare to take the field without the aid of the foreigners.

Sapieha returned to his previous encampment before the Trinity monastery, and the Muscovites did not trouble him until Jakob de la Gardie arrived from Sweden. After this battle Sapieha sent a small detachment of Germans, Poles, and Cossacks from his camp to find out whether it was possible either to capture several towns or to persuade them to submit voluntarily. Their captain was a Spaniard called Lord Juan Cruzati. The first town they arrived at was called Pereiaslavl, which swore allegiance to the second Dmitry. A second town, Rostov, situated twelve miles further on into the country, which had earlier sworn allegiance to Dmitry, wanted to rebel, but things went badly for it. On 12 October it was totally destroyed. All the buildings were reduced to ashes, and many precious items of gold, silver, gems, and pearls were pillaged; in the churches robes were even torn off the saints. The reliquary of St Levonty,[28] which was of pure gold, weighed two hundred pounds, and lay in a silver sarcophagus, was hacked to pieces by the soldiers' axes, and each grabbed what he could. They seized the metropolitan[29] of Rostov, Prince Fedor Nikitich,[30] and sent him to Dmitry in the great encampment before Moscow. Dmitry received him graciously and even appointed him patriarch over the lands and towns under his authority. This metropolitan presented the second Dmitry with his staff, containing an oriental ruby equal in value to a whole barrel of gold.

The fate of this town, Rostov, served as a lesson to the rich commercial city of Yaroslavl, situated twelve miles beyond Rostov. It agreed to surrender voluntarily on the following conditions: if the tsar would let them keep their own laws, forbid the Poles to attack or raid them or to dishonour their wives or children, then they would voluntarily make their submission, be loyal to him, and endeavour eagerly to do all that they could. Then a certain Swede, called Laurens Buick, a doubly baptized Mameluke of the Russian religion, was appointed as governor, to receive the allegiance of the inhabitants, German, English, and Russian, and govern them on behalf of Dmitry. This was on 21 December of the same year 1608.

The city sent the second Dmitry thirty thousand rubles, which is equivalent to 83,888 ordinary thalers and eight good groschen, at a reckoning of twenty-four groschen to a thaler. They also maintained, at their own expense, a garrison of a thousand cavalrymen, providing them with forage and flour all the year round. But the Poles nevertheless were not content with this, doing great violence to the merchants among the market stalls, the ordinary man on the street, to the boyars in their houses and courtyards, pilfering in the market place whatever they laid their eyes upon or whatever they could use, which was the cause of much misfortune, as will be related later on.

The cities of Kostroma, Galich, and Vologda surrendered to Dmitry, swore allegiance to him, and truly would have remained steadfast in their allegiance had they not been persuaded, to the ruin of himself and all the city, by an accursed apostate Dutchman named Daniel Eyloff, who was living in that place in Russia and was in business as a salter.[31] He wrote to them that they were not obliged to observe their oath, for they had sworn to remain loyal to Dmitry Ivanovich, the son of the Tyrant, the legitimate heir of the Muscovite land. But now he knew for sure that this person was neither the Tyrant's son nor the first Dmitry, but another, a new deceiver.

The apostate collected in his saltworks two hundred Muscovite infantrymen armed with bows, arrows, axes, and pikes, and with this force he intended to expel all the Poles. But when the Poles came after him, he hid in his cellar with his three grown daughters, leaving the two hundred Muscovites to the mercy of the Poles, who killed them all. The Poles found him and his three daughters in the cellar on 11 December, took him prisoner, and demanded that he and his daughters ransom themselves and buy their freedom for six hundred thalers. If a certain good and honourable man named Johann Schmidt, whom the second Dmitry had appointed as governor in Yaroslavl, had not intervened and forestalled disaster, and advanced him the six hundred thalers, he would doubtless have received his daughters back in a different state from that in which they were when they were taken from him. For which reason he and his daughters ought in justice to have been grateful to him to the end of their lives, but the manner in which they recompensed him will soon be described in the fifteenth chapter. On 12 December a thousand Russians were killed not far from the apostate's saltworks and many villages were burned down.

On that same day Aleksandr Jozef Lisowski came to Yaroslavl from Dmitry's encampment, and Sapieha with five thousand Cossacks, and Ivan Shuminsky with nine hundred lancers. They proceeded to the house and saltworks of the apostate, burned everything to the ground, and killed everyone who stood in their way. Then they turned upon Kostroma and Galich, dealing likewise with these treacherous and perfidious cities. They burned down the cities, killed all those whom they encountered, plundered many goods, both gold and silver, ravaged the whole district, and returned with much booty to their encampment. So ended the year 1608, during which the second Dmitry caused an indescribable amount of misfortune on one side of the unfortunate land of Russia.

---

xv *How Russia in the Year 1609 Was Beset on All Sides by War and Tribulation*

In that year misfortune increased all the more in all places of Russia, from which it was easy to understand that the Lord God had become angry at this land, and was severely visiting punishment upon all its inhabitants. There was bloody war throughout the land. The second Dmitry was besieging Moscow and the Trinity monastery closely, and wherever harm could be inflicted upon the Muscovites, tens of thousands of men spared no effort as they burned and plundered on all sides as they came. Their camp was filled with all kinds of victuals, butter, flour, honey, mead, malt, brandywine, and all kinds of livestock, in such abundance that it could only be wondered at. Heads, legs, livers and lungs and all discarded parts of carcasses were thrown out, and so many lay on the streets everywhere in the camp that even the dogs could not devour them all. Because of this there arose in the camp such a fearful stench that people had to beware of the pestilence. Daily even the most lowly sort of people boiled and roasted meat, and ate only the most delicate parts. They drank more mead than beer, in such quantities were honeycombs found in the houses of peasants and in the monasteries.

In that year the Polish king, Sigismund III, also came to Smolensk with twenty thousand soldiers, demanding that the town and fortress surrender to him voluntarily, since of old it had belonged to the Polish kingdom.[1] The inhabitants of Smolensk sent him no reply except powder and lead. He remained there for a year and a half, until 13 June 1611, losing so many of his German soldiers in the course of assaults that there remained only four hundred men out of all the regiment. The inhabitants of Smolensk suffered from lack of salt and vinegar, which led to a devastating pestilence from which they died in great numbers. When the city was taken only three or four hundred healthy persons remained, who could in no wise defend the town, which had been besieged for so long; had it been

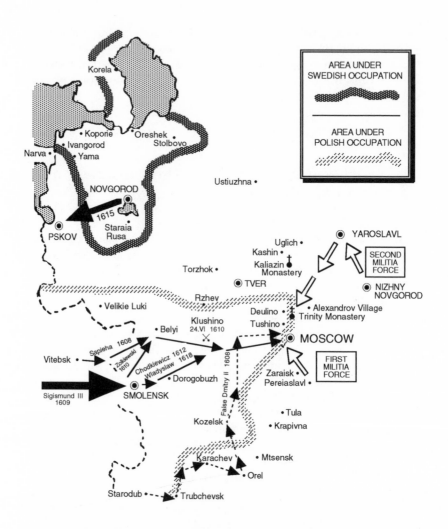

POLISH AND SWEDISH INTERVENTION
1609 – 18

AREA UNDER SWEDISH OCCUPATION

AREA UNDER POLISH OCCUPATION

Korela

Koporie
Ivangorod
Narva
Yama
Oreshek
Stolbovo

Ustiuzhna

NOVGOROD

1615

PSKOV
Staraia
Rusa

Uglich
Kashin
Kaliazin
Monastery

Torzhok

TVER

YAROSLAVL

SECOND
MILITIA
FORCE

NIZHNY
NOVGOROD

Rzhev

Velikie Luki

Belyi
Klushino
24.VI 1610

Deulino
Tushino
Alexandrov Village
Trinity Monastery

MOSCOW

Vitebsk
Sapieha 1608
Zolkiewski 1610
Chodkiewicz 1612
Wladyslaw 1618
Dorogobuzh
False Dmitry II 1608

Zaraisk
Pereiaslavl

FIRST
MILITIA
FORCE

Sigismund III
1609
SMOLENSK

Kozelsk
Tula
Krapivna

Karachev
Mtsensk
Orel

Starodub
Trubchevsk

otherwise, the king would have been put to much more trouble before he could have taken the fortress.[2]

During this time many thousands of Muscovites came out of the fortress and swore allegiance to His Majesty, but most of them betrayed their oath and went to Moscow when they had the opportunity. The walls around the city are twenty-three feet thick and so high that scaling ladders with thirty-five rungs cannot reach the top, unless the breastworks are demolished. The besieged loaded up many carts with stones and brought them up to the walls, and if they had had enough healthy men to allow one to be placed at each embrasure, they still could have held out, even though they had run out of powder, firearms, spears, or swords. Even heavy artillery did not make much impact upon the walls.[3]

The king was able eventually to take the fortress only because the wall was blown up by a mine near the river Dnieper, which was ten fathoms deep, and through the breach the infantry poured with colours flying, which threw the inhabitants of Smolensk into such panic that many threw down their weapons and let themselves be killed. Those who had abandoned the town to seek refuge in the fortress blew themselves up, together with their wives and all that they had with them, and thus took their own lives. The commander[4] and his son were captured and taken away to Poland. How an army of a mere twenty thousand could cause so much devastation over all the land is difficult to comprehend.

One year before the capture of this town Shuisky had sent a messenger with letters to King Sigismund while he was before Smolensk, in which he proposed to surrender the Russian monarchy to His Majesty if only he would come to Moscow and chase away the second Dmitry.[5] Two days after the arrival of this messenger Polish troops seized a Muscovite agent who had been proceeding to the commander of Smolensk with letters from Shuisky, saying that he should hold out while Shuisky convinced the king to give him aid in getting rid of the second Dmitry, and then, if this should come about, he should deal with the king and his followers in such a way that few of them would ever be able to return to Poland. When this was read to the king, His Majesty was amazed at the treachery and crafty wiles of the Muscovites, had both messengers killed, and said: "**No Muscovite can be trusted.** I shall settle accounts with that rogue Shuisky, so that he will never be able to trick me again."

In the same year 1609, Prince Skopin returned from the kingdom of Sweden, bringing with him Jakob de la Gardie as well as three thousand Germans and troops from other nations. When he reached Great Novgorod, he also gathered the local princes and boyars to his colours, intending with their help to liberate Moscow, as will be told later. The foreign troops that he brought with him also left behind only what was too hot or heavy for them.

On the third front, in the year 1609, the Tatars attacked with forty thousand men, and on three occasions carried off innumerable people and livestock, not counting the number of old and young and livestock that they killed and left lying there because they were too weak to travel. As for the fearful depredations that they visited upon the country by their incendiarism, it is impossible to describe them. At this time such a fearful lament could be heard from the people of the land, who had lost not only their livestock but also part of their families, whether wives who had lost their husbands, or men who had lost their wives and children, that even a stone would be moved.

In that same year a certain Muscovite[6] boyar named Liapunov came forward, rallied to his cause a number of towns that were subject to Moscow, and waged war against Dmitry, against Shuisky, and also against His Royal Majesty the King of Poland. He called himself the White Tsar and wished to fight, he said, for the Muscovite Christian faith. Wherever his host went, there was scarcely a blade of grass left growing.

On the fourth side of the Russian land, in February, March, and April of the same year, several of the towns which had sworn allegiance to the second Dmitry, namely Vologda, Galich, Kostroma, Romanov, Yaroslavl, Suzdal, Mologa, Rybinsk, and Uglich, now deserted him. On all the corners thousands of peasants gathered in crowds. They dealt many times more rudely and mercilessly with those Germans and Poles whom they encountered out in search of forage,[7] than these same Poles had dealt with them.

Once peasants rise up in rebellion, they usually become like reckless madmen and wild boars, not hesitating to devour and tear apart whatever they can, not sparing anything, and, having struck once, they continue striking the same place. May God prevent any honest warrior from falling into their hands.

The cause of their defection was the lawlessness and great indiscipline of the Poles, who could not abstain from pillage and violence, and pushed the peasants under the ice, slit their throats, or even hanged them. They used force against poor people, even those who had sworn allegiance to Dmitry, taking all that they had, as if they were their bitterest enemies, even though these poor people had contributed much to the camp in order to support the army. Because of this the poor were forced to hide and conceal themselves in the countryside from the Polish predators, who were hard for these people to endure, and who gave them the pretext, even before they had heard of the arrival of Skopin and de la Gardie, to rise up in rebellion against Dmitry's plundering soldiers and to desert him.

They killed several Poles, pushing them under the ice and saying: "You pigtails,[8] you have plundered our region clean, you have slaughtered all our cows and calves, so now you can go to the fish in the Volga, that they may in turn devour you to death."

From the encampment, in order to curb the rebellious peasants, Samuel Tyszkiewicz was sent to Romanov, while Pan Lisowski was sent to Suzdal and later to Yaroslavl, but the peasants had fortified their camps so well, surrounding them with palisades or stockades, that the Poles could do nothing against them, but had to leave them in peace.

Joachim Schmidt, whom we have mentioned earlier, was governor in the city of Yaroslavl, which had defected, but he had fled from there at the time of the defection, together with the Poles who were with him. The Poles sent this same Schmidt back to Yaroslavl to try and persuade the inhabitants to reconsider and not give rise to greater bloodshed. Their tribulations would be ended, for Tsar Dmitry would place a great lord in command of the town, whom the Polish soldiers would respect. They beguiled Schmidt with deceitful words near the city gate and, before he was aware of it, he was completely surrounded, and the poor man was dragged forcibly into the city. Then they played a grisly passion play[9] with him. Having boiled a great cauldron of mead, they stripped Schmidt of his clothes, threw him into the cauldron, and boiled him until there was no flesh left on his bones.

This unspeakable cruelty towards this good and honest man, as well as the defection and insurgency of this town, was caused by none other than the perfidious and evil apostate, the salter Daniel Eyloff, who once before, as has been narrated earlier, had defected from Dmitry. At that time he had been taken captive together with his three daughters, but had been rescued by this same Joachim Schmidt, who paid on his behalf six hundred reichsthalers, which allowed his daughters to preserve their honour. Now this Eyloff rendered him the gratitude of this world.[10] Not only did he mock his loyal old friend in misfortune but even urged the Russians to make short work of him. When Schmidt had been sufficiently boiled, they took his skeleton out of the cauldron and cast it out onto the city wall, so that the pigs and dogs could tug at it. Nor were his wife and friends permitted to gather up the bones and bury them. The poor and greatly grieving widow and friends had to enjoy ten times as much mockery and ribaldry from their false friend, the perfidious apostate and his companions, as from the Russians themselves.

Pan Lisowski later amply avenged the death of this honest man. He reduced the entire suburbs of Yaroslavl to ashes, then proceeded further into the depths of the countryside, killing and destroying everything which lay in his path, men, women, children, nobles, townspeople, and peasants. He burned to the ground the large settlements of Kineshma and Yurievets Polsky, returning to his encampment before the Trinity monastery with great booty. What palpable damage was done in that year by murders, plunder, and fire to those cities which had defected, both within their walls and also outside, it is impossible to describe. I have often wondered how such a land could endure all this for so long.

I too had fine estates in Russia. One of them, Fedorovskoye, together with eight hamlets, was situated fourteen miles from Smolensk. The armies of His Majesty the King of Poland reduced it all to nothing. A second was called Rogozhna. It belonged to two owners, and each had his manor there. It was an extensive estate, along with a large productive woodland and rough grazing, which alone was six miles wide, and was situated only seven miles from the city of Moscow. The third and smallest was called Krapivna, had three villages, and was thirty-six miles from Moscow. The two latter estates, Rogozhna and Krapivna, were so severely burned by the Tatars, and so many people were slaughtered or carried off, that in the two together there remained scarcely twenty[11] houses of peasant homesteads that had not suffered from fire, and no more than forty persons.

XVI *Concerning the Return of Skopin and the Arrival of Jakob de la Gardie with Three Thousand Foreigners*

When Skopin, accompanied by Jakob and the foreign soldiers he had brought with him, arrived in Novgorod in January 1609, the second Dmitry sent a certain Polish colonel, Kernozicki, with four thousand lancers to engage him. He attacked them with such force that when they met they had to retreat to the city of Novgorod. There Kernozicki besieged them all winter, until March.

On account of this Dmitry was greatly pleased and thought that he had won a complete victory, so he consummated his marriage with the consort of the first Dmitry (who was, as we have related, with him in the camp before Moscow), despite the oath which he had sworn to her father, the governor of Sandomir, that he would not lie with her until he was seated upon the tsar's throne. He generally began to behave very haughtily, and began to call himself the only Christian emperor under the sun, and so forth, as can be seen from his title, which was as follows: **We, Dmitry Ivanovich, Tsar of All Russia, of the Muscovite realm, Autocrat of the Grand Principality of Moscow, given to us by God, being elected by God, anointed by God, raised by God far above all sovereigns, guided and protected by God as a second Israel, the only Christian emperor under the sun, lord and suzerain of many principalities.**

Shortly before Whitsuntide the foreign troops stole by night out of Novgorod through the marshes on the far side, attacked the Poles in their encampment, and inflicted upon them such heavy damage that Pan Kernozicki and all his forces were compelled to retreat to Dmitry's large encampment before Moscow. When the second Dmitry learned that it was the foreigners who had inflicted these losses upon him, he conceived a great hatred against all Germans and became their enemy. Therefore he began also to hate his own Germans who were with him, even though they were entirely innocent in this matter.

Having won this victory, Skopin, Jakob, and his foreigners advanced further, arriving at Tver, on the Volga. After Trinity Sunday Dmitry sent against them Pan Zborowski with five thousand lancers. On the first day these lancers gave them such trouble that they were compelled, if they did not wish to be killed quickly, to cross over the deep and wide Volga, which also caused them considerable losses. On the next day Jakob, having crossed that same river again in a different place, once again attacked the Poles, struck bravely at them, and inflicted such damage upon them that they retreated, being forced to return with great losses and ignominy to Dmitry's encampment.[1] This greatly angered the second Dmitry and incited him further against the German nation.

On the feast of St Peter and St Paul, Skopin and Jakob arrived at the Kalyazin monastery. Skopin and his boyars remained in the monastery, while Jakob and his people were in the open field before the monastery. To redeem his reputation Dmitry once again sent this same Pan Zborowski against Skopin and Jakob, as well as the regimental commander Sapieha, who had been stationed before the Trinity monastery with twelve thousand lancers. They attacked Skopin and Jakob several times, but each time suffered ignominious defeat. Thus they stood facing each other until September, when Skopin and Jakob attacked the Poles with all their forces, killed about a hundred of their men, and routed them so completely that the Poles abandoned the field without a backward glance until they had reached the encampment before the Trinity monastery.[2]

XVII *Concerning Aleksandr Jozef Lisowski, the Second Dmitry's Commander Over Several Thousand Cossacks, and How He Proceeded with Them Too Deep into the Country, and How the Enemy Cut Off His Retreat to the Encampment, and How for This Reason He Was Compelled to Retreat to Suzdal, and How, Finally, Having Effected a Wide Diversion, He Withdrew Towards Pskov*

At this time the Lord Lisowski decided to undertake a military stratagem relating to the defection of Yaroslavl.[1] He proceeded there on a forced march, day and night, halting three miles from that city. In this he wished to imitate Skopin and Jakob and also attempt to seize the city. But he received timely intelligence that Skopin and Jakob had already taken Yaroslavl, and because of this he was forced to withdraw, in order to attempt to regain his encampment.

This hindered his intention with regard to the city; moreover, that very night, when he was making ready to return to his encampment, de la Gardie's followers, having captured the city, were already advancing against him in the field. In this manner the road back to the Trinity monastery was denied him, and had he not received as a prisoner a certain boyar, from whom he learned that Jakob's Germans were already in pursuit and within a few hours would be advancing together with David Zherebtsov, things would have gone very badly for him. He did not wish to await their arrival, so he turned aside at Suzdal and barricaded himself there with palisades as best he could. There he operated for the whole winter, occasionally emerging to attack the neighbouring cities and monasteries and returning with excellent booty. Then he received intelligence that the career of his lord, the second Dmitry, had come to an end, and that his forces had gone over to the Polish king, so once again, in March 1610[2], he set out again, made a wide diversion through the entire country, and finally moved towards Pskov.

There the inhabitants of Pskov not only received him very graciously but also requested and persuaded him to stay with them for some time, to give them help against the Germans, who were daily attacking and assaulting them out of Narva, which belongs to the Swedish kingdom and is situated on the Livonian frontier. He eagerly complied, and not only cleared the borderlands of Pskov of the Narva forces but also by secret stratagems and negotiations arranged that five hundred Englishmen and three hundred Irishmen deserted them and joined his forces, after which the Narva forces left the inhabitants of Pskov entirely in peace.

Having rendered the inhabitants of Pskov this service, Lisowski went over to the side of the Polish king, and spent his winter in Voronezh. But learning that the Cossacks and Russians under his command were preparing to betray him, he left them and proceeded with only eight hundred foreign troops to Krasnoe, captured it in the summer of 1611, paid off the foreigners, and once again recruited three hundred Poles, remaining in that same fortress and holding it on behalf of His Majesty the King of Poland. These adventures befell Lisowski because Jakob's followers had at that time blocked off his retreat and he had, like a crafty fox, to go the long way around in order to find another lair in Russia and so escape the spite of the Russians.

Skopin and Jakob once again brought Yaroslavl into obedience to Shuisky, and went with all their forces to the Alexandrovskaia Sloboda[3], erected new defences out of planks or wooden benches, took cover in them, pitching their autumn camp there until the freeze-up came and they could proceed on frozen ground. And although the Poles occasionally visited them, they were not keen on gaining glory at the expense of the Germans, who on each occasion compelled them to retreat.

At Martinmas[4] the Germans wanted to be the Poles' uninvited guests before the Trinity monastery and help them eat the St Martin's goose. The Poles were excellently prepared for this, making room for them with pipes playing, while they themselves celebrated the feast at Dmitrov, awaiting the Germans there for some time.

XVIII *Concerning the Embassy of His Majesty the King of Poland to the Poles in Dmitry's Encampment*

During the Advent of 1609 King Sigismund sent a delegation to Dmitry's encampment before Moscow, not to him, but to his chief commander, Roman Rozynski and the Polish knights. The delegates and messengers were: Lord Stadnicki, Lord Zborowski, Lord Ludwig Wieger, and Pan Martzin, a cavalry commander. **The king's instructions to the soldiers were as follows.** They should recall that in recent years, by their rebellion in Poland, they had committed the crime of *lèse majesté*. All this would be forgiven and forgotten, and all the property confiscated from them in Poland would be restored, if they would arrest and bring before Smolensk the impostor,[1] to whom they had sworn allegiance and whom they were now serving, and who called himself Dmitry but was not in fact Dmitry. But this was to be kept secret throughout Advent.

Dmitry was surprised that the ambassadors did not appear before him or request an audience, but it did not occur to him that the purpose of the embassy was to encompass his ruin. But as time went by and the ambassadors had still not requested an audience, Dmitry became alarmed, and on the fourth day of our Christmas he summoned his commander Roman Rozynski, enquiring as to the business of the king's ambassadors, in that they had tarried for several weeks in the encampment but had not yet requested permission to come to him and receive an audience.

Rozynski, who had already spoken with the senior commanders and nobles, had decided, like them, to comply with the king's wishes, but on this occasion he was dead drunk and, uttering unseemly abuse and threats, he said: **"You Muscovite whoreson!"** He swung at him with his mace, and continued, "Why do you want to know what business the emissaries have with me! **The Devil knows who you are.** We Poles have for so long shed our blood for your sake, but have not yet received our pay." And there followed similar expostulations.

Dmitry tore himself away from him, went to his consort, fell at her feet, and tearfully and with sighs bade her good night, saying: **"The Polish king has entered into conspiracy against me** with my commanders, and I am in great peril. I shall not be worthy for you to set eyes upon if I should countenance this. **Either he must die or I**

must perish, since he and the Poles do not wish me well. May God protect me upon the road which I am about to travel, and may God also preserve you from evil as you remain here."

Having dressed himself in peasant clothes, he mounted a dung sled and on 29 December 1609 with his jester, Peter Koshelev, left the encampment for Kaluga, so nobody knew where the tsar was hidden or whither he had gone, whether he had been killed or whether he had fled. Most people thought that he had been killed and privily disposed of.

Dmitry, however, did not go directly to Kaluga, but first past Kaluga to the nearest monastery, whence he sent several monks to the inhabitants of Kaluga, commanding that they be told that the pagan Polish king had repeatedly demanded of him that he cede to him the Severian lands, which in earlier times had belonged to Poland, but he had refused him, not wishing a pagan faith to take root in these lands. So now the king was conspiring with his commander Roman Rozynski and the Poles who had for so long served him, demanding that Rozynski arrest him and deliver him to the king before Smolensk, but he, Dmitry, having learned of this, had concealed himself, so now he was appealing to the people, asking them what they had decided to do, and entreating them to decide upon his cause. If they would remain loyal to him, he would come to them, and with the help of St Nicholas and the aid of all the estates which had sworn fealty to him he would take his revenge, not only upon Shuisky but also upon the perfidious Poles, in a way that they would never forget. He was also prepared to die beside his people for the sake of the Christian Muscovite faith and to root out all alien pagan faiths, nor would he cede to the Polish king a single village or even a tree, let alone any city or principality.

This greatly pleased the Russians who were in Kaluga. They themselves came to him in the monastery, brought him bread and salt, and escorted him to the fortress of Kaluga, to the house of the governor Lord Skotnicki. They gave him clothing, horses, and sleds, and equipped his kitchen and cellar. This occurred on 17 January of the new year 1610.

HOW DMITRY, SHUISKY, AND LATER HIS MAJESTY THE KING OF POLAND FARED IN THE YEAR 1610

Dmitry wrote thereafter to Prince Grigory Shakhovskoy, who had advanced with several thousand Cossacks against the King of Poland and had pitched his camp at Tsarevo-Zaimishche, not far from

Viazma, commanding him to turn back and make all haste to Kaluga. He arrived in Kaluga on the fifth day after the feast of Epiphany,[2] and there a new royal court was founded. Dmitry wrote to all the towns on his side, commanding that all Poles who were in those places, or who came thither, were to be killed, and all their possessions forfeited to him in Kaluga. If any merchant or soldier owned property in the countryside or in the city, then it should be confiscated, nor should anybody be left alive within it.

Merciful God, how many well-born Poles piteously lost their lives during this unforeseen turn of events, were dragged to the river, and thrown as food for the fishes! Hundreds of merchants who were proceeding to Putivl or Smolensk, bringing to the encampment velvet, silk, muskets, weapons, wines, and spices, were seized by the Cossacks and brought to Kaluga. Dmitry took everything from them, leaving them nothing to live on, so that they who before had been rich and had thousands were compelled to live by begging in Kaluga, while others were even deprived of their lives.

Only God and those Germans who lived in Kaluga, Peremyshl, and Kozelsk to the very end know how much anguish, scarcity, and fear they often had to endure along with the Poles. At first Dmitry was very well disposed towards the Germans, but when de la Gardie and his mercenaries, who were mostly Germans, caused him so much harm, he became the Germans' bitterest enemy, especially after, through the wiles of the Polish king, he had been forced secretly to leave his encampment and his army and take flight.

At first he confiscated all the Germans' estates, then he took away all their houses and homesteads with all that there was in them, and all this he gave to the Russians for the sole reason that those who wished them ill, the Russians, had made denunciations against them, saying that they would rather be with the Poles than with the Russians, and that they had secretly carried on negotiations with the Polish king, whose soldiers frequently had come out from the king's encampment to wherever Dmitry was. Therefore the Germans had to expect death hourly.

He even forbade us and our families our religious services, and we, poor people, lived at that time in considerable fear and dread, especially our preacher and spiritual pastor, Master Martin Beer, whom twenty-five priests had tried to deprive of his life and property in Kozelsk; but the Lord God in His miraculous fashion shielded him from harm and preserved him.

On the day after Dmitry fled from the encampment, the Poles and the Muscovite princes and boyars, together with Patriarch Fedor Nikitich, who was with them in the encampment, called together an assembly and council to decide what to do now that Dmitry had fled. They all swore to be at peace[3] with one another, neither to go over to the Polish king or Shuisky, and if anyone should arise who claimed to be Dmitry, they would neither believe nor acknowledge him, still less would they receive Dmitry himself back. They heaped abuse upon the tsaritsa, Maryna Yurievna, in such a manner as it is not befitting to write, and this prompted her to slip secretly out of the encampment to Lord Sapieha in Dmitrov.

On 3 January 1610 the second Dmitry sent a certain boyar named Ivan Pleshcheev from Kaluga to the encampment to find out what was the sentiment of the Polish rank and file, what they were saying, whether they thought it would have been better had he stayed with them. If anyone should say that they would gladly receive him back again, then he should be told that Tsar Dmitry had ordered him to convey the following information: he had gone away to collect some money, and with this money he would give them several quarters' pay as soon as possible, if they would send to him in Kaluga that perfidious traitor Roman Rozynski, dead or alive.

The Poles would readily have agreed to this, had the aforementioned oath they had given after Dmitry's flight not served as a constraint and an impediment. Since Pleshcheev had achieved no result from these efforts, he betook himself to Ivan Martynovich Zarutsky, who was commanding twenty thousand Cossacks, attempting to induce him and his Cossacks to leave the encampment and go over to Dmitry in Kaluga, but he was also unsuccessful in this. The regimental commander Zarutsky moved off with most of his Cossacks from the encampment to the Polish king before Smolensk. Many Cossacks, who were weary enough of this extraordinary war, went back to the Wild Steppe, while only about five hundred Cossacks came to their Lord Dmitry in Kaluga, pursued by Poles from the encampment, so that on the way many were trampled by horses or cut down.

Shortly afterwards, Dmitry sent to the encampment Pan Kazimierz, the governor of Kaluga, a veritable chameleon.[4] With the Poles he was a true Pole, and with the Russians a true Russian. When he realized that he could achieve nothing with the Poles, he spent a long time ingratiating himself with Lord Rozynski, from whom he received permission to return to Kaluga and secretly to remove all his remaining property; but he was obliged thereafter to steal away and return to the Poles in the encampment. Rozynski gave Kazimierz a missive for Lord Skotnicki, who had long been governor there but who had subsequently fallen into Dmitry's disfavour and been replaced since he had refused to fight against the Polish king. The letter urged Skotnicki to gather around him all the Poles who were quartered in the Kaluga district, and then to seize Dmitry and bring him to the encampment.

The court flatterer Kazimierz gave the letter personally to Dmitry, saying that he should read it and see what his perfidious general Rozynski had written to the governor Skotnicki. Dmitry, having read the letter, was led to believe that he was to have been seized secretly by Skotnicki. He fell into a rage and straight away, without investigating the matter or questioning anyone, ordered the executioner and his assistants to arrest Skotnicki by night, take him to the Oka river, which flows close to Kaluga, and push him under the ice.

When the unfortunate man asked why they were treating him in such a manner, what he was supposed to have done, what crime he was supposed to have committed, why they were dealing with him so without a hearing and at dead of night, the executioner's assistants told him that Tsar Dmitry had ordered that they were not to dispute with him, but should plunge him into the river. They placed a halter around his neck and dragged him to the water as they would drag a dead dog. His last words were these: "**Such is my reward, in that for two long years I have served faithfully, enduring such a hard siege. May God have mercy upon me.**" His wife and children had everything taken from them, to be given to Pan Kazimierz for the betrayal he had committed. Dmitry then in his anger swore that if God placed him back upon his throne, he would not leave a single foreigner[5] alive, not even a babe in its mother's womb.

On 13 January of the same year Jurgen Krebsberg, a native of Pomerania, a very devoted chamberlain of the tsaritsa, arrived at Kaluga dressed in peasant's[6] clothes. The tsaritsa had sent him from Dmitrov with a verbal commission to her consort, Dmitry. He received him joyfully, rewarded him handsomely, and sent him back in haste also with a verbal answer to the effect that the tsaritsa should spare no pains or effort but as soon as possible make her way to Dmitry in Kaluga, and not to let the Poles take her to the king before Smolensk, which Dmitry had reliable intelligence that the Poles were intending to do.

At that time Skopin and de la Gardie had finally decided to attack Dmitrov, of which Sapieha remained in continual fear, for which reason he counselled the tsaritsa that if she did not wish to go to Poland to her father and mother, or fall into the hands of Skopin and de la Gardie, she should leave secretly and join her husband in Kaluga. The tsaritsa replied: "How can I, a Russian tsaritsa, return in shame to my kinsfolk in Poland? It would be better for me to have perished in Russia. I shall share with my husband whatever fate has decreed us." Whereupon she immediately ordered to be prepared for her a man's costume in velvet, in the Polish fashion. She put it on, armed herself with a musket and sabre, put on boots and spurs, and chose a swift horse for herself.

Sapieha gave her an escort of Muscovite Germans who were with him in Dmitrov and fifty Cossacks. With them she travelled the forty-five German miles no worse off than any fighting man, and on the night of Candlemas[7] arrived at Kaluga. Before the gates of Kaluga she told the sentry that she was one of Dmitry's trusted chamberlains and was coming in haste with an important dispatch, concerning which nobody else was supposed to know. The tsar immediately knew what was afoot and ordered the Cossacks to guard the gates closely and admit the chamberlain. She immediately rode into the citadel, to the tsar's steps, sprang from her horse and came into her lord's presence, which caused great rejoicing. And since the ladies-in-waiting whom the tsaritsa had brought from Poland had returned with the tsaritsa's father to Poland, she chose a new suite from those German damsels whose parents lived in these parts. A German chief lady-in-waiting was also chosen to supervise them and all this time the tsaritsa was very gracious and well disposed towards the Germans, as she showed by her deeds, as soon will be related, when she saved us from extreme danger and death and preserved our lives.

Soon thereafter, just as soon as the tsaritsa had departed, Skopin captured the stockade[8] close to the fortress of Dmitrov. Sapieha and those who were serving with him soon abandoned the fortress of Dmitrov, skirted Dmitry's camp before Moscow and proceeded to the monastery of St Joseph,[9] left several hundred Cossacks there and went off to the king at Smolensk.

The remainder of his army pitched their camp for the winter by the Ugra river, in a very fertile region rich in cattle, which hitherto had not been visited by any army but which during this winter and spring would have to endure much. The aforementioned skirting movement by Lord Sapieha determined the Poles and Cossacks in their resolve not to hold out in the great encampment.

Certain Muscovite lords, such as, for instance, Ivan Tarasovich and Mikhail Glebovich Saltykov,[10] appeared with many other Muscovite princes and boyars at the king's headquarters before Smolensk and, as befitted evil and cunning men, counselled the king that, since there was no longer in Russia any legitimate sovereign who could be tsar of such a monarchy, he should set forth and try his fortune because, thanks to the second Dmitry, a splendid causeway had been built all the way to Moscow, for all the land as far as Moscow had become enfeebled and pacified. Therefore, while the city was still standing, he should seize the opportunity, which would not come again should he let it slip. At the same time they should strive among their fellow countrymen in Moscow and so contrive Shuisky's overthrow, so that either he or his son might be elected and acknowledged.

The Poles whom Dmitry had left behind also sent their emissaries to the king before Smolensk, bidding His Majesty come and attack the Muscovites, provided that they were paid all that the second Dmitry owed them. His Majesty sent his refusal and replied that if they wished to serve His Majesty, they would be paid the same as any other of his soldiers, from the time they entered his service.

But the Poles were neither content nor happy with such a decision. Some began to abuse the commander Rozynski for having expelled Dmitry for the king's sake, and themselves for having behaved so dishonourably towards Dmitry, violating the oath they had sworn to him and on account of which they had for so long served him. A very few overlooked the pay that Dmitry owed them and went over to the king. Most of them went to the Ugra, to Sapieha's host, and there awaited what reply Sapieha brought back from the king regarding their pay. Meanwhile they continuously plundered this rich region, raided it, and stripped it absolutely bare.

Skopin and de la Gardie, with all their foreign troops, reached Moscow without encountering any resistance. All that side, from Livonia and the Swedish realm as far as Moscow had been cleared of Dmitry's forces in the space of one year, so that not one Pole or Cossack could be seen of the hundred thousand who for nearly two years had invested Moscow and the Trinity monastery and had lorded it everywhere, since they had been compelled to withdraw by a small squad of Germans and soldiers of other nationalities under de la Gardie's leadership.

HOW JAKOB DE LA GARDIE AND HIS HOST WERE RECEIVED BY SHUISKY IN MOSCOW, AND HOW SKOPIN WAS REWARDED FOR HIS SERVICE

Jakob and all the mercenaries whom he had brought with him were made very welcome by Shuisky. He frequently sent them splendid gifts from his kitchen and cellars, and honoured all the officers as they arrived, giving them gold and silver vessels from his treasury. He paid all the soldiers in full all that they were owed, in gold, silver, and sable. But when Jakob and his brother Veit had filled their purses with money, they became so overbearing, and committed so many improprieties within the city, that the Muscovites became disgusted with them and wished God would soon send fair weather to melt the snow, free the rivers of ice, and make the way clear for these hirelings to be sent against the enemy in the field and the city to be rid of them.

The unfortunate courageous hero Skopin, who had been in the Swedish realm and for the benefit of his tsar and his country had brought with him foreign troops, had even remained with them for a whole year, never once complaining about his lot, and had fought valiantly against the foe, was rewarded graciously for his pains, in that Shuisky ordered that he be given venom and poisoned to death.[11] The reason for this was simply that the Germans and other nationalities, and even many of the Muscovites themselves, esteemed him for his prudence and bravery more highly than Shuisky. His death was a misfortune for all Moscow.

At Easter Lord Sapieha returned from the king to his and Rozynski's army on the Ugra with the following final answer. The king was unwilling to pay anyone for service rendered Dmitry, but as long as they would serve His Royal Highness, they would be paid in full. Having received this answer, all the knights of the army of Sapieha and Rozynski sent a delegation to Kaluga to their lord Dmitry, telling him that they were not guilty of the conspiracies that Rozynski had hatched against him, since not once in their lives had they even contemplated betraying him, for which reason they had not gone over to the king but had remained in the encampment, and further-more, God had rewarded Rozynski for his services, for he died shortly thereafter, whereas his fellow conspirators were already no longer with him in the encampment but had deserted and gone over to the king.

If Dmitry paid them off for three quarters, the delegation of knights said they would wait for the balance, and continue to serve him, and try for a second time in his company to capture Moscow. Since Dmitry was very pleased at this proposal, he ordered that the Poles be sent a favourable reply, namely that they would only have to wait a little while. He had already made arrangements for the money, which he was expecting hourly, and as soon as the money was available, he would send it to them with all dispatch. In order to collect this money he placed an extraordinary and heavy tax upon the whole country and collected many thousands of rubles. He met with his newly recruited Russians, Cossacks, Tatars, and Poles on the Ugra, negotiated with them, paid them off for three quarters, once again received their allegiance, and made dispositions that as soon as possible after Whitsun they would once again move back towards Moscow.

At exactly the same time Shuisky sent his own foreign troops, together with some Russians, to clear the way to Smolensk and to pay a visit to the king there before Smolensk, and to this end he gave Jakob sufficient money to give his men their pay when it fell due. Jakob himself and his people, as well as the bulk of the Muscovite army, remained in Moscow, while Grigory Valuev was sent with a small detachment to reconnoitre, to see whether they would encounter any resistance from the royal army in the field.

When Valuev reached Tsarevo-Zaimishche, and had received detailed information that Lord Stanislaw Zolkiewski was not far off, and had with him an excellently equipped force, he quickly pitched his camp right in the open field, fortified himself there as best he could, and sent a dispatch post haste to Mozhaisk. Learning of this, Zolkiewski quickly advanced and besieged Valuev there. Receiving news that Zolkiewski was so close at hand, they who were in Mozhaisk quickly advanced to relieve Valuev. This was on 23 June.

Zolkiewski, receiving important intelligence that the principal army was also advancing, pitched a dummy camp before Valuev's trenches, ordered a number of hop staves to be driven in around the camp, and ordered that only several hundred light cavalry remain on guard and be visible to Valuev's forces. When dawn broke the two camps kept diligent watch upon each other, and those who were on sentry duty began to converse with one another, the Poles deciding to urge Valuev's forces to surrender to the king voluntarily.

Meanwhile Zolkiewski had caught up with the Muscovites and Jakob, and on the feast of John the Baptist, 24 June, they met six miles from Mozhaisk and engaged in battle in the open field before Klushino. The battle had scarcely begun when two regiments of French horsemen deserted Jakob, went over to Zolkiewski, and together with the Poles opened fire upon Jakob's men and the Muscovites. Because of this the Muscovites fell into such despondency that they turned their backs upon the enemy and returned to Moscow, leaving the German infantry detachment in the lurch. All the same, they defended themselves valiantly for some time against the Poles, killing several notable Poles, in the hope that the Muscovites would return and come to their rescue. But since there was no sign of the Muscovites' return, and since it was becoming more and more impossible to withstand the Poles, they parleyed with the Poles, promising to surrender if the Poles promised on oath that their lives would be spared. If they would not, then they would hold out and fight to the last man, but the Poles themselves would not profit from this.[12]

The Poles withdrew a little way, took counsel, and agreed unanimously that they would spare the Germans. They sent Pan Zborowski to them, who swore that no harm would come to them. But since there were among the German soldiers some who knew very well how the Poles had observed their oath in Livonia, before Dünamünde, when the soldiers had given up their muskets and then were slaughtered like dogs by the Poles, they reminded the Poles of this perfidy, stating that they could not rely on the oath of an isolated individual. Then the most exalted magnates appeared before them and they all swore that they would deal honourably with the Germans, and would moreover allow them to keep their weapons and sidearms, so that they should not fear any treachery.

After this they surrendered, and all that had been promised was honestly fulfilled. The oaths of those who wished to serve the king would be accepted. Those who did not wish to remain but wished to leave the country were to be permitted to do so.

Having gained this victory, chasing the Muscovites from the field and plundering their camp with all its military supplies and all that was in it, and also the money which Shuisky himself had given to Jakob to pay his soldiers, Zolkiewski returned with rejoicing and great triumph to Tsarevo-Zaimishche, bringing with him many captive boyars. He led these boyars in front of Valuev's trenches, so that Valuev himself might hear how the Muscovite host had been defeated and had fled back to Moscow, and how Zolkiewski had received as booty all the encampment and everything that was in it. He also related to him how the Germans had surrendered to him and sworn allegiance to the king.

Valuev could now see this with his own eyes, for they were coming in friendship to persuade him to reconsider and not offer any further resistance to Zolkiewski and the military forces of His Royal Majesty who were with him, but to choose a course that would preserve both his own life and possessions and those of the men under his command. If he would listen to their advice, neither he nor anyone else would come to harm.

Thereafter Valuev declared that it was now sufficiently obvious to him that God had given the victory to the royal army and he would cease to oppose His Royal Majesty and his forces and voluntarily surrender, together with all those who were with him. After this had occurred Lord Zolkiewski, with all the Poles, Germans, Frenchmen, and Russians, proceeded as one force back to Moscow, to the camp where the second Dmitry was situated, besieging the city from the same side, often being kept busy as the Muscovites made sorties.

At that time Monsieur Laville and Colonel Eberhard von Horn arrived from Pogoreloe, which is also in Russia, with all their regiments, Germans and Frenchmen. The king's men captured the monastery of St Joseph, where there still remained some of Dmitry's forces, whom Sapieha had left there when he had sent the rest of his army to the Ugra, while he himself proceeded to the king before Smolensk. They were all defeated by the aforementioned Germans and Frenchmen, nor were any left alive.[13] Dmitry was so enraged at this that he was about to order that all the Germans remaining with him were to be drowned, and he said scornfully: "**Now I see that the Germans are not at all devoted to me.** They have gone over to the infidel king of Poland and they are killing the followers of the only Christian emperor under the sun. **When I attain the throne, all the Germans shall pay dearly for this.**" This devilish vow was very pleasing to the princes and boyars, and therefore they shamelessly defamed the Germans in all the places occupied by Dmitry, bearing all sorts of false tales against them, especially against those who lived in Kozelsk.

These false denunciations against the Germans were the work of Dmitry's counsellors, namely Prince Grigory Shakhovskoy, Trubetskoy, Ryndin, Peter Alekseevich, Mikhail Konstantinovich Yushkov, Tretyakov, Nikoforovich, and several others. They all received and occupied splendid estates, which had formerly been awarded the Germans by Dmitry for their faithful service. Therefore they feared that if the Germans remained in favour, these estates would be taken from them and restored to the Germans. For that reason, by day and by night, they sought pretexts to get rid of us for good, to deprive us of our lives and hold on to our estates, despite the fact that for three whole years we had served Dmitry loyally, shed our blood for him, and had lost our health and many of our kinsfolk.

Since these godless people had repeatedly heard that Dmitry had sworn, while moved to anger, not to leave a single German alive because of the harm that the King's Germans had caused him (as has been related earlier), they appeared before him, saying: "**The Germans in Kozelsk have written to the Polish king**, proposing to surrender the city to him, and the king has also sent a letter in reply." They also said the Germans would rejoice if Dmitry were to suffer any reverse upon the battlefield or lose any fortresses. They would drink and jump for joy within the fortress day and night, while the Muscovites mourned and wept.

On account of this Dmitry was yet more angered against the Germans, and straight away sent a verbal command to Kozelsk, ordering that the Germans living there, fifty-two persons in all, men and youths, be brought thither without stopping by day or night, and come in disfavour to Kaluga so that they, together with the Germans who were living in Kaluga, might be thrown into the Oka river without a hearing. This would indeed have happened if the pastor and chaplain of the Kozelsk Germans, Master Martin Beer of Neustadt (who had together with them been expelled from Kozelsk, so that he might suffer with them), had not interrogated everyone, from captain down to the humblest ranker, strictly enquiring of each one in person whether he had written to the Polish king before Smolensk, had received any letter from that quarter, or knew of any other kind of treasonous dealings in relation to Tsar Dmitry. If anyone knew of any such thing, he should testify on oath to it and not conceal anything, so that they might be ready for an investigation, which could proceed without danger or harm to them since none of them would be implicated.

After they had all together sworn under the open sky that they did not acknowledge any offence against the tsar, the pastor said in turn: "I swear that I do not know of any such treason against the tsar," and added: "Almighty God sees and hears all this. He knows that we are guiltless. So let us proceed without fear. God well knows His children, and no one can pluck them from His right hand. The tsar's heart is in His hands, and He will so govern him, that he will not do us any harm. He shall turn the crafty spirits of those who wish us ill to foolishness, and all these evil designs will be brought to nothing, if this is the will of God, however skilfully they go about it. God walks by other paths, and we are all in His right hand."

Although the pastor very much desired by these words to inspire the Germans with undismayed courage, most of them still remained troubled and sad, thinking of miraculous means to avoid death, for **life is natural and sweet, but death is grim and abhorrent.** At last they came to the Oka river, which flows by the city of Kaluga, where Dmitry held his court. Here the pastor ordered that the horses be left to graze upon the meadow and that the people wait for him there until he called them. Meanwhile he went over to the other side of the river to find out from some of his spiritual daughters within the tsaritsa's household what had been the cause of such mighty disfavour. He took with him Colonel Daniel Gilberts, Ensign Thomas Moritzon, and two nobles from Livonia, Johann von Reinen and Reinhold Engelhardt. They were ferried across the river and stole into the women's quarters, which caused the chief lady-in-waiting and all her damsels much consternation. They asked why he had come, and what business did he have with people in the court, and why had he not stayed at his own house, and they wept at the tsar's anger against the Germans, saying that no plea could move the tsar, and that all who had been brought hither were to die.

The pastor replied: "May the Lord help us now. He knows that we are guiltless. If we are fated to die, then we shall reconcile ourselves to it, for in truth we shall not suffer as transgressors but as Christians, who were often falsely denounced and killed but who nevertheless remained servants of God, Who in His time will judge and avenge all."

"The Russians," he continued, "also seized me, even though I am not in the tsar's service but that of God and my small congregation, and have not in any way sinned against the tsar but on the contrary I have prayed for him earnestly, together with my small congregation, that God might aid him. Now he is rewarding us in the same way that the world always rewards true Christians. Among us here there is not one who has sinned against the tsar in any way, for each one has sworn this to me on the way here, on pain of being deprived of his share of the heavenly kingdom. Therefore we have proceeded in peace, entrusting our ways to the All-merciful God, that He may do with us as He sees fit. If there are any among us whose conscience is unclean, they would have found out other ways and paths."

After that the pastor requested the chief lady-in-waiting and all her damsels to fall humbly upon their knees before the gracious tsaritsa and with pitiful pleas and tears move her to address the tsar to intercede for the Germans, not to the effect that he pardon traitors and those who had acted against him but that he should not cause the innocent and guilty to suffer together without a hearing. Let them also say that among those who had been brought there were a number of innocent youths and also their chaplain, the German pastor, and that many of them were blood relations, who had remained alive in these three years of war, of those who had laid down their lives on the battlefield in His Majesty's service, so that they would be the most unfortunate people in all of Russia were they now to be drowned. Let the gracious tsaritsa strive to convince His Majesty, with her most earnest pleas, that he sort out the guilty, and punish them in an exemplary fashion, but in the name of God to spare the innocent. The poor, deeply mourning German women, bending lower and even more devotedly, undertook to plead this cause to the tsar and tsaritsa.

With these instructions all the ladies-in-waiting together went to the tsaritsa with tears and sighs, so that neither old nor young could speak, and the tsaritsa almost burst into tears when she heard of this mission. She bade them rise, and said: "What, the Germans have come from Kozelsk?" Sighing, they replied: "Yes, the Russians have driven hither all the men and youths, and also their chaplain." They then plaintively narrated all that they had been instructed to say. The tsaritsa said: "My children, cease to weep. It is true that my lord has conceived great anger against them, as also against those who live in Kaluga, and has sworn not to admit a single one to his presence, and has also ordered that as soon as they arrive they are all to be taken to the Oka river and drowned, but all the same I shall try, on account of your lamentation and distress, and see if I can plead mercy for them this time."

To this end she sent one of her chamberlains to the bloodthirsty Prince Grigory Shakhovskoy, who had been entrusted with the execution of the tsar's wrath against the Germans. As soon as they arrived she sent word to him that, on pain of death and confiscation of all his property, he should hold back from carrying out the orders he had received until he heard from her further. She sent a second chamberlain to the tsar with instructions to ask His Majesty to deign come and have a word with her, but he refused, saying: "I know very well that she will intercede for her pagan Germans, so I shall not go. If they do not die today, I shall not be Dmitry, and if she pesters me too much, I shall order her to be drowned together with her Germans."

This angry and tyrannical reply greatly troubled the kind tsaritsa, and her women and damsels even more so. The tsaritsa said: "God knows what evil these men have done." One damsel fled with lamentations and sighs to the pastor, and told him what an ungracious reply the tsaritsa had received to her petition, and that there was no hope for mercy, for the tsar had said that they would all die, otherwise he would not be Dmitry.

The pastor replied: "So be it. Let God's will ever be done." He sent one of the nobles, named Reinhold Engelhardt, over the Oka to bring the others over to this side of the Oka, and to bring with them the ecclesiastical vessels so that first they might take the sacrament together and then in the name of God take up their cross and follow their Lord Jesus Christ. When they had arrived the pastor prayed and sang many prayers which he himself had composed in this extremity, and which may be found at the end of this book.[14]

Meanwhile the tsaritsa gathered together her ladies, and herself went to call upon her husband. Together with her ladies and damsels she threw herself to her knees before him, and with sighs and tears most humbly begged that he should not forgive scoundrels, brigands, and traitors, but also that he should not in unconsidered anger spill innocent blood lest he should have to repent of it later, even as he had had occasion to repent of the execution of the governor Skotnicki when he had discovered his innocence. Let him simply consider that fifty-two souls had come from Kozelsk, in addition to all those who lived in Kaluga. Among them were a pastor, some innocent youths, and also some married men, whose wives and children would be left in a pitiful state and would immediately cry and wail, complaining against him. He should not in his anger and without cause increase the number of widows and orphans and bring down upon himself their tears, sighs, complaints, and curses. If he knew of any traitors, he should single them out and punish them according to their deserts.

Although at first the tsar remained relentless and severe, in the end he was moved and won over by the pathetic words of the tsaritsa. He arose, went to her, took her by the hand and raised her up, also bidding the ladies-in-waiting to arise. He asked his valet how far Kozelsk was from Kaluga, and when he was told twelve miles, he remarked that even though that was so far, they had made the journey by evening. Only the previous day he had sent thither his command to bring them here. It seemed therefore that the princes and boyars in their hatred had accused them of more misdeeds than was possible. He also marvelled at the speed of their arrival. Turning to the tsaritsa, he said: "**So be it. These are your people, they have been pardoned.** Take them and do with them what you wish."

The Germans were assembled in great grief at my house, and each was preparing to make his confession and receive absolution and communion. The tsaritsa's senior chamberlain then came with this joyful mission, saying that we should no longer grieve but rejoice, for the tsar's wrath had abated. The tsaritsa had obtained clemency for us, and we should therefore render heartfelt thanks to Almighty God and the tsaritsa, and also pray for her and the tsar, that both might remain in good health and fortune. For the tsaritsa was to the Germans not only tsaritsa, but also a gracious mother, and all we Germans should behave in all things in such a manner that we might once again be considered faithful, obedient, and pious children.

The pastor replied on our behalf: "May the Lord God preserve our pious and most worthy tsaritsa and her gracious consort, our all-merciful tsar and lord, and may he have long life and health. We most humbly thank our kind and praiseworthy tsaritsa with all our hearts for all her great efforts and all her additional strivings on our behalf. We will call unceasingly upon the just God, and ask that in

His omnipotence He will give our all-gracious tsar and our all-gracious tsaritsa continual success and victory over all their enemies, and give them his paternal protection and defence against all their assaults. We also vow to be prepared at any time, without any hesitation, to put ourselves and our lives at his disposal for any service demanding loyalty, as before, by day or night, as the need arises. With the help of God we will in all places conduct ourselves so that His Majesty will never again have just cause for his disfavour."

After the chamberlain had departed, the pastor said: "Dear friends! This is the third time that we have been shamefully denounced and slandered before the tsar. We may again be denounced and slandered at a time when we will not have the opportunity to turn to the tsaritsa, and that would be the end of us, for whosoever is dead stays dead. Our wives and children will draw little consolation from the fact that we died guiltless. Let us present a petition to the tsaritsa, most sincerely and humbly thanking her for her constant and earnest intercession, thanks to which she saw to it that the tsar's wrath did not descend upon us, and we, the innocent along with the guilty, were not cast into the waters. And let us plead with the tsaritsa, since we know nothing about any treason towards the tsar, that she may by her pleas persuade His Majesty to summon those who denounced us, so that judgment can be rendered between us in the presence of all. If by letters or any other means any disloyalty or treason can be demonstrated or proven, then let us all, innocent as well as guilty, bear the punishment for it and die."

Since this counsel was pleasing to us all, such a petition was immediately drawn up for presentation to the tsaritsa. She read it through to herself and immediately transmitted it to the tsar. When the tsar had also read the petition, he smiled and said: "That is true, I never imagined **that my Germans were ever untrue to me.** For more than two years they have rendered me arduous and difficult service. **Tomorrow I shall do justice to them under the open sky, before all the community.**" This is in fact what occurred.

When on the following morning he was on his way to church for prayers, he cast his eyes upon some Germans, recognizing them at once and calling them by name. "You Germans from Kozelsk and Kaluga," he said, "have served me for long, and I have rewarded you well, granted you the estates of princes and boyars, and have also seen to it that you have not lacked for anything, and all of you have become rich men, as you yourselves must acknowledge and all your neighbours know. Now I have taken away these estates and distributed them among my princes and boyars, because you had betrayed me, were disloyal to me, since you offered the fortress of Kozelsk, where you live, to the pagan Polish king, and were wishing to go over to him. That is why I summoned you here and intended to drown you."

We bowed low before him, and said: "God give you, our tsar, good health! We are guiltless, we have shed our blood for you, we have served you loyally and do not know of any treason. We have never even contemplated doing what is alleged against us to Your Majesty. We do not beg for mercy if we are guilty; that is why we are standing here and, **for God's sake, are demanding a trial.** Whosoever among us is guilty, punish him according to his deserts, only command our accusers to say their piece before us, so that we may hear of what they have accused us before Your Majesty, and we can refute the charges."

The tsar descended the steps with his lords and said: "Here are some of them before your eyes." He pointed to the princes and boyars, and said: "We were informed of this by the governor of Kozelsk and several priests, boyars, townspeople, and peasants." We replied: "All are subject to Your Majesty, whether princes, boyars, governors, priests, townspeople and peasants, even as we foreigners are. Let them make amends to us, otherwise put them in our place."

The tsar meanwhile mounted his horse, turned to his lords and said: "**I see the innocence of my foreigners** and reject what you have falsely and treasonably alleged against them. Mark well what they say. If you have letters, or if any of you has knowledge of them, then come forward." And since they had none, nor could they produce any, they abused us foreigners, saying: "*Yebti matir, latushi,*"[15] that is to say: "You German lads fuck your mothers, etc. We are the inhabitants of this land, you are our guests, not we yours."

Then the tsar spoke kindly to us and said: "**I see that you have been treated unjustly, and that my lords are hostile towards you and hate you.** What has been taken away from you shall be restored in full." At the same time he said to the Russians: "You princes and boyars, **return them their estates**, for the sake of which you have subjected these honest folk to such peril that if God had not decreed otherwise you would by now be rejoicing at their destruction. You Germans, henceforth be as loyal to me as you have been hitherto and I will give you even more estates and, apart from that, you will no longer have to live in Kozelsk among your enemies. Live here in Kaluga so that you will be in my presence, and my princes and boyars will leave you in peace." **Thus out of evil came good, and great honour for the just, but the great evil-doers were brought to shame.**

On the return journey the pastor said to his flock: "Dear friends, let us not despise the means whereby we may extricate ourselves from misfortune. We heard plainly enough from the tsar that we are surrounded by our enemies, who covet our houses and homesteads and all that is in them. I shall abandon these transitory goods and be the first to bring his wife and children hither, and then seize the first opportunity to move on. Whosoever is like-minded, let him prepare himself for the morrow. Let us not tempt God, we have been crucified enough. He who loves danger will die through it.[16] God will assuredly not leave such murderous people unpunished. May the scourge come hither when it listeth!"

Several people then went with the pastor, brought thence their wives and children, and lived peacefully with the tsar in the city of Kaluga. Those who did not heed the faithful-hearted admonition and heed the warning in God's word but thought more on avarice, thinking that subsistence in Kaluga would cost them too dear whereas upon their estates it would cost them nothing, preferring to remain there in Kozelsk among the blasphemers and persecutors of Christ, were shortly thereafter, together with the godless barbarian people, visited by the scourge of God.

There were four thousand freebooters[17] who had been serving the Polish king before Smolensk, who left the king's camp with the intention of roaming throughout the land in search of plunder. On 1 September they quickly, suddenly, and completely unexpectedly appeared before Kozelsk, which at that time had no garrison. When they became aware of this, they attacked so skilfully that within two hours they had captured the town and fortress, killing in the process seven thousand persons, both old and young, reducing the town and fortress to ashes. The princes and boyars, along with the Germans, those who refused to put their trust in their pastor's sincere words of caution and had remained there in Kozelsk, were there led off captive, together with their wives and children. Many of them were severely wounded, and they had to leave all their property to the whim of fate.

What happened to the women and girls who fell into the hands of these Polish freebooters is, alas, not difficult to imagine. None of this would have happened if they had heeded their pastor's advice and gone to live with him and the other Germans in Kaluga. So perished the persecutors and enemies of the Germans through God's wondrous providence, in such a swift fashion that they who before had sought to destroy the innocent were destroyed themselves, and together with their families were shamed and brought to nothing, for which may dear God constantly be praised.

XIX Concerning Shuisky's Deposition; Also the Destruction of the Second Dmitry and the Election of Lord Wladyslaw, Son of King Sigismund of Poland

After Zolkiewski, as has been previously narrated, was fortunate in winning a victory at Klushino, and had driven the Muscovites from the battlefield, and had overcome de la Gardie's Germans who had not been relieved, and induced Valuev in Tsarevo-Zaimishche to come over to the king, the city of Moscow was tightly blockaded in the direction of Mozhaisk. News also came to Moscow that the second Dmitry with his troops at the Ugra had struck camp and taken to the field again, had forcibly taken the monastery of St Paphnutius, had killed all the monks, priests, princes, boyars, and the five hundred musketeers who had been dispatched there from Moscow, and had plundered and burned the monastery. Because of this the Muscovites were greatly afraid that they would be besieged again, this time by two enemies simultaneously, when they had only just been liberated from the last long siege.

Therefore three prominent boyars, who had long been in collusion with Zolkiewski and had become proper Poles, namely Zakhar Liapunov, Mikhail Molchanov, and Ivan Rzhevsky,[1] decided to stage an uprising against Shuisky. On 14 July they came out onto the platform on the Red Square,[2] where the most important matters are deliberated upon, summoned the people together, bewailed the sad and lamentable state of the Muscovite land and how it had been devastated as wolves devour a sheepfold, how Christians had been so horribly annihilated, and how there was nobody who could or would defend the country.

Everyone could well see that for the third year Tsar Shuisky was having neither success nor luck in his governance, since he had seized power by such irregular means. On this account many hundreds of thousands had lost their lives and there was to be no end to the bloodshed as long as he sat upon the throne. Moreover, whenever he or his brothers engaged the enemy in battle, they always suffered defeat and abandoned the battlefield. The land was being destroyed and brought to nothing, people were perishing, and no end to the war was in sight. If perchance their words carried any weight, they would earnestly counsel the Christian community to set Shuisky aside and, with unanimous consent of all the estates, choose another tsar, who would be elected and chosen by God.

The common people were not at all displeased at this, saying: "The advice is good, so now we must bring it to fruition." Then these three boyars, hearing that the common people were favourably disposed, ordered all the people to proceed to the fortress and summon Shuisky's senators to appear before the people, and announce to them their intention, which is exactly what happened, though many[3] important people and merchants were not pleased.

The common multitude rushed together with the three aforementioned boyars to Shuisky in the palace. They took the imperial crown and sceptre from him and laid them aside, and he himself was led out of the royal palace and out of the fortress altogether, to his former house. They tonsured the crown of his head, placed a cowl and skull cap on him, and against his will and inclination made him a monk.[4]

On the next day they all gathered in the open air outside the city on that side which was not blockaded, so that each of the estates might deliberate as to who of the prominent lords should be chosen as the new tsar. Since one cast his vote for one candidate, another for another, and so on, several people emerged from the crowd, saying: "Out of all this high estate of princes, from whom it is befitting that a tsar be chosen, there is not one who could exalt himself and say that he is higher or more exalted than the others. If we now choose one of them to be tsar of all the land, then all the others will hate and privily work against him, for nobody willingly swears allegiance to his equal, as we have all well seen from the example of Boris Fedorovich Godunov. If people had not envied his high estate and persecuted him but let him enjoy the crown and sceptre, then the present misfortune and divisions would not have overtaken this land. Therefore we propose that it would be more prudent **to choose a completely foreign prince**, who would inherit royal status from his father and mother and would not have any equal in this land. Both the lords of our land and the rest of us would justly make our obedience and submission to him.

It is true and well known that there are many worthy princes and lords in the Holy Roman Empire worthy to take over our realm. But there is no better placed neighbouring sovereign more suitable in speech, customs, and clothing, than the King of Poland, Sigismund III. He has a son, Wladyslaw, who is a fine, young, and pious lord. His father is the son of a King of Sweden, his lady mother is from the Imperial stem of the Holy Roman Empire. Let us choose him as our tsar and hand over our realm to him, so that we may receive peace and tranquillity. If not, let us choose another. It will be equally good if he be willing, so that there might be an end to this bloodshed.[5]

Concerning the present Dmitry, it is known to everyone that he is a brigand, deceiver, and tempter, that he was a schoolmaster in White Russia and the servant of a parish priest, and is more deserving of the gallows and wheel than a crown and sceptre.

If all the lords in this Christian assembly are now like-minded, then we must deliberate upon the conditions under which we will hold this election, in order that we may retain our rights, customs, practices, and forms of worship. We should not be subjected to any novelties, and attention should also be paid as to what else might be conducive to the welfare of our country and ourselves. Let the lords without delay inform us what they, in their opinion, think best."

Then all the estates cried out that such a counsel was good and it would be prudent to pursue it, after which they returned in harmony and gladness to the city, concluded an armistice with Zolkiewski, the king's commander, announced their intention to him, and sent their ambassadors to the king before Smolensk, to inform His Majesty that they had decided to choose as their tsar his son WLADYSLAW, earnestly begging His Majesty that he graciously give his consent and approval and help them further this end and co-operate with them in all that was necessary to bring about a successful conclusion to this matter, so that they would once again receive a constant tsar, and they themselves might be delivered from the internecine struggles, bloody war, and ruin of the country and finally return to a state of blessed peace and tranquillity.[6]

The king gave the ambassadors a gracious reply, was favourably inclined to the matter, and sent his most trusted counsellor to his military commander Zolkiewski[7] at Moscow, giving the latter plenipotentiary powers and authority to carry on negotiations with the Muscovites as he thought best. His Majesty undertook to approve any undertakings and without any reservations to fulfil all that Zolkiewski agreed to with the Muscovites, and on which he would irrevocably swear to them.

Only two points were excepted and reserved, namely that, first, under no circumstances should he be rebaptized or converted to the Muscovite faith, and secondly, that he should have a court, since His Majesty would not entrust his own solely to the Russians. In return, the Russians would keep and preserve inviolate their religion, customs, usages, statutes, and laws, and under the rule of his son they would prosper and flourish, not fade and diminish.

The Muscovites were very content and satisfied with these conditions, which both sides swore to observe; the Muscovites that they would accept and acknowledge Lord WLADYSLAW as their sovereign, and would honour and swear fidelity to him provided he kept the conditions of the treaty. Zolkiewski swore on behalf of the king's son, Lord WLADYSLAW, that the aforementioned clauses would also be preserved inviolate and Wladyslaw would soon come in person, accept the tsardom, and begin his reign.

After all this had been achieved Zolkiewski, together with his followers and officers, was conducted to the tsar's palace within the fortress and was splendidly entertained and honoured with valuable presents, after which he and his suite were accommodated in special apartments as befitted the representative of the tsar. The remainder returned to their quarters in the camp.

There followed a period of good and peaceful relations between the Poles and the Muscovites, the latter going to the Poles in the camp and the Poles coming into the city. They carried on all manner of transactions with each other, and there was great amity and unity between them. The second Dmitry, to whom several boyars and Cossacks came running out of Moscow, was told of this election and reconciliation. They also brought good news, namely that the lesser people of Moscow were on his side and that, if he approached the city, they would create dissension within against the greater people, and when that had started, he should co-ordinate his attack and so easily capture the city. Dmitry advanced with his Poles, Germans, Cossacks, Russians, and Tatars from the monastery of St Paphnutius, pitching his camp between Moscow and the Kolomenskoe monastery[8] in the firm hope that such disorder as he had been told of would begin in Moscow and the lesser people would declare for him and he would come to their assistance and gain victory over the entire city.

But his hopes were frustrated; he was fishing behind the nets. The Muscovites daily made sorties, bravely engaged his people and held out valiantly, from which it became apparent to him that the matter was not going as planned. Therefore he ordered that on the next day, when the Muscovites came out, his soldiers should surround them on all sides and strike them hard.

That is what happened when the Muscovites next ventured out, and they were so soundly thrashed that they scarcely knew how they got back into the city. From that day they did not dare come out except when accompanied by several hundred Polish lancers from Zolkiewski's encampment. Accompanied by these, they attacked Dmitry's encampment with all their forces.

When Dmitry perceived what company he had, and that many hundreds of Polish lancers were under the Muscovite banner, he quickly saw how things were shaping and that his hopes were in vain, and especially that his own Poles did not enter the fray with much bravery and daring. He once again beat a retreat, and on St Bartholomew's Day[9] withdrew to Kaluga with great shame and ignominy but with only a small army, several hundred Cossacks and the Romanov Tatars.[10]

The Poles, however, once they had in this manner helped the Muscovites repel their enemy Dmitry, took advantage of this situation and stealthily, day by day, gradually and further infiltrated more men into Moscow, until they had a force of five thousand men within, as well as eight hundred foreign mercenaries. The latter were stationed in the Kremlin, in the citadel, which is the best fortress in Moscow, called "the seat of empire,"[11] and they had at their disposal powder, shot, and all kinds of munitions.

The five thousand were stationed in the bailey and within the third wall, which in fact encompasses the city proper, and did not wish to be quartered in any other place, nor could they be persuaded or compelled to return to their encampment, as the Muscovites would have wished, because it was warmer here and better than out in the field. They received fodder and flour for themselves, their servants, and their horses, and also monthly payment out of the Muscovite treasury, because of which the treasury became even more emptied and exhausted than it had been under Shuisky.

Dmitry was greatly displeased by this latest reverse, for once again the Poles had played him false and his fellow-countrymen, the Russians, had told him a pack of lies. Expecting no good from the one group or the other, he said to himself: "I must hire Turks and Tatars to help me recover my birthright,[12] otherwise I shall obtain nothing. If I do not win these possessions, I shall waste and destroy them, so that they will be almost worthless. As long as I am alive, Russia shall never be at peace."

Thereafter he sent Pan Kernozicki, one of the few Poles remaining with him, who was more devoted to Dmitry than to the Poles, to the Tatar tsardom (as the Muscovites call it, though it is only a kingdom) of Astrakhan, situated five hundred miles from Moscow. He was to be Dmitry's John the Baptist and forerunner,[13] having to prepare the way to Astrakhan through the uninhabited steppes, and was to present his greetings and express his great favour to the inhabitants of Astrakhan, and tell them that he and his tsaritsa were coming to them and would keep their court among them for this reason, that the Muscovite and Severian lands had been so polluted by non-Christians.[14]

If this journey had been made, things would have gone even worse with Russia, but God did not wish it so and in a miraculous fashion averted this catastrophe. He deprived Dmitry of his reason and contrived it so that he behaved tyrannically even towards those few Tatars and Cossacks who were his most loyal and beloved warriors, who guarded him day and night, accompanied him on the hunt and in other diversions, and were dearer and closer to him than any German or Pole. He secretly ordered the Tatar Khan of Kasimov privily to be cast into the Oka river and drowned, because this khan's very own son had maliciously and falsely denounced him to Dmitry, saying that he wished to depart and go over to Moscow.

When the Tatar prince Peter Urusov heard of this cruel murder, he was greatly incensed at Dmitry and at the son of the drowned Tatar khan, who was the source of this treason against his own father and the original cause of his death.[15] This Urusov decided to stalk him by night in Kaluga and kill him as he left the tsar's house and was going home. But he encountered another prominent Tatar, who in dress and appearance was very similar, and took off his head with his sabre. Dmitry, to whom this was reported, and to whom a complaint was carried against Peter Urusov, ordered him to be cast into prison, even though he had great affection for him, especially since he knew the roads to Astrakhan very well.

He also ordered fifty other Tatars to be placed under arrest and severely tortured for several days. But subsequently he restored them to favour, reinstated them in all their former positions, and trusted them as much as before, taking them with him on hunting expeditions and sending them out on reconnaissance, not only to find out information about the king's army but also, if they chanced upon any Polish soldiers or merchants on the highways, or Polish serfs or servitors on estates belonging to their masters, to seize them and send them to him in Kaluga with all they had.

The Tatars discharged this service obediently and diligently, regardless of the fact that they bore in their hearts towards Dmitry, on account of the shameful and disgraceful manner in which he had treated them, a hatred which nevertheless they concealed skilfully for nearly two months, and then took fearful revenge upon him, as will be related hereafter. They frequently each brought ten, eleven, or twelve Poles, whom they had taken from their beds at dead of night on their estates, and many merchants whom they had encountered on the highways with rich wares and all kinds of goods. Several of these Poles, at Dmitry's command, were deprived of their lives in a pitiful and tyrannical fashion. Almost every morning there were found in the marketplace six to twelve corpses of those who had been killed during the previous night, being mercilessly wounded, hacked to pieces, and tortured to death, then cast out under the open sky for so long that they were half devoured by dogs, and then were taken away and buried secretly in a ditch. They were mostly well-born and respectable people.

Many of the Polish soldiers and merchants so captured were, as soon as they were brought to Kaluga, taken to the Oka river and immediately thrown live into the water and drowned. The Tatars showed so much zeal in the task of seizing the Poles, and showed such enthusiasm for each and every service, that Dmitry thought they had forgotten the imprisonment and ignominy and trusted them even more. While going out hunting or riding he took with him only his jester Peter Koshelev, an utter villain and bloodhound, and two or three of his household servants, but never any of the Germans, Poles, or Russian boyars,[16] but twenty or thirty Tatars. He entrusted his person to them, not being mindful of the proverb: "Watch out if even your own horse runs away."[17]

These Tatars often came and went with him and were very diligent and servile, all the while waiting for the chance and opportunity. Then they gave instructions to all the Tatar army to be at the ready with all that they had, and that the next time that the tsar went hunting, they should move their families secretly out of Kaluga and themselves leave, so that none remained there. They should make for the Pchelna river and wait there until Peter Urusov came to them from the tsar's hunt to lead them out of Russia to their homeland of Tatary.

The eleventh of December was an infamous and unfortunate day, especially for this Dmitry. On this morning he made an excursion by sled, taking with him, according to his previous custom, only his jester Peter Koshelev, two servants, a Tatar prince, and twenty other Tatars. When the other Tatars learned of this, they all left, some by one gate, others by another, together with their wives and children, taking with them all that they could carry, and assembled at the Pchelna. There were more than a thousand assembled, not counting women and children.

When Dmitry had gone out into the open country, at a distance of a quarter mile, the pent-up hatred of the Tatars was suddenly unleashed. The Tatar prince Peter Urusov, having loaded his musket with two bullets, came as close as he could to Dmitry's sled, flattered him and spoke with him so submissively that Dmitry could not suspect anything amiss. The prince, however, who had carefully prepared the attack, fired at Dmitry, who was seated in the sled, and for good measure seized his sabre and took off his head, saying: "**I will teach you how to drown Tatar tsars in the river and throw Tatar princes into prison.** You were just a mean and worthless Muscovite, **a traitor and a rascal.** You claimed to be the rightful heir to the land, and we served you loyally. **See, now I have placed upon you the very hereditary crown to which you are entitled.**" The jester Peter Koshelev and the two servants, not wishing to see any more of this tragic coronation, slipped away, hurried to Kaluga, and related how they had been at this unusual and evil hunting expedition and ambush, and how the Tatar prince had crowned Tsar Dmitry.

After Prince Peter Urusov had so craftily placed the hereditary crown upon Dmitry's head, he moved off, together with his Tatars, out of Russia back to Tatary, taking with them all they could carry. In Kaluga they signalled by cannon fire that something was amiss and that they should assemble quickly within the city. But by the time they had gathered, the Tatars were already far off, and so it was impossible to pursue or capture them.

Nevertheless a small number of Tatars remained in Kaluga, largely because they had known nothing about this conspiracy, nor did they have horses on which they could have made so long a journey. These poor people were pursued like hares in the field from one street to another, and when they were too exhausted to run any further, they were hacked or beaten to death with swords or clubs and thrown like dogs into a single heap, having to pay the price of the others' deeds, even though they had not heard a word of what was afoot, for if they had, surely they would have betaken themselves elsewhere like the others.

After this Tatar hare-hunt, the princes, boyars, Cossacks, and townspeople came out to view the hunting ground, found their Tsar Dmitry in two pieces and lying clad only in his shirt, placed him back in the sled and brought him to the tsaritsa within the fortress, where he was washed spotlessly clean, brought into a hall, and laid out on a large table; his head was replaced on his body so that anyone who wished could come and look upon him.

A few days later he was buried according to the Muscovite rite in the castle church at Kaluga. There he remains to this day and as long as the world endures, one generation after another will call him to mind and forever thank the Tatar prince for so signally bestowing upon him a fitting crown, and putting an end to his frenzy, on account of which there was so much misfortune, murder, and death in all of Russia.

How grievous and sad a day was this 11 December for the pious tsaritsa, Maryna Yurievna, can easily be imagined, for in the space of just a few years both her husbands had been slain one after another, the first Dmitry on 17 May 1606 in Moscow, and the second here in Kaluga on 11 December 1610, when she was in the last months of her pregnancy. Shortly after this she gave birth to a son, whom the Russian lords, with her agreement and consent, took from her, promising to rear him in secrecy, lest he be killed by his persecutors and, if God gave him life, he would in the future be tsar of Russia. The tsaritsa herself was at that time entertained and honoured in imperial fashion.[18]

What new tumults and uproar her son will cause Russia when he grows up, if God preserves his life, those who are alive twenty years from now will know, if in the meantime the Muscovites, according to their practice, do not destroy him. On account of this, he will live in great danger. This second Dmitry perished by a fearful death, nor did he attain the rulership after which he had striven for so long, and for which he had fought against Shuisky and spilled so much blood. Dmitry lost his life and Shuisky his crown and sceptre and, instead of a monarch, he became a monk against his will. The king's son in Poland was chosen as Tsar of All the Russias, so the prize for which the two of them had been contending was given to the third without contest, but he did not keep it long, as will soon be related.

Shortly after Shuisky had been deposed from the imperial dignity, the Muscovites sent him and his two brothers, Dmitry and Ivan Ivanovich Shuisky, together with the most noble princes of the Golitsyn family, as prisoners to the king of Poland before Smolensk. He sent them further on into Poland, where they were also held captive.

Some reliable witnesses, who had been sent as deputies of the city of Riga in Livonia to the Diet, were present at the time, and saw and heard it, and affirm that at the recent Diet at Warsaw, in Poland, which took place recently at Martinmas in 1611, an ambassador of the Turkish emperor was present, whom, it is said, His Majesty the King of Poland one day entertained and showed great honour. When this ambassador expressed a great desire to see the Russian tsar, and persisted in this request, his wish was granted. They brought Shuisky, splendidly dressed in Muscovite costume, and seated him opposite at the ambassador's table. The Turkish ambassador looked and gazed upon Tsar Shuisky for a long time, and at length praised the good fortune of the Polish king, in that he had held Maximilian[19] as prisoner for several years, and now held the mighty Russian monarch in his power.

Shuisky, who took these words very much to heart, apparently answered the ambassador in these words: "Do not be surprised that I, a former potentate, am now sitting here, since this is the work of inconstant fortune, and if the Polish king conquers my Russia, he will then be the most powerful ruler in the world, so even your sovereign could be sitting where I am sitting now. As the saying goes, **today it is my turn, tomorrow yours.**"[20]

The Turkish ambassador apparently made no answer, but in the course of the following year, 1612, the Turkish emperor sent the Polish king a dreadful missive containing a declaration of war. As can be seen from it and as it bears witness, it was partly inspired by the reply of the captive tsar:

HERE FOLLOWS THE TURKISH EMPEROR'S LETTER CONTAINING THE DECLARATION OF WAR AGAINST THE KING OF POLAND

"Sultan Akhmet Khan, the Most Illustrious, son of the Great Emperor, Son of the Highest God, Emperor of the Turks, Greeks, Babylonians, Macedonians, Sarmatians, King of Upper and Lower Egypt, Alexandria, India, and also lord and monarch of all the peoples and inhabitants of the earth, sovereign and illustrious son of Muhammad, protector and defender of the cities of Persia and the Earthly Paradise, protector and defender of the tomb of the Earthly God, King of Kings, Emperor of Emperors, Prince of Princes, lord of all the earthly gods and all who will never be seen on this earth, lord of the Tree of Life and the Holy City of God, as well as the cities of the Red Sea, Lord and Inheritor of all Inheritors, sends greetings to you the King of Poland.

You have taken counsel with your petty kings and princes, and have opposed us, the powerful and invincible Emperor, whom no man on earth has defeated, and have heeded ill-considered and reckless counsel to do evil, and not fearing, together with these petty kings, princes, and nobles, to do any evil, even though up to now you have only spoken to us of friendship, peace, and alliance, now you have turned and declared war upon us. Therefore, I will invade your country, since you do not wish to keep the peace, and am confident of defeating you. I shall attack your possessions with my followers, plundering, looting, killing, burning, and devastating at will.

Be aware of the power I can raise within my dominions, which I have held from the beginning of the world, and will hold until its end. With this power I shall subject you to my way, O petty kings, and I shall establish my throne in Cracow, and you shall see it with your very eyes. And do not count on living in peace with us, for I do not fear your subjects, and I shall leave my memorial in your kingdom, that I can promise you.

In perpetual memory of which I send you a naked bloody sword, a bloody spear, and a bloody bullet. I shall so trample your land with all my horses and camels that it will be known and famed throughout the world and among all the peoples of the earth. As God has avenged himself and vented His wrath upon those who swear oaths and perfidiously break them, so shall I, the earthly God and equal of God himself, also punish and prove your faith, and shall so execute judgement before I write again. All this you can deliberate upon and comprehend at your convenience. If you do not comprehend, then you will feel it.

SULTAN AKHMET KHAN

The All-Illustrious Emperor."

---

xx What Occurred in the Year 1611 in Russia, Especially in the Capital City of Moscow, and Why the Polish King Did Not Allow His Son Wladyslaw, Who Had Been Chosen Russian Tsar, to Proceed Thither, and What Great Misfortune and Irreparable Harm Resulted Therefrom

After the death of the second Dmitry, all the towns and fortresses that had been under his sway and had assisted him against Moscow wrote the following to the inhabitants of Moscow: that their sins (as they are proverbially wont to say) had caught up with them and Dmitry, who had claimed to be the true tsarevich, had been a scourge for them and the whole Russian land. They wished to make their peace again with the inhabitants of Moscow and live in harmony with them, provided that once again they would expel from the city the pagan Polish army, those un-Christians, so that thereby unfortunate Russia might once again be pacified, and Christian blood cease to be shed within her borders. The inhabitants of Moscow were very pleased with this, and thanked them for having come to their senses and being willing to turn over a new leaf, and urged them not to refuse to swear allegiance to Lord WLADYSLAW, to whom they themselves had already sworn allegiance, so that thereby the land might once again be at unity with itself.

Together with this letter, the inhabitants of Moscow secretly sent yet another letter with the following content: Let them not refuse to administer the oath of allegiance to the king's son in the presence of all the people, for in that way the internecine struggle which for so long had divided them would be pacified and the Russian land once again united. All the same, let them consider privately how they might destroy underhandedly those Poles who had estates within their districts, or lived within their towns, and so diminish the number of unbelievers in the land.

They themselves, the Muscovite community, were strong enough to take care of the Poles in their midst, and would deal with them when the time was ripe. Even though they were clad in steel armour and helmets, they could beat all of them to death with cudgels. After this, on 2 January 1611, the towns and fortresses took the oath and swore allegiance to the elected tsar, Lord WLADYSLAW, which deceived the Poles yet further,[1] but the proverb "Evil counsel is even worse for the counsellor"[2] in the end recoiled upon the perfidious Muscovites, as will be related hereafter.

On 25 January, the feast of the Conversion of St Paul, the populace in Moscow assembled and complained that Polish soldiers caused them great hardship, did all kinds of violence to them, mocked their religious services, dishonoured their saints by firing upon them with muskets, beat their brethren, and treated them with force and arrogance within their own houses, and furthermore were exhausting the tsar's treasury, levying contributions upon the people so that every month money was being disbursed to pay six thousand soldiers, while all the time the elected WLADYSLAW had yet to appear.

They also said they should consider how to change all this, for it was becoming obvious that the king was about to devastate, not strengthen, their land, as could readily be understood from the fact that, despite his oath, he had not yet allowed his son to travel to Moscow. Therefore they declared openly to the lieutenant and governor of the king, Lord Gasiewski, and all his colonels and captains, that they should see to it that the chosen tsar arrived within a matter of days, otherwise, if they knew what was good for them, they should go back to where they had come from or they would be chased out and the Muscovites would find an alternative groom for such a stately bride.

Lord Gasiewski answered them calmly, and asked them to reconsider and not stir up misfortune for themselves, and also not to worry, for the king had many concerns within his kingdom, but wished to equip his son for the journey in such a manner as was fitting, both for the kingdom of Poland and for the tsardom of Russia. Furthermore, he wanted first to reduce and occupy the fortress of Smolensk, since this city had of old belonged to the Polish crown, so that there might not later be a dispute with his son over it.

He, Gasiewski, promised to write to His Majesty requesting that the young ruler be dispatched as quickly as possible; meanwhile, in the king's name, he would sit in judgment over the Poles who had committed wrong. Let the Muscovites present their complaints, and they would be shown justice. Thereupon several immediately complained against a certain Polish noble, who three times when intoxicated had fired upon the image of St Mary, whom they call *Prechista*, that is to say, the Intercessor,[3] at the Sretensk Gates, and said that if he were punished they would for the time being forget about the other injuries.

The governor immediately ordered this man arrested and subsequently condemned to death. He was led to the aforementioned gate and first both his hands were cut off at the block and nailed to the wall before the image of St Mary. He himself was brought out through the same gates and was burned to ashes in the middle of the marketplace.

Then Lord Gasiewski ordered a letter to be read out to the people, saying that His Majesty, the chosen tsar Lord Wladyslaw, would soon come to Moscow. They should earnestly petition him. His Majesty had ordered strict judgment, to put an end to indiscipline, to protect the Muscovites, and not transgress their religion. This was what had just occurred before the eyes of all, as an example of what would happen in the case of any indiscipline among the Poles. In this manner the Muscovites were to have been pacified and assured that henceforth all would be well.

Even though this appeared to have pacified the Muscovites, all the same the Poles were on their guard, for some of them already knew that the Muscovites could not be trusted very far. Therefore they kept a strong and vigilant watch in full armour, day and night, on all the gates, and forbade the Russians to carry any arms. They searched any carts or sleds that entered, to see if there were any concealed weapons. The Muscovites protested at this, but the Poles replied: "We are only a handful as opposed to your whole community. It is only right that we should be wary and keep on our guard. We do not intend any evil towards you, but you Muscovites mean us no good. We are not about to pick any quarrel with you, nor have we received any such order from our sovereign. Just keep calm and do not yourselves start any trouble, and you will have nothing to fear."

The Muscovites, however, were very vexed that the Poles had deprived them of their advantage. They hung their heads and said among themselves: "If things are so now, how will it be when yet more of these calfheads arrive? From their conduct it is plain that they wish to subjugate and lord it over us, and this we must prevent before it is too late. It is true that we have chosen a Polish tsar, but this does not mean that each and every Pole should be lord over us. If so, we Muscovites will all perish, unless we are masters in our own house.

"The king, the old dog,[4] has tarried for a whole year with his son, the puppy,[5] who has yet to come here. So let him stay away for good. We do not wish to have him as our ruler, and if these six thousand pigtails[6] do not take themselves off willingly, we will beat them out like dogs, even though they have the great advantage of us. We have seven hundred thousand inhabitants,[7] so if we undertake something in earnest, we will have something to show for it."

They mocked the Poles to their faces as they stood on sentry duty, or as they strolled along the streets towards the marketplace to buy what they needed. "Ah, pigtails," said the Muscovites, "it will not be long before the dogs tug at your pigtails and calfheads, nor will it be otherwise unless you willingly clear out of our city." When a Pole bought something, he had to pay twice the price a Muscovite paid or go away empty-handed. From this it could be observed how much the Poles were hated. Several prudent Poles spoke fairly to them, saying: "Keep mocking us, we are prepared to put up with a lot from you, nor will we be the cause of any bloodshed between us, unless we are extremely provoked. But if you should start something, take care that you do not regret it later." So they went away amid great mockery and ridicule.

On 13 February several Polish nobles commanded their squires[8] to buy oats in the grain market, which lies on the other side of the Moskva river, and one of these guides paid particular attention to how much the Russians paid for a cask and then measured out a full cask and offered to pay for it a Polish florin, the same as the Russians were paying. When the Muscovite profiteer would not be satisfied with one guilder but demanded two guilders for each cask, the squire said: "You mother-fucking Muscovite son of a bitch.[9] You Muscovite whoreson, fuck your mother, why are you fleecing us Poles? Are we not your lord's men?" The Muscovite answered: "If you do not wish to pay two florins a cask, take your money back, and let me sell my oats to a better market. No Pole shall buy from me. You can go to the Devil."

Whereupon the Polish servitor, enraged at this, seized his sabre and wished to strike the grain profiteer; but forty or fifty Muscovites rushed on the scene, armed with sleigh runners, and beat three Polish squires to death, and gathered together such a large crowd that the Polish mounted guards who were stationed at the pontoon by the watergate were ordered to go and investigate what was happening. When the Polish servitors caught sight of them, they ran towards the Polish guards, pursued by many Muscovites armed with sleigh runners and cudgels. They called upon the guards to help them, saying that three of them had already been slain without any provocation except that they had wanted to know why Poles had to pay two florins for a cask of oats whereas the Russians only had to pay one. Then twelve Polish soldiers attacked many hundreds of Muscovites in the marketplace. They killed fifteen of them and emptied the marketplace.

When all this became known in the suburb, and in that part of the city which is enclosed by the white encircling wall, there rushed into the streets an innumerable crowd of people, who spoke very ill of the Poles, saying that they had shot so many of their brethren. The Devil would soon have had his sport on this day had not this been forestalled and prevented by the lieutenant, or governor. He pronounced a moving oration before the whole community and warned them earnestly against inflicting any harm.

"You Muscovites," he said, "you consider yourselves to be the best Christians in the world. Why do you not fear God, but are so athirst to spill blood and become traitors and perjurers? Doubtless you think that God will not punish you for it? Assuredly He will do so. You will experience God's scourge. You have killed so many of our rulers. You have only just elected our king's son as your ruler, sworn obedience and fidelity to him, yet, now that he cannot come as speedily as you would wish, you abuse him and his father. You call him a puppy, and his Lord father an old dog. The Lord in heaven has commanded that you honour him as His vicegerent on earth, but you give him less honour than if he were one of your swineherds. Now you do not wish to observe your oath, you also do not want him as your ruler, whom you have elected of your own free will, and even earnestly had begged the king to give his consent thereto and allow his son to become your tsar, for which reason you received us into your fortress. You murder his people, not considering that it is we who have saved you from your enemy, the second Dmitry. What you are doing to Lord WLADYSLAW, your lord and ours, you are not doing to an ordinary mortal but to God himself, Who will not be mocked.

Do not rely, my dear sirs, on your might, on the strength of your numbers, on the fact that we are only six thousand against your seven hundred thousand. Victory does not depend upon masses or numbers of men but on the intercession and aid of Almighty God. He can help the few as easily as He can help the many, of which many numerous examples can be cited, as you yourselves indeed have experienced in recent times when more than once you in your thousands were defeated in the field by an insignificant force. Think, dear sirs, for what reason are you fomenting all this unrest? You are the servants and subjects also of him whom we serve. Your ruler is our ruler. If now you wish to embark upon murder and bloodshed, truly God will not give you any success in it but will intervene on our behalf, as for his own small army, for our cause is just and we will go into battle in the name of our sovereign."

Then some of the common multitude interrupted the lieutenant's speech, saying: "Now you are just a morsel for us. We do not need to take up arms or cudgels, but could stone you to death within an hour with our felt hats."

He answered: "Dear sirs, you could not even beat a whore to death with a felt hat, let alone well-armed heroes and well-trained soldiers. By all means cast and throw your felt hats at six thousand whores in vain, but what would happen if you came up against the valour of six thousand armed soldiers? I beg, implore and beseech you in all earnest, do not start a bloodbath."

Thereupon they answered: "So go away from here and vacate our fortress and our city."

He answered yet again: "Our oath will not permit it, nor were we placed here by our sovereign in order to flee at your convenience but in order to remain here until he arrives."

They said: "Then in the next few days none of you will be left alive."

He replied: "It will be according to God's will, not yours. If you start something you cannot finish in the way you want, then may God have mercy upon you and upon your children. I have given you enough warning. We will let you deliberate, while we set our affairs in order. If God is with us, you will not be able to overcome us." With these words he left and went back into the fortress, while the people dispersed stiff-necked and hard of heart.

After this several weeks went by, yet nothing was heard of Wladyslaw's coming but, on the contrary, it was said secretly that His Majesty the king did not wish to entrust his son to a perfidious people. They became even more enraged and incensed, especially when on *Judica* Sunday[10] the governor and officers demanded provisions and money for their soldiers. At that time the Muscovites did not wish to feed them anything but powder and lead, but told them to go to their lord and demand remuneration from him. They also shamefully mocked those Muscovite lords who were supporting the king, namely Mikhail Glebovich Saltykov, Fedor Andronov, Ivan Tarasievich Gramotin, and several others, demanding that these be sent out to them since they had betrayed Russia and by their guile had contrived that it should be handed over to the king's son.

In answer to this Lord Borkowski, the chief commander of the Germans and foreigners, immediately ordered the drums to beat quarters and bring the musketeers to arms, which so alarmed the Muscovites, about three thousand of whom had crowded into the fortress and were about to rebel, that they quickly scurried out of the fortress.

The soldiers wanted to shut the fortress gates and ambush the perfidious Muscovites, and would have done so except that the chief commander would not allow it but said: "Stand fast and wait until they attack us. Then we will continue. Let them abuse us; sticks and stones will break our bones, but insults never hurt us. If they come looking for blood, then let them come in good time." So in the space of a quarter of an hour there was not a single Russian in the fortress, but it became quite clear that the Muscovites would stir up trouble next on the pretext that the general and chief commanders would not allow the Muscovites to celebrate Palm Sunday (which after the feast of St Nicholas is among them the most important of the year) in order to prevent uprising and mutiny.

For on that day it is the custom for the tsar to come from the Kremlin to the church which they call Jerusalem, while the patriarch rides seated on a donkey, which the tsar leads by a bridle. Before them go the clergy in their priestly vestments, singing Hosanna in their ceremonies. Twenty or more boyar children, clad in red, go before the tsar and spread their garments, over which the tsar walks, as well as the donkey on which the patriarch sits. When the tsar has gone by they pick up the garments, run forward, and once again strew them in his way, and this continues until he reaches Jerusalem church. On sleighs there stands a full-grown tree, which they drag behind the patriarch, and on the sleighs there are also three or four boys, who also sing Hosanna. On the branches of this tree there hang various apple-like fruits. Behind the tree all the princes, boyars, and merchants follow in procession. Many thousands of people converge in order to take part in this festivity. Anyone who can walk will head there, resulting in such a conflux of people that the weak and puny should not be there if they know what is good for them.

But since because of the prohibition of this festival the people had become even more incensed and were given the excuse to say that it would be better for them all to die than leave this festival uncelebrated, they were permitted to observe it, only instead of the tsar one of the Russian lords, Andrei Gundorov, was to hold the bridle of the donkey on which the patriarch was seated as far as the Jerusalem church.

But the German and foreign regiments and all the Poles were fully armed and on the alert. Their commanders had received sufficient information that the Muscovites had some mischief in mind and were planning to start something, and that the patriarch was one of the instigators of all the disorders, having ordered the people that, if the rebellion did not take place on Palm Sunday, they should rise up during Holy Week.

They also found out that the princes and boyars had in their courtyards sleds loaded with timber which, as soon as the uprising started, could be brought out onto the streets and be set sideways so that not a single horseman could go through the streets, nor would the Poles be able to rescue one another, since they were scattered in various localities throughout the city.

Therefore the lieutenant and governor Lord Gasiewski, and Borkowski, the commander of the foreign regiment, gave orders that no German, Pole, or foreigner should remain beyond the third or fourth encircling wall on pain of flogging, but straight away proceed within and around the fortress so that they might be together should any disorders break out and not be caught off guard as the wedding guests of the first Dmitry had been, dispersed and scattered all over the place.

Seeing that on Monday the Germans were proceeding to the fortress with all their possessions, and that the foreign troops were doing likewise, the Muscovites became aware that truly their plans had been discovered. They took counsel day and night on how to prevent all the soldiers from assembling in or near the fortress and then on Tuesday, 19 March, the Muscovites made the first move and slaughtered many Poles who were spending one last night in their previous quarters. They put up barricades and dug trenches in the streets and assembled many thousands strong.

The governor sent several squadrons of lancers against them to prevent such measures, but the Muscovites did not pay any attention to them. The Muscovite musketeers (or harquebusiers) fired upon them, so that they had to abandon many men and horses in their flight. If there had not been in the fortress a regiment of musketeers hired from among the Germans and other nationalities, and also the Poles, not one of the five thousand lancers would have been left alive on that day, for the Muscovites' spirits were greatly roused when they saw so many Poles fall to the ground and so many squadrons retreat.

They so shouted and cried out that the heavens resounded, while at the same time a thousand bells sounded the alarm.

When the Poles had been so ingloriously repulsed by bullets and arrows back to the gates of the fortress, and had been seized by great fear, the captain[11] of the foreign troops, Jacques Margeret, at the eighth hour according to our reckoning, sent out into the Nikitsk street three[12] companies of musketeers, altogether numbering about four hundred men. This street, which is about a quarter of a mile long, had many intersections, where about seven thousand Muscovites were crouching behind their barricades or in their trenches and inflicting many heavy losses upon the Poles. The four hundred musketeers, **in the name of the Lord**,[13] attacked the Nikolaites behind the first barricade, and their volley was so effective that the Muscovites fell like sparrows before buckshot. Thereafter, hour by hour, was heard the fearful wail of the Muscovite battle cry, the ringing of so many thousands of bells, the crackle and snap of musket fire, the noise and howling of an extraordinarily fierce wind storm, that it was truly dreadful to hear or see. The soldiers nevertheless attacked so resolutely along all the length of the street that the Muscovites ceased to utter their battle cry but dived for cover like hares.

The soldiers set about them with their rapiers as fiercely as dogs, and since the musket fire was no longer to be heard, the other Germans and Poles within the fortress thought that these three companies had been annihilated, and great dread fell upon them. But they returned, looking like butcher's apprentices. Their rapiers, hands, and clothes were covered in blood, and they were a gruesome sight. They had destroyed many Muscovites but had lost only eight of their own soldiers.

On the other side of the Neglinnaia, which is a small brook within the city, the battle cry of the Muscovites was heard anew, since they were building fresh barricades there and were sounding the alarm loudly. Then those same three companies ventured there also, and God helped them once again to gain the victory. In the course of two hours they fought the Muscovites in one place or another until they defeated them.

But yet again another crowd gathered upon the Pokrovsk street. Since these four hundred soldiers had soon become fatigued with carrying heavy muskets for so long and for such a distance, and had tired themselves out by shooting, hacking, and thrusting against the enemy, the chief commander Borkowski sent out some lancers to aid them.

Since, because of the barricaded streets, they could not attack the Russians on horseback, the chief commander ordered them to set fire to the corner houses, and the wind blew to such effect that in twelve and a half minutes all of Moscow from the Arbat to the Kulizhek was engulfed in flames, thanks to which our men were victorious. The Russians were not able at the same time to defend themselves against the enemy, put out the fire, and save their possessions, so they had to turn to flight, leaving their houses with their wives and children and abandoning all that they had. Thus the old military Latin proverb held true, which was spoken of old in Rome, and is repeated in Virgil's Bucolics, book nine: "**As the owner of the plot said, This is mine: move on, former settlers.**"[14] On this day a third part of Moscow burned down, while many people perished from bullets, the sword, and the fire that engulfed them.

The streets where the shops of the goldsmiths and armourers had stood were so full of the corpses of those who had been slain that the feet of those who passed through them in places could hardly touch the ground. The soldiers obtained excellent booty from the goldsmiths' and other shops in the form of **gold, silver, precious stones, pearls, gems, cloth of gold**, velvet, and silk.

During the following night the Russians dug in right next to the fortress on the Chertolie, which the fire had not reached the previous day. At the very same time those who lived on the opposite shore of the Moskva river also built a redoubt, and raised their banner above the redoubt and wandered from one barricade to another.

Those who were on the Chertolie occupied a triangle bounded by the Great White Wall, and there were about a hundred[15] musketeers within it. In a like manner they erected barricades in the streets on both sides of the wall, thinking that we would launch a frontal attack. The others, on the opposite bank of the Moskva, built redoubts by the pontoon outside the watergates, placed cannon there, and fired heavily on our men from over the river, thinking, like the others, that we were intending a frontal assault.

But Captain Jacques Margeret employed a fine stratagem. He let them complete their redoubt and guard it. Since the ice on the Moskva was still firm enough, he led his men out through the watergates of the fortress onto the river and so, thus finding himself between the enemy and their fortifications, could attack to left and right at will. Apart from this, twelve regiments of Polish cavalry were stationed on the ice to guard against a possible assault from the left by the men on the Chertolie, but these remained within their redoubt. Captain Jacques Margeret proceeded along the ice with his soldiers, along the White Wall as far as the fifth tower, and then skirted the city and re-entered the city gates, being at the rear of the enemy, who had not expected any danger from that quarter and had kept the gates open for their friends who were behind other barricades or in the redoubts. Thanks to this the Russians lost, since they were defending the forward redoubts more strongly than the gates in their rear. Unexpectedly for them, in an instant our men attacked the redoubts and quickly came upon them, slaughtering all who were in them, setting fire to the redoubts and all of the Chertolie.

When those in the redoubts on the other side of the river saw this, their spirits fell, and it must have caused much consternation when, in an instant, as our Poles rode out onto the shore in order to have more room, Pan Struys arrived from Mozhaisk with one thousand hand-picked cavalry who roamed about the city, burning, killing, and plundering all that lay in their path.

Having levelled the Chertolie to the ground, our soldiers also went over to the other bank of the Moskva and there set fire to the redoubts and all the houses they could reach. No war cries or bells could help the Muscovites. Our soldiers were aided by wind and fire, for wherever the Muscovites fled they were followed by the wind and the flames, and it was plain that the Lord God wished to punish them for their **bloody murders, perfidy, avarice, and Epicurean sodomy**.

Next, crowds were seen fleeing from the city to the nearby monasteries. Towards midday there was not the slightest resistance; neither were any Muscovite soldiers anywhere to be seen. So in the course of two days the great metropolis of Moscow, having a circumference of more than four German miles, was reduced to dung and ashes, and nothing remained except the imperial fortress and its suburb, which were occupied by the king's men, and some stone churches. Most of the other churches within and without the White Walls were built, like all other buildings in Russia, like blockhouses, only of wood. Whatever else was built of wood, like the outer and fourth circular wall, which surrounded all of Moscow, with all the houses and homesteads that stood within, and also the fine palaces of princes, boyars, and rich merchants by the White Walls, was all reduced to ashes.

In this manner an insignificant detachment, perhaps eight hundred Germans and other foreign mercenaries and six thousand Poles, chased out of house and home, with all that they had, seven hundred thousand people capable of wielding a sabre, musket, bow and arrow, together with all their wives and children. They were also compelled to see the place of their splendour and all the city blazing, to consume themselves in their own fat, to be killed with their own powder and lead, and to give over to the rapine of foreigners their rich treasure, which was indescribable and, for some, unbelievable. Out of this they paid the king's army up to 1612. Seven imperial crowns and three sceptres, one of which was fashioned out of an entire rhinoceros horn and beautifully inlaid with rubies and diamonds, and also very many invaluable gems were about to travel the world and wander in foreign lands.[16]

After the uprising the Poles deposed the patriarch, who was the leader and author of all this sedition,[17] and kept him under a guard of thirty archers in the monastery of St Cyril to await WLADYSLAW's arrival and the reward he had earned by inciting this mutiny and uproar, as a result of which so many people had been so piteously slain, while all of Moscow had undergone ruin and suffered irreparable damage by fire and plunder.[18]

In other words: **If you do not desire peace, then you can have war: if you do not desire a blessing, then you can have a curse.** The Muscovites brought upon themselves the calamities of this day, like putting on a shirt, as it is written in the Book of Wisdom: **that with which ye shall sin, thereby shall ye also be punished.** Several years before this they had displayed fearful cruelty against the Germans in Livonia by plundering, murder, arson, revelry, carousing, dishonouring, or seduction of women and maidens. This was now repaid a hundredfold in kind. They had taken out of Livonia riches to the value of a hundred thousand guilders; they now had a hundred times as much gold taken from them. The few German women and maidens whom they mistreated and abducted from Livonia to Moscow were as nothing compared to the huge number, in their thousands, of their women and maidens who were now dishonoured or seduced by the Poles.

The harm caused in Russia by fire was so great that the places destroyed were four or five times as many as in the whole of Livonia. In these seven years of war more than six hundred thousand Muscovites were killed, according to the registers that were compiled while I was there, not counting those who were secretly murdered or pushed under the ice or drowned in the water, and it is to be wondered how many more of them must bite the dust[19] before they will enjoy a lasting peace!

Since for the space of fourteen days the Muscovites showed no sign of returning, the soldiers did nothing but roam around in search of booty; clothing, linen, pewter, brass, copper, and utensils, which they dug out of cellars and ditches and could have sold for more money, they left behind, taking only velvet, silk, gold coins, precious stones, and pearls. In church they stripped the saints of their silver vestments embroidered with gold thread, their stoles and the collars so richly ornamented with precious stones and jewels. Many Polish soldiers obtained ten, fifteen, or twenty-five pounds of silver torn from the idols, and those who set out in bloodstained muddy clothes returned to the fortress in costly garments.

Beer and mead were not at this time good enough, for they distributed choice wines, of which there was a profusion in the Muscovites' cellars – French, Hungarian, and Malmsey. Whoever wanted to help himself did so, which gave rise to such degeneracy, whoring, and godless living that no gallows could have deterred them, until Liapunov,[20] with the help of his Cossacks, put a stop to it. The soldiers shamefully abused their victory, not giving thanks to the Lord God. In their arrogance the soldiers shot a great number of pearls as big as peas or beans out of their muskets at the Russians, and gambled away at cards the children of prominent boyars and rich merchants, who were eventually taken away from them by force and sent back to the enemy, their parents and friends.

At that time nobody, or almost nobody, gave thought to the splendid **provisions, such as bacon, butter, cheese, all kinds of fish products, rye, malt, hops, honey, etc.**, all of which there were in abundance, but which were thoughtlessly burned or destroyed by the Poles. It would have been enough to have sustained the whole army for several years, and even then with some left over. Doubtless the Polish soldiers thought that simply because they wore silk clothes and bedecked themselves with gold, jewels, and pearls, hunger would never touch them. Now although gold and jewels have splendid virtues when they are employed in the alchemist's art, nevertheless they are powerless to satisfy a hungry stomach. Within the space of two or three months neither bread nor beer could be bought at any price. A measure of beer cost half a Polish guilder, that is fifteen mariagroschen, a small piece of bacon fifteen florins, a scrawny cow fifty florins (which formerly would have fetched barely two florins), and the loaf was very small.[21] It was also impossible to go out to the burned-out cellars and courtyards, where there had been enough provisions that had actually been dug up, because Liapunov, whom we have mentioned earlier, had rallied the fleeing Muscovites and in the third week after the uprising, on *Misericordia Domini* Sunday[22] of 1611 the Russians had retaken the White City, since it was impossible for us with such a small number to man and defend it. Because of this the Muscovites and Cossacks took from the burned-out cellars all the remaining provisions, while we had to watch. If we wanted to obtain anything, we had to do so at great risk, nor could we find anything. As the saying goes: "Opportunity knocks only once,"[23] or: "Strike while the iron is hot."[24]

Such was the state of affairs when on *Misericordia Domini* Sunday of 1611 the king's forces in Moscow were once again besieged by the

Muscovites, and everyday stiff engagements took place, which kept the chaplains and surgeons busy, and which only sixty soldiers from the regiment of Germans and mercenaries of other nations survived. The fortress would have surrendered long since by reason of famine if Jan Piotr Pawel Sapieha had not come to their assistance on St James's Day,[25] skilfully skirting the White City, which was occupied by the Muscovites, and bringing to the fortress, apart from other provisions, two thousand rusks of coarse bread.

In the absence of Lord Sapieha, who was bringing up the provisions, the Muscovites stormed and captured the New convent, situated half a mile from the fortress and occupied by our men, thereby denying us the use of gates of the White City either to enter or to come out; not even a dog or cat could get out, on account of which our men suffered greatly.

On the day that Lord Sapieha succumbed to a severe bodily sickness from which he died, the defenders were once again aided by a general of the Polish crown from Livonia, Lord Karol Chodkiewicz, who had been sent by His Majesty the King of Poland to Moscow with several thousand experienced warriors, bringing to the Poles on this occasion enough provisions to enable them to hold out for some considerable time. This was about St Bartholomew's Day.[26]

But since Chodkiewicz could not bring them any more provisions subsequently, nor repel or chase away the Muscovites in order to relieve the Poles within the fortress, the blockade became ever tighter, for the longer the siege went on the stronger the Muscovites became. They did not spare any efforts, pains, toil, or blood to regain the city and all that pertained to it, while the Polish army daily diminished and became weaker. Then the Muscovites attacked on all four sides in a relentless and terrible assault, finally capturing and occupying by force the **fortress of Moscow, the imperial seat**, fearfully slaying and killing everyone except for a few Polish nobles who could later be exchanged for some of their own who had been held prisoner in Poland.

After they had recovered the imperial seat and the fortress of Moscow, they chose as tsar their fellow countryman, a well-known magnate from the Nikitch family,[27] and crowned him. His father was called Fedor Nikitich, the same Fedor Nikitich whom, as we have related earlier, the second Dmitry had appointed patriarch, but who later, together with Shuisky and his brothers, had been deported to Poland. **If this tsar holds onto his throne for very long, he will be lucky.**[28]

For the Muscovites and His Majesty the King of Sweden (whose brother they had also chosen previously as tsar but later did not wish to receive)[29] also concluded an agreement, whereby the Muscovites were to pay a large sum of money to the king and cede to the king, as his hereditary possession, renouncing their title to them forever, six powerful fortresses; Kexholm, Noteborg, Koporie, Gdov, Yamgorod, and Ivangorod (called Narva by the Russians, and situated exactly opposite the Swedish Narva in Livonia, on the other side of the river called Narova, the course of which for several miles constitutes the boundary between Russia and Livonia), and also Korela,[30] with all the Grand Principality that pertains to it. In exchange the Muscovites received back the great commercial city of Novgorod, with the huge Grand Principality of Novgorod pertaining to it, and in this fashion concluded a perpetual peace with Sweden,[31] which is not very likely, since His Majesty the King of Poland (who now has in his hands the fortress and Grand Principality of Smolensk, which extends over a hundred miles as far as Putivl, though to win it cost him dear) and His Majesty's son Prince Wladyslaw will not leave unavenged the great dishonour done to them.

Therefore it must necessarily be feared that, if any decisive move is taken from that quarter, all will be over for the new tsar, for even now the Russians are not very pleased with him, since it is said he does not personally attend to state affairs but, contrary to their customs, delegates everything to the marshal and other lords, and only occupies himself with drunkenness. Moreover, there are some even more prominent lords who, judging from rumours, are supporters of the King of Poland and Prince Wladyslaw and are endeavoring strenuously to incline His Majesty to try and take to the field again, since if this should happen many thousands of Muscovites would without a doubt go over to the king and help him, according to their custom, to overthrow their new tsar.[32]

O just God, to whom all are subject, in Thy mercy bring to an end these long and bloody wars, and show Thy mercy that these obdurate Egyptians might be turned away from their idolatry to the true Christian faith, admit and acknowledge their guilt and sinfulness, repent before the Lord God, come to peace and tranquillity, and serve their ruler more truly and loyally than they have up to this time.

May this come about and be achieved by the omnipotent will of God, to the glory and praise of His most honourable name, to the spreading of His holy divine word, to the increase and benefit of all Christendom, especially for the consolation of all poor Christians who live in this land, especially those who have been preserved through all these dreadful wars, among whom, alas, is also my eldest son, named Conrad Bussow, and several other close relatives who, as has been mentioned earlier, came from Livonia during the reign of Boris Fedorovich. **For the sake of Thy beloved Son, the true Prince of Peace, Jesus Christ. Amen! Amen! Amen!**

Appendices

Duke Friedrich Ulrich of Braunschweig-Wolfenbuttel. Herzog August Library, Wolfenbüttel

Conrad Bussow's Missive to Duke Friedrich-Ulrich of Brunswick, 28 November 1613

Most illustrious, noble and gracious Prince and Lord:[1]
Having served since the year 1569 beyond the borders of Germany, in Livonia and Russia, at the court of various princes and lords, I have now been back for a year among the German nation and in my beloved fatherland, the praiseworthy principality of Lüneburg, having survived, may God be praised and thanked, many and great dangers to body and life. Out of these foreign lands (where I have, unfortunately, left behind one of my sons,[2] about eight hundred miles, as it is reckoned, beyond the capital city of Moscow, in the Siberian Tatar lands, in harsh captivity and bondage) I, however, have brought out nothing except my naked body and the description of the internal disorders and fearful wars (on account of which that fair land, over the extent of hundreds of miles, has been pitifully devastated, and many foreigners who were living in Russia, for safety's sake had to leave all, abandoning their fine estates and many possessions), from which we, a certain worthy gentleman[3] and I, have attempted, as best we could with our imperfect understanding, to compile the present book, since we have had better opportunity to do this than others, for we could not only witness and note all that occurred during the time of this ruin in various places, in which we were in part witnesses and participants, but also to pursue the events which occurred at that court beforehand, and which had given rise to these internecine wars, insofar as we were successful in obtaining testimony therefor, not only from Muscovites, but also from Germans who had lived in Russia for many years, and who had noted down

these events as they occurred. And although it is true that many worthy military men (of those who were active on the side of the Swedes or Poles against the Muscovites, and also on the side of the Muscovites against their enemies) have returned from thence, and have related truly concerning these events, all the same it is scarcely probable that these people received, or could have received, completely reliable information concerning the original causes of this internecine war, since not everything was known, either to the German settlers, or to the hundreds of thousands of Muscovites.

For which reason we, my comrade and I, have expended great pains and effort, partially to find out about all these matters from honest and credible people, and partially, as has been stated earlier, since we ourselves experienced them, and know this to be the true succession of events, without any admixture of falsehood or deceit, I conceived a great desire to publish this among the Germans in the form of a printed book, but have been prevented through lack of means, for a printer charges much.

I would like most humbly to dedicate and present to you this account of these Muscovite events, as a gift to Your Princely Grace, since soon after my arrival I learned that you are a great connoisseur of such and similar historical narratives. I am further moved to do so by the fact that when Your Princely Grace's uncle, His Highness the late Prince and Lord Johan, Hereditary Prince of Norway, Duke of Schleswig-Holstein, Stormarn and Dittmarsch, Count of Oldenburg and Delmenhorst, of Christian memory, so unexpectedly and so piteously came to the end of his young life there in Moscow, I, like all the other foreigners, with great weeping and mourning, accompanied the princely corpse to its burial place, which is at the very altar of the German church, at about a quarter of a mile's distance from the city of Moscow, concerning which Klaus Müller, Your Princely Grace's most devoted servant and my dear friend, reported and narrated to you recently in Wolfenbüttel. And insofar as I, as was befitting, have included this also in this present book, with befitting reverence I most humbly offer and present it as a gift to Your Grace, with the humble request that you graciously accept it, even though it is insignificant and unpolished, and declare the wish to be my gracious prince and lord, and, if it is your gracious wish, to publish it among the Germans by means of the Wolfenbüttel printing press which belongs to Your Highness, in which case I request that several copies be set aside for me.

Apart from that, Most Gracious Prince and Lord, insofar as I, as has been stated earlier, from my youth have been in service with princes and lords, I humbly make bold to offer my services to Your

Grace, and if Your Grace will most graciously deign to receive me into the number of the least of your servitors, I hope, with the help of God, that my conduct will give satisfaction to Your Grace, and vouchsafe my promotion. If there does not happen to be a vacant post in which I could be placed, I most humbly beg of Your Grace to grant me asylum, perhaps at Your Grace's court,[4] until Your Grace will deign to give me the opportunity to perform some kind of service, for which I, in order that I may humbly deserve it in the eyes of Your Grace, shall be found to be obedient and indefatigable in your service.

I pray to Almighty God to grant Your Grace and the praiseworthy House of Brunswick a long life, good health, a fortunate and peaceful reign, and all manner of success, and to me, an insignificant person, Your Grace's benevolence and protection.

Given in the City of Hanover,
Your Grace's hereditary possession.
28 November 1613.[5]
Conradt Busso
Manu propria
[HAB COD. GUELF 56 EXTRAVAGANTES, fol. 339–342]

Conrad Bussow's Letter to J. Peparino, 3 February 1614

To the Most Highly Esteemed and Most Learned Master Johann Peparino,[1] Doctor *utriusque juris* and Most Noble Privy Counsellor, my Most Gracious and All-powerful Protector.

Most Highly Esteemed, Most Learned, and Most Gracious Master Doctor! Together with the expression of my constant readiness to be of service, I most cordially thank you, in that you, Most Esteemed and Most Learned Sir, several days ago graciously received from me my *Muscovite Relation*, and forwarded it to our Most Gracious Prince and Lord. In the petition appended to the *Relation*, I offered His Princely Grace my most devoted service, and told concerning myself that I had brought nothing with me out of the Muscovite land but, on the contrary, I was unfortunately obliged to leave there my extensive wealth, and have not found in my own country anything whereby to support myself. And since I have spent most of my life in service to princes and lords, for this reason once again I am compelled by need to plead with them for their most gracious patronage. Thus my most eager and diligent plea is transmitted to you, Most Esteemed and Most Learned Sir, to find out whether you might not intercede for me, a poor outcast, before His Princely Grace, so that I might receive a favourable response, not only in the matter of my *Relation*, which I have offered to him, but also be accepted among the least of his servitors. But since it is difficult for me to support myself until I am given a service post, I would wish to enjoy a place at the table in the Prince's court. In order to merit all these vital favours from you, Most Esteemed and Most Learned Sir, I shall remain your servant forever. May the All Highest God not leave you, Most Esteemed and Most Learned Sir, without a fitting reward.

Wolfenbüttel
3 February 1614

I remain, Most Esteemed and Most Learned Sir, always your obe-dient servant

Conradt Bussou
manu propria.

[HAB COD. GUELF 56 EXTRAVAGANTES, fol. 343–344.]

APPENDIX THREE

Bussow's Map of Moscow

This map inked on a scrap of paper, numbered f. 96, found between ff. 95v and 97 of Cod. Guelf. 86 Extravagantes in the Wolfenbüttel Library. The handwriting differs from that of the codex, but corresponds to that of Bussow's autograph letter, which apparently accompanied it. It appears that the map's inclusion in the codex was fortuitous, since it has no relation to the surrounding text. It is a very rough sketch, with a number of corrections and deletions. The terminology found on the map, however, corresponds with that used in Bussow's text; hence the Dormition cathedral is labelled as *Templum Precista*, the church of St Basil the Blessed as the "Jerusalem Church," etc.

There are extant several other maps of Moscow pertaining to the same period; the late sixteenth-century Petrov map, the one attributed to Fedor Borisovich Godunov, the map done for Isaac Massa by his nameless Muscovite friend, and the map commissioned by King Sigismund III of Poland. Bussow's map differs from all of these in that it is a ground plan, rather than an aerial relief. It is also obviously drawn by a soldier, concerned with objects of military significance such as walls, towers, bridges, and gates. The actual toponymy tends to be rather vague: "Water Gates," "Other Kremlin monasteries" (*Andere Kloster im Schloß*), "New Lodgings" (*Neue Gemächer*), etc. The belfry of Ivan the Great, at the time this map was compiled a very new structure, is simply labelled "Tall Tower" (*Lange Thurm*). The "Tsaritsa's Convent" (*Kaiserin Kloster*), which we know to have been the Ascension, is correctly placed, just behind the Frolov or Saviour gates of the Kremlin. The *Kirilo monastir*, on the south side of the

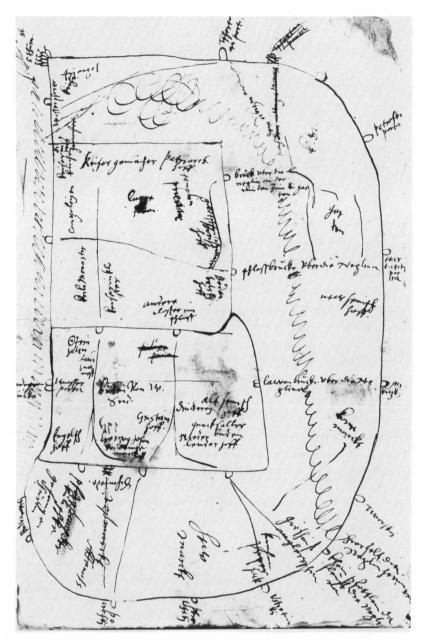

Bussow's Map. Codex Guelf, 86 Extravagantes, f. 96. Herzog August Library, Wolfenbüttel

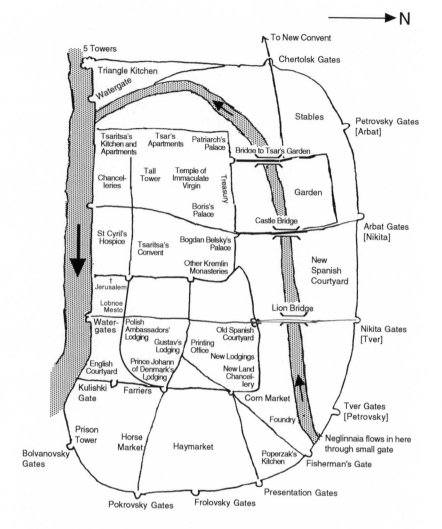

N

To New Convent

5 Towers

Chertolsk Gates

Triangle Kitchen

Watergate

Stables

Petrovsky Gates
[Arbat]

Tsaritsa's
Kitchen and
Apartments

Tsar's
Apartments

Patriarch's
Palace

Bridge to Tsar's Garden

Chancel-
leries

Tall
Tower

Temple of
Immaculate
Virgin

Treasury

Garden

Boris's
Palace

Castle Bridge

St Cyril's
Hospice

Tsaritsa's
Convent

Bogdan Belsky's
Palace

Arbat Gates
[Nikita]

Other Kremlin
Monasteries

New
Spanish
Courtyard

†
Jerusalem

Lobnoe
Mesto

Lion Bridge

Water-
gates

Polish
Ambassadors'
Lodging

Old Spanish
Courtyard

Nikita Gates
[Tver]

Gustav's
Lodging

Printing
Office

New Lodgings

English
Courtyard

Prince Johann
of Denmark's
Lodging

New Land
Chancel-
lery

Kulishki
Gate

Farriers

Corn Market

Tver Gates
[Petrovsky]

Foundry

Neglinnaia flows in here
through small gate

Prison
Tower

Horse
Market

Haymarket

Poperzak's
Kitchen

Fisherman's Gate

Bolvanovsky
Gates

Presentation Gates

Pokrovsky Gates

Frolovsky Gates

KEY TO BUSSOW'S MAP

Kremlin, is obviously an error, but the Beloozero monastery of that name is known to have maintained a hospice in Moscow.

The area covered by the map consists of the Kremlin, the Kitay-gorod and the White City, each enclosed by a ring of stone fortifications. The diagram accompanying the map is largely self-explanatory, but a few comments might be appropriate. The five gates of the Kremlin, though marked, are not labelled, and only one of the five gates of the Kitay-gorod, the Kulishki, is actually named. The outer gates, those of the White City, are accurately named, except those on the north side, which for the most part are in the right sequence, but in the wrong place. Where appropriate I have appended the correct name in square brackets on the diagram.

From the location of the lodgings of Prince Gustav, Prince Johan of Denmark, and the English Courtyard, we can see that the Foreign Quarter was at that time located in the southeast sector of the Kitay-gorod. Unfortunately I am unable to offer any explanation for the labels pertaining to the "Old" and "New Spanish Courtyards." As for Poperzack's Kitchen, it is known that there was at that time an expatriate of that name among the foreign merchants hoping to do business with the court of False Dmitry I, but who were robbed of their wares in the disorders of 17 May 1606. Would it be too fanciful to suggest that Poperzack tried to recoup his fortunes by opening a hostelry where the foreign community could repair for refreshment?

Notes

ABBREVIATIONS

The following abbreviations or shortened references are used in the notes.

AAE   *Akty sobrannye i izdannye v bibliotekakh i arkhivakh Rossiiskoi Imperii Arkheograficheskoiu Kommisseiiu* (Acts Collected and Edited from the Libraries and Archives of the Russian Empire by the Archeographical Commission)

CHOIDR   *Chteniia otdeleniia istoriia i drevnostrei rossiiskikh* (Readings of the Section for Russian History and Antiquities)

MERSH   *Modern Encyclopedia of Russian and Soviet History* (Gulf Breeze, Florida: Academic International Press, 1976–82)

PSRL   *Polnoe sobranie russkikh letopisei* (Full Collection of Russian Chronicles)

RIB   *Russkaia istoricheskaia biblioteka* (Russian Historical Library)

SGGD   *Sobranie gosudarstvennykh gramot i dogovorov* (Collection of State Documents and Treaties)

SRIO   *Sbornik Imperatorskogo Russkogo Istoricheskogo Obshchestva* (Collection of the Imperial Russian Historical Society)

INTRODUCTION

1   See Ivan's own account in his first letter to Prince Kurbsky, *The Correspondence between Prince A.M. Kurbsky and Tsar Ivan IV of Russia*, edited with translation and notes by J.L.I. Fennell (Cambridge: Cambridge

University Press, 1963), 68–81. This narrative may, of course, be exaggerated or even spurious, but it nevertheless contains an element of truth.

2 D.P. Makovskii, *Razvitie tovarno-denezhnykh otnoshenii v sel'skom khoziaistve russkogo gosudarstva XVI v.* [Development of commodity relations in the economy of the sixteenth-century Russian state] (Smolensk: Izdatel'stvo Moskovskii Rabochii, 1960). The contents of this volume are summarized by Richard Hellie, "The foundations of Russian capitalism," *Slavic Review* 27 (1967): 148–54.

3 S.F. Platonov, *Ivan the Terrible*, edited and translated by Joseph L. Wieczynski (Gulf Breeze, Fla: Academic International Press, 1974), 86–7.

4 Ruslan G. Skrynnikov, *Ivan the Terrible*, edited and translated by Hugh F. Graham (Gulf Breeze, Fla: Academic International Press, 1981), 49–50.

5 Alexander Yanov, *The Origins of Autocracy: Ivan the Terrible in Russian History* (Berkeley: University of California Press, 1981), 15.

6 Ibid., 201–2. Many orthodox historians claim that Yanov's work on Ivan the Terrible is more polemical journalism than properly documented history, but I feel that here at least he has a point.

7 Skrynnikov, *Ivan the Terrible*, 157.

8 Robert O. Crummey, "The Fate of the Boyar Clans 1565–1613," *Forschungen zur Osteuropäische Geschichte* 38 (1986): 241–56.

9 N.E. Nosov, *Stanovlenie soslovno-predstavitel'nykh uchrezhdenii v Rossii* [Establishment of states-representative institutions in Russia] (Leningrad, 1969), 9.

10 See the excellent anthology of essays edited by Rodney Hilton, *The Transition from Feudalism to Capitalism* (London: New Left Books, 1976).

11 Perry Anderson, *Passages from Antiquity to Feudalism* (London: Verso, 1978), 245. See also Jerome Blum, "The Rise of Serfdom in Eastern Europe," *American Historical Review* 77, no. 4 (1957): 812–25; M. Malowist, "The Problem of Inequality of Economic Development in Europe in the Later Middle Ages," *Economic History Review* 19 (1966): 15–28.

12 See entry by V.I. Koretskii, "Forbidden Years," MERSH 11 (1979): 205.

13 Hellie, *Slavery in Russia* (Chicago: Chicago University Press, 1982), 692.

14 G.E. Orchard, "The Frontier Policy of Boris Godunov," *New Review* (Toronto) 9, no. 1 (1969): 113–23.

15 Bussow's account is unique in that it depicts Grigory Otrepiev as a kind of "talent spotter," used to find somebody to play the part of Tsarevich Dmitry. Once he had succeeded, he went off to the steppe to recruit Cossacks on behalf of the Pretender.

16 Anderson, *Lineages of the Absolutist State* (London: Verso, 1979), 333.

17 Although Margeret was of course a Frenchman, he enlisted in the mercenary corps, in which German was the language of command. Indeed, Margeret's only known autograph (1603 or 1604) is in that language: *Ich Jacob Margeret Capitain hab Kaiserliche Majestät begnadigung empfangen.*

18 Norman Davies, *God's Playground* (Oxford: Clarendon Press, 1981) 1: 341–3.

19 The crown hetman was one of the sixteen officers of state, and his function was to act as field commander of the armed forces. The officers of state were chosen by the king, but could not be dismissed unilaterally.

20 Sigismund's rightful successor was his younger half-brother Johan (1589–1618). Karl waited until Johan came of age in 1604, at which time the latter renounced the succession and was confirmed in the royal duchy of Östergötland. In 1612 Johan married Karl's daughter Marie-Elisabeth.

21 Michael Roberts, *The Early Vasas: A History of Sweden 1523–1611* (Cambridge: Cambridge University Press, 1968), 453–4.

22 Sergei M. Soloviev, *History of Russia*, vol. 15 (Gulf Breeze, Fla: Academic International Press, 1989), 139.

23 *Russkaia istoricheskaia biblioteka* 13 (1909): col. 1304.

24 Orchard, "The election of Michael Romanov," *Slavonic and East European Review* 67, no. 3 (1989): 378–402.

25 Kazimierz Waliszewski, *La crise révolutionnaire* (Paris: Plon-Nourrit, 1906), 99–100.

26 Similarly Ivan the Terrible was a hero to the gentry, since serf legislation, which began under his rule, was designed to protect them against unfair competition with large-scale landowners for scarce labour resources.

27 K.V. Chistov, *Russkie narodnye sotsial'no-utopicheskie legendy XVII-XVIII vv.* [Russian popular socio-utopian legends in the seventeenth and eighteenth centuries] (Moscow, 1967).

28 Maureen Perrie, "Popular Socio-Utopian Legends in the Time of Troubles," *Slavonic and East European Review* 60 (1982): 221–43.

29 "The rationalistic myth of the monarch as usurper had been born, apparently, during the reign of Boris Godunov following the extinction of the Riurikid dynasty and had gained force during the 'Time of Troubles' in the seventeenth century. The succession crises of the eighteenth century served to strengthen its popularity as a means of legitimizing social action, and 'just tsars,' however doubtful their credentials, became increasingly effective in rallying fractionalized groups of discontented people. Indeed, by the latter part of the eighteenth century, with a real usurper

on the throne, only a pretender could serve as a magnet to attract mass support for an insurrectionary grass-roots movement directed towards change." Philip Longworth, "The Pretender Phenomenon in Eighteenth Century Russia." *Past and Present* 66 (February 1973): 75.

30 During the peasant revolt at Bezdna in 1863, its leader Anton Petrov announced that "true freedom" would come in a letter from the tsar borne by "a young man … seventeen years old, and on his right shoulder he will have a gold medal and on his left shoulder a silver one." Franco Venturi, *The Roots of Revolution* (London: Weidenfeld and Nicholson, 1960), 215.

31 Perrie, "Popular Utopian Legends," 242.

32 Skrynnikov, "The Civil War at the Beginning of the Seventeenth Century (1603–1607): Its Character and Motive Forces," *New Perspectives on Muscovite History*. Selected Papers from the Fourth World Congress for Soviet and East European Studies, Harrogate, 1990: 78.

33 Makovskii, *Pervaia krest'ianskaia voina v Rossii* [The First Peasant War in Russia] (Smolensk: Izdatel'stvo Moskovskii Rabochii, 1967), 398; Denise Eeckaute, "Brigands en Russie du XVIIe au XIXe siècle," *Revue d'histoire moderne et contemporaine* 12 (1965): 165.

34 See Hellie, *Enserfment and Military Change in Russia* (Chicago: Chicago University Press, 1971).

35 A.K. Leont'ev, *Obrazovanie prikaznoi sistemy v russkom gosudarstve* [Creation of the Chancellery System in the Russian State] (Moscow, 1961).

36 This theme is developed in Nancy Shields Kollmann, *Kinship and Politics: the Making of the Muscovite Political System* (Stanford: Stanford University Press, 1987), and Edward L. Keenan, "Muscovite Political Folkways," *Russian Review* 45, no. 2 (1986): 115–181.

37 In fact the Polish Vasas were to maintain their claim to the Swedish crown until 1660, when under the provisions of the Treaty of Oliva it was renounced by Jan Kazimierz. In any case the line became extinct in 1672.

38 Paul Pierling, S.J., *Lettre de Dmitri dit le Faux à Clément VIII* (Paris: Alphonse Picard et Fils, 1898). Translation in Sonia E. Howe, *The False Dmitri: a Russian Romance and Tragedy* (London: Williams and Norgate, 1916), 1–4.

39 David Kirby, *Northern Europe in the Early Modern Period* (London: Longman, 1990), 122–3.

40 See Daniel B. Rowland, *Muscovite Political Attitudes as Reflected in Early Seventeenth-century Tales about the Time of Troubles*, PhD dissertation, Yale University, 1976.

41 Karl himself was married to Maria of the Palatinate (1574) and then to Kristina of Holstein-Gottorp (1592). Through his sisters he was related

to the ruling houses of East Frisia, Baden, Pfalz-Vedenz, Saxe-Lauenburg, and Mecklenburg.

42 Peer Peerson de Erlesunda (1570–1622), who wrote under the name
Petreius, was a Swedish diplomat and historian. He first entered royal
service in 1595, and was resident agent in Moscow between 1602 and
1606, when he was sent back to Sweden on an unspecified mission on
behalf of Tsar Vasily Shuisky. In July 1607 he was sent to Moscow by
Karl IX with an offer of military help, which was ungraciously refused
by Shuisky. In 1609 he was sent to repeat the offer, to which this time
the tsar was more receptive. In 1611 Petreius was sent to report on the
authenticity of Sidorka, a pretender who had appeared at Pskov and
appealed for Swedish help. Petreius gave a negative report, and in any
case Sidorka was captured and slain by his own Cossack supporters. At
Stockholm, in 1615, Petreius published the first version, in Swedish, of
his treatise on Russia, which he dedicated to King Gustav Adolf. The
earlier part of the work is devoted to description of the land, customs,
and early history of Russia, the latter part to a more detailed history of
the Time of Troubles, much of which he had personally witnessed. An
expanded version, in German, appeared at Leipzig in 1620, and it
seems that Petreius was actually there to supervise the printing and
publication. He borrowed extensively, word for word without acknowl-
edgement, from the writings of Sigismund von Herberstein, Alessandro
Guagnini, and more especially from Bussow. With the latter he was on
terms of personal enmity, since in the Swedish version he reveals Bussow's treasonable dealings with the Muscovites while still in Swedish
service prior to his defection in 1601. Apart from the fact that Petreius
got into print first, these revelations doubtless prevented Bussow from
obtaining the patronage necessary to get his own manuscript printed
and published. Notwithstanding the shameless plagiarism practised by
Petreius, his history does contain considerable original material, and is
therefore of value as a primary source.

43 See chapter II, note 25.

44 The last religious service in Polabian was conducted at Wustow, near
Lüneburg, in 1751.

45 *"Sein Styl ist an vielen Stellen unbeholfen, ja roh und sprachwidrig."* A.A.
Kunik, "Aufklärungen über Konrad Bussow und die verschiedenen
Redaktionen seiner Chronik," *Bulletin des Sciences Historiques, Philolo-
giques et Politiques de l'Académie Impériale des Sciences de Saint-Pétersbourg*
1849: col. 359.

46 *Een wiss och egentlich Beskriffing om Rydsland* [A True and Unique
Description of Russia] (Stockholm, 1615); *Historien und Bericht von dem
Großfürstenthumb Muskhow* (Leipzig, 1620).

47   The present collection contains about 750,000 volumes, including 350,000 imprints earlier than 1830, about three thousand incunabula, 75,000 sixteenth-century imprints, and 120,000 eighteenth-century imprints.

48   The Rotunda was unfortunately demolished during the renovations to the Biblioteca Augusta between 1884 and 1887. It remains, however, the official emblem of the Library.

49   There are, of course, also significant departures. Karamzin discards Bussow's "helper theory" concerning Grishka Otrepiev, neither does he share Bussow's evident sympathy for the widowed Tsaritsa Maryna.

50   The Academy manuscript contains 397 folio pages. There is a notation that the author died at Lübeck in 1617 before the proposed book could be printed. The manuscript is written on paper dating from the late eighteenth century, with a watermark containing the motto "Pro Patria" with the monogram "CR" on the reverse.

51   Christoph Schmidt-Phisildek, *Versuch einer neuer Einleitung in die russische Geschichte* (Riga, 1773), 303.

52   Friedrich von Adelung, *Kritisch-literärische Übersicht der Reisenden in Rußland bis 1700 deren Berichte bekannt sind* (St Petersburg, 1846) 2: 46–111. Adelung was born in Prussia, but migrated to Russia in 1794, became a Russian citizen and accepted Orthodox baptism under the name Fedor Pavlovich, under which some of his Russian-language publications appeared.

53   Kunik, "Aufklärungen ... "; E. Hermann, *Geschichte des russischen Staates* (Hamburg, 1846), 780–2; Ya. K. Grot, "Deistvitel'no li Martin Ber avtor khroniki?" [Was Martin Beer really the author of the chronicle?], *Zhurnal Ministerstva Narodnogo Prosveshcheniia* 1849, no. 5 (Russian translation of an article previously published in Swedish).

54   *Rerum Rossicarum Scriptores Exteri*, vol. 1 (St Petersburg, 1851). The title used is that of the Academy manuscript, *Summarische Erzehlung vom eigentlichen Ursprung dieser itzigen blutigen Kriegs-wesens in Moscowiter-Landt oder Reußland*.

55   *Istoriia Rossii s drevneishikh vremën*. Subsequent editions of this volume appeared in his lifetime, in 1866 and 1873, and the whole history was reissued by the *Obshchestvennaia Pol'za* publishing house in 1893–5, 1895–6, and 1911. The latest Russian-language edition was published in Moscow between 1960 and 1966. An English translation of Soloviev's eighth volume (my own) is contained in S.M. Soloviev, *History of Russia* (Gulf Breeze, Fla: Academic International Press, 1976+), vols 14–15.

56   S.F. Platonov, *Ocherki po istorii smuty v moskovskom gosudarstve XVI-XVII vv.* (St Petersburg, 1899). Subsequent editions appeared in 1901 and 1910. The third edition was reprinted in 1937 and 1967.

57 R.G. Skrynnikov, *The Time of Troubles: Russia in Crisis*, translated and edited by Hugh F. Graham (Gulf Breeze, Fla: Academic International Press, 1988).

58 I.I. Smirnov, *Vosstanie Bolotnikova* [Bolotnikov's Uprising] (Leningrad, 1949, 2nd edition Moscow, 1951). This monograph won the 1950 Stalin Prize for history.

59 Conrad Bussow, *Zeit der Wirren: Moskowitische Chronik der Jahre 1584 bis 1613*, herausgegeben und kommentiert von Gottfried Sturm, Übersetzung aus dem Frühhochdeutschen von Marie-Elisabeth Fritze (Berlin [DDR]: Union Verlag, 1989).

CHAPTER I

1 The Sunday after Cantate Sunday, i.e., the fifth Sunday after Easter or 31 May in 1584. Bussow, following the Roman Catholic and early Lutheran practice, designates the fourth Sunday after Easter according to the first word of the Introit of the Latin propers pertaining to that particular Sunday. In any case, this information is inaccurate, since Ivan IV died 18 March, more than a month *before* Easter, which in 1584 fell on 19 April.

2 Ivan's eldest son, also called Ivan, was slain in 1581 as a result of a quarrel between father and son. Accounts differ as to whether the dispute in question was over the father's conduct of the Livonian War or his alleged mistreatment of the tsarevich's wife.

3 It appears that the accession to the throne of Fedor Ivanovich was not uncontested, since there was an attempted coup by Ivan IV's erstwhile favourite Bogdan Belsky in favour of Dmitry and a regency which would maintain in power the group which had benefited from the former tsar's *oprichnina* policies. (The oprichnina was a set of crown estates set aside for his personal use by Ivan IV, who used them to establish a reign of terror over his entire realm). The coup was defeated and Fedor was established upon the throne, after which the reversionary interest was removed to the distant principality of Uglich. Dmitry died there under suspicious circumstances on 15 May 1591.

4 The "German mile" is reckoned at 7,500 metres, or 4.6 English miles. The verst is an ancient Russian measure of distance, equivalent to 1.06 km. Bussow in fact notes in the margin of his manuscript that "5 versts is equal to a German mile," and at the next reference to 90 versts adds "18 German miles."

5 Both here and repeatedly in his chronicle Bussow has the mistaken impression that St Nicholas the Thaumaturge was venerated as a god. The "Immaculate Virgin" here referred to was probably the Dormition cathedral in the Kremlin. In his map of Moscow, Bussow refers to this

particular church as *Templum Precistae* (Temple of the Immaculate
Virgin). "St Nicholas" here probably does not refer to any specific
church building, though there were several churches with that dedica-
tion in Moscow, but rather to the peculiarly Russian devotion to the
Thaumaturge.

6 Marginal note: *Kneesen sind Fürsten, Boyaren – Edelleute und Räthe*
(boyars are noblemen and councillors). *Kneesen* is Bussow's attempt to
render the plural of the Russian *kniaz'*, meaning "prince" (the correct
Russian plural is *kniazia'*. *Fürst* is the German title for princes not of
the blood royal.

7 "Yesterday's slave, a Tatar." Actually the epithet contained in Pushkin's
drama, intended to be pejorative, in the sixteenth century might well
have been intended to elevate Boris's status, since the descendants of
the Tatar "tsars" were considered to have been of comparable throne-
worthiness to those of Rurik or Gedimin (the eponymous ancestors of
the Russian and Lithuanian ruling families respectively), as witness the
temporary elevation of the baptized Tatar princeling Semeon Bekbulatovich in 1575. In fact, despite the often repeated claim that Boris was
descended from the Tatar Murza Chet, said to have entered the service
of the Muscovite Grand Prince Ivan Kalita early in the fourteenth century, the Godunovs were in fact a cadet branch of the Zernov family,
which had its origins in the Kostroma region. The Godunovs owed
their rise to Ivan IV's oprichnina, to which Boris's father, Fedor Ivanovich "Krivoi" and his uncle Dmitry were admitted. Shortly afterwards Boris, his elder brother Vasily, and his sister Irina were
orphaned, becoming wards of their uncle Dmitry Ivanovich, who
became chamberlain of the oprichnina court in 1567. Boris therefore
grew up in the intimate circle of the tsar's household and his sister
eventually married the tsar's second son. Boris himself married Maria
Grigorievna, daughter of Ivan IV's henchman Maliuta Skuratov.

8 Boris's accession to power was not as smooth as Bussow relates but was
rather the result of a three-year power struggle. Boris was not named
to the regency council that took over after Ivan's death, but he used his
position as brother-in-law to the new tsar to further his position at the
expense of his rivals, whose ranks were thinned by natural death,
retirement through ill health, or disgrace caused by ill-considered political initiatives. See R. G. Skrynnikov, *Boris Godunov*, chapter 2.

9 Even commentators generally unfavourable to Boris concede that
during his regency he acquitted himself well.

10 *Lupi und Corycaci.*

11 In fact Irina, after several miscarriages, gave birth in May 1592 to a
daughter, Feodosia, who died 25 January 1594.

12 Several sources, both Russian and foreign, remark upon the young
Dmitry's sadistic tendencies, as well as his particular animosity towards
Boris. See Giles Fletcher, *Of the Russe Commonwealth*, 16v; Avraamii Palitsyn, *Skazanie Avraamiia Palitsyna*, 101–2; Isaac Massa, *A Short History
of the Muscovite Wars*, 30; Petreius, *Historien und Bericht*, 259–60.

13 *Melius est praevenire quam praeveniri.*

14 *Man muß dem Jungen Herrn das Gelbe vom Schnabel wischen.* The meaning
of this idiom is uncertain.

15 Bussow's opinion concerning Boris's guilt in the murder of Tsarevich
Dmitry probably derives from the official view as reflected in the documents issued by the Shuisky regime in connection with the tsarevich's
canonization and also in the *Tale of the Year 1606*, later incorporated
into the *So-called Other Tale*, the only chronicle of the period uniformly
favourable to Shuisky. Modern scholarship tends to discount the
murder theory and accept the report of the investigation commission
sent to Uglich in 1591, which found that the tsarevich's death was acci-
dental and that his Nagoy relatives were responsible for stirring up the
subsequent sedition in the town of Uglich. See Vernadsky, "The Death
of the Tsarevich Dmitry," and Skrynnikov, *Boris Godunov*, chapter 6.
The official report of the 1591 inquest is contained in SGGD, 2, no. 60,
and is also edited with commentary by V. I. Klein, *Uglichskoe sledst-
vennoe delo o smerti tsarevicha Dmitriia 15-go maia 1591 g.* (Moscow: Zapiski Moskovskogo Arkheologicheskogo Instituta, 1913).

16 Bussow is not alone in thinking that Boris instigated the fires in
Moscow to deflect attention from the events at Uglich. It is noticeable,
however, that all accounts attributing the blame to Boris are of foreign
origin (as well as Bussow, see Margeret, *The Russian Empire*, 16–17,
Massa, *Short History*, 32 and Petreius, *Historien und Bericht*, 261). The
New Chronicler (*Novyi Letopisets*), 42, while generally hostile to Boris,
reports these conflagrations, even confirming some of the topograph-
ical details contained in the foreign sources, but does not blame Boris.

17 7 January 1598. Although Bussow relates this *sub anno* 1597, it must be
remembered that most of Europe still operated under the "March calendar," while the Russians still followed the Byzantine usage of com-
memorating the New Year on 1 September.

18 This story is repeated, in a slightly different version, by Massa (*Short
History*, 46). It is probably untrue, though it was widely current at the
time when Bussow was writing and was to gain momentum as support
grew for the Romanov candidature in 1612–13. Yet the *New Chronicler*
(49), which might have been expected to use this story to reinforce the
legitimation of the Romanov dynasty, merely states that the rulership
devolved upon Irina, and only after she had irrevocably renounced the

world for the cloister did the question arise of an election which, if not unanimous, was at least legitimate. Moreover only the Shuisky princes, not the Romanovs, are cited as being actively opposed to the Godunov candidature.

CHAPTER II

1 For administrative and police purposes the urban inhabitants were divided up into units of hundreds and fifties, each headed by a responsible official, a hundredman or fiftyman (*sotnik* or *piatidesiatnik*). Bussow uses these terms untranslated in his text.

2 "*... was hinter dem Berge verborgen*," literally, "what was hidden behind the hill."

3 Literally "which way the bell was tolling."

4 *Vox populi, vox Dei.*

5 The Novodevichy [New] convent was founded in 1525 to commemorate Vasily III's conquest of Smolensk from the Poles. Its fortifications guarded the south-western approaches to Moscow.

6 The official version of these events is confirmed in the dispatch of the Austrian ambassador Michael Schiele, who was an eyewitness of the events. The people were urged to swear allegiance to the "princes and boyars," but instead they put pressure on a reluctant Boris to assume the throne. "Donesenie o poezdke v Moskvu pridvornogo rimskogo imperatora Mikhaila Shiliia," CHOIDR 1875, kn. 2, otd. 4, 12–13.

7 Here for the first time Bussow uses the scornful term *Herr Omnis*, "Lord Everybody," which frequently occurs in his narrative.

8 Ivan Timofeev (55) states that a youth "was placed like a false orator" near the tsaritsa's cell, and that he importuned Irina to urge Boris to accept the throne. In place of Timofeev's single youth, Bussow has a small group, which Petreius (268), borrowing for the most part from Bussow, magnifies to several thousand.

9 Massa (41–2) gives a very different version of the role of the tsaritsa, wherein she urges Boris to repent of his sins and renounce the tsardom.

10 The 1598 Assembly of the Land is discussed by R. G. Skrynnikov in chapter 9 of his *Boris Godunov*, and more fully by the same author in his article "Boris Godunov's struggle for the throne," *Canadian-American Slavic Studies* 11, no. 3 (1977): 325–53. A *zemsky sobor*, or Assembly of the Land, was a gathering of representatives of various strata of society to discuss matters of national importance. Some historians have seen the *zemsky sobor* as an abortive step towards a permanent "states-representative monarchy," but this view is generally discounted. Ivan IV used the *zemsky sobor* several times to gain public approval for his fiscal

and military policies, and such assemblies also met for the election of Fedor Ivanovich, Boris Godunov, and Michael Romanov. Some kind of rump *zemsky sobor* was hastily convoked to legitimize Vasily Shuisky's seizure of power in 1606. The *zemsky sobor* remained in more or less continuous session from the election of Michael Romanov in 1613 until the return of Filaret (Fedor Nikitich Romanov) from Polish captivity in 1619. Thereafter the sobor was only convoked infrequently. See entry by Richard Hellie, MERSH 45 (1987): 226–34. Job was the first patriarch of the Russian church, elected in 1588 largely through the support of Boris Godunov, who was then regent. However disinterested his actions at the *sobor* of 1598, Job was perceived as returning a favour. He vigorously supported Boris against the pretensions of the False Dmitry. Seized while celebrating the liturgy in the Dormition cathedral in June 1605, he was deposed and sent to his former monastery at Staritsa. He was briefly recalled during the reign of Vasily Shuisky to reinforce the proclamations of Patriarch Hermogen against the second Pretender. He died in 1607 and was canonized in 1652 at the instigation of Patriarch Nikon. See entry by Nicholas Lupinin, MERSH 15 (1980): 136–8.

11 The account of the review of the troops at Serpukhov and the reception of the Tatar ambassadors is also given in Massa (42–3) and the *Novyi Letopisets* (50–1). Apart from Petreius (269–70), whose account is almost certainly derived from Bussow, there is no mention elsewhere of any Persian ambassadors.

12 Emphasized in the original (Wolfenbüttel II).

13 Actually 3 September 1598.

14 Prechista in fact means "Immaculate." The church in question is the Cathedral of the Dormition, or *Uspenskii Sobor* (see Chapter I, note 5).

15 1 September. Bussow uses the Latin form, *Aegidius*. St Giles was an obscure hermit somewhere in France, whose feast became popular in the west around the ninth or tenth century. For the Muscovites 1 September was the New Year, and therefore the taxation thus remitted was in fact a New Year offering, though Bussow may not have been aware of the fact.

16 *Sappass, das ist Victualien. Sappass* is Bussow's faulty rendering of the Russian *zapas*.

17 There is no actual documentary evidence for this oath, but the story is repeated in so many sources that there must have been some basis in reality.

18 The foregoing provisions, though Bussow does not make this clear, evidently applied to the expatriate community.

19 This is a reference to the first foreign settlement, or "German suburb" in Moscow. The foreign settlement was more or less disbanded during

the Time of Troubles, but with the restoration of order the expatriates returned and settled principally in the northwestern sector of the White City. In 1652 all foreigners were required to move to the new "German suburb" beyond the Yauza river. See Lindsey A.J. Hughes, "Foreign Settlement," MERSH 11 (1979): 216–18.

20 Actually *Jakob* de la Gardie, son of Pontus, the celebrated French soldier of fortune who saw many years of Swedish service. Jakob commanded the Swedish contingent sent to aid Tsar Vasily Shuisky against the Poles in 1609, and led the Swedish forces occupying Novgorod and large areas of Northern Russia until the 1617 Treaty of Stolbovo.

21 Petreius (272): "Since this project did not come about, he nevertheless sent eighteen youths from the lesser nobility forth to learn foreign languages and arts, of whom eventually three ended up in Sweden, and served at the court of King Karl IX of blessed memory, and were provided with honourable remuneration."

22 Gustav (1568–1607) was an illegitimate son of King Erik XIV by Katharina Monsdotter, the daughter of a military servitor. His father was deposed in the same year as Gustav's birth. The child was sent to Poland and subsequently wandered from one country to another, at different times seeking the protection of King Sigismund III of Poland (who considered himself the rightful king of Sweden, as opposed to the usurper Karl IX), and the Holy Roman Emperor Rudolf II. In 1599 Boris invited Gustav to Moscow, where he arrived 19 August.

23 The passage between parentheses is omitted from the Adelung MS.

24 Other foreign accounts (Massa, *Short History*, 46–8, and Petreius, *Historien und Bericht*, 272–5) corroborate the obsequious attention Boris accorded Gustav, also relating that he was very learned but mentally unstable, and the baneful influence exerted upon him by Mistress Kater. Having disappointed Boris's hopes, Gustav was exiled to Uglich in 1601, transferred to Yaroslavl by the False Dmitry in 1605, and sent by Vasily Shuisky to Kashin in 1607, where he died shortly thereafter. Petreius gives a different account of the reasons for Gustav's disfavour: "This Grand Princely favour lasted for two years, until the Grand Prince let it be proposed to him that he cast off his religion and be rebaptized, adopting the Russian religion, and then he would not only be as a father to him, and give him his daughter to wed, but would also be prepared to assume the rule of the kingdom of Sweden. The praiseworthy lord would in no wise consent to the Grand Prince's proposals and said that if he could not obtain a wife without casting off his religion and dismembering his beloved fatherland, he would be willing to spend all his life in captivity and die the most dreadful death."

25 Again Petreius (276–7) provides an interesting variation: "After the
    death of Grishka, at the order of the Grand Prince Vasily Ivanovich
    Shuisky, he was brought from there to the town of Kashin, where he
    was provided with somewhat better food, drink, and other commodities
    than he had been given under Grishka. He remained there until he
    departed through death in the year 1607, and was buried in the town
    in a fine mausoleum within a birch thicket, which not only I, but also
    the Swedish general Jakob de la Gardie and various other people have
    seen with their own eyes and can bear witness to the fact. Therefore
    what Martin Beer writes cannot be credited, namely that he buried
    him and received a fee of twenty rubles, and that he was buried in the
    monastery named after Dmitry Solunsky, for it is the Russian custom
    that in no way is it permitted for anyone, be he of high or of lowly
    estate, to be buried in any consecrated ground, or in any monastery or
    church, who is not of their religion." Note that Petreius, unlike Bussow,
    gives de la Gardie's name correctly, or rather, names the right de la
    Gardie. He then (277) continued with damaging testimony against
    Bussow, whose would-be patron the Duke of Brunswick was a friend of
    the Swedish king: "Since the Grand Prince Boris Godunov could in no
    way persuade Lord Gustav to fight against his fatherland, he intrigued
    with certain foreign persons, *of whom one named Conrad Bussow was the
    principal and ringleader*, how they might by their craft and guile bring
    the fortress of Narva over from the Swedish crown under the Musco-
    vite yoke and servitude. But he was no more successful, since several
    were arrested on account of this, and were beheaded or broken on the
    wheel, and thus received their just reward, for which they had none
    but their traitorous seducers to thank." [emphasis mine]
26 Martin Beer (1577–1646), a native of Neustadt, pursued theological
    studies at Leipzig, and in 1600, together with two other ordinands, was
    called to minister to the Lutheran community in Moscow, where he
    taught in the parochial school for three years prior to his ordination in
    1605. He also married one of Bussow's daughters and collaborated
    with his father-in-law on an early draft of his chronicle. Beer was in
    Moscow during the reign of the False Dmitry and the early part of
    Shuisky's reign, though later he resided in Kozelsk and Kaluga in terri-
    tory controlled by the second Pretender, from whose wrath, according
    to Bussow's highly dramatized account (see chapter XVIII, below) he
    was largely instrumental in saving the lives of the German mercenaries
    suspected of disloyalty. In 1611 he fled to Riga, became a military
    chaplain at Dünamünde in Polish-held Livonia, and finally settled at
    Narva, where he became pastor of St John's Lutheran church. In 1615
    he is known to have taken a leading part in the prosecution of a witch

trial, ending in the defendant being burned at the stake. Fragments of a sermon delivered by him in 1627 show him to have been a stern and unbending champion of the Lutheran faith.

27 Christopher Reitlinger entered Russia in the suite of Ambassador Richard Leigh. He had been preceded by a Scotsman, a certain Captain Gabriel whom Bussow later shows, *sub anno* 1602, depriving Bogdan Belsky of his luxuriant beard for alleged treasonable utterances against Boris.

28 Vasmar was the only one of the physicians recruited by Boris to be allowed to remain in Moscow after the death of the False Dmitry. It seems that by then he had become Vasily Shuisky's personal physician.

29 The Adelung MS reads Benoki, but all the other MSS read Benski.

30 Marginal note: "A ruble is worth 100 mariagroschen." The maria-   ,
groschen was equivalent to one-tenth of a reichsthaler, though the exact exchange rate between the latter and the ruble fluctuated greatly. In the early seventeenth century in Russia the Joachimsthaler, which represented the purest silver currency of the Holy Roman Empire, was overstamped and placed in circulation on a par with the ruble. Such a piece of coinage was known in Russia as an *efimok*, plural *efimki*.

31 Bussow uses the Russian term *korm*.

32 Adelung MS: a large jug of aquavit and a large jug of vinegar.

33 *"Ein schön Zimmer Zobeln."* Smirnov translates this as *"sorok prekrasnykh sobolei."* A literal translation would be "a roomful of fine sables." Sables generally were presented in multiples of forty.

34 Ivan IV had been far more indulgent towards Lutheranism than any other non-Orthodox creed, permitting the German Protestants in his service to hold their own religious gatherings. In the 1560s there was a resident pastor, Johannes Wettermann, and in 1575–76 the first Lutheran church was built, dedicated to St Michael the Archangel. Ivan ordered it destroyed in 1580, but a second St Michael's church was built outside the city in 1584. Bussow apparently is referring here to a third church, which was built in 1601. A second Lutheran parish, that of St Peter and St Paul, was added, and so it continued until 1643, when St Michael's church was moved and all private Lutheran chapels were closed. With the removal of the foreign community beyond the Yauza in 1652, the Lutheran congregations were reorganized once again. See Daniel Rowland, "Lutherans in Russia and the Soviet Union", MERSH 20 (1981): 199–201.

35 Martin Beer later married Bussow's daughter.

36 In fact no such treaty was concluded. The Imperial ambassador Michael Schiele (see note 6, above) was in Moscow in 1598 and in this capacity conveyed the Emperor Rudolf II's felicitations on Boris's accession. A return embassy, led by Afanasy Vlasiev, did not mention the

possibility of an anti-Turkish coalition; its chief aim was to obtain Austrian aid against Poland. Though both sides professed sincerest amity, no concrete agreement was reached.

37 Most MSS read *Blianten*, but Wolfenbüttel II has a correction *Brillanten* inked in (f. 11v). This occurs in several places in the MS.

38 There is no record elsewhere of such an exchange between Russia and Turkey during the reign of Boris Godunov. Bussow's account can therefore be dismissed as fictitious.

39 There were abortive negotiations in 1601 in which the Russians demanded the retrocession of Narva and part of Estonia, but in the end relations between the two countries continued to be governed by the 1595 Treaty of Teusen.

40 The Truce of Yam Zapolsky concluded the Livonian War in 1582 and was to last for ten years. It was renewed in 1592, and then was extended for twenty-one years in 1601 after stormy ambassadorial exchanges between Leo Sapieha and Afanasy Vlasiev.

41 A fuller account of the arrival, sojourn, death, and burial of the prince is to be found in Massa, 56–63, and Petreius, 277–82. Massa gives the date of the prince's death as 28 October. There is also a detailed account by the Danish diplomat Aksel Gyldenstierna (1602–03), and an anonymous account, published in German in 1604 and in Danish in 1606. See Adelung, *Kritisch-literärische Übersicht der Reisenden in Russland*, 2:111–27.

42 The Prince's remains were removed to Denmark in 1637 and reburied in the royal crypt.

43 Sigismund Vasa (1566–1632) was elected King of Poland in 1587 and in 1592 succeeded to the throne of Sweden where, however, he was distrusted on account of his ardent Catholicism. He was overthrown in 1599 after several attempts to assert his royal prerogative. The leader of the Protestant interest, Duke Karl of Södermanland, formally accepted the throne in 1604 as King Karl IX, reigning until his death in 1611. Sigismund fought three unsuccessful wars (1599–1611, 1617–20 and 1621–29) to regain his Swedish throne. Livonia was a major bone of contention between Poland and Sweden in the course of these years. Sigismund also had to contend with the *rokosz* (rebellion) of 1606–08, in which the Protestant party among the Polish gentry played a major role. Sigismund also encountered much opposition among the Polish nobility to the furtherance of his extraneous dynastic ambitions in Sweden and Muscovy.

44 The adjective "*gut*" is frequently translated by Smirnov as "poor" or "unfortunate." Apparently in Bussow's time it could be used in such an idiomatic fashion.

45 Rendered as *Hirriempe* by Bussow. It was a minor fortress situated between Dorpat and Walck.

46 Neuhausen (in Russian Novgorodok) was situated right on the border-lands of the Pskov territories. During the course of the Livonian War (1558–82) it had been successively in Russian, Polish, and Swedish hands. In this particular round of the Polish-Swedish contest, the Swedes enjoyed the initial success, conquering the whole of Estonia, but in the spring of 1601 the Poles counterattacked. Boris's cordial wel-come to the thirty-five Livonian nobles was doubtless designed to gain popularity in that quarter in order that he himself might fish in these troubled waters. Bussow himself had previously been commandant of the Neuhausen garrison.

47 If Petreius's assertions (see note 25, above) are correct, Bussow's moral indignation against Vittinghofen is singularly misplaced. The only dif-ference is that the latter intended to hand the fortress over to the Poles rather than to the Russians.

48 The Caves (Pechersky) monastery near Pskov, named after its ancient Kiev prototype, was founded in the middle of the fifteenth century. Its principal church was built in 1473 and the monastery as a whole was rebuilt after being destroyed by the Livonian knights in 1519. Between 1553 and 1565 it was surrounded by fortifications, and withstood a major siege by King Stefan Bathory in 1581–82. It also resisted attempts by both the Poles and the Swedes to capture it between 1611 and 1616.

49 *Ex duobus malis minimum esse eligendum.*

50 Academy MS reads *21 Dec. 1601.* Wolfenbüttel II – *21 Novembris Anno 1601.*

51 *Zum prestauen.*

52 "tapestries and" is omitted from the Adelung MS.

53 The term *Latuschen* is used. Wolfenbüttel II has a marginal note: "*Latuschen* are non-Germans."

54 In Russia the offering of bread and salt is a token of welcome.

55 The Wolfenbüttel II and Academy manuscripts add "father."

56 The Razriad. The Academy and Wolfenbüttel II MSS have a marginal note: *Razereth ist eine Canzley oder Gemach darauf Kayserl. Sachen verrichtet werden.*

57 Trading post – Bussow uses the word *Comthore.*

58 The embassy from Lübeck and the other Hanseatic towns is also recounted by Petreius, 283.

59 The construction of stone fortifications (1585–91) enclosed the so-called White City as a third line of fortifications, after the Kremlin and the Kitay-gorod. A fourth set of defences also enclosed the so-called Earthen City. The fortifications built at this time around Smolensk enabled the city to hold out against the Poles for the space of twenty-one months. Both of these projects were executed by the Russian

engineer and architect Fedor Savelev Kon and were commissioned by Boris Godunov while still regent.

60 Boris did build a frontier town called Tsarevo-Borisov in the year 1600. Bussow is evidently confused by this double-barrelled name and thought that two towns had been built. Tsarevo-Borisov was on the Donets river below Belgorod. The site was abandoned during the Troubles.

61 *Das jus talionis traf ihm endlich. Quod fecerat idem ipsi Deus retribuebat.*

62 Bogdan Belsky (d. 1611) was the nephew of Ivan IV's favourite Maliuta Skuratov and came to enjoy the particular confidence of the tsar. Tradition has it that Ivan died while playing chess with Bogdan. He led a clique in 1584 which favoured a regency on behalf of Tsarevich Dmitry, and almost certainly was saved from the power of the mob by Boris, who temporarily sent him into honorific exile. During the reign of Tsar Fedor he returned to Moscow and resumed the office of Armourer, to which he had originally been appointed in 1578. He and Boris fell out in 1598 when the latter made his bid for the throne. Once again the rift was healed by yet another period of honorific exile, this time to Tsarevo-Borisov. Following the events related here by Bussow, Belsky was stripped of his estates and banished to the Volga frontier, where he remained until Godunov's death in 1605. He was promoted to boyar rank by the False Dmitry, but under Shuisky he was once again sent to a remote command, this time as governor of Kazan, where he was assassinated in 1611 by the townspeople who wished to support Pseudo-Dmitry II. See entry by Hugh F. Graham, MERSH 4 (1977): 1–2.

63 Other variants give this figure as fifteen.

64 *Cacoëthes regnandi.*

65 The Romanov affair began in 1601 with a denunciation by Vtoroy Bartenev, treasurer to Alexander Nikitich Romanov, saying that there were certain roots hidden in his master's treasury. These roots had been placed there by Bartenev himself at the instigation of S. N. Godunov, who at that time was responsible for the police network. A search was initiated, following which the Romanovs were accused of wishing to poison the tsar and were punished severely. The eldest brother, Fedor Nikitich, was tonsured as a monk and sent to the Antoniev-Siisky monastery. His wife was forced to take the veil in one of the settlements beyond the Onega river. Alexander Nikitich was sent to Luza, near the shores of the White Sea, Mikhail Nikitich to Perm, Vasily Nikitich to Yaransk, Ivan Nikitich to Pelym. All the brothers except Fedor and Ivan died in exile. The blow also fell upon families related to the Romanovs— the Cherkassky, Sitsky, Repin, Shestunov, Sheremetev, and Karpov families [Note 32 in Smirnov edition of Bussow].

66   *Non audet Stygius Pluto tentare, quod audet / Effraenus monachus plenaque fraudis anus.*

67   Most sources take it for granted that the False Dmitry and Grishka Otrepiev were one and the same person. Nevertheless the "helper" theory propounded by Bussow, who was so knowledgeable on other matters, cannot be dismissed lightly. Another theory, to which Bussow also alludes, was that the Pretender was a natural son of the late Polish king Stefan Bathory. Sapieha allegedly boasted of the Polish achievement in placing Bathory's son on the Muscovite throne in his conversation with the author. See below, chapter VIII.

68   Interpolation in some MSS "the grandfather of Michael Wisniowecki, King of Poland." Michael Wisniowiecki Koribut reigned from 1669 to 1673. The interpolation is absent from the Wolfenbüttel II and Academy MSS.

69   The most common Russian version of this story is related by the *New Chronicler* (60–1). The Pretender, living incognito in Lithuania, feigned mortal illness and made a deathbed confession, which the priest reported to Prince Adam Wisniowiecki.

70   There is no confirmation elsewhere of Boris's alleged message and offers to Prince Adam Wisniowiecki. For "brigand," Bussow here uses the term *den Worrn*, which is a Germanized version of the Russian *Vor*. Thus False Dmitry II was commonly referred to as the Tushino Brigand (*Tushinskii Vor*), or simply as "the Brigand" (*Vor*).

71   *Wolan Boch da thy.*

72   Narva was at that time in Swedish hands. It had been captured from the Livonian knights in 1558 by the Russians in the opening stages of the Livonian War, but was captured in 1581 by the Swedes, in whose hands it remained until 1704.

73   Ivangorod was originally founded by Ivan III on the site of the fishing village of Novoye Selo, on the opposite bank of the Narova estuary to the town of Narva. It was burned to the ground by the Swedes in 1495 but subsequently recovered. During the Livonian War, in 1581, it was captured by the Swedes but was retaken by the Russians in 1590. Between 1612 and 1704, like Narva, it was in Swedish hands.

74   According to Massa (68) S. S. Godunov was sent to receive the submission of the Nogay Tatars, who had decided to exchange Muscovite for Turkish tutelage, but he was prevented from proceeding further than Samara by reason of cossack piracy on the Volga.

75   Most historians accept the hypothesis that there was a connection between the princely-boyar opposition to Boris and the forces backing the Pretender. The early Soviet historian Golubtsov presented an alternative thesis, namely that the idea originated with certain "Polish diplomats" and was eagerly received by service people and townsmen in the border

regions, where social discontent was rife. See A. I. Golubtsov, "'Izmena' smolian pri Borise Godunove," *Uchenye zapiski* RANION (Scholarly Nota-tions of the Russian Association of Scientific Research Institutes in the Social Sciences), vol. 5, 1929. This theme is also dealt with at length in D. P. Makovskii, *Pervaia krest'ianskaia voina v Rossii* (Smolensk, 1967).

76   The thaler is probably the Joachimsthaler, first minted in 1518. It became standard currency throughout Europe, including Russia where they were used in the absence of silver coins with large denominations and even became for a short time official currency in 1655, over-stamped with the Russian official die and called *efimki s priznakami*. A groschen was a silver coin of small denomination of German or Polish origin whose exchange value varied. At one time sixty Polish groschen were held to be equivalent to half a ruble.

77   (*credas*).

78   *Boschtumb* , doubtless Bussow's rendition of *Bozhii Dom*.

79   *ziemlich exhaurieret*.

80   Here, as elsewhere in Bussow's narration, actual figures must be treated with caution since they are not so much concerned to provide accurate statistics as to impress or appal. Most historians agree that the entire population of Moscow at this time barely exceeded 100,000.

81   Palitsyn (105–6) and Massa (52–4) give similar account of the famine. Palitsyn gives the number of those buried at the tsar's expense as 127,000, but hints that this only represents a fraction of the total fatali-ties. Both Palitsyn and Massa emphasize speculation in grain, Massa in particular pointing the finger at the Patriarch. Margeret (58) gives the number of those who died in the famine as 120,000.

82   *Klafftern*.

83   Actually Rudolf II (1576–1612). His younger brother, Archduke Mat-thias, reigned from 1612 to 1619, though in 1608 he gained consider-able power and territory at the expense of the mentally unstable Rudolf.

84   Andreas Logau, ambassador of Rudolf II, arrived in Moscow in July 1604. Bussow's information, that in preparation for Logau's reception measures were taken to conceal the grave internal situation in the country, corresponds to reality. For instance, it is specified in the instructions to V. I. Buinosov, governor of Novgorod, that "wherever the ambassador may be in Great Novgorod, ensure that whatever streets the ambassador may travel are thronged with people, and in good order." Concerning the execution of these orders, the governor reported as follows: "And in whatsoever place the ambassador went in Novgorod, or beyond the city limits, O sovereign, every place was thronged with people and was in a good state of repair, according to your previous instructions. Gentry, boyar sons, and officials patrolled

these places on horseback and in clean attire, while other boyar sons, Novgorod merchants, and townspeople were also on foot in the streets, in the market rows, and in front of the houses, likewise in clean attire." Obviously, as Bussow's notations show, much greater attention would have been given to the good appearance of the capital at the moment of Ambassador Logau's entry [Note 39 in Smirnov's edition of *Moskovskaia Khronika*].

85 Marginal note in Wolfenbüttel II: "How the war in Livonia in the year 1600 between the crowns of Poland and Sweden raged, how the wolves set up so great a howling, also appearing in broad daylight in villages and public places, doing great mischief."

86 *des Ortes, da das Schwert herkam.*

87 Marginal note: "A ruble is equivalent to a hundred mariagroschen."

88 The bright star was probably the Supernova, which is known to have appeared in June 1604. Practically every account of the events of that year, perhaps with the benefit of hindsight, reports unusual portents and apparitions.

89 Afanasy Vlasiev (dates of birth and death unknown) is first mentioned in 1595 as one of the ambassadors sent to Rudolf II at Pilsen. Between 1596 and 1603 he was one of the officials in charge of the Kazan Chancellery and he also served with the Ambassadorial Chancellery from 1601 to 1605. In the latter capacity he took part in many diplomatic receptions during the reign of Boris Godunov and was sent to Poland in 1601, in the company of Mikhail Glebovich Saltykov, to negotiate an extension of the truce with Sigismund III. He was also present at an audience between Boris and the Crimean emissary and in February 1602 received the English agent John Merrick. Again in the company of Saltykov, he was sent to the frontier to escort Duke Johan, Boris's prospective son-in-law, to the capital. He was also the chief negotiator regarding a possible English marriage for Boris's son Fedor. After the fall of the Godunovs, Vlasiev was one of the delegates sent by the city of Moscow to greet the Pretender at Tula. In July 1605 he was promoted from conciliar secretary to the rank of *okol'nichii*. The following month he was sent to Poland to claim the hand of Maryna for Dmitry, and on 20 November, N.S., stood as Dmitry's proxy at the betrothal ceremony. In the last days of Dmitry's reign, as treasurer, he was virtually in sole charge of state affairs. It is said that it was he who interceded for Shuisky as the latter was about to be executed for treason. If so, Shuisky's ingratitude to Vlasiev was exceeded only by that shown to Dmitry himself. After Shuisky's seizure of power he was removed from office and his estates were confiscated, his former house being requisitioned for the incarceration of the Mniszech family. He

himself was later sent in semi-honorific exile to be governor of Ufa. In 1610 he petitioned King Sigismund for the restoration of his estates.

90 Note that Bussow considers Otrepiev and the False Dmitry to be two distinct persons. See note 67, above.

91 *Das Diabolicum Instrumentum.*

92 Bussow's account of Dmitry's initial incursion into Moscow is over-simplified. In fact he captured Moravsk and Chernigov without a struggle but suffered his first reverse at Novgorod-Seversk, held by Peter Basmanov (later to be Dmitry's chief collaborator but at this time still loyal to Boris). Detachments from the main invading force fanned out in all directions, occupying various towns in Dmitry's name. Putivl was surrendered to the invaders by the governor, Vasily Rubets-Mosal-sky. Other towns, such as Rylsk, Kursk, Sevsk, Kromy, and Karachev, followed suit. Bussow's description of the methods used by the government to compel servitors to report for duty is confirmed in official sources. The battle in which Mstislavsky was wounded took place 21 December 1604. Massa (86) states that Peter Basmanov and Prince Yury Trubetskoy arrived back at Moscow 14 February 1605.

93 Actually Fedor Ivanovich Mstislavsky.

94 11 November.

95 *Blindlings (wie man pflegt zu reden).*

96 Literally "did not spin any silk from it" (*aber selbst spann er auch keine Seide dabey).* See also below, chapter XVIII, note 12.

97 Bussow probably exaggerates the number of Muscovite forces, which other sources estimate to have been forty or fifty thousand.

98 Jacques Margeret (1565–1619), a Protestant veteran of the French wars of religion, who in 1595 became an international soldier of fortune in the service of various rulers in their wars against the Turks. In 1600, while seeking employment in Austria, he was recruited by the Russian ambassador Afanasy Vlasiev (see note 89, above) and within several years rose to over-all command of Boris Godunov's foreign troops, playing a decisive role in the defeat of Dmitry's forces at Dobrynichi (though see note 99, below). After the death of Boris, Margeret was graciously received into Dmitry's service and in January 1606 assumed command of the palace guard. He was indisposed on the night of Dmitry's assassination and for a short while continued in the service of Tsar Vasily Shuisky. Discharged honourably towards the end of the summer of 1606, he returned to France, where King Henri IV commissioned him to write an account of his experiences in Russia. This was completed in the winter of 1606–07 and has since proved to be a valuable primary source for this period of Russian history. Unfortunately Margeret has left no account of his second, and equally

fascinating, period of participation in the Muscovite wars. In late 1608 he joined the Tushino camp, but when it broke up in December 1609 he rallied to the forces of King Sigismund III before Smolensk. He took part in Hetman Zolkiewski's advance on Moscow, particularly distinguishing himself at the battle of Klushino, 24 June 1610. He was among the Polish occupying forces in Moscow and, according to Bussow (see chapter XX), was outstanding in conducting a daring sortie against the numerically superior Muscovite besieging forces, doing much to restore the flagging Polish morale. Margeret was recalled in October 1611 to Poland, where he was richly rewarded by King Sigismund. In January 1612 he was at Hamburg, trying to organize an expeditionary force to aid the Muscovites. Prince Dmitry Pozharsky, commander of the Muscovite forces, made it clear in no uncertain terms that Margeret's services were not required and ordered the local authorities at Archangel to prohibit his entry. He seems thereafter to have retired from active service, settling down in the Palatinate. See entry by Chester Dunning, MERSH 21 (1981): 96–9; Margeret, *The Russian Empire*.

99 According to Bussow, the day was saved by a cold steel counterattack by the foreign mercenaries under Walther von Rosen and Jacques Margeret. Yet Margeret (63), who is not exactly given to false modesty, gives credit to the Russian infantry, who "seeing the Poles so near, fired a volley from ten or twelve thousand harquebuses which so frightened the Poles that they turned back in great confusion. Meanwhile the rest of Dmitry's cavalry and infantry approached as quickly as possible, thinking to have gained a great victory. But on seeing their own cavalry turn back in such disorder, they took to their heels and were pursued by five or six thousand horses for more than seven or eight versts."

100 *Lumpen-haus.*

101 Similar accounts of atrocities committed in the Komaritsk district are contained in Massa (77) and Timofeev (84).

102 According to the *Chronograph of the Third Redaction* (Popov, *Izbornik*, 226), the inhabitants of Putivl threatened to hand Dmitry over to Boris, rather than allow him to flee to Poland and leave them to face the music!

103 The town of Kromy is first mentioned in 1147, but was of scant importance until the 1595 construction of a wooden fortress intended to forestall Tatar attacks. A similar account of the events at Kromy is contained in Massa (87–90).

104 Prince Mikhail Petrovich Katyrev-Rostovskii, father of the more famous Prince Ivan Mikhailovich who married Tatiana, sister of the future tsar Michael Romanov. Prince Mikhail is notable for having been one of the few Muscovite commanders to remain loyal to Boris's son Fedor when

the rest of the army declared for Dmitry. During the reign of the Pretender he was sent into semi-honorific exile as governor of Nizhny Novgorod, where both he and his wife died of plague within the year.

105 The notion that Boris committed suicide, though widely current at the time, appears to be unfounded. It is also unlikely that the *skhima*, or highest order of monasticism, would be conferred upon a suicide. Boris is known to have been in poor health for several years and suffered partial paralysis from a stroke in 1604. The most circumstantial accounts indicate that a massive cerebral haemorrhage was the cause of death. Margeret (64) states that Boris died of apoplexy. Both the *Chronograph of the Third Redaction* (Popov, *Izbornik*, 228) and Terenty's *So-called Other Tale* (col. 39) state that Boris took poison, but the English ambassador, Sir Thomas Smith, who was in Moscow at the time, states: "His death was very sudden, and as was in it felt, very strange: for within some two hours after dinner having (as he usually had) his Doctors with him, who left him in their judgments in health, as the good meal he made could witness, for he dined well, and plentifully, though presently after as may be thought, feeding over much, he felt himself not only heavy, but also pained in his stomach: presently went into his chamber, laid himself upon his bed, sent for his doctors (which always speeded) yet before they came, he was past, being speechless and soon after dying." *Voyage and Entertainment in Russia* [Spelling modernized].

106 *Da traf den guten Herrn das jus talionis wieder.*

107 *O mala conscientia, quam timida tu es.*

108 Actually 1598 (see chapter I, note 17). In actual fact Fedor Ivanovich died 7 January and Boris was elected 17 February, though his coronation took place 1 September.

CHAPTER III

1 *New Chronicler* (64) denounces Basmanov as "the instigator of all the evil misfortune," who after the administration of the oath to Fedor Borisovich "soon took counsel to his own evil perdition and forgot his solemn oath." Massa (98–100) states that the treason was premeditated, and that there was also considerable confusion, "that it seemed that heaven and earth were coming to an end." He also states that after some hesitation the German mercenaries agreed to serve Dmitry, and only a remnant of about seventy men remained loyal to Fedor and returned to Moscow. Margeret (see note 224 of the Dunning translation) was apparently in Moscow at the time. He also (66) gives the interesting detail that Saltykov was arrested by Dmitry's supporters. It could be, as Dunning suggests, that Margeret was simply misinformed,

or otherwise that Saltykov, like Golitsyn in the *New Chronicler* account, was simply hedging his bets.

2 ... *das große Dorf Crasna Cella, sonsten auch das Kayserdorff genannt ...*

3 *Powina.* Marginal note: "A *Powina* is a letter in which one acknowledges one's guilt and asks for pardon."

4 Dmitry's missive, which Bussow paraphrases here, is printed in AAE, 2, no. 34. In actual fact Dmitry sent not one but two emissaries to Krasnoye Selo, namely Gavrilo Pushkin and Naum Pleshcheev.

5 Bussow is evidently referring to the Church of Basil the Blessed, officially the Church of the Intercession, erected 1555–60 to commemorate the conquest of Kazan and Astrakhan. The chapel, which contains the remains of the famous *yurodivyi* Basil the Blessed, was built in 1588 on the northeast side of the original church.

6 *Lobnoe Mesto*, or *Laubenmesse* in Bussow's rendition. The stone pulpit, still to be seen in the Red Square, is first mentioned under the year 1547 and was originally surmounted by a roof. It was used for reading aloud decrees and proclamations, and state executions were carried out close by.

7 See Chapter II, note 62, above.

8 The *povinnaia gramota* from the inhabitants of Moscow was carried to Dmitry by Prince I. M. Vorotynsky and Prince A. A. Teliatevsky. The latter was kept waiting while Dmitry entertained a Cossack delegation and was subsequently ill-treated by the Cossacks. *New Chronicler*, 65.

9 Bussow is correct when he states that Fedor and his mother were murdered, actually by strangulation, though it was officially given out that they had committed suicide. Their remains and those of Boris (which were exhumed from the Archangel Cathedral) were interred in the Varsonofiev monastery, the lack of ceremony being intended to reinforce the suicide story, which was widely believed and is echoed in a number of sources. During the reign of Vasily Shuisky the remains of the Godunovs were more honourably reinterred in the forecourt of the Trinity Monastery, in a large stone sarcophagus which can still be seen today. Xenia, now the nun Olga, was present at the reburial, and was among those besieged in the monastery by the Poles in 1608–10. In 1622 she petitioned Tsar Michael for permission to be buried beside her parents and brother.

10 Actually based upon the prophecy of his predecessor Celestine V: "Thou hast climbed like a fox, thou shalt reign like a lion, thou shalt die like a dog."

CHAPTER IV

1 The Academy MS reads "three days," Wolfenbüttel II and Adelung "five days."

2 *Reichs-Senatoren.*

3 Bussow is the only author to mention the whirlwind, though the *New Chronicler* (66) mentions an eclipse of the sun, which was not seen anywhere outside Moscow. Massa (109) gives the date of Dmitry's entry into Moscow as 20 June, and on this detail and many others is in agreement with Bussow. Margeret (67) likewise gives the date as 30 June, N.S. (20 June O.S.).

4 Smirnov (note 51) considers it unlikely that the cross in question bore the image of St Nicholas, since the only image on crosses at that time was the crucifixion. The only cross-shaped objects to bear the image of saints were reliquaries.

5 Bussow is probably in error as to the date of Dmitry's coronation. Massa (112) gives the date as 20 July and Margeret (68) as 31 July, N.S. (21 July O.S.). This would accord with the repeated assertions by Dmitry that he would not be crowned until his "mother," the nun Martha, had arrived back in Moscow. This event, according to most accounts, occurred 18 July. Bussow therefore appears to have these events in reverse order.

6 Actually Maria-Martha was consigned to a convent near Beloozero. The Trinity monastery, as is well known, was a male conventual establishment.

7 Bussow, in his plan of Moscow, plots the monastery of St Cyril, though there was actually no such monastery in the Kremlin. The wealthy community of St Cyril of Beloozero very likely maintained a hospice in Moscow, as did several other powerful religious foundations. Martha was actually lodged in special apartments in the Ascension convent, close to the Saviour gates.

8 This account of Dmitry holding open house every Wednesday and Saturday to receive petitions is unique to Bussow.

9 Argamaks were hardy horses of Tatar origin, much favoured as mounts by the Muscovites.

10 *Daninsky.*

11 *Galeats.* Dmitry's assembly of a large cache of arms for the forthcoming campaign against the Turks is also related in Massa (123), the *New Chronicler* (68) and Palitsyn (118).

12 The new wooden palace in the Kremlin is described by Massa (115), together with a sketch (illustration facing xxiv).

13 *Multo alius Hector.*

14 *Marinae Gorgonae.*

15 *Affenas Iwanowitz Flassow.*

16 Doubtless a reference to Margeret's Protestant faith, which he shared with Bussow, the son of one Lutheran pastor and the father-in-law of another.

17 Dmitry's foreign bodyguards are also described in detail by Massa
(116–17), who gives the name of the Scottish captain, called Albert
Wandmann by Bussow, as Albert Lanton (?Lambton). Knudson is mentioned by Massa, with the additional detail that he had formerly been
in the retinue of the late Duke Johan.

18 *Periculum est in mora.*

19 *Terrae inutilibus ponderibus et otiosis monachis.*

20 Soloviev (book IV, 450) thought that Bussow mistook a simple demand
for clerical taxation for a crusade against the Tatars, for which there
were precedents under Ivan IV, for such an attempt. Soloviev further
points out that, far from being hostile to religious foundations, Dmitry
confirmed charters for some of them and even issued new charters of
immunity.

21 *Tsertori und Narbat.*

22 Massa (121–3) also described the fate of the plotters among the musketeers in similar gruesome detail, concluding, "The remains of the
corpses were gathered into a cart and thrown to the dogs in the open
field. The sight of this cart on which these human remains had been
placed on view, and which thus crossed the city, made the hair stand
up on the heads of all the beholders." The incident is also related by
the *Novyi Letopisets* (68) and Petreius (323–4), who follows Bussow's narrative very closely.

23 *Coriphaeum.*

24 *Carnificem.*

25 Bussow seems to use the term "Mameluke" pejoratively of Germans
and other foreigners who became converted to the Orthodox religion
while in Muscovite service.

26 It is not clear why Bussow relates the occurrence of Shuisky's near-
execution *sub anno* 1606, when most other sources relate it to the
summer of 1605. Massa (113) gives the date as 25 August 1605, while
the most generally accepted date, late June, is given in the Russian
sources, the *So-called Other Tale* and the *Chronograph of 1617* [RIB, 13,
col. 52, and Popov, *Izbornik*, 235, 240]. Margeret (68), in a tantalizingly
brief reference, hints that Shuisky was tried by a body somewhat
resembling a *zemsky sobor*: "A short time later Prince Vasilii Shuiskii was
accused and convicted, *in the presence of persons chosen from all estates,* of
the crime of lese majesty." [Emphasis mine]. Concerning the possible
intervention of Dmitry's "mother," it is possible, as Margeret's translator
points out (164, note 241) that "although the nun Martha had not yet
arrived in Moscow, she could possibly have sent word to her 'son' not to
execute such a high-born prince at the outset of his reign."

27 *Wesom.*

28 Marginal note: "Tsar is not a Muscovite but an Arabic word, and means king. The Russians, however, believe that Tsar and Caesar have the same significance and therefore they call their lord an Emperor, though formerly they were only called *Kniaz Velikii*, which means Grand Prince. The Tatars however call their rulers Tsar, meaning a king."

29 Actually in 1606 Easter Sunday fell on 23 April.

30 Haiduks were mounted frontier troops of Hungarian or South Slav origin, who were occasionally employed by the Polish crown.

31 Marginal note: "*Nabaten* [the term used in the German text] are larger than military kettledrums [*Heerpaucken*]."

32 Maryna's entry is also described in great detail by Massa (127–9).

33 *malum omen.*

34 *diese Regiments Mutation.*

35 Some MSS: "all the power of Muscovy."

36 *Sotnicken und Petdeßotniken.*

37 Both the *New Chronicler* (68) and Massa (132) comment on the indignation of the Russians at having their sacred cathedrals profaned by "unbaptized" Latins.

38 Marginal note: "Russians do not eat veal."

39 Veal was regarded by the Russians as a forbidden dish. Some of Dmitry's accusers asserted that he had eaten veal during Lent, which of course would be doubly reprehensible. Nevertheless, it was also said of Shuisky that he, too, was partial to the same forbidden viands.

40 Annotations here and in the next note are appended in a different and later hand by someone acquainted with the travel account of Adam Olearius, published in 1656. Olearius was apparently acquainted with Martin Beer. "This pastor, Reverend Martin Bäer [sic] who spoke was Pastor in Narva in the year 1635, and is mentioned by Master Adam Olearius in his oriental Travel Description, page 129, stating that he had lived in Moscow during the reign of Boris Godunov. Concerning the election of Boris Godunov, see p. 125." This note is on a separate slip of paper between ff. 47v and 48 of the Wolfenbüttel II MS.

41 Notation in the same hand on the margin of f.48: "After the bath it was customary to take an afternoon nap. Olearius, p. 148."

42 Academy MS: "and 16."

43 *Citius venit periculum cum spernitur: item, accidit in puncto, quod non speratur in anno.*

44 Bussow's account of the events of 17 May 1606 is partly an eyewitness record and partly derived from first-hand information from his countrymen among the German bodyguards. His narrative is therefore of particular value as a primary source.

45 *Furor arma administrabat.*
46 *Achty mney, thy, Aspodar moia, sam Winewacht!* (Bussow then repeats it in German).
47 *Schwenzhoff* in the Adelung MS.
48 *"Infer stuprum tuae matri una cum imperatore tuo!"*
49 *10 Klafftern hoch war hinunter auf die Erde.* The Academy and Wolfenbüttel II manuscripts give the distance as twelve spans.
50 *Den Worn.* Marginal note: *"Worn ist ein Schelm."*
51 *Volumus nos omnes, unus post alium stuprum inferre, unus in p ...: alter in v ...: audivimus Polonicas vestras meretrices plurimum concubitus bene sustinere posse: nec ipsis unus vir sufficere. Et postea nudabant sua equina pudenda (proh Sodomia!) coram toto Gynaeceo, dicentes: Videte meretrices, videte nos multo fortiores Polonicis vestris. Probate nos!* These words, which in the original are in Latin, are only to be found in print in note 78 of Ustrialov's translation. The editors of the 1851 edition, as well as Smirnov in 1961, seem to have been overly solicitous of the susceptibilities of their readers. Rather than leave these words in the decent obscurity of a learned language, they have chosen to omit them altogether.
52 *ut intra actum anni tempus ex virginibus matres fierent.*
53 *Magna haec est injuria, trahi et trudi simul. Zugleich getreckt und gestoßen werden mag wohl ein unbillig Ding seyn.*
54 *Eto Zayr, pfse Russi.*
55 *Scammaroth* (Bussow's rendition of *skomorokh*).
56 A reference to the St Bartholomew massacre, 25 August 1572, a black day in the Protestant calendar, when about two thousand Huguenots were massacred, having gathered for the marriage of Henri of Navarre to Marguerite of Valois.

CHAPTER V

1 Literally "bite the grass."
2 See above, Chapter IV, note 25.
3 Massa (141–2) also describes the despoliation of the foreign merchants, and even gives some specific names, such as Philip Holbein of Augsburg and Ambrogio Cellari of Milan.
4 *Secci, secci Bledini deti! Haue tod, haue tod die Hurenkinder.*

CHAPTER VI

1 *dennige.* Marginal note: "Thirty-six dennige equals one thaler, and a ruble is one hundred dennig."
2 According to the Polish diarist Waclaw Dyamentowski, who was Maryna's chamberlain, the ladies of the tsaritsa's suite hid all their posses-

sions before being conducted by the boyars to another room for their own safety. Hirschberg, *Polska a Moskwa*, 52.

3 *Polluschen*. Marginal note: "Polluschen are worth forty to a penny."

4 *Mihi vindicta: Et ego retribuam. Mein ist die Rache, ich wills vergeltern.*

5 The official record of the interview between the boyars and Jerzy Mniszech, contained in sGGD 2, no. 139, is somewhat less dramatic.

6 Marginal note: "Beloozero (*Belesar*) is a fortress in a great deep morass where man can come to evil, and where the tsar's treasure is stored, and which also is called the White Lake."

7 Maryna and her father were transferred to Yaroslavl 16/26 August under the guard of three hundred musketeers. Prince Adam Wisniowiecki was interned at Kostroma, Martin Stadnicki at Rostov (later being transferred to Vologda and Beloozero), Pan Tarlo at Tver, and Pan Kazanowski at Ustiug.

CHAPTER VII

1 *virile.*

2 *juxta pudendum.*

3 The mask and bagpipe were two tools of the trade of the *skomorokhi*, or minstrels, who were regarded as suspect by the Orthodox church, which refused them burial in consecrated ground.

4 These two sentences are found only in Wolfenbüttel II (f. 6ov.).

5 *Die Bulwanische Pfordte.*

6 Most accounts agree that there were unnatural portents, which were attributed to the presence of the False Dmitry's corpse, and that as a result the Muscovites resolved to burn the body in order to exorcise his evil spirit. See Massa, 145; the Book of Annals, RIB 13, cols 656–7; Margeret, 73; the *So-called Other Tale*, RIB 13, col. 59. Massa and the *Book of Annals* state that the body was incinerated within the wooden fortress Dmitry had built, which was called by the Muscovites the "Monster of Hell." Peyerle (*O puteshestvii iz Krakova v Moskvu i obratno*, 196–7) also adds that after they had burned the body they placed the ashes in a cannon and fired it through the same gates by which he had entered Moscow, "so that even of his ashes nothing should remain."

7 *Gloriosos terrae humiliabo.*

8 *Quod uni accidit, pluribus accidere potest. Similes causae, similes producunt effectus.*

9 *Sunt demissa Deo curae sublimia tutus.*

10 *Deposuit superbos de sede.*

11 *Summisque negatum est stare diu.*

12 *Memento te esse hominem, gedencke, daß du ein Mensch bist, &c.*

13 *Redemptorem patibulo suspendere.*

14 *In matutino interficio peccatores.* Bussow then continues the quotation in German.

15 *Canis mortuus non mordet.*

16 *Fiat justitia et pereat mundus.*

CHAPTER VIII

1 *in partu et in educatione caesarei infantis.*

2 *Starost.* Literally "elder," but Bussow has a marginal note "*Starost ist ein Wächter.*"

3 Some variants read "did away with" (*umgebracht*) but this reading (*unterbracht*) in the Wolfenbüttel II and Adelung MSS is more factually correct.

4 *Quod Romanis non essent minores, imo majores.*

5 *Nostris viribus nostraque armata manu id facimus.*

6 An interesting autobiographical detail, namely that Bussow was present at Sapieha's siege of the Trinity monastery.

7 See chapter I, note 12.

8 On the other hand, another foreign mercenary, Margeret (90–1), believed Dmitry to have been genuine.

CHAPTERS IX AND X

1 In fact Shuisky was proclaimed tsar on 19 May and was crowned on 1 June 1606.

2 *Piroschnicken und Saposchnicken.* Marginal notes: "*Piroschnicken sind Pasteten Becker. Saposchnicken sind Stiefelmacher.*" (Wolfenbüttel II)

3 The assembly on the Red Square was at best a rump *zemsky sobor*. Bussow is therefore correct in characterizing Shuisky's accession as having taken place "without the knowledge or consent of the Assembly of the Land" (*ohne Wißen und Bewilligung sämtlicher Land-Stände*). The *Novyi letopisets* (69) confirms this assessment: "When the Renegade Monk was slain, the boyars began to consider sending out messages to the whole land, so that all manner of people might come from all the towns to Moscow, and that they in counsel with them might choose a sovereign for the Muscovite realm who would be beloved by all. But God did not see fit to pardon our sins or spare the bloodshed of so many Christians, for, being moved by Prince Vasily Ivanovich Shuisky, and not in consultation with the whole land, for even in Moscow there were not many people to be seen, on the fourth day after the slaying of the Renegade Monk they entered the city and took Prince Vasily to the Lobnoe Mesto, proclaimed him tsar, and accompanied him into the city, to the cathedral of the Most Pure Mother of God."

Palitsyn (115–16) is even more sweeping: "On the fourth day after the slaying of the Renegade Monk, Prince Vasily Ivanovich Shuisky was favoured as tsar by certain lesser people of the tsar's household and was brought to the tsar's palace without being proclaimed by any of the magnates or being petitioned by any of the people. And all of Russia was divided, for some loved him and others hated him."

4   Vasily Shuisky's embassy to the Polish king Sigismund III was dispatched 29 May 1606. The ambassadors, Prince G. K. Volkonsky and the secretary Andrei Ivanov, arrived in Krakow 16 December. They were received by the king on 24 December, and on 26 and 29 December carried on negotiations with the lords of the council. On 31 December the king gave them a farewell audience. As can be seen from the list of instructions given to Volkonsky and Ivanov, Bussow gives the gist of the talks fairly accurately [Smirnov's edition of *Moskovskaia Khronika*, note 72].

5   *Scilicet.*

6   *Davidem Vasmarum Lubecensem.*

7   A similar ironical account of the translation of the remains of Dmitry and its attendant miracles is contained in Massa, 159–61.

CHAPTER XI

1   *Nimca.*

2   This account of Bussow concerning the flight of Shakhovskoy and his fabrication of the new Dmitry legend is inaccurate. Shakhovskoy remained in Moscow and was later appointed governor of Putivl, replacing Prince Rubets-Mosalsky. The more likely initiator of the rumour would be Dmitry's boon companion Mikhail Molchanov, who in fact did flee Moscow on 17 May 1606. The ambassadors to King Sigismund were furthermore instructed, if asked about the rumour that Dmitry was alive and living in Sambor, to say that this person was probably Molchanov. SRIO 137, 301–2.

3   Bussow is probably correct in saying that it was Shakhovskoy who called upon Putivl to rise up in favour of Dmitry, since this is also mentioned in the *Novyi letopisets* (70): "In the town of Putivl Prince Grigory Shakhovskoy betrayed Tsar Vasily with all of Putivl, and told the inhabitants thereof that Dmitry was alive and was living in hiding."

4   *Parlament.*

5   *Galecz.*

6   Marginal note: "*Subenick ist ein Pelzmacher.*" *Subenick*, i.e., *shubnik* is a pun on Shuisky's name.

7   *Blynen.* Marginal note: "Blynen are cakes baked from oatmeal."

8 Bussow is mistaken here. Irina Fedorovna was Boris's sister, who had
   taken the religious name of Alexandra. His wife's name, of course, was
   Maria Grigorievna. The name is omitted from the Academy MS.
9 *Man soll den alten Freund nicht eher verwerfen, bis den neuen zuvor wohl
   probiert habe.*

CHAPTER XII

1 *Iwan Isaiwitz Polutnik.*
2 Bussow provides the most detailed biography of Bolotnikov contained
   in any source. The author had by now left Moscow and was, as he
   relates, living in semi-retirement at Kaluga. His son, also named
   Conrad, was fighting in the ranks of Bolotnikov's forces and the elder
   Conrad evidently knew Bolotnikov personally and had great respect for
   him – the respect of one soldier of fortune for another.
3 Two encounters have been compressed into one here. Pashkov had
   agreed to defect some time before, but was persuaded to remain in
   place until battle was engaged on the night of 26–27 November.
   Bussow also gives the interesting detail that out of the forty thousand
   troops commanded by Pashkov he was only able to take "several thousand" with him. The siege of Moscow was finally relieved on 2
   December.
4 Marginal note: "Kaluga is thirty miles from Moscow."
5 Actually "Dmitry" would have been the "uncle" rather than the "cousin"
   of "Tsarevich Peter." The correspondence between Shakhovskoy and
   Tsarevich Peter is borne out by the testimony of the bogus prince himself (AAE 2, no. 81). Tsarevich Peter was in fact Ileika Muromets, the
   illegitimate son of a petty trader of Murom. For a while he worked as a
   labourer in various towns along the Volga and then joined the Terek
   Cossacks, by whom he was chosen from a short list of two candidates to
   become the "Tsarevich Peter." During the winter of 1605–06 he and his
   men moved to the Volga basin, where they received a letter from the
   False Dmitry inviting them to Moscow, but when they heard of the Pretender's death they withdrew to the Lower Volga and eventually found
   their way to Putivl. They advanced to join the forces of Bolotnikov, at
   that time in Kaluga, which they relieved, and then together with Bolotnikov withdrew to Tula. After the fall of Tula on 10 October 1608,
   Ileika was captured and was hanged at Moscow outside the Serpukhov
   gates early in 1608.
6 Bussow consistently refers to him as Pontus, but this is incorrect (see
   chapter II, note 20, above). I have taken the liberty of amending the
   translation accordingly. Shuisky took the King of Sweden up on his
   offer in August 1608.

7 *Wenn einem Ferkel angeboten wird, daß man den Sack offen solle.*
8 *Woitzschin, ist ein Erbgut ...*
9 The Wolfenbüttel II and Adelung MSS give the date as 1 May.
10 Marginal note: "Tula is fourteen miles from Kaluga."
11 The battle described here was fought on the Vosma river, 5–7 June 1607.
12 This clause occurs only in the Wolfenbüttel II and Adelung MSS.
13 Zarutsky was not in fact a Pole, but a Ukrainian, a native of Tarnopol. After escaping the collapse of Bolotnikov's rebellion, he commanded a body of Don Cossacks on behalf of the second False Dmitry, upon whose death he assumed the guardianship of Maryna and her infant son. He took part in the abortive attempt to liberate Moscow in 1611, but after falling out with the commander of the second national army, Prince D. M. Pozharsky, he once again took up the cause of Maryna and her son, and finally withdrew to Astrakhan. Driven out of there by forces loyal to the new tsar, Michael, and a popular uprising within the city, he fled to the Urals, where he was handed over to the Muscovite authorities by local Cossacks. He was executed at Moscow in 1614.

CHAPTERS XIII AND XIV

1 The Academy MS reads *Ruschnitz.*
2 *Solcher Schreiberey war der gute Canzler ungewöhnt.* Literally, "The poor chancellor was not used to this kind of writing."
3 Marginal note: "Nicholas is their patron saint."
4 *Ja winewat Aspodar, Herr ich bin schuldig ...*
5 Most historians agree that the second False Dmitry was backed by Polish interests from the very start. Soloviev (book 4, 478–9) is a notable exception, since he considers the Pretender to have arisen spontaneously and only subsequently to have received Polish backing. In so doing he follows Bussow, whom he extensively quotes verbatim.
6 *Ismenick.* Marginal note: "*Ismenick ist ein Verräter.*"
7 28 October.
8 Bussow's account of the siege and surrender of Tula is especially valuable, since he was either an eyewitness or had a very direct interest in the events because of the presence of his son among the besieged. The information that Shuisky made a "separate peace" with the townspeople, and that Bolotnikov, far from being a revolutionary hero, was in fact a typical soldier of fortune, has a special ring of authenticity. This would explain why Bussow, normally so contemptuous of *Herr Omnis*, had so obvious a respect for Bolotnikov.
9 A marginal comment in the Academy manuscript reads, "they spent all the next nine years there, until 1617, enduring hardship." (*haben nun biß 1617 Jahr gantzer 9 Jahr lang sich allda im Elende drücken müssen*).

10 *Je ärger der Schalk, je beßer Glück.*

11 Marginal note: "*Sergius ist ein Abgott.*" Another instance of Bussow's odd notions about the Orthodox religion. Sergius of Radonezh, the founder of the Trinity monastery, was of course revered as a saint, not a god.

12 This paragraph only appears in the Academy and Wolfenbüttel II MSS.

13 " ... as will be related at the end of this book." (Adelung MS).

14 Aleksandr Jozef Lisowski (1575–1616) was a colonel of the Polish royal army and the organizer of irregular military bands known long after his death as *lisowczyki*. He joined the forces of the second False Dmitry at Starodub and the rest of his life was spent campaigning in Russia, either in the service of the Pretender or of King Sigismund. See the entry on Lisowski in MERSH 20, 60–2.

15 "Bergh" in some MSS.

16 Bussow is apparently mistaken about the timing of the defections and counter-defections of Hans Borck, which in fact occurred about a year earlier than stated here. He deserted Shuisky for Bolotnikov in October or November 1606 and fled to Kaluga, but when that city was besieged he was induced by rich gifts to transfer his allegiance again to Shuisky. After the forces of the "Tsarevich Peter" had relieved Kaluga, he once again joined the rebel camp. It is possible that he was sent to Tula as Shuisky's agent. See Smirnov's edition of *Moskovskaia Khronika*, note 105.

17 Ustrialov's translation gives I. I. Godunov in place of I. I. Nagoy. This seems to correspond with the information in the Sheremetev *Book of Boyars*, except that the drowning took place in 1610. *Drevneishaia Rossiiskaia Vivliofika* 20 (Moscow, 1791), 84, cited by Smirnov, note 105.

18 Most accounts agree as to the indecisive nature of the engagements around Briansk. The *Novyi letopisets* (78) states that Shuisky's forces "fought against them unceasingly, and there was a great conflict, and then they dispersed." Jozef Budila, a Polish colonel in the forces of the second False Dmitry, stated that his forces arrived at Orel on 6 January 1608 and wintered there (*Historya Dmitra falszywego*, RIB 1, col. 130).

19 *Welches St. Gregori Tag War.* Probably an error, as it is in fact St George's day. However, all variants read "*St. Gregori.*" Smirnov (150) nevertheless translates it *Sv. Georgiia.* i.e., St George's Day in the spring, as distinct from 16/26 November, St George's Day in the autumn. Actually the fourth Sunday after Easter in 1608 fell on 27 April. Easter was 30 March.

20 The place name Bussow gives for this engagement, Kaminsk, is impossible to identify precisely. Perhaps he means the Kamenka, a tributary of the Sukhaya river, where there was a battle on 30 April (not 23 April, as Bussow states), which lasted four days. The information concerning treason and defection of two hundred Germans under Albert

Lamsdorff is probably correct. There must be some doubt as to Bussow's account about the wholesale slaughter of the Tushino Germans.
This is inconsistent with the constant policy of the second False Dmitry
to welcome defectors into his camp. See Smirnov's edition of *Moskovskaia Khronika*, note 109.

21 *Sontags Cantate.*
22 *Novyi letopisets* (80): "The Lithuanians and the Russian brigands came
that night and attacked the Russian regiments and defeated them,
taking whole formations captive. And they all fled, and only managed
to regroup outside the city, where they turned around on them and
began to fight against them, chasing them fifteen versts back to the
Khodynka stream, so that they could barely get back to their encampment, and so they were repulsed."
23 Marginal note: "Five versts is one German mile."
24 *Klaffen zum Creuz bringet manchen Mann / Der sonst wohl Fried und Ruh
mocht han.*
25 *Bey ihrem Herrn Demetrio (scilicet) bleiben.*
26 *est verus Demetrius, der rechte Demetrius seyn.*
27 *... et quod grande, nefas, et morte piandum, ...*
28 Marginal note: "Levonty is the patron saint of Rostov."
29 Marginal note: "Metropolitan is the highest ecclesiastical rank after the
Patriarch."
30 Marginal note: "His son has since become tsar in Moscow."
31 Possibly related to Johan Eyloff (see Massa, *Short History*, 21), a Dutch
physician and Anabaptist, who was active against the Catholic interest
during the mission of the Jesuit Antonio Possevino in 1581. He was
also engaged in commerce while in Muscovy.

CHAPTER XV

1 The principality of Smolensk had been part of the Kievan polity, but
after the Mongol conquest had come increasingly under the influence
of the Grand Principality of Lithuania, by which it was absorbed in
1404. The city of Smolensk was conquered for Moscow by Vasily III in
1514, but from 1611 to 1654 was once again under Polish-Lithuanian
rule.
2 Marginal note: "Smolensk has a circumference of one German mile."
3 The city of Smolensk was refortified between 1596 and 1602 by the
renowned Russian military engineer Fedor Savelevich Kon, at the order
of the then regent Boris Godunov. On the defence of Smolensk against
Sigismund III, see the entry in MERSH 36: 46–53.
4 Mikhail Borisovich Shein, who also commanded the unsuccessful
attempt to regain Smolensk in 1632. On the latter occasion failure cost

him his life, as he was executed 23 April 1643. See entry by Daniel B. Rowland, MERSH 34: 196–8.

5 There is no other record of such a proposal, except in Petreius (419–20), which is almost certainly derived from Bussow.

6 The Adelung MS erroneously calls Liapunov a Polish boyar. See also below, chapter XIX, note 1; chapter XX, note 20.

7 *Sagon, das ist auf der Fütterung* ...

8 *Glagolen.* Marginal note: "*Glagolen* are people who wear their hair in long braids, as the Poles and Tatars do." See also chapter XX, note 6.

9 *Polter-Passion.*

10 *der gab ihm ietzo dafür der Weldt Deo gratias.* Some variants read "*ago gratias.*" Marginal note: "*Der Weldt Dannk.*"

11 Some variants read "ten."

CHAPTER XVI

1 The conflict between the Polish supporters of the False Dmitry and the Russian-Swedish expeditionary force is described also by Budila (col. 158).

2 The engagement around the Kalyazin monastery is described also in the *Novyi letopisets* (91), and its decisive nature is confirmed by Skopin himself, who stated that "from this battle the Lithuanians went away in retreat." A. M. Gnevushev, *Akty vremeni pravleniia tsaria Vasiliia Shuiskogo* (Moscow, 1914), no. 67.

CHAPTER XVII

1 Actually Pereiaslavl.

2 All other variants read 1609. The Academy MS, however, gives the date correctly as 1610.

3 The Alexandrovskaia Sloboda, situated on the approaches to the Trinity monastery, was liberated on 9 October 1609. Its liberation opened the approaches to the Trinity monastery to the Russians and posed a threat to Tushino. Bussow writes that at this time the Poles attacked the Russians in the Alexandrovskaia Sloboda but, not gaining any success, made haste to retreat. Polish and Swedish sources complement Bussow's testimony with a description of the battle of 29 October 1609, which ended in the defeat of the Polish-Lithuanian forces. Bussow is mistaken when he writes that Skopin and de la Gardie (the latter was entirely absent from the vicinity of the Trinity monastery) made a sortie and attacked the Poles on Martinmas. This fact should probably be related to the January activities of the Russian forces. According to Palitsyn (192–3), on 9 January 1610 a detachment of

soldiers under the command of Grigory Valuev was despatched by Skopin from the Alexandrovskaia Sloboda and reached the Trinity monastery at 4 a.m. The sortie was successful, and as a result "many Lithuanians were slain and prisoners were taken." After Valuev's reconnaissance expedition, Skopin moved his forces closer to the monastery. The interventionists, seeing the numerical superiority of the Russians, retreated to Dmitrov and held out there until the end of February, not against the Germans, as Bussow writes, but against Skopin's forces. (Adapted from Smirnov *Moskovskaia Khronika*, note 141).

4 11 November 1609.

CHAPTER XVIII

1 *impostorem*. Some variants read *imperatorem*.
2 *Funfften Tagh nach den Heiligen drey Königen.*
3 *Friede*. Some variants read *Freundschaft* (friendship).
4 *Vertumnum.*
5 Some variants read "Russian."
6 Some variants read "blue clothes" (*blauen Kleidern*) instead of "peasant clothes" (*Bauernkleidern*).
7 2 February.
8 *Ostrog*, rendered by Bussow as *Astroga*, with marginal note: "*Astroga ist eine Vorstadt.*"
9 The monastery of St Joseph of Volokolamsk was founded in 1479, about twenty kilometres from the present town of Volokolamsk, near Moscow, by Joseph Sanin, abbot of the St Paphnutius monastery of Borovsk, who was the chief opponent of the non-possessor movement within the Russian Orthodox church as well as of the various heretical tendencies which developed late in the fifteenth century. By the end of the sixteenth century the monastery had become a wealthy landowner, and in 1594–95 experienced a serious peasant revolt. The monastery gave considerable material help to Tsar Vasily at the time of the Bolotnikov rebellion but suffered considerable loss during the events of 1610. Much of its wealth was restored by Tsar Alexis late in the seventeenth century. After the October Revolution the monastery became a local history museum, while its rich manuscript collection was deposited in the Lenin Library. The monastery suffered extensive damage by the German invaders in 1941–42 but has been restored since the war.
10 Ivan Tarasievich Gramotin (d. 1638) first appeared at the court of the first False Dmitry as a crown secretary. Appointed secretary to the governor of Pskov by Vasily Shuisky, he distinguished himself for his rapacity, which doubtless contributed to the revolt which broke out there in September 1608. Being in disfavour with Shuisky, he fled to

the Tushino encampment, from which he and Saltykov were sent in 1609 to the Trinity monastery with the false information that Moscow had surrendered and that Shuisky had made his submission to Tsar Dmitry. This ruse failed and the defenders continued their heroic defence. After the fall of the Tushino encampment, Gramotin proceeded to King Sigismund at Smolensk, where he was appointed keeper of the seal and conciliar secretary to the collaborationist government within the Kremlin. In September 1612 he was sent on behalf of the captive Russian boyars to urge King Sigismund to send his son Wladyslaw to Moscow without delay. While he was absent on this mission, Moscow surrendered to Pozharsky. Gramotin remained in Poland, but managed to ingratiate himself with Filaret, with whom he returned to Moscow in 1619 to enjoy a distinguished career under Michael Romanov. See entry in MERSH 13: 92–4.

Mikhail Glebovich Saltykov (d. 1621), a veteran of the Livonian wars, was employed on a number of diplomatic missions with Afanasy Vlasiev. They negotiated the betrothal of Prince Johann of Denmark to Boris's daughter Xenia and, after the prince died unexpectedly, travelled to Germany to solicit the hand of Prince Philip of Schleswig instead. He served in the boyar council under the first False Dmitry, but was in disfavour under Vasily Shuisky and eventually aligned himself with the Polish interest, being one of the leading lights in the collaborationist regime in Moscow, which he fled in March 1611 for permanent exile in Poland-Lithuania. See entry in MERSH 33: 45–9. See also Chapter II, note 89, and Chapter III, note 1.

11 It seems that Shuisky was not directly responsible for the death of his kinsman but rather some other of his jealous relatives. Skopin had been approached by the Liapunovs and others with a view to supplanting Vasily Shuisky. He had refused to have anything to do with such plans, but had at the same time failed to denounce the plotters. The most generally accepted version is that Skopin was poisoned during a christening banquet by Ekaterina, the wife of the tsar's brother Prince D. I. Shuisky and a daughter of Maliuta Skuratov. After the death of Skopin (23 April 1610) and the defeat of the tsar's brothers at Klushino (24 June), the popularity of the Shuisky regime plummeted and the tsar was himself deposed on 17 July.

12 *Wobey den auch die Pohlen keine Seide spinnen sollten.* Literally: from which the Poles would not spin any silk. See also above, Chapter II, note 96.

13 Petreius (443–7), perhaps with better knowledge of the doings of his Swedish countrymen, diverges somewhat from Bussow at this point. After Klushino, de la Gardie made a separate truce with Zolkiewski but, instead of going home, the Swedes and their foreign auxiliaries set

up their headquarters next to Novgorod and seized a number of strongholds on the Baltic littoral. The French captain Laville is also mentioned in Petreius's account as having led the Swedish force which captured Ladoga.

14 The order of service on this occasion is reprinted in RRSE 1 (1851): 132–6. The hymn consists of twelve stanzas, the first letter of each comprising the acrostic MARTINUS BEER.

15 *Latushi* = "Latins," a pejorative term applied to foreigners.

16 Marginal note: "*Qui amat periculum peribit in eo.*"

17 *Wolnoludi.* Marginal note: "*Wolnoludi seind Freybauter, Räuber.*"

CHAPTER XIX

1 Molchanov and Rzhevsky are not mentioned in this connection in any other source. The chief fellow conspirators of Zakhar Liapunov were Fedor Khomutov and I. N. Saltykov. Liapunov, at least, cannot be considered to have become a "proper Pole," since it was his brother Prokopy who was to lead the first effective national resistance to the Poles.

2 *Laubenmoest.*

3 *Viele.* The Adelung MS reads *vier.* Once again the Wolfenbüttel II and Academy MSS readings make better sense!

4 Nevertheless, his captors did not hold him to his involuntary monastic vow when he became a prisoner of the Poles. In August of the same year he and his brothers were removed to Smolensk and then finally to Poland. Vasily and his brother Dmitry both died in 1612 and were buried at Warsaw. With the death of the last brother Ivan, in 1638, the Muscovite branch of the Shuisky clan died out, though during the 1640s there were two pretenders who claimed to be sons of Vasily Shuisky.

5 This paragraph occurs only in the Academy MS. There is a mark "B" in the Wolfenbüttel II MS (f. 123) and the marginal zodiac sign of Mercury, perhaps indicating that an interpolation was intended here.

6 The so-called "seven boyar" administration, fearful of the approach of the forces of the second False Dmitry to Moscow, and also of the possibility of a social uprising within the city, came to an agreement with Zolkiewski and admitted a Polish garrison to the Kremlin and Kitay-gorod on the night of 21 September. One of the conditions laid down by the boyars and Patriarch Hermogen was that Prince Wladyslaw should immediately be rebaptized into the Orthodox faith. After the fall of Smolensk on 3 July 1611, King Sigismund repudiated the treaty concluded by Zolkiewski and began to advance his own claims to the Muscovite throne. Zolkiewski quit the king's encampment in disgust and took no further part in Sigismund's Russian campaigns.

7 Marginal note in a different (and later) hand: "*Olearius Reisebeschreib., p. 196.*"

8 The monastery of St Paphnutius is in the vicinity of Kaluga, while Bussow probably mistook the large church at Kolomenskoe for a monastery.

9 25 August.

10 A number of Tatars, under their own prince, had been settled in the Volga town of Romanov since the mid-fifteenth century.

11 *Stulnitzki, (welches die beste Festung in der Moscau ist, Imperatoria Sedes genannt)* ...

12 Marginal comment: "Yes, my dear Dmitry, you obtained your rightful inheritance on 11 December of this year."

13 *derselbe Johannes und des Demetrius Prodromus.*

14 Bussow, as a resident of Kaluga, is particularly well informed as to the events leading up to and following upon the murder of the second False Dmitry.

15 Other variants read: "and could not deny that he had been the original cause of his death."

16 Some variants read "Russians, some of whom were boyars."

17 *Trau wohl, reit das Pferd davon.*

18 Maryna's son, Ivan Dmitrevich, became the heir to Dmitry's claims and was later championed by the Cossack chieftain Ivan Martynovich Zarutsky, whose fate he shared. Late in 1614 Zarutsky was impaled, while the young Ivan, the "Little Brigand," was hanged outside the Serpukhov gates of Moscow, being not quite four years old. Maryna is said to have died of grief in her tower prison at Kolomna shortly afterwards.

19 In 1587 Archduke Maximilian, brother of Emperor Rudolph II, was the Austrian-backed candidate for the Polish throne. When Sigismund III was elected, a civil war ensued with the partisans of Maximilian, who was captured and not released until Vienna had undertaken to abandon all pretensions to the Polish throne.

20 *Heute mir, morgen dir.*

CHAPTER XX

1 ... *und machten damit den Pohlen einen neuen blauen Dunst für die Augen* ... made yet another blue mist before the Poles' eyes.

2 *Malum consilium consultori pessimum.*

3 *Prechista* actually means Immaculate. Another example of Bussow's misinformation about the Russian Orthodox religion.

4 *der Starra sabacca.*

5 *den Tashchanok.*

6 *Glagolen.* Marginal note: "*Glagolen sind beschorene Köpfe mit Zöpfen.*" See also above, chapter XV, note 8.

7 In fact the population of Moscow at this time was only barely in excess of a hundred thousand, as Bussow himself elsewhere states.

8 *Pagoleken,* in Polish *pacholiki,* meaning either young boys or else, as here, military servitors of lesser rank. Marginal note: "*Pagolcken sind Diener.*"

9 *Ey thi scurbosin moskal, yepstfo matir.*

10 Passion Sunday (two weeks before Easter), from the opening words of the Introit.

11 *Obriste Lieutenant.*

12 The Wolfenbüttel II ms reads "6 Campagnien," though the Academy and Adelung mss read "3 Campagnien." The latter would appear to be correct, since later on in the narrative we twice read in all variants: "these three companies" (*diese drey companeyen*).

13 *in nomine Domini.*

14 Marginal note in Wolfenbüttel II: "Virgil Eclog 9 Bucol: *Ut possessor agelli diceret: haec mea sunt, veteres migrate coloni.*"

15 Most variants read "1000," but Wolfenbüttel II clearly reads "*und darauff bey hundert Strelitzen.*"

16 *Musten das ite in orbem universum lernen und in fremden Ländern wandern.*

17 *Dux und Author omnis seditionis war.*

18 In fact Patriarch Hermogen was imprisoned in the Miracles monastery, where he was starved to death for refusing to discountenance the national liberation movement led by Minin and Pozharsky. He died 17 February 1612 and was canonized as a saint of the Russian church 12 May 1913.

19 *ins Gras beißen müßen.* See also chapter V, note 1.

20 In fact Liapunov was the commander of the Riazan gentry contingent, to whom the Cossacks were bitterly hostile. Liapunov was murdered by the Cossacks in June 1611.

21 In the seventeenth century the price of a loaf of bread was always the same, though the size of the loaf varied according to the price and availability of grain.

22 Second Sunday after Easter.

23 *Post haec occasio calva.*

24 *Cudendum igni tum ferrum.*

25 25 July.

26 25 August.

27 In Wolfenbüttel II (f. 144v) "*Michäel Fedorowitz*" is added in a later hand, with the marginal note in the same hand: "*A° 1591 Oct. 22 ann. Olear. Reisebeschr. Nikititz. p. 157, A° 1613.*" Michael's name is altogether missing from the Academy ms.

28 In fact Michael was to occupy the Muscovite throne for just over thirty-two years, though Bussow at the time of writing can scarcely be blamed for thinking that his hold upon the rulership was at best tenuous.

29 Karl Filip, brother of King Gustavus Adolphus, was strongly favoured as an alternative candidate by both Prokopy Liapunov and Dmitry Pozharsky.

30 Korela is the Russian name for Kexholm, mentioned earlier in this paragraph. After its reconquest by Peter the Great it retained its Swedish name, but in Soviet times was renamed Priozersk.

31 The Peace of Stolbovo, concluded 27 February 1617, shortly before Bussow's death. See entry by Daniel B. Rowland, MERSH 37: 146–9.

32 Prince Wladyslaw made a determined effort in 1618 to substantiate his claim to the Muscovite throne, but was thwarted through determined Russian resistance and the refusal of the Polish nobility to vote further taxation to finance the dynastic ambitions of the Vasa kings. A fourteen-year truce between Poland and Russia, on the basis of *uti possidetis*, was concluded at Deulino, a village near the Trinity monastery, on 1/11 December 1618. See entry in MERSH 9: 103–4. Upon his accession to the throne as King Wladyslaw IV, Russia intervened in the Thirty Years' War, attempting to recover Smolensk. Although they failed in this objective, under the Truce of Polianovka the Polish king was obliged to renounce for ever his claim to the Russian throne, in return for a indemnity of two hundred thousand rubles.

APPENDIX ONE

1 Friedrich-Ulrich was Duke of Brunswick from 1613 to 1634. The German of the original letter is extremely tortuous and I have accordingly relied very heavily upon Smirnov's Russian translation.

2 Apparently the younger Conrad was released from Siberian captivity some time in 1617. See chapters XIII–XIV, note 9, above.

3 Probably his son-in-law, Pastor Martin Beer.

4 *in dero Kloster*, which Smirnov has translated literally (*v monastyre*). Since, however, Brunswick was solidly in Protestant territory, Bussow is undoubtedly using the term idiomatically for some kind of refuge or protection.

5 *den 28 9bris Anno 1613*. Smirnov was under the impression that this letter had no signature, but the handwriting was identical to the Peparino letter which follows. Having seen the letter for myself, I can vouch for the fact that it is signed in an identical manner. In discussion with the librarian, Professor Wolfgang Milde, it was suggested that Smirnov, although he did visit Wolfenbüttel briefly, did not have time

to examine all the codices closely, and may have been working from a defective microfilm copy.

APPENDIX TWO

1 Johannes Peparino was one of the privy councillors to Duke Friedrich-Ulrich, the addressee of the preceding letter.

Bibliography

The following abbreviations are used in the Bibliography.

AAE   *Akty sobrannye i izdannye v bibliotekakh i arkhivakh Rossiiskoi Imperii Arkheograficheskoiu Kommisseiiu* (Acts Collected and Edited from the Libraries and Archives of the Russian Empire by the Archeographical Commission)

AI   *Akty istoricheskie, sobrannye i izdannye Arkheograficheskoiu Kommissieiu* (Historical Acts Collected and Edited by the Archeographical Commission)

BAN   Biblioteka Akademii Nauk (Library of the Academy of Sciences)

CHOIDR   *Chteniia otdeleniia istoriia i drevnostei rossiiskikh* (Readings of the Section for Russian History and Antiquities)

GBL   Gosudarstvennaia Publichnaia Biblioteka imeni V. I. Lenina (V. I. Lenin State Public Library)

GPB   Gosudarstvennaia Publichnaia Biblioteka imeni M. E. Saltykov-Shchedrina (M. E. Saltykov-Schedrin State Public Library)

HAB   Herzog August Bibliothek Wolfenbüttel (Duke August Library)

MERSH   *Modern Encyclopedia of Russian and Soviet History* (Gulf Breeze, Fla.: Academic International Press, 1976–82)

PSRL   *Polnoe sobranie russkikh letopisei* (Full Collection of Russian Chronicles)

RIB   *Russkaia istoricheskaia biblioteka* (Russian Historical Library)

RRSE   *Rerum Rossicarum Scriptores Exteri* (Foreign Writers on Russian Affairs)

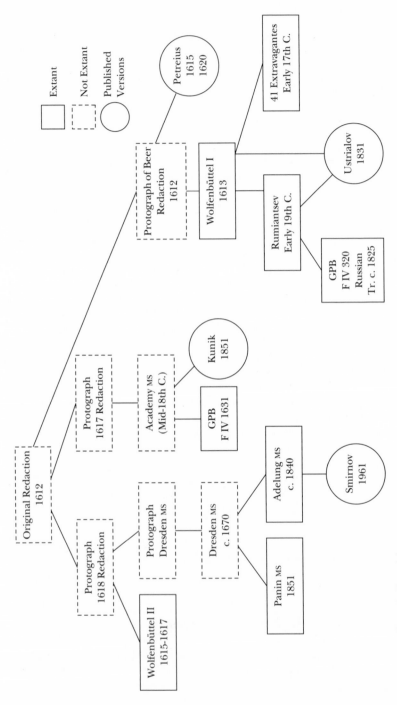

Stemma of Bussow's Chronicle

SGGD   *Sobranie gosudarstvennykh gramot i dogovorov* (Collection of State Documents and Treaties)

SRIO   *Sbornik Imperatorskogo Russkogo Istoricheskogo Obshchestva* (Collection of the Imperial Russian Historical Society)

TSGADA   Tsentral'nyi Gosudarstvennyi Arkhiv Drevnykh Aktov (Central State Archive of Ancient Acts)

NOTE ON MANUSCRIPT SOURCES

The manuscript tradition of Bussow's chronicle is extremely tortuous, but with the help of the accompanying diagram it is possible to disentangle the provenance of the distinct manuscript "families." The original redaction of 1612, no longer extant, was completed at Riga or Dünamünde on 1 March 1612 by Conrad Bussow, in collaboration with his son-in-law Martin Beer.

THE BEER-KARAMZIN-USTRIALOV FAMILY

The Protograph of the Beer redaction (1612)

Beer took the original redaction and recast it as his own, as far as possible expunging the name of Bussow and excluding autobiographical information. *Petreius*, or Peer Peerson de Erlesunda, somehow came into possession of the Beer redaction and incorporated much of it, word for word, in the Swedish version of his history, published in 1615, and the modified German version, published in 1620. Petreius also included information that was damaging to Bussow and contradicted Bussow's testimony on a number of details. *Wolfen-büttel I* is a defective copy of the original Beer redaction, which was entitled *Summarische Relatio*. This manuscript was sent by Bussow from Hanover to Duke Friedrich-Ulrich of Braunschweig-Wolfenbüttel, with a covering letter asking for the duke's assistance to defray publication costs. Both the codex and the covering letter are to be found in the Herzog August Bibliothek, Codex Guelf 86 Extravagantes and 56, fol. 339–42v. respectively. A second copy of this version was made in the early seventeenth century and is bound with a manuscript of the travel account of the Augsburg merchant Hans Georg Peyerle in Codex Guelf 41 Extravagantes. The *Rumiantsev manuscript* is a copy of Wolfenbüttel I made for Count N. P. Rumiantsev early in the nineteenth century. It was used by Karamzin in the writing of his *History of the Russian State* (published 1819). The manuscript was originally preserved in the Moscow archive of the Ministry of Foreign Affairs. In the 1840s it was sent to the offices of the Archeographical Commission in St Petersburg at the request of A. A. Kunik. For a long time thereafter its whereabouts were unknown. In 1960 it was rediscovered among a miscellaneous batch of foreign documents in the Central State Archive of Ancient Acts in Moscow.

Unfortunately I have not been able to ascertain its call number. *GPB F IV No. 320* is a Russian translation of the Rumiantsev manuscript, possibly a duplicate of the translation done by Ustrialov while preparing his 1831 anthology. It is deposited in the Saltykov-Shchedrin Library, St Petersburg.

In 1831 *Nikolai Gerasimovich Ustrialov* (1805–1870) published the first printed version of the chronicle in his anthology *Tales of Contemporaries concerning Dmitry the Pretender*, though the authorship is attributed to Martin Beer. A second edition was published in 1859. Ustrialov seems to have remained unconvinced of the mounting evidence that Bussow was in fact the author.

THE 1613 REDACTION

The *Protograph of the 1613 redaction* is no longer extant. It was done by Bussow himself on the basis of the original redaction, with the addition of autobiographical details and various other emendations. *Wolfenbüttel II* (Cod. Guelf. 125.15 Extravagantes) is the only extant contemporary manuscript derived from it. The codex came into the possession of the Herzog August library as a gift from Gottfried Leonhard Baudis of the Collegium Carolinum in Brunswick. Both the short title and the extended title page give 1613 as the terminal date of the chronicle. Smirnov, Bussow's Soviet editor and translator was of the opinion that Wolfenbüttel II was compiled "about the middle of the seventeenth century" (80). According to the recent study by Myl'nikov and Milde (86–7) it is of a much earlier provenance, although I cannot agree with the authors in accepting the 1613 date on the title page at face value. I have also consulted personally with Milde, who points out that the handwriting and orthography correspond to those used in the second decade, rather than the middle, of the seventeenth century. The codex was also written in its entirety by the same scribe, except for a few marginal comments and corrections in a different and later hand. The difficulty with the 1613 dating is that the final chapter of the manuscript contains details of the peace concluded between Russia and Sweden. The actual peace treaty was concluded in February 1617; consequently Wolfen-büttel II might only be slightly earlier than the protograph of the Academy manuscript, which differs from the former chiefly in containing further autobiographical details, news of the younger Conrad's release from captivity, omission of the *Register* (Table of Contents) and mention of the author's death in Lübeck. Alternatively, Wolfenbüttel II might have been composed as early as the autumn of 1615, since active hostilities between Russia and Sweden ceased when Gustavus Adolphus lifted the siege of Pskov in September, and peace feelers had already gone out. Although the two sides quibbled over fine points for sixteen months, the general principles of

the peace treaty had been agreed upon in advance. The dating of Wolfenbüttel II therefore may be narrowed to between late 1615 and early 1617.

THE DRESDEN "FAMILY"

At the basis of this manuscript tradition is the Dresden manuscript, a secondary copy (c. 1670) of the 1613 redaction, preserved until late in the
Second World War at the Royal Public Library, Dresden. This manuscript,
long regarded as the most authoritative, was destroyed in the Allied bombing,
but fortunately two notarized copies had been made during the nineteenth
century. The *Adelung manuscript* is a transcription of the Dresden manuscript,
made early in the 1840s at the request of Friedrich von Adelung. It is
deposited in the Manuscript Division of the Library of the Academy of
Sciences, St Petersburg. It forms the basis of Smirnov's critical edition,
though Smirnov also includes variants from the Panin, Wolfenbüttel II and
Academy manuscripts. The *Panin manuscript* is also a notarized transcription
of the Dresden manuscript, commissioned by the Minister of Justice, Count
V. I. Panin in 1851. It is preserved in the Manuscript Division of the Lenin
Library, Moscow, call number *fond* 183, No. 850.

THE 1617 REDACTION

The *Protograph of the 1617 redaction* was compiled in Lübeck shortly before
Bussow's death. It was a reworking of the 1613 redaction, except that some
of the earlier autobiographical information was excluded, though other
materials were added, such as the return of the younger Conrad from
Siberian exile. The *Academy manuscript* is a copy of the lost protograph of
the 1617 redaction. It is probably the version known to Christian Kelch and
Gottlieb Treuer. The manuscript itself was acquired by the library of the
Imperial Academy of Sciences from Johann Christoph Brotze late in the
eighteenth century. Both the manuscript itself and the catalogue entry
relating to it are in the same hand. The Academy manuscript (call number
F No. 14) was the basis for the 1851 printed version edited by A. A. Kunik.
GPB F IV 163 is a late eighteenth-century copy of the Academy manuscript,
preserved in the Manuscript Division of the Saltykov-Shchedrin Library,
St Petersburg.

PRINTED VERSIONS OF BUSSOW'S ACCOUNT

Letopis' moskovskaia. Russian trans. N. G. Ustrialov (who attributes the account
to Martin Beer), *Skazaniia sovremennikov o Dmitrii Samozvantse* (St Petersburg 1831, 2nd edition 1859).

C. Bussovii Chronicon. Ed. A. Kunik, *Rerum Rossicarum Scriptores Exteri* I (St Petersburg, 1851), 1–136.

Konrad Bussow, *Moskovskaia khronika 1584–1613,* trans. and ed. by I. I. Smirnov, with annotations by A. I. Kopanev and M. V. Kukushkina (Moscow and Leningrad, 1961)

Conrad Bussow, *Zeit der Wirren: Moskowitische Chronik der Jahre 1584 bis 1613,* herausgeben und kommentiert von Gottfried Sturm, Übersetzung aus dem Frühhochdeutschen von Marie-Elisabeth Fritze (Berlin [DDR], 1989).

CONTEMPORARY PRIMARY SOURCES

Akty sobrannye i izdannye v bibliotekakh i arkhivakh Rossiiskoi Imperii Arkheograficheskoiu Kommissieiu, II (St Petersburg, 1836).

Book of Annals, RIB 13: cols 625–712. 2nd ed. (St Petersburg, 1909). (Attributed formerly to Prince I. P. Katyrev-Rostovsky, but now thought more likely to have been written by Prince S. I. Shakhovskoy.)

Borsza, Stanislaw, *Wyprawa czara moskiewskiego Dymitra do Moskwy z Gerzim Mniszkiem, woiewoda Sendomierskim y z inszym rycerstwem, roku 1604.* RIB 1: 365–426 (St Petersburg, 1872).

Budila, Jan. *Historya Dmitra Falszywego,* RIB 1: 81–364 (St Petersburg, 1872).

Dyamentowski, Waclaw. *Dyaryusz Waclawa Dyamentowskiego.* In Hirschberg, *Polska i Moskwa,* 1–166.

Fletcher, Giles. *Of the Russe Commonwealth* (London, 1591).

Hirschberg, Aleksandr. *Polska a Moskwa w pierwszej polowie wieku XVII* (Lwow: Nakladem Zakladu n. im Ossolinskich, 1901).

Howe, Sonia E. *The False Dmitri: A Russian Romance and Tragedy Described by British Eye-witnesses, 1604–1612* (London: Williams & Norgate, 1916).

Job, Patriarch. *Povest' o chestnem zhitii tsaria i velikogo kniazia Fedora Ivanovicha vseia Rusii.* PSRL 14 (St Petersburg: Tipografiia M.A. Aleksandrova, 1910), 1–22.

Marchocki, M. *Historya wojny moskiewskiy* (Poznan, 1841).

Margeret, Jacques. *The Russian Empire and Grand Duchy of Muscovy: A 17th-Century French account,* trans. and ed. Chester S. L. Dunning (Pittsburgh: University of Pittsburgh Press, 1983). Based upon *L'estat de l'Empire et Grand Duché de Moscovie* (Paris, 1607).

Massa, Isaac. *A Short History of the Muscovite Wars.* Trans. with an introduction by G. Edward Orchard (Toronto: University of Toronto Press, 1982).

Novyi letopisets. PSRL 14 (St Petersburg, 1910), 33–154.

Palitsyn, Avraamy, *Skazanie Avraamiia Palitsyna.* Ed. L. V. Cherepnin (Moscow and Leningrad: Izdatel'stvo Akademii Nauk SSSR, 1951)

Pamiatniki diplomaticheskikh snoshenii drevnei Rossii s derzhavami inostrannymi. SRIO 137 (Moscow, 1912).

Pamiatniki drevnei russkoi pis'mennosti otnosiashchiesia k Smutnomu Vremeni. RIB 13, 2nd ed. (St Petersburg, 1909).

Petreius (Per Peerson, Peter Petreius de Erlesunda). *Een wiss och egentelich Beskriffing om Rydsland* (Stockholm, 1615). (Swedish text.)

– *Historien und Bericht von dem Großfuerstenthumb Muschow* (Leipzig, 1620). (German text – except where otherwise noted, I have cited from this edition.)

– *Ex Petri Petrei Chronicis Moscoviticis.* RRSE (St Petersburg, 1851), 1: 142–325. (German text with Swedish variants.)

– *Istoriia o velikom kniazhestve moskovskom* (Moscow, 1867). (Russian translation by A. Shemiakin from the German version.)

– *Reliatsiia Petra Petreia o Rossii.* Ed. by Yu. A. Limonov and V. I. Buganov (Moscow, 1976). (Swedish text, with Russian translation and commentary, of the portions relating to the Time of Troubles.)

Peyerle, Georg. *O puteshestvii iz Krakova v Moskvu i obratno.* In Ustrialov, *Skazaniia sovremennikov o Dmitrii Samozvantse*, 153–234.

Popov, Andrei N. *Izbornik slavianskikh i russkikh sochinenii i statei vnesennykh v Khronografov russkoi redaktsii* (Moscow: Tipografiia A. I. Mamontova, 1869).

Rude and Barbarous Kingdom: Russia in the Accounts of Sixteenth-Century English Travellers. Ed. Lloyd E. Berry and Robert O. Crummey (Madison: University of Wisconsin Press, 1968).

Sapieha, Jan-Piotr. *Dziennik Jana Piotra Sapiehy.* In Hirschberg, *Polska a Moskwa*, 167–332.

Smith, Sir Thomas. *Voyage and Entertainment in Russia* (London, 1605).

Sobranie gosudarstvennykh gramot i dogovorov, vol. 2 (St Petersburg, 1819).

Terenty, Archpriest. *The So-called Other Tale* [Tak nazyvaemoe Inoe Skazanie]. 2nd ed. RIB 13: cols 1–144 (St Petersburg, 1909).

Timofeev, Ivan. *Vremennik Ivana Timofeeva.* Ed. with trans. into modern Russian by O. A. Derzhavina and V. P. Adrianova-Peretts (Moscow and Leningrad: Izdatel'stvo Akademii Nauk SSSR, 1951).

Ustrialov, N. G. *Skazaniia sovremennikov o Dmitrii Samozvantse*, 2nd ed. (St Petersburg, 1859).

Zolkiewski, Stanislaw. *Poczatek i progres wojny moskiewskiej.* Ed. Jarema Maciszewski (Warsaw: Panstwowy Institut Wydawnicsy, 1966). English trans. by M. W. Stephen, *Expedition to Moscow* (London: Polonica Publications, 1966).

TEXTOLOGICAL MATERIAL

Apart from the able textological analysis contained in the preface to the Smirnov edition of Bussow's chronicle, the main contributions to the controversy over the authorship of the work are to be found in the following:

Friedrich von Adelung. *Kritisch-literärische Übersicht der Reisenden in Rußland bis 1700 deren Berichte bekannt sind* (St Petersburg, 1846), 2: 46–111.

A. Kunik. *Aufklärung über Konrad Bussow und die verschiedenen Redaktionen seiner Moskowischen Chronik* (St Petersburg, 1851). See also Introduction, note 5.

Myl'nikov, Aleksandr S., and Milde, Wolfgang. "Handschriftliche Slavica der Herzog August Bibliothek," *Wolfenbütteler Beiträge* 7 (1987): 79–98.

Ya. K. Grot. "Deistvitel'no Ber avtor Khroniki?," *Trudy* 4 (St Petersburg, 1901), originally published in the *Zhurnal ministerstva narodnogo prosvesh-cheniia* 12, no. 5 (1849). See also Introduction, note 5.

SECONDARY WORKS IN ENGLISH

Avrich, Paul. *Russian Rebels* (New York: Shocken Books, 1972).

Barbour, Philip. *Dimitry, Called the Pretender, Tsar and Grand Prince of All Russia, 1605–1606* (Boston: Houghton Mifflin, 1966).

Crummey, Robert O. *The Formation of Muscovy, 1300–1613* [Longman History of Russia, vol. 3] (London and New York: Longman's, 1987).

Grey, Ian. *Boris Godunov, the Tragic Tsar* (New York: Charles Scribner's Sons, 1973).

Modern Encyclopedia of Russian and Soviet History. Ed. Joseph L. Wieczynski (Gulf Breeze, Fla.: Academic International Press, 1976–92). 55 vols.

Orchard, G. Edward. "The Election of Michael Romanov," *Slavonic and East European Review* 67, no. 3 (July 1989): 378–402.

Platonov, S. F. *Boris Godunov*. Trans. L. Rex Pyles, with introductory essay by John T. Alexander (Gulf Breeze, Fla.: Academic International Press, 1972).

Platonov, S. F. *The Time of Troubles*. Trans. John T. Alexander (Lawrence: University of Kansas Press, 1970).

Skrynnikov, R. G. *Boris Godunov*. Ed. and trans. Hugh F. Graham (Gulf Breeze, Fla.: Academic International Press, 1982).

Skrynnikov, R. G. *The Time of Troubles*. Ed. and trans. Hugh F. Graham (Gulf Breeze, Fla.: Academic International Press, 1988).

Soloviev, S. M. *Boris Godunov and the False Dmitry* [History of Russia, vol. 14]. Trans. G. Edward Orchard (Gulf Breeze, Fla.: Academic International Press, 1988).

Soloviev, S. M. *Vasily Shuisky and the Interregnum* [History of Russia, vol. 15]. Trans. G. Edward Orchard (Gulf Breeze, Fla.: Academic International Press, 1990).

Vernadsky, George. "The Death of the Tsarevich Dimitry: A Reconsideration of the Case," *Oxford Slavonic Papers* (1954), 5: 1–19.

Vernadsky, George. *The Tsardom of Muscovy, 1547–1682*. 2 vols (New Haven: Yale University Press, 1969).

Index

Åbo, 31
Adelung, Friedrich von, historian, xxxvi, 186
Adelung, Nicholas von, xxxvi
Agrippa, 80
Ahlden, Ensign Jurgen von, 108
Akhmet Khan, Turkish sultan, 153
Alekseevich, Peter, counsellor to False Dmitry II, 136
Alexander Nevsky, xviii
Alexandra, nun, 212. See also Irina Fedorovna, tsaritsa
Alexandria, 153
Alexandrovskaia Sloboda, 125, 216
Alexis Mikhailovich, tsar, xxiv, xxv, xxviii, xxix
Alexius, scribe, 101
Ambassadorial Chancellery, 200
Anastasia, first wife of Ivan IV, xxv
Andronov, Fedor, 160
Anton Ulrich, duke of Brunswick, xxxiii

Antoniev-Siisky monastery, 197
Arbat (Moscow), 163
Archangel, 202
Archangel cathedral (Moscow), 204
Argamaks (Tatar horses), 205
Ascension church (Kolomenskoe), xxiv
Ascension convent (Moscow), 205
Assembly of the Land, xv, xxiii, xxiv, 84, 190, 210
Astrakhan, xiii, 31, 148–9, 204, 213
Augsburg, 69, 208, 227
August, duke of Brunswick, xxxiii
Austria, 114
Azov, 53, 56

Babylonians, 153
Baden, 185
Baltic sea, xxviii, 219
Bartenev, Vtoroy, 197
Basil the Blessed, holy fool, 204
Basil the Blessed, church (Moscow), 204

Basmanov, Peter Fedorovich, 201, 203; besieged in Novgorod Seversk, 38, 201; rewarded by Tsar Boris, 38; declares for Dmitry, 44; death, 63–4; conversation with Bussow, 82
Beer, Martin, Lutheran pastor: chronicle attributed to, xxiv–xxvi; collaboration on chronicle, xxxi, 222, 227–8; preaches at Duke Johan's funeral, 15; appointed to Lutheran church in Moscow, 17; preaches in Kremlin, 61; pastor to German community in Kozelsk, 128; intercedes with False Dmitry II for Germans, 137–42, 219; summary of career, 193–4
Belev, 103
Belgorod, 197
Beloozero, 75, 205, 209

Belsky, Bogdan, 194;
revolt against Boris, 26,
187; disgrace and exile,
26–7: return, 46–7,
greets False Dmitry I,
50; summary of career,
197
Benski, Erasmus, medical
student, 16
Bergk, Lieutenant Joa-
chim, 108
Bezdna, 184
Bezzubtsev, Georgy, boyar,
105
Bolkhov, 103, 107–9
Bolotnikov, Ivan Isaevich,
rebel leader, xvi, xix,
xxiii, xxvi–xxviii, xxxi,
xxvi, 212–14, 217;
early career, 91;
appointed to command
False Dmitry II's forces,
91–3; besieges Moscow,
94–5; retreats to
Kaluga, 95–6; besieged
in Tula, 96–100; sur-
render, 103–4; capture
and death, 104
Bolvanovsk Gates
(Moscow), 77, 209
Boniface VIII, Pope, 48
Bonoparte, Jérome, king
of Westphalia, xxxiv
Book of Annals, 209
Borck, Hans, 107, 214
Boris Fedorovich
Godunov, tsar, xvi,
xviii–xx, xxiv, xxvi,
xxix–xxxi, xxxiv, 44,
46, 59, 63, 74, 82, 83,
96, 145, 168, 195, 201,
202; election, 10–13;
coronation, 13, 191;
reforms, 14, 26, 196–7;
relations with Prince
Gustav, 15, 192;
recruits foreign experts,
16–20; generosity to
Livonian exiles, 19–25;
conflict with Bogdan

Belsky, 26–7; conflict
with Romanov family,
27, 197; measures
during famine, 32–4;
entertains Austrian
ambassador, 34–5, 194–
5, 199–200; measures
against False Dmitry I,
37–43; death, 43, 105;
reinterred in Varsono-
fiev monastery, 48;
reburial in Trinity mon-
astery, 89–90
Borisgorod, 26
Borkowski, Polish com-
mander, 160–1
Brambach, Johannes,
town secretary, 25
Brest, Union of, xxviii
Briansk, 107–8, 214
Brotze, Johann Christoph,
xxxv
Brunswick, xxxii–xxxiv,
222
Budila, Józef, Polish
colonel, 214, 216
Buick, Laurens, Swedish
"Mameluke," 115
Buinosov, Vasily Iva-
novich, governor of
Novgorod, 199
Bussow, Conrad: chroni-
cler, xxiv, 190–1, 193–
208, 210–18, 220–3,
227; authorship of
chronicle established,
xxv–xxvi; career of,
xxix–xxxvii; in Swedish
service, xxx, 19; prose
style, xxxii, 185;
"helper theory", 27–8,
186, 198; conversation
with Sapieha, 28, 83;
opinion on authenticity
of Dmitry, 81–3; con-
versation with Bas-
manov, 82; seeks
patronage of duke of
Brunswick, 171–5; map
of Moscow, 178–9; trea-

sonable dealings with
Russians, 193
Bussow, Conrad, the
younger, xxxi, 97, 104,
168, 171, 222

Carles, Johann Heinrich,
Austrian, 114
Caves monastery (Pskov),
20, 196
Celestine V, Pope, 204
Cellari, Ambrogio, mer-
chant, 208
Cherkassky family, 197
Chernigov, 201
Chertolie street (Moscow),
163–4
Chertolsk Gates (Moscow),
65
Chet Murza, alleged
ancestor of Godunov
family, 188
Chistov, K.V., ethnogra-
pher, xxv
Chmieliewski, Pawel,
Polish colonel, xx
Chodkiewicz, Jan Karol,
Polish hetman, xxiii,
167
Christian IV, Danish king,
18, 68, 90
Chronograph (1617),
xxix, 206
Chronograph of the
Third Redaction, 202
Church of Jerusalem, 45
Cicero, xxxii
Clement VIII, Pope, xxv,
xxviii
Constantine Pavlovich,
grand duke, xxv
Cossacks, xvi–xvii, xxii–
xxiii, xxvii, 28, 31, 37,
41–4, 54, 57, 88–9, 95–
6, 99–100, 105–6, 109,
111, 115–16, 124–5,
127–9, 131, 133, 147–
9, 151, 166, 204, 213,
221
Crimean khanate, xiii

Crimean Tatars, xv, 12,
88
Croesus, 80
Crown hetman (Poland),
183
Cruzati, Lord Juan, Span-
iard, 115

Daniel, prince of Moscow,
xviii
Danzig, 15
David, biblical king, xvii,
xxiv, 81
Decembrists, xxv
de la Gardie, Jakob,
Swedish soldier and
diplomat: subsequent
movements, xxviii, 136,
218–9; sent to aid
Shuisky, 96–7, 115;
advances from Nov-
gorod, 119; relieves
Moscow, 122–5;
received in Moscow,
132–4; defeated at
Klushino; 134–6
de la Gardie, Pontus, 123,
192, 212
de la Gardie, Veit, 132
Delmenhorst, 172
Denmark, xxi, 18, 48,
195, 218
Deulino, truce, 222
Dionysius, 80
Dittmarsch, 172
Dmitrov, 125, 129–31,
217
Dmitry Ivanovich, tsar-
evich, xxv, xxxv, 7;
birth, xvii, 82; exile to
Uglich, xvii, 7, 82;
death, xvii, xxiv, 8, 48,
83, 86; sadistic tenden-
cies, 8, 83, 189; alleged
escape, 28, 31, 37;
Bogdan Belsky claims
to be godfather of, 47;
alleged remains trans-
ferred to Moscow, 85–
6, 211; attempted coup

in favour of, 187,
197
Dmitry Solunsky, monas-
tery, 15, 193
Dmitry, scholar, 14
Dnieper, river, 27
Dobrynichi, battle, xviii,
xx, 40, 42, 49, 201
Don Cossacks, 213
Donets river, 197
Dormition cathedral
(Moscow Kremlin), 187,
191
Dorogobuzh, 57
Dorpat, 14, 195
Dresden, xxxv–xxxvii
Dünamünde, xxxi, 193,
227
Dyamentowski, Waclaw,
209

Earthen City (Moscow),
196
East Frisia, 185
Egypt, xxiv, 153
Eighty Years War, xix
Elets, 53, 89, 205
Engelhardt, Reinhold,
Livonian noble, 137,
139
England, 14
English, 16, 125
English Courtyard
(Moscow), 77, 179
Erik XIV, Swedish king,
15, 192
Erlau, 19
Estonia, xxvii–xxxv, 195–
6
Eyloff, Daniel, Dutch
apostate, 116, 121
Eyloff, Johan, 215

False Dmitry I, xxxi, 68,
71, 85, 89, 96, 111,
113, 179, 191–4, 197,
210, 212, 217–18; as
"just tsar," xvi; con-
tempt for Russian cus-
toms, xviii, 51–2, 61–2,

74, 78–9, 207; Polish
support for, xx, 59; ini-
tial favourable response
from Muscovites, xxiv,
xxvii, 53, 59, 72, 83;
social programme, xxvi,
83; papal support for,
xxviii; "helper theory,"
27–8, 31, 186, 198;
rumours of survival,
31, 37; invades Mus-
covy, 37–8, 201–2;
defeat at Dobrynichi,
40–1; urges Muscovites
to submit, 41–2, 45,
204; Basmanov declares
for, 44; acclaimed by
Muscovites, 45–8, 204;
entry into Moscow, 48–
51, 205; receives Ger-
mans into service, 49,
202; coronation, 52, 72,
205; reign and lifestyle,
52–3, 205; sends Vla-
siev to Poland, 53;
Shuisky conspires
against, 53–5, 58–9,
80–1, 206; foreign body-
guard, 53–4; war
games, 55–6; sends for
Maryna, 56–6, 200;
marriage, 60–2; con-
spiracy against, 62–7;
death, 65–7, 207; body
exposed to public view,
67, 76–7, 209; portents
occurring around
corpse, 77–8; body
incinerated, 78, 209;
Bussow's opinion of,
78–9, 82–3; alleged son
of Stefan Bathory, 83;
rumours of escape, 87–
8, 100, 105–6. See also
Otrepiev, Grishka
False Dmitry II, xvi, xx,
18, 76, 78, 84–5, 90,
97, 119, 132, 154, 158,
167, 191, 193, 197;
advance on Moscow,

xix, 103–11, 214–15;
Bolotnikov acting on
behalf of, xix, xxvii,
91–5, 99–100, 211; col-
lapse of Tushino
encampment, xxi, 126–
7; at Kaluga, xxi, 126–
7; advances on Moscow,
xxii, 147, 219; social
program, xxvi; Shak-
hovskoy promotes
rumours of, 88–9, 94,
100, 211; fails to
appear, 95–6; reveals
himself, 101–2; and
Miechowicki, 102;
advances on Briansk,
107; and Rozynski,
107–9, 126; victory at
Bolkhov, 108–9; battle
at Taininskoe, 110–11;
Tushino encampment,
111, 117, 198; abducts
Maryna and retinue,
111–12; marriage to
Maryna, 113, 123; dis-
patches Sapieha to
Trinity monastery, 114–
15; towns surrender to,
116, 120; anger against
Germans, 123, 128,
136–40; king recalls
Tushino Poles, 126;
recalls Shakhovskoy
from Tsarevo-
Zaimishche, 127–8;
unjustly condemns
Skotnicki, 129–30, 140;
rejoined by Maryna,
131; negotiations with
Sapieha, 133–4; relents,
140–3; captures St
Paphnutius monastery,
144; origins, 146;
retreats to Kaluga, 148;
alienates service Tatars,
149–50; death, 150–2,
220; Polish backing,
213–14
Famine, 32

Fedor Borisovich
Godunov, tsar, xviii,
xxiv, xxxv, 44, 46–8,
72, 89, 178, 200, 202–4
Fedor Ivanovich, tsar, xvi–
xvii, xxiv, 7–9, 27, 82,
96, 187, 191, 197, 203
Fedorovskoye, 122
Fellin, 14
Feodosia Fedorovna, tsar-
evna, xxiv, 188
Fiedler, Friedrich, 97
Fiedler, Kaspar, physician,
16
Filaret, metropolitan, later
patriarch, xxiv, xxix,
115, 128, 191, 215,
218. See also Romanov,
Fedor Nikitich
Finland, 31
First Militia Force, xxii–
xxiii
Forbidden Years, xvi
France, xix, xxxi, 14, 201
Frenchmen, 136
Friedrich-Ulrich, duke of
Brunswick, xxxii–xxxv,
171, 174, 193, 222–3
Fuerstenberg, Wilhelm,
Livonian noble, 66

Gabriel, Scottish captain,
26, 47, 194
Galich, 75, 116, 120
Gasiewski, Polish com-
mander, 155–6, 161
Gdov, 168
German Suburb, xxiv, 17,
61, 68, 191
Germans, xiv, xxxii, 13–
18, 20, 22–4, 26, 31,
33–5, 38, 40–2, 44, 49,
53–4, 66, 68–9, 77–8,
82, 87, 91, 96–7, 100,
104, 107–9, 114–15,
117, 119–20, 123–5,
128, 131–44, 147, 149–
50, 160–2, 164–5, 167,
171–2, 193, 203, 206,
215, 217

Germany, xx, 14, 218
Germers, Konrad, burgo-
master, 25
Gilberts, Colonel Daniel,
137
Godunov, Boris Fedo-
rovich: ability as
administrator, xvi, 7–8;
clash with Shuisky
family, xviii; assumes
regency, 7, 188, 197;
plot to assassinate
Dmitry, 8, 189; sets fire
to Moscow, 8–9, 189;
seizes sceptre from
dying tsar, 9; intrigues
to gain throne, 10–11,
189–90; refuses tsar-
dom, 11–12; gathering
at Serpukhov, 12–13,
191; coronation, 13. See
also Boris Fedorovich
Godunov, tsar
Godunov, Ivan Ivanovich,
214
Godunov, Semeon Niki-
tich, 197
Godunov, Stepan Stepa-
novich, 31, 198
Godunov, Vasily Fedo-
rovich, 188
Godunovs, 44–7, 72
Golden Horde, xiii
Golitsyn, Prince Ivan Ivanovich, 77, 204
Golitsyn family, 152
Golubtsov, A.I., historian,
198–9
Göttingen, xxxiv
Gramotin, Ivan Tara-
sievich, 160, 217–18
Greeks, 153
Grot, Jakob, historian,
xxxvi
Guagnini, Alessandro,
185
Guelph family, xxxiii–
xxxiv
Gundorov, Andrei,
161

Gustav, Swedish prince, 15, 179, 192
Gustav II Adolf, Swedish king, xxviii, xxxii, 185, 222
Guzów, battle, xx

Haiduks, 207
Halberdiers, 54, 58, 62–4, 66, 78
Hamburg, 202
Hanover, xxix, xxxii, xxxiv, 173
Hanseatic league, 25, 196
Hector, 53
Heinrich Julius, duke of Brunswick, xxxiii
Helmstedt, xxxiv, xxxv
Henri of Navarre, later King Henri IV of France, 201, 208
Henry VII, English king, xxv
Herberstein, Sigismund von, 185
Hermann, E., historian, xxxvi
Hermogen, patriarch, xxii–xxiii, 165, 219, 221
Herod, 8, 26, 80
Herzog August Bibliothek, Wolfenbüttel, xxxiii–xxxiv, xxxvii, 186
Heyde, Lubert von der, 108
Hildesheim, xxxiii
Holbein, Philip, Augsburg merchant, 208
Holy Roman Empire, 23, 145
Hoper, Berndt, merchant of Riga, 82
Horn, Colonel Eberhard von, 136
Huguenot wars, xx
Hullemann, Woldemar, pastor, 17
Hungarians, 16

Hungary, 114
Hyschlenius, Johannes, physician, 16

Ilten, xxix
Immaculate Virgin church, Moscow, 7, 59
India, 153
Intercession church (Moscow), 204
Irina Fedorovna, tsaritsa, 8–10, 12, 188–90, 212
Irishmen, 125
Italy, 14
Ivan Dmitrievich, son of Maryna, xxiii, 152, 213, 220
Ivan IV, tsar, xxv, xxix, 14, 26, 28–9, 31, 37, 50, 66–7, 82–3, 89, 116, 188, 197, 206; accession, xiii; promise of early reign, xiii; and Livonian War, xiv; oprichnina, xiv–xv; institution of serfdom, xv; problems of succession, xxiv; death, 7, 187; indulgence towards Lutherans, 17, 194
Ivangorod, 31, 33, 168, 198
Ivan Ivanovich, tsarevich, xvi, 187
Ivanov, Andrei, crown secretary, 211
Ivanov, Russian agent, xxx

Jan Kazimierz, Polish king, 184
Jerusalem, 32, 35
Jerusalem church (Moscow), 160–1, 178
Jerusalem Gate (Moscow), 51, 76
Jesuits, xviii, xxiv, xxviii–xxix
Jews, 32, 35–6
Joachimsthaler, 199

Job, Patriarch, xvii, 13, 191, 199
Johan, Danish prince, 206; burial, 17–19, 195; suitor to Boris's daughter, 18, 48, 90, 195, 200, 218; death, 68, 172, 195; lodging in Moscow, 179, 195
Johan, duke of Östergötland, 183
Jonas, metropolitan, locum tenens, xxix
Joseph, biblical character, xxiv
Josephus, xxix, xxxii, 32
Julius, duke of Brunswick, xxxiii

Kaliazin monastery, 123
Kalmar, War of, xxi
Kaluga, xxi–xxii, xxxi, 79, 91, 95, 98, 102, 105–7, 127–31, 133, 137, 139–52, 193, 212–14, 220
Kalyazin monastery, 216
Kamenka, river, 214
Kaminsk, 109, 214
Karachev, 201
Karamzin, Nikolai Mikhailovich, historian, xxxiv–xxxv, 186
Kargopol, 75, 104
Karl IX, Swedish king, 14; assumes throne, xxi, 183; unsuccessful war in Livonia, xxi, 19; rulership disputed by Sigismund, xxvii, 184, 192; offers aid to Shuisky, xxviii, 96, 185, 212; promotes son's candidacy for Muscovite throne, 167. See also Karl, duke of Södermanland.
Karl, duke of Södermanland, regent, xxi, xxx, 18, 21, 195. See also Karl IX, Swedish king.

Karl Filip, Swedish prince, xxiv, xxviii, 222
Kashin, 15
Kashnets, Grigory, 101
Kater, mistress of Prince Gustav, 15
Katyrev-Rostovsky, Prince Ivan Mikhailovich, 42, 202
Kazan, xiii, 31, 197, 204
Kazan Chancellery, 200
Kazanowska, chief lady-in-waiting, 58, 65, 72
Kazanowski, Polish lord, 209
Kazimierz, Polish lord, governor of Kaluga, 129, 130
Kelch, Christian, xxxv
Kerckling, Heinrich, alderman, 25
Kernozicki, Polish colonel, 122–3, 148
Kexholm, 168, 222
Khodynka river, 215
Khomutov, Fedor, 219
Kiev, 196
Kievan state, xv
Kineshma, 122
Kirkholm, battle, xxi
Kirrumpä, 19, 195
Kitay-gorod (Moscow), xxii, 67, 179, 196, 219
Klushino, battle, xx, xxii, xxviii,134,144, 202, 218
Knudson, Matthias, captain, 54, 206
Kokenhausen, 19
Kolomenskoe, xxiv, 90, 220
Kolomenskoe monastery, 147
Kolomna, 220
Komaritsk district, 41, 91, 202
Kon, Fedor Savelev, 197, 215
Königsberg, 97
Kopanev, A.I., historian, xxxvi

Koporie, 168
Korela, town, 168, 222. See also Kexholm, Priozersk
Korela, Cossack ataman, 42
Koshelev, Peter, jester, 127, 150–1
Kostroma, xxiii, 75, 116, 120, 188, 209
Kotly, 90–1
Kozelsk, 102, 105, 128, 136–7, 139–43
Kraków, 154, 211
Krapivna, xxxi, 122
Krasnoe, 125
Krasnoye Selo, 45, 204
Krebsberg, Jürgen, 130
Kremlin (Moscow), xxii, 14, 16, 22, 27, 35–6, 38, 43, 45–8, 50–5, 57, 60–3, 66–7, 69, 76–7, 82, 89, 148, 160, 178–9, 205, 218
Kristina of Holstein-Gottorp, wife of Karl IX of Sweden, 184
Kromy, 41, 42, 44, 201–2
Kuddelin, Arndt, 108
Kukushkina, M.V., historian, xxxvi
Kulisha Gate (Moscow), 77
Kulizhek (Moscow), 163
Kunik, A.A., historian, xxxvi–xxxvii
Kurland, 54, 63
Kursk, 201

Ladoga, 219
Lamsdorf, Albert, 215
Lamsdorff, Colonel Barthold, 108–10
Lapps, 78
Laville, Monsieur, French mercenary, 136, 219
Leibniz, Gottfried Wilhelm, xxxiii
Leigh, Richard, English ambassador, 194

Leipzig, xxxiii,185, 193
Leo XI, Pope, xxviii
Lessing, Gotthold Ephraim, xxxiv
Levonty, St, 215
Liapunov, Prokopy, xxii–xxiii, 120, 144, 166, 216, 219, 221–2
Liapunov, Zakhar, 219
Likhvin, 103
Lion Bridge (Moscow), 58
Lisowski, Aleksandr Józef, Polish commander, xix–xx, 107, 116, 121–2, 124–5, 214
Lithuania, Lithuanians, 31, 198, 215–6
Livonia, xiv–xv, xxi, xxvii, xxx, 14, 17, 19–23, 31, 36, 40, 54, 63, 66, 68, 82, 107–8, 114, 125, 132, 135, 137, 152, 165, 167–8, 171, 193, 200
Livonian Order, xiv, 196, 198
Livonians, 19, 22, 23, 54, 63, 107, 114, 125
Livonian War, xiv–xvi, 187, 195–6, 198, 218
Lobnoe Mesto (Moscow), 210
Logau, Freiherr Andreas von, Austrian ambassador, 34, 199–200
Lower Saxony, xxxii
Lübeck, xxxiii, 14, 16, 196, 229
Lüneburg, 171
Luza, 197

Macedonians, 153
Maliuta Skuratov, xxi, 188, 218
Mamelukes (apostates), 55, 68, 114, 115, 206
Margeret, Jacques, French mercenary, chronicler: returns to France, xix, 201; publishes account

of experiences, xxxi; at battle of Dobrynichi, 40; appointed to Dmitry's bodyguard, 54; leads couterattack against Muscovites, 162–4; chronicle cited, 189, 199, 203–4; career, 201–2

Marguerite of Valois, 208

Maria Fedorovna Nagaia, 7

Maria Grigorievna, wife of Boris Godunov, xviii, 89, 188, 204, 212

Maria of the Palatinate, wife of Duke Karl of Östergötland, 184

Marie-Elisabeth, Swedish princess, 183

Marienburg, 19

Martha, nun, 205. See also Nagaia, Maria Fedorovna

Martzin, Pan, cavalry commander, 126

Maryna, daughter of governor of Sandomir, tsaritsa, 148; betrothed to False Dmitry I, xvii, 53, 200; marriage, xviii, 60–1, 85; under protection of Zarutsky, xxiii; lavish gifts to, 53, 74; journey to Moscow, 56–7; entry, 57–8, 207; escapes from riot in Kremlin, 65, 208–9; allowed to rejoin father, 71; reviled by Muscovite womenfolk, 77; reflections in captivity, 79; internment, 111, 209; abducted by supporters of False Dmitry II, 111–12; informed Dmitry not her husband, 112; marriage to second pretender, 113, 123; Dmitry confides

despair, 126–7; abused by Dmitry's supporters, 128–9; escapes to Sapieha's encampment, 129; rejoins Dmitry, 130–1; intercedes for Kozelsk Germans, 137–41; birth of son, 152, 220; death, 220

Massa, Isaac, Dutch merchant apprentice, chronicler, 178, 189, 190–2, 198–9, 201–3, 205–9, 211, 215

Matthias, archduke, later emperor, 34, 199

Maximilian, archduke, 152, 220

Mecklenburg, 185

Merrick, John, English agent, 200

Michael Fedorovich Romanov, tsar, xvii, xxiii–xxv, xxviii–xxix, 167, 191, 202, 204, 213, 215, 218, 221–2

Michael Koribut Wisniowiecki, Polish king, 198

Miechowicki, Mikolaj, xx, 101, 102, 108

Mikhailov, xxiii

Milan, 208

Minin, Kuzma, xxiii, 221

Miracles monastery (Moscow), 221

Mistress Kater, 15, 192

Miulnik, Muscovite merchant, assassin of False Dmitry I, 66

Mniszech, Jerzy, governor of Sandomir, 65, 91, 100–1, 105, 123; Dmitry betrothed to daughter, xvii, 53; patron of False Dmitry, 31; journey to Moscow, 57; besieged by Muscovites, 67; altercation with Muscovites, 71–6; alleged misdeeds of fol-

lowers, 84–5; internmant, 85, 209; abducted by followers of False Dmitry II, 111; returns to Poland, 113

Molchanov, Mikhail, 144, 211, 219

Mologa, 120

Mongol conquest, 215

Monsdotter, Katharina, mother of Prince Gustav, 192

Moravsk, 201

Moritzon, Ensign Thomas, 137

Mosalsky, Prince Vasily, 113

Moskva river, 157, 163, 164

Mozhaisk, 57, 134, 144, 164

Mstislavsky, Prince Fedor Ivanovich, 201

Mstislavsky, Prince Ivan Fedorovich, 28, 37–8, 42, 44, 57, 201

Müller, Klaus, 172

Murom, 212

Muromets, Ileika. See Peter, "tsarevich"

Musicians, 52, 58, 67, 73, 74

Musketeers, 11, 27, 37, 55, 57, 65, 144, 160–3, 206

Mussorgsky, Modest, xxxiii

Nagaia, Maria Fedorova, 7, 51, 82

Nagoy, Ivan Ivanovich, 107, 214

Nagoy family, 189

Narova river, 198

Narva, xxx, 14, 31, 33, 96, 125, 168, 193, 195, 198, 207

Nebuchadnezzar, 80

Neglinnaia river (Moscow), 8, 162

Nero, Roman emperor,
xxv
Neuhausen, 19, 21, 196
Neustadt, 15, 17, 61, 137
New Chronicler. *See* Novyi
Letopisets
New Convent (Moscow),
11, 48, 190
New Spanish Courtyards
(Moscow), 179
Nikitsk street (Moscow),
162
Nikitsk Gates (Moscow),
58
Nikoforovich, counsellor
to False Dmitry II,
136
Nikon, patriarch, 191
Nizhny Novgorod, xxiii,
202
Nogay Tatars, 198
Norway, 172
Noteborg, 168
Novgorod, xv, xviii, xxviii,
21, 96, 123, 168, 199–
200, 219
Novgorod Seversk, 37–8,
101, 201
Novgorodok, 196. *See also*
Neuhausen
Novoye Selo, 198
Novyi Letopisets (New
Chronicler), 189, 198,
203–7, 210, 216

Oka river, 87, 106, 137,
139, 150
Old Believer schism, xxiv,
xxviii
Oldenburg, 172
Olearius, Adam, 207, 220
Olga, nun, 204. *See also*
Xenia Borisovna Godu-
nova, tsarevna.
Oliva, treaty, 184
Onega river, 197
Oprichnina, xiv–xv, 187–8
Otrepiev, Grishka, rene-
gade monk, 193, 210;
probably true identity

of False Dmitry I, xvii;
flees to Poland, 27;
seeks someone to
impersonate tsarevich,
28; recruits Cossacks,
31, 37; encourages
Dmitry after Dobryn-
ichi, 41; "helper
theory," 186, 198, 201.
See also False Dmitry I.

Palatinate, 202
Palitsyn, Avraamy, xxix,
189, 199, 205, 216
Panin, Count V.N., xxxvi
Papal curia, 96
Pashkov, Istoma, 88, 90–
1, 93–5, 212
Paul V, Pope, xxviii
Pausanias, 80
Pchelna river, 150
Pelym, 197
Peparino, Johann, cham-
berlain, xxxii, 174,
222–3
Pereiaslavl, 115
Peremyshl, 128
Perm, 197
Perrie, Maureen, histo-
rian, xxv–xxvi
Peter, "tsarevich," 96,
98–9, 103–4, 212,
214
Peter I, Russian emperor,
xxix, 222
Peter III, Russian
emperor, xxv
Petreius (Peer Peerson de
Erlesunda), chronicler,
xxx, xxxii–xxxv, 185,
189–93, 196, 206, 216,
218–19
Petrov, Anton, rebel
leader, 184
Peyerle, Hans Georg,
Augsburg merchant,
209
Pfalz-Vedenz, 185
Philip, prince of
Schleswig, 218

Phisildek, antiquarian,
xxxv. *See also* Schmidt,
Christoph
Pilsen, 200
Platonov, Sergei Fedo-
rovich, historian, xiv,
xxxvi
Plautus, xxix, xxxii, 65
Pleshcheev, Naum, 204
Pogoreloe, 136
Pokrovsk street (Moscow),
162
Polabian, xxxii, 185
Polyanovka, truce, 222
Pomerania, xxxv
Pomestie landholding, xvi
Pompey, 80
Poperzack's Kitchen, 179
Possevino, Antonio, Jesuit,
215
Pozharsky, Prince Dmitry
Mikhailovich, xxiii, 202,
213, 218, 221–2
Prague, 16
Priozersk, 222
Prussia, 97
Pskov, xviii, 21–2, 124–5,
185, 196, 217, 228
Pugachev, Emilian, rebel
leader, xxv
Pushkin, Alexander,
xxxiv, 188
Putivl, 31, 37, 41–4, 87–
91, 93–6, 101, 128,
168, 201–2, 211

Razin, Stenka, rebel
leader, xxv–xxvi
Red Square (Moscow),
xxiii, 210
Regensburg, 16
Reinen, Johann von,
Livonian noble, 137
Reitlinger, Christopher,
physician, 16, 194
Repin family, 197
Riazan, 221
Riga, xvii–xviii, xxx–xxxi,
xxxv, 16, 82, 152, 193,
227

Rogozhna, xxxi, 122
Romanov, Alexander
Nikitich, 9, 197
Romanov, Fedor Nikitich,
xvii, 9, 115, 167, 191.
See also Filaret, metro-
politan, later patriarch
Romanov, Ivan Nikitich,
9, 197
Romanov, Mikhail Niki-
tich, 9, 197
Romanov family, xvii, 27,
197
Romanov, town, 120, 148,
220
Romanova, Tatiana, 202
Rosen, Walther von,
Livonian noble, 40,
202
Rostov, 75, 111, 115, 209,
215, 230
Rozynski, Roman, 107–9,
126–7, 129–30, 132–3
Rubets-Mosalsky, Prince
Vasily, 201, 211
Rudolf II, emperor, 17,
192, 194, 199–200, 220
Rumiantsev, Count N.P.,
xxxv
Rybinsk, 120
Rylsk, 41, 201
Ryndin, counsellor to
False Dmitry II, 136
Rzhevsky, Ivan, 144, 219

St Bartholomew massacre,
208
St Cyril monastery
(Beloozero), 51, 205
St Cyril monastery
(Moscow), 178, 205
St Joseph monastery
(Volokolamsk), 131,
136, 217
St Nicholas, 7, 50, 59, 61,
70, 83, 101, 114, 127,
187, 205, 213
St Paphnutius monastery
(Borovsk), 144, 147,
217, 220

Saltykov, Ivan Nikitich,
219
Saltykov, Mikhail Gle-
bovich, 131, 160, 200,
203–4, 218
Samara, 198
Samov, 103, 105, 107
Sandomir, 31, 53, 57, 65,
67, 84–5, 88, 91, 100–
1, 105, 111, 123
Sanin, Joseph, 217
Sapieha, Jan-Piotr, Polish
military leader, xix, xx,
136; conversation with
Bussow, xxxi, 83, 198;
joins forces with False
Dmitry II, 110;
besieges Trinity monas-
tery, 114–15, 210;
destroys Yaroslavl and
other cities, 116–17;
fights against Skopin
and de la Gardie, 123–
4; Maryna seeks his
protection, 129; coun-
sels Maryna to leave
Russia, 130; aids her
escape to Kaluga, 131;
negotiations with King
Sigismund, 132; king
refuses terms, 133;
death, 167
Sapieha, Leo, chancellor,
42, 195
Sarmatians, 153
Saviour Gates (Moscow),
205
Saxe-Lauenburg, 185
Schiele, Michael, Aus-
trian ambassador, 190,
194
Schleswig, 218
Schleswig-Holstein, 172
Schmidt, Johann, gov-
ernor of Yaroslavl, 116,
121
Schneider, Hans,
Livonian, 114
Schroeder, Heinrich, phy-
sician, 16

Schwartzkopf, Wilhelm,
Livonian noble, 63
Sebastian, Portugese king,
xxv
Second Militia Force,
xxiii, 213
Semeon Bekbulatovich,
Tatar princeling, 188
Sergius of Radonezh, St,
105, 214
Serpukhov, 12, 47–8, 87,
95, 99, 191
Serpukhov Gates
(Moscow), 77, 212, 220
Sesswegen, 19
Seth, 81
"Seven boyar" administra-
tion, 219
Severia, 38
Severian lands, 127, 149
Sevsk, 201
Shakhovskoy, Prince Gri-
gory: spreads rumour
of Dmitry's escape, 87–
8, 93; appointed gov-
ernor of Putivl, 88,
211; False Dmitry sends
Bolotnikov with letter
to, 91–3; receives Mus-
covites' demands, 94;
summons bogus tsar-
evich Peter, 95–6;
defenders of Tula
incensed at, 99–100;
arrested, 100; treated
leniently by Shuisky,
104–5; advances
against Poles at
Tsarevo-Zaimishche,
127; denounces Kozelsk
Germans, 136, 139
Shakhovskoy, Prince
Semeon Ivanovich, xxix
Shein, Mikhail Borisovich,
119, 215
Sheremetev family, 197
Sheremetev Book of
Boyars, 214
Shestunov family, 197
Shklov, 101

Shuiskaia, Princess Eka-
terina Grigorievna, xxi,
218
Shuisky, Prince Dmitry
Ivanovich: jealousy of
Skopin, xxi, 218; inep-
titude as military com-
mander, xxii; conspires
against False Dmitry I,
53–4; Pashkov demands
extradition from
Moscow, 90; Polish cap-
tivity, 152; death, 219
Shuisky, Prince Ivan Iva-
novich, 53–4, 90, 114,
152, 219
Shuisky, Prince Ivan
Petrovich, xviii
Shuisky, Prince Vasily Ivanovich, 197; heads
Uglich commission,
xvii; conspiracy against
False Dmitry I, xviii,
53–5; sentenced to
death but reprieved,
xviii, 55, 80–1; renewed
conspiracy, xviii, 58–60;
seizes power, xviii, 66,
68–9, 84. See also Vasily
Ivanovich Shuisky, tsar
Shuisky family, xvii, 53,
190
Shuminsky, Ivan, 116
Siberia, xxxi, 27, 98, 104,
171, 222
Sidorka, Pskov pretender,
185
Sigismund III, Polish
king, xxviii, 19, 75, 79,
201, 214, 220; receives
False Dmitry, xvii; and
Zebrzydowski rebellion,
xix–xx, 127, 195; also
king of Sweden, xx–
xxi, xxx, 195; overt
intervention in Mus-
covy, xxi; besieges Smo-
lensk, xxi, 26, 117–19,
132, 168, 202, 215;
appeal to Tushino
Poles, xxi, 132, 135,

216; loses Swedish
crown, xxi, 195;
advances own claims to
Muscovite throne, xxii,
xxiv, 218–19; maintains
claim to Swedish
throne, xxvii, 183, 192,
195; relations with Tsar
Dmitry, 53, 72; receives
embassy from Shuisky,
84–5, 211; approached
by Bolotnikov and
Shakhovskoy, 100;
Shuisky offers to cede
Muscovy, 119; opposed
by Liapunov, 120;
forces destroy Bussow's
estate, 122; Lisowski
rallies to, 125; nego-
tiations with Sapieha
and Rozynski, 133;
Muscovite approach
concerning Wladyslaw's
candidacy, 145–7;
response, 146; enter-
tains Turkish embassy,
152–3; disparaging
remarks of Muscovites,
157–8; dispatches
Chodkiewicz to relief
of Moscow, 167; com-
missions map of
Moscow, 178; extends
truce with Muscovy,
200
Simnel, Lambert, xxv
Simonides, 80
Sirach, 80
Sitsky family, 197
Skåne, xxi
Skopin-Shuisky, Prince
Mikhail Vasilievich:
advances with Swedish
auxiliaries to relief of
Moscow, xxi, xxviii,
119–22; death, xxi,
133, 216, 218; at battle
of Taininskoe, 110; dis-
patched to obtain
Swedish aid, 113–14;
fighting around Tver,

123; holds Kaliazin
monastery, 123–4, 216;
occupies Yaroslavl and
Alexandrovskaia Slo-
boda, 125, 216–7;
attacks Dmitrov, 130–1;
relieves Trinity monas-
tery, 132, 217; entry
into Moscow, 132–3
Skotnicki, Pan (Albert
Wandmann), 54, 106,
127, 129–30, 140
Skrynnikov, Ruslan Grigo-
rievich, historian, xiv,
xxvi, xxxvi, 190
Smirnov, Ivan Ivanovich,
historian, xxxvi–xxxvii,
187, 194–5, 197, 200,
205, 208, 214–15, 217,
222
Smith, Sir Thomas, 202
Smolensk, xxi–xxii, xxxi,
26, 56–7, 79, 117, 119,
122, 126–32, 134, 136–
7, 143, 146, 152, 156,
168, 196, 215, 218–19,
222
So-called Other Tale, 202,
206, 209
Solovetsk monastery, xxviii
Soloviev, Sergei Mikhailovich, historian, xxi,
xxxvi, 186, 206, 213
Spain, xix, 14
Sretenka, Moscow street,
48
Sretensk Gates (Moscow),
156
Stadnicki, Martin, Polish
lord, 111, 209
Staritsa princes, xvi
Starodub, 100–2, 214
Stefan Bathory, Polish
king, xviii, xxx, 28, 81,
83, 196, 198
Stockholm, 185
Stolbovo, Peace of, 222
Stormarn, 172
Struys, Dutch mercenary,
164
Sukhaya river, 214

Supernova of 1604, 200
Suzdal, xviii, 120–1, 124
Sweden, xv–xvi, xx–xxi,
. xxiv, xxvii–xxviii, xxx,
15, 19–20, 23, 113,
115, 125, 145, 192,
195, 200, 212
Swedes, 15, 23, 44, 96,
172, 196, 198, 218
Sybelski, Martin, German
renegade, 55

Taininskoe, 53, 110
Tarlo, Polish lord, 209
Tarnopol, 213
Tatars, xv–xvi, xxii, 12,
18, 23, 26–7, 35–6, 44,
53–4, 57, 88–9, 91, 98,
104, 111, 120, 122,
133, 147–51, 206, 216,
220
Tatary, 150
Tatishchev, 63
Täysinä, Peace of, xvi,
195
Teletin, commander, 99
Teliatevsky, Prince A.A.,
204
Terek Cossacks, 212
Terenty, archpriest, xxix
Thierfeld, Master Johann,
31
Thiesenhausen, Dietloff
von, Livonian noble, 23
Thirty Years War, 222
Time of Troubles, xiii,
xix–xx, xxii–xxiii,
xxviii–xxix, xxxi, xxxiv,
183, 185, 192, 197
Timofeev, Ivan, chroni-
cler, xxix, 190
Tonnies von Wissen,
Livonian, 107
Tretyakov, counsellor to
False Dmitry II, 136
Treuer, Gottlieb, xxxv
Trinity Gates (Moscow
Kremlin), 89
Trinity monastery, xix,
xxxi, 51, 83, 89, 105,
114–15, 117, 122–5,

132, 204, 210, 214,
216, 218, 222
Trubetskoy, Andrei Vasil-
ievich, governor, 22
Trubetskoy, counsellor to
False Dmitry II, 136
Trubetskoy, Prince Dmitry
Timofeevich, xxii–xxiii
Trubetskoy, Prince Yury,
201
Tsarevo-Borisov, 197
Tsarevo-Zaimishche,
57,127, 134, 135, 144
Tsargorod, 26
Tula, xxxi, 96–9, 102–5,
107, 200, 212–14
Turkey, Turks, 17, 23, 36,
53–4, 91, 98, 114, 148,
153, 195, 205
Tushino, xix, xxi, xxviii,
111–12, 198, 202, 215–
16, 218
Tver, 21, 123, 209
Tyszkiewicz, Samuel,
Polish commander, 107,
121

Uglich, xvii, xxx, 7–9, 15,
27–8, 82–3, 85, 120,
189
Ugra river, 131–3, 136,
144
Ukraine, xxiv
Uniate church, xxviii
Upa river, 99
Upper Poland, 31
Urals, 213
Urusov, Peter, Tatar
prince, 149–51
Ustiug, 209
Ustrialov, Nikolai Gerasi-
movich, historian, xxxv,
214

Valuev, Grigory, Muscovite
commander, 134–5,
144, 217
Varsonofiev monastery
(Moscow), 204
Vasily III, grand prince,
xxiii, 215

Vasily Ivanovich Shuisky,
tsar, xxvi, xxxi, 15, 94,
115, 119–20, 125, 148,
191, 193; seizes throne,
xviii, 84, 210; throne-
worthiness, xviii; per-
sonality defects, xix,
145, 207; and Bolot-
nikov rebellion, xix,
96–104, 212; sends for
Swedish aid, xxi, 113–
14, 119–20, 185; depo-
sition, xxii, xxviii, 144–
5, 152; fictitious son as
pretender, xxv; embassy
to King Sigismund, 84–
5, 211; orders intern-
ment of Poles, 85, 209;
transfers alleged
remains of Tsarevich
Dmitry to Moscow, 85–
6; summons army to
combat forces of False
Dmitry II, 88–9; orders
reburial of Godunov
family at Trinity mon-
astery, 89–90, 204;
refuses Swedish aid,
96–7, 185; hires Fiedler
to assassinate Bolot-
nikov, 97–8; defeat at
Pchelna river, 98–9;
besieges Tula, 99–100,
213; negotiates sur-
render terms, 103–4,
212; false promises to
Bolotnikov, 104, 212;
exiles Germans in Bol-
otnikov's service, 104;
leniency towards Shak-
hovskoy, 104–5; pilgi-
mage to Trinity
monastery, 105; offers
terms to kaluga, 105;
failure to reduce
Kaluga, 106–7; rela-
tions with German ren-
egades, 107, 214;
defeat at Bolkhov, 109–
10; repels False Dmitry
II at Taininskoe, 110–

11, 215; releases
Maryna and retinue,
111; resorts to necro-
mancy, 113; offers to
surrender Muscovy to
Sigismund, 119;
relieved by Skopin and
de la Gardie, 132–3,
217; orders death of
Skopin by poisoning,
133, 218; sends troops
against Zolkiewski, 134;
defeat at Klushino,
134–6; involuntary ton-
sure, 145, 219; Polish
captivity, 152–3, 167,
219; exiles Prince
Gustav to Kashin, 192;
appoints Vasmar his
personal physician,
194; exiles Vlasiev to
Ufa, 200–1; death, 219.
See also Shuisky, Prince
Vasily Ivanovich
Vasmar, David, physician,
16, 85, 194, 211
Venice, 91
Vervins, Peace of, xx
Viazma, 57, 12
Vienna, 220
Virgil, xxxii
Vittinghofen, Otto von,
Livonian nobleman, 19,
21
Vlasiev, Afanasy Iva-
novich, 36, 53, 194–5,
200–1, 218
Volga, river, xiii, 121, 123,
197–8, 212, 220
Volkonsky, Prince G.K.,
211
Vologda, 76, 116, 120,
209
Volokolamsk, 217
Voronezh, 125
Vorotynsky, Prince I.M.,
204
Vosma river, 213
Vozdvizhenskoe, 114

Vyborg, Treaty of, xxi
Vykhodets, Timofey, xxx

Walck, 195
Wallachian House
(Moscow), 68
Wandmann, Albert, Scot-
tish captain, 54, 206.
See also Skotnicki
Warbesk, Perkin, xxv
Warsaw, 219
Watergates (Moscow), 158,
163, 178
Westphalia, 17
Westphalia, kingdom of,
xxxiv
Wettermann, Johannes,
Lutheran pastor, 194
White City (Moscow), 67,
166–7, 179, 192, 196
White Russia, 27–9, 31,
37, 101, 146
White sea, 197
White Walls (Moscow), 164
Wieger, Lord Ludwig, 126
Wild Steppe, 28, 31, 37,
88, 91, 96
Wisniowiec, 30
Wisniowiecki, Prince
Adam, xvii, xxxi, 28–
31, 37, 107, 198, 209
Wissen, Tonnies von,
Livonian, 107
Wladyslaw, Polish prince,
later King Wladyslaw
IV of Poland, xxxi, 84,
144, 154, 168; pro-
posed as candidate for
Muscovite tsardom,
xxii, xxiv, xxvii, 145–6;
supported by papacy,
xxviii; Muscovites agree
on candidacy, 147, 152,
155, 158, 219; fails to
appear, 155, 159, 165,
218; Muscovites reject
him, 155, 157–8; fur-
ther attempts to gain
Muscovite throne, 222

Wolfenbüttel, xxxii–xxxv,
xxxvii, 172, 178, 222

Xenia Borisovna, tsar-
evna, xviii, 15, 18, 48,
90, 204, 218. See also
Olga, nun

Yamgorod, 168
Yam Zapolsky, treaty, 195
Yanov, Alexander, Russian
author, xiv
Yaransk, 197
Yaroslavl, xxiii, 75, 111,
115–16, 120–2, 124–5,
192, 209
Yauza, river, xxiv, 69, 192,
194
Yauza Gates (Moscow), 77
Yurievets Polsky, 122
Yushkov, Mikhail Kon-
stantinovich, counsellor
to False Dmitry II, 136

Zamoyski, Jan, chancellor,
xxx
Zaporozhian Cossacks,
109
Zarutsky, Ivan Mar-
tynovich, xxii–xxiii,
100, 102, 129, 213,
220
Zborowski, Polish lord,
123, 126, 135
Zebrzydowski, Nicholas,
xix–xx
Zebrzydowski rebellion,
xx, 195
Zernov family, 188
Zolkiewski, Stanislaw,
Polish hetman: defeats
Zebrzydowski rebels,
xx; reaches agreement
with Muscovites, xxii,
146–7; victory at
Klushino, 134–5, 144;
advances on Moscow,
202; truce with Swedes,
218–19; memoirs, 231